武井宏之
(SOUVENIR GIFT COLLECTOR)

I'm probably the biggest tourist working at *Weekly Shonen Jump*. During my first year of publication I've traveled all over Japan, starting with Kamakura. I've ravaged Izu, Ikaho, Izumo, Nikko, Kawaguchiko, and Kawagoe. Why? For one thing, of course: *souvenir key holders.*

—Hiroyuki Takei, 1999

MANTANNIAN DICTIONARY

Unconventional author/artist Hiroyuki Takei began his career by winning the coveted Hop Step Award (for new manga artists) and the Osamu Tezuka Award (named after the famous artist of the same name). After working as an assistant to famed artist Nobuhiro Watsuki, Takei debuted in **Weekly Shonen Jump** in 1997 with **Butsu Zone**, an action series based on Buddhist mythology. His multicultural adventure manga **Shaman King**, which debuted in 1998, became a hit and was adapted into an anime TV series. Takei lists Osamu Tezuka, American comics and robot anime among his many influences.

SHAMAN KING VOL. 4
The SHONEN JUMP Graphic Novel Edition

This graphic novel contains material that was originally published in English in **SHONEN JUMP** #16-19.

STORY AND ART BY
HIROYUKI TAKEI

English Adaptation/Lance Caselman
Translation/Lillian Olsen
Touch-Up Art & Lettering/Dan Nakrosis (pages 7-129),
Kathryn Renta (pages 131-191)
Cover Design/Sean Lee
Graphics & Layout/Sean Lee
Design Assistant/Walden Wong
Editor/Jason Thompson

Managing Editor/Elizabeth Kawasaki
Executive V.P./Editor-in-Chief/Hyoe Narita
Director of Production/Noboru Watanabe
Senior Director of Licensing & Acquisitions/Rika Inouye
V.P. of Marketing/Liza Coppola
V.P. of Sales/Joe Morici
V.P. of Strategic Development/Yumi Hoashi
Publisher/Seiji Horibuchi

PARENTAL ADVISORY
Shaman King is rated "T" for Teen. It contains fantasy violence. It is recommended for ages 13 and up.

Printed in the U.S.A.

Published by VIZ, LLC
P.O. Box 77010 • San Francisco, CA 94107

SHONEN JUMP Graphic Novel Edition
10 9 8 7 6 5 4 3 2 1
First printing, August 2004

www.viz.com

THE WORLD'S MOST POPULAR MANGA
SHONEN JUMP
GRAPHIC NOVEL
www.shonenjump.com

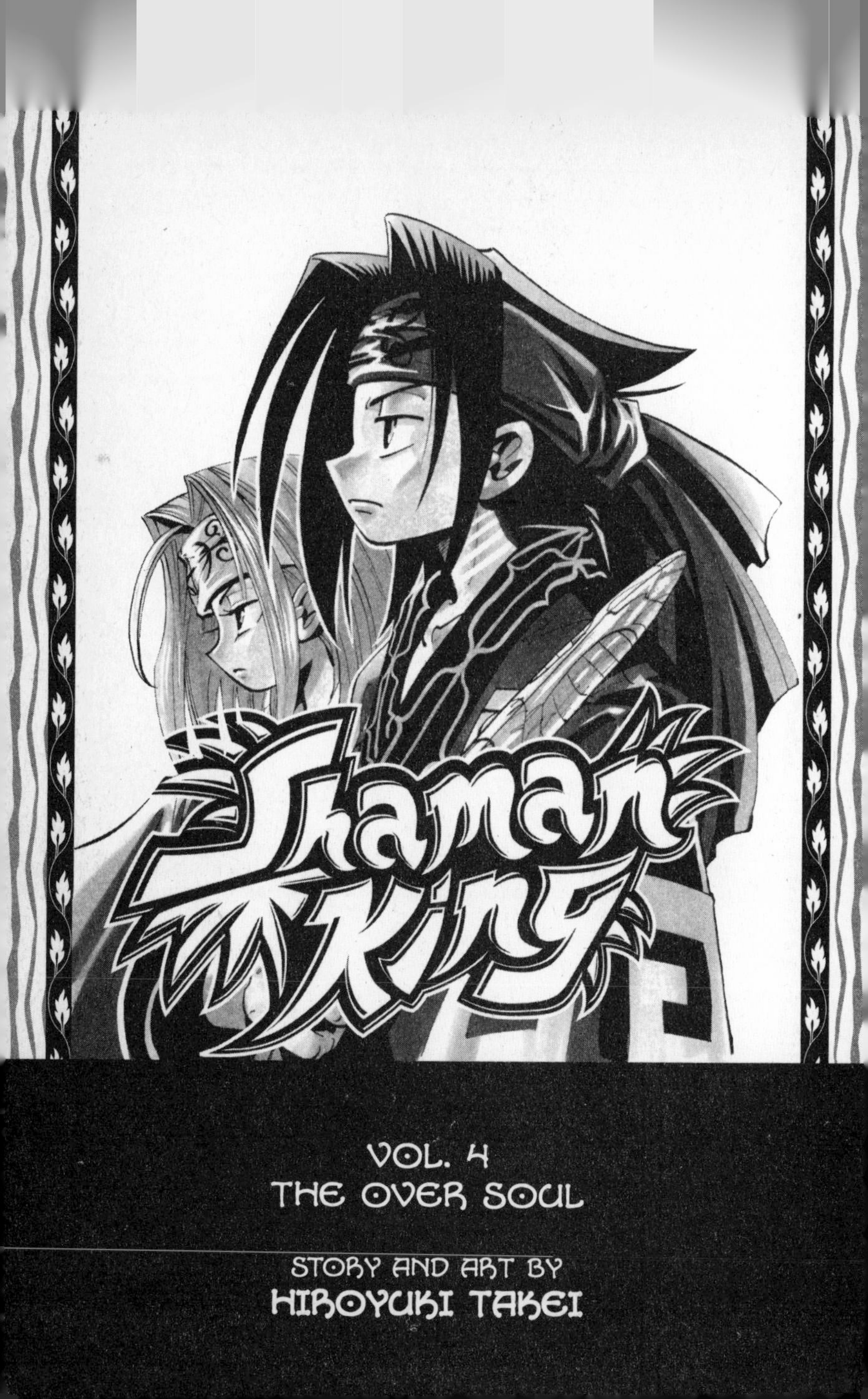
Shaman King

VOL. 4

THE OVER SOUL

STORY AND ART BY
HIROYUKI TAKEI

阿弥陀丸 *(あみだまる)*

AMIDAMARU
Known in legends as "the fiend," Amidamaru was a samurai who died in Japan's Muromachi Era (1334-1467). His soul haunted Funbari Hill for 600 years, until he became Yoh's ghost companion. His name is based on a Buddhist prayer.

麻倉 葉 *(あさくら よう)*

YOH ASAKURA
Cheerful and easy-going, Yoh seems to be a slacker, but he is actually the heir to a long line of Japanese shamans. His first name means "leaf."

恐山アンナ *(きょうやま)*

ANNA KYOYAMA
Yoh's no-nonsense fiancée (it's an arranged marriage). She is an *itako* (a traditional Japanese village shaman).

小山田まん太 *(おやまだ まんた)*

MANTA OYAMADA
An easily panicked student who always carries a huge dictionary. He has enough sixth sense to see ghosts, but not enough to control them. In the anime he's named "Mortimer."

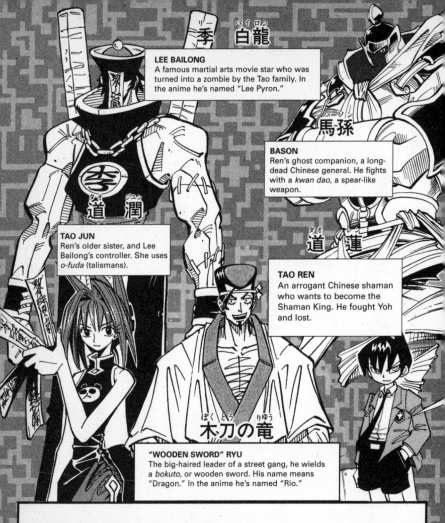

季 白龍

LEE BAILONG
A famous martial arts movie star who was turned into a zombie by the Tao family. In the anime he's named "Lee Pyron."

馬孫

BASON
Ren's ghost companion, a long-dead Chinese general. He fights with a *kwan dao*, a spear-like weapon.

道 潤

TAO JUN
Ren's older sister, and Lee Bailong's controller. She uses *o-fuda* (talismans).

道 蓮

TAO REN
An arrogant Chinese shaman who wants to become the Shaman King. He fought Yoh and lost.

木刀の竜

"WOODEN SWORD" RYU
The big-haired leader of a street gang, he wields a *bokuto*, or wooden sword. His name means "Dragon." In the anime he's named "Rio."

THE STORY SO FAR...

Yoh Asakura is a *shaman* -- one of the gifted few who, thanks to training or natural talent, can channel spirits that most people can't even see. With the help of his fiancée Anna, Yoh is in training for the ultimate shaman sports event: the "Shaman Fight in Tokyo," the once-every-500-years tournament to see who can shape humanity's future and become *the Shaman King*. But who are the organizers of the Shaman Fight? How do you get in? Where can you get tickets? Like it or not, Yoh's questions are about to be answered...

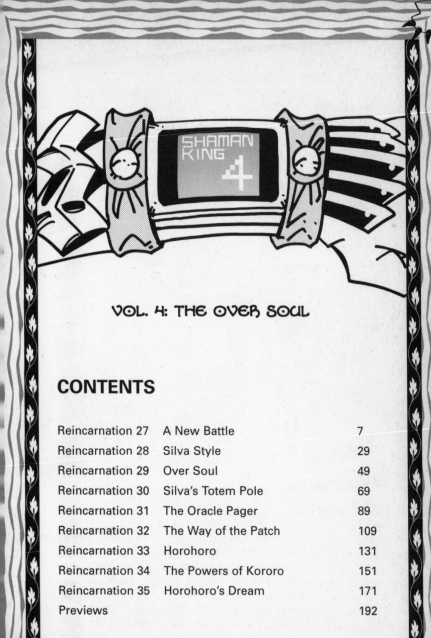

VOL. 4: THE OVER SOUL

CONTENTS

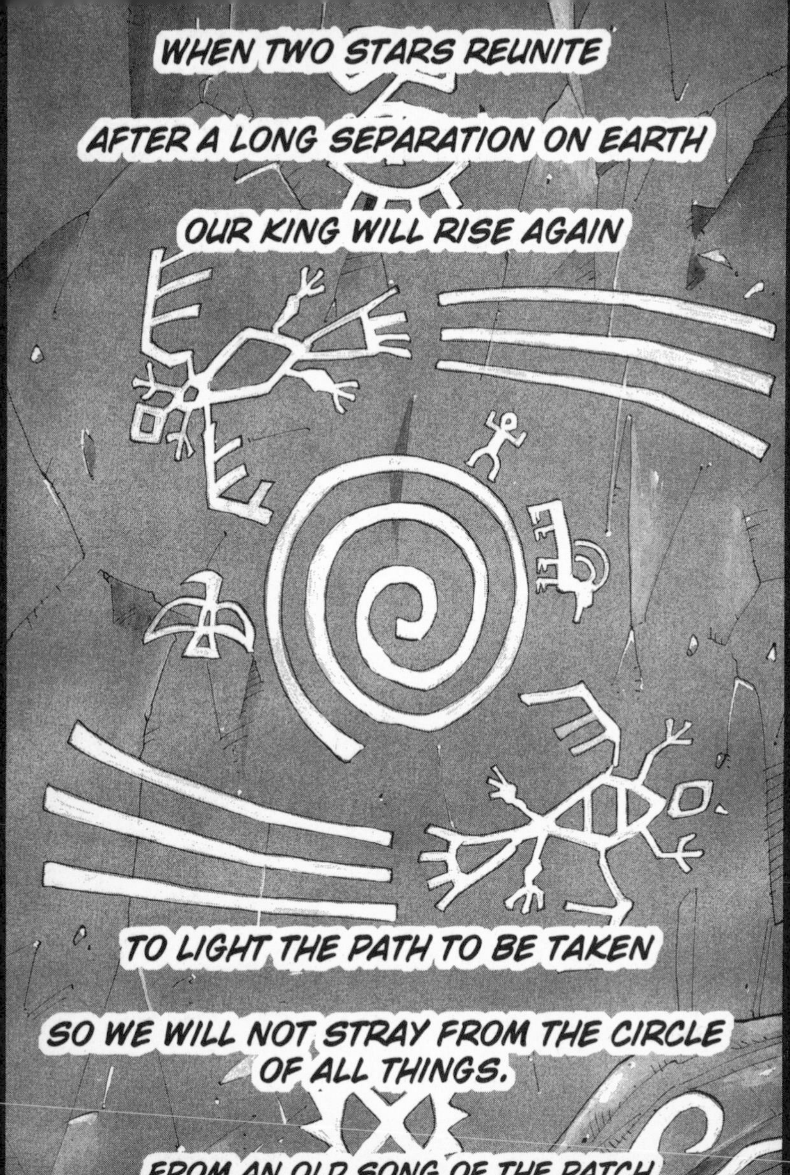
WHEN TWO STARS REUNITE
AFTER A LONG SEPARATION ON EARTH
OUR KING WILL RISE AGAIN
TO LIGHT THE PATH TO BE TAKEN
SO WE WILL NOT STRAY FROM THE CIRCLE OF ALL THINGS.
— FROM AN OLD SONG OF THE PATCH A NATIVE AMERICAN TRIBE —

REINCARNATION 27: A NEW BATTLE

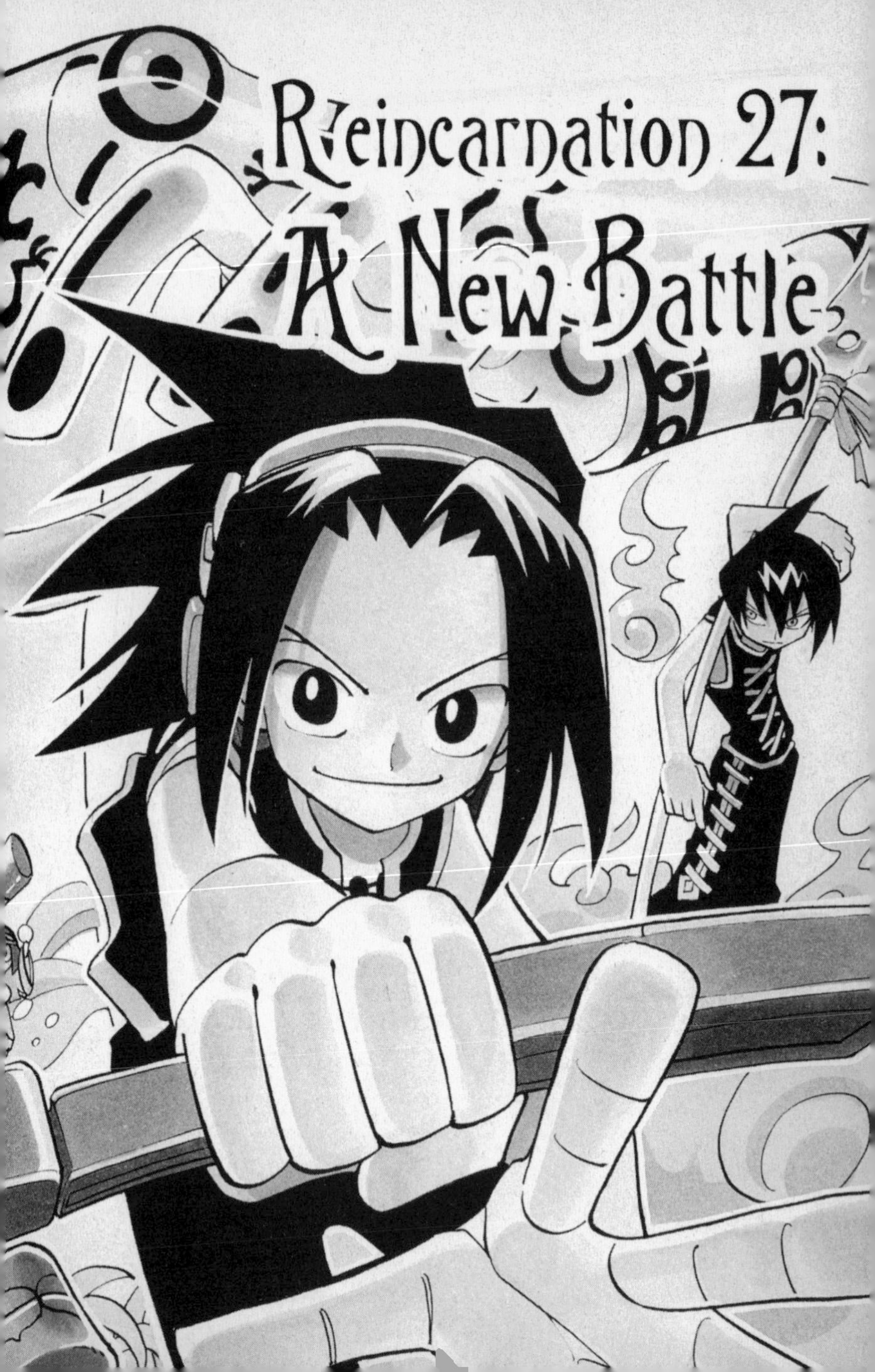
Reincarnation 27:
A New Battle

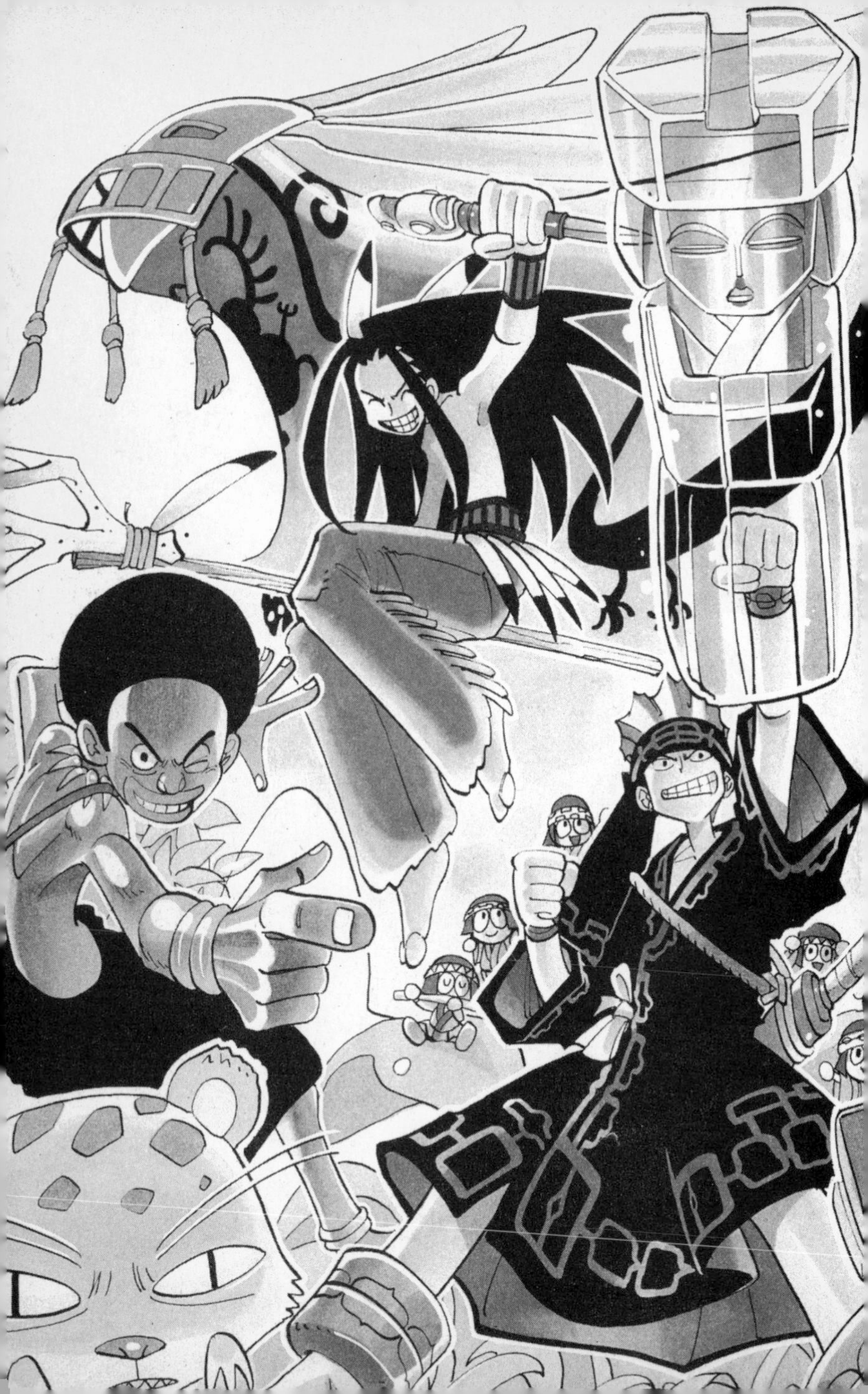

SHAMAN KING CHARACTER FILE No.14

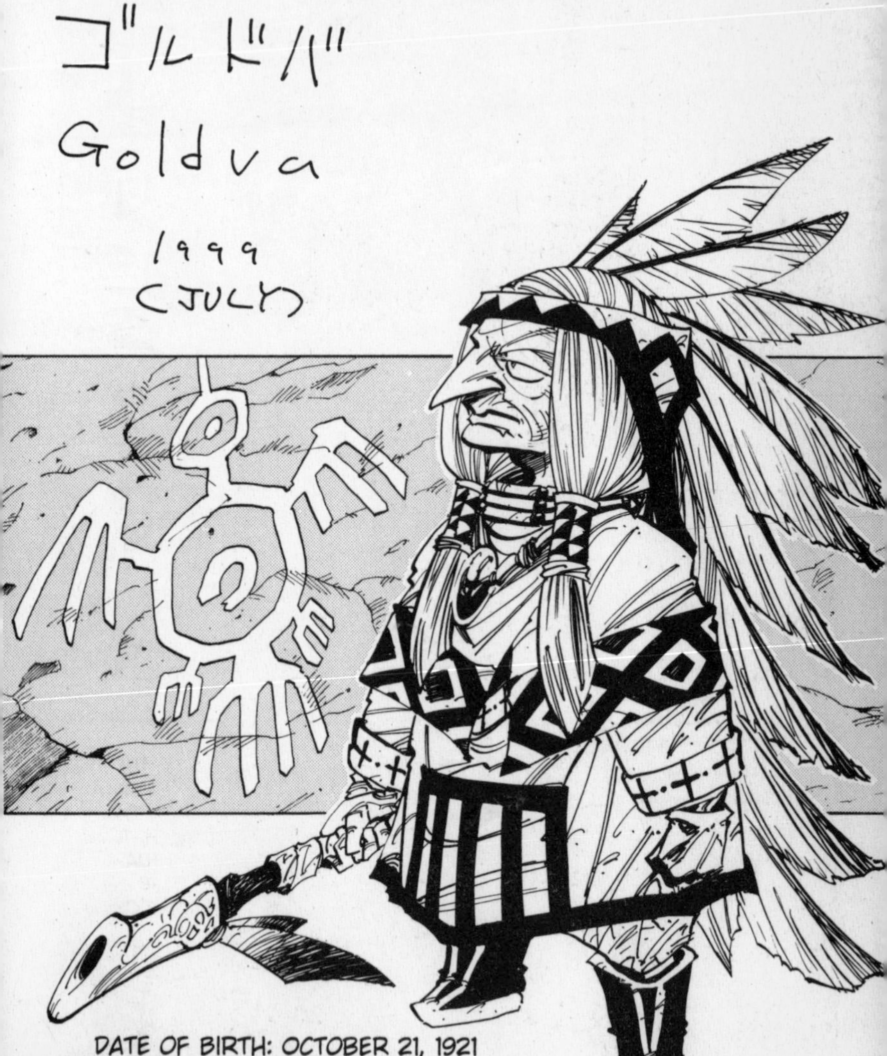

ゴルドバ
Goldva
1999
(JULY)

DATE OF BIRTH: OCTOBER 21, 1921
ASTROLOGICAL SIGN: LIBRA
BLOOD TYPE: O

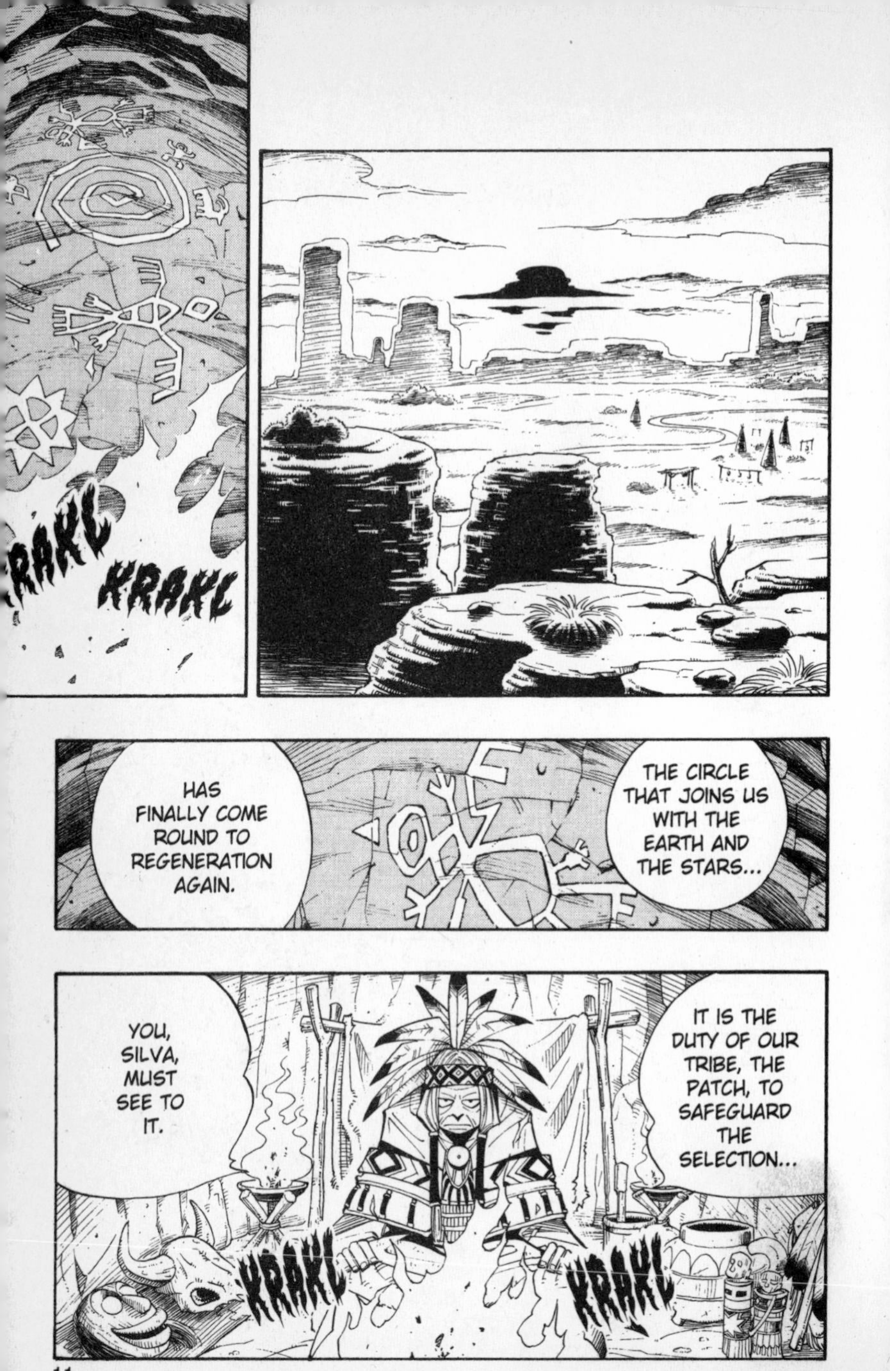
KRAKL
KRAKL
THE CIRCLE THAT JOINS US WITH THE EARTH AND THE STARS...
HAS FINALLY COME ROUND TO REGENERATION AGAIN.
IT IS THE DUTY OF OUR TRIBE, THE PATCH, TO SAFEGUARD THE SELECTION...
YOU, SILVA, MUST SEE TO IT.
KRAKL
KRAKL

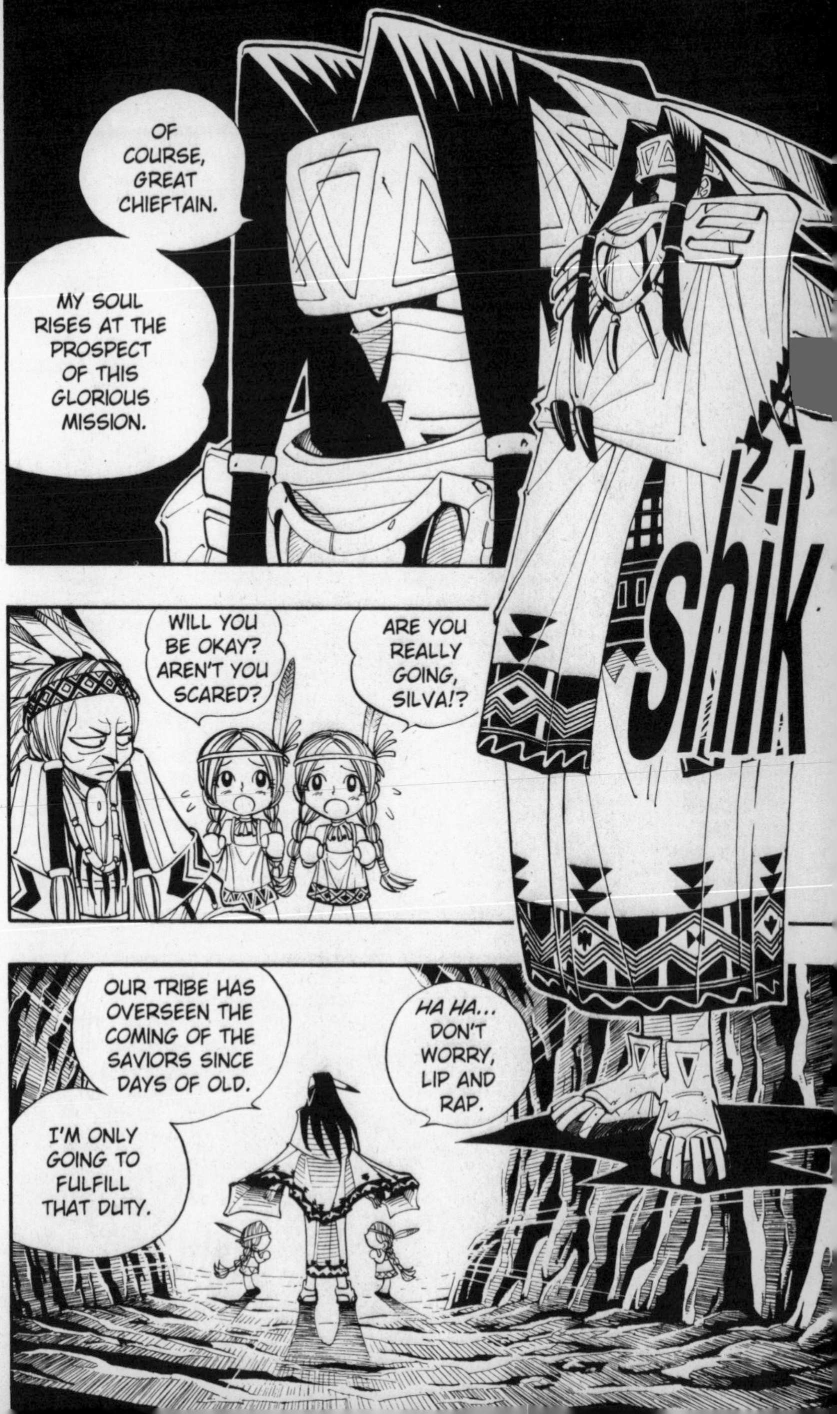
OF COURSE, GREAT CHIEFTAIN.
MY SOUL RISES AT THE PROSPECT OF THIS GLORIOUS MISSION.
shik
ARE YOU REALLY GOING, SILVA!?
WILL YOU BE OKAY? AREN'T YOU SCARED?
HA HA... DON'T WORRY, LIP AND RAP.
OUR TRIBE HAS OVERSEEN THE COMING OF THE SAVIORS SINCE DAYS OF OLD.
I'M ONLY GOING TO FULFILL THAT DUTY.

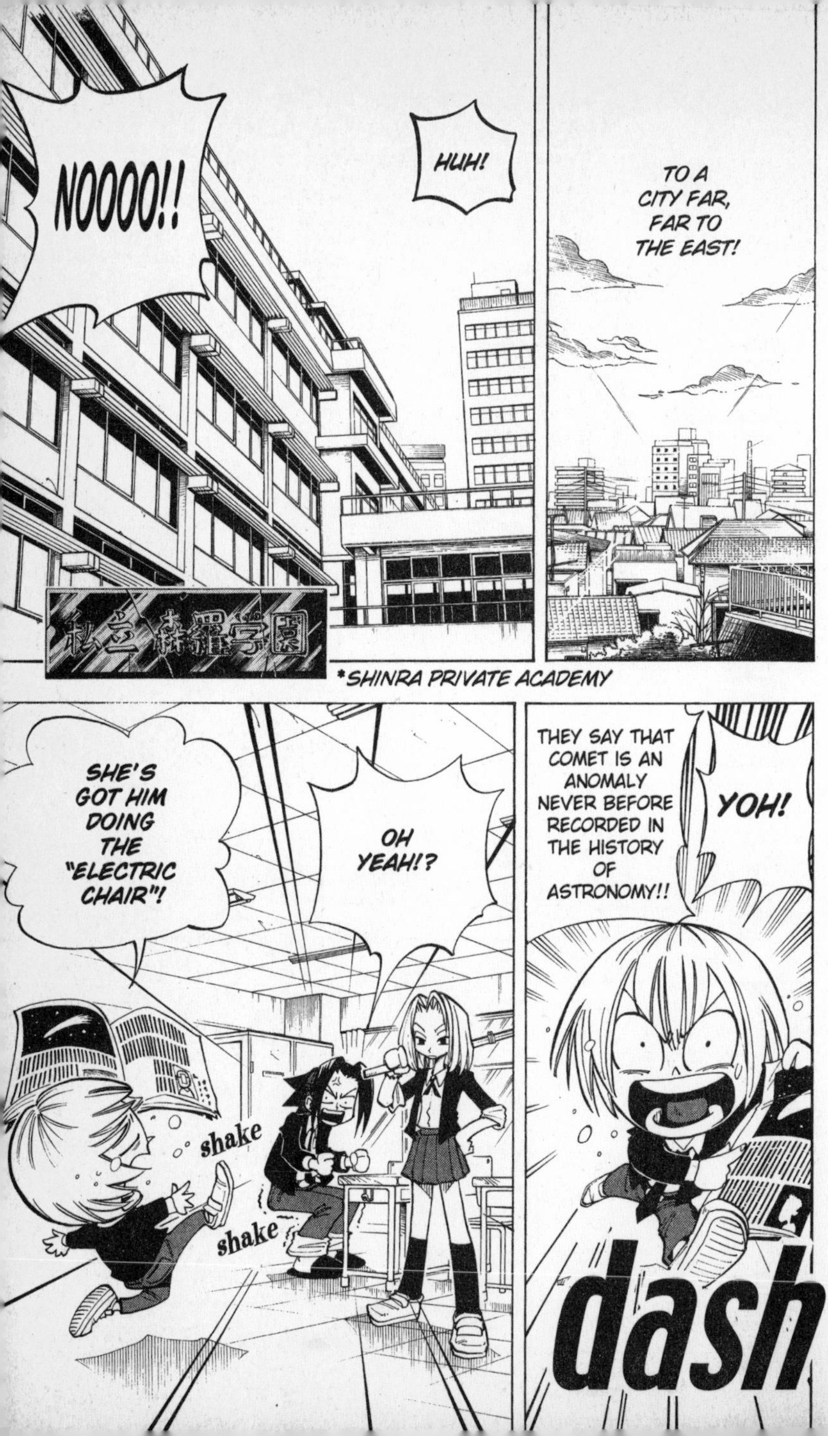
TO A CITY FAR, FAR TO THE EAST!
HUH!
NOOOO!!
私立森羅学園
*SHINRA PRIVATE ACADEMY
THEY SAY THAT COMET IS AN ANOMALY NEVER BEFORE RECORDED IN THE HISTORY OF ASTRONOMY!!
YOH!
dash
OH YEAH!?
SHE'S GOT HIM DOING THE "ELECTRIC CHAIR"!
shake
shake

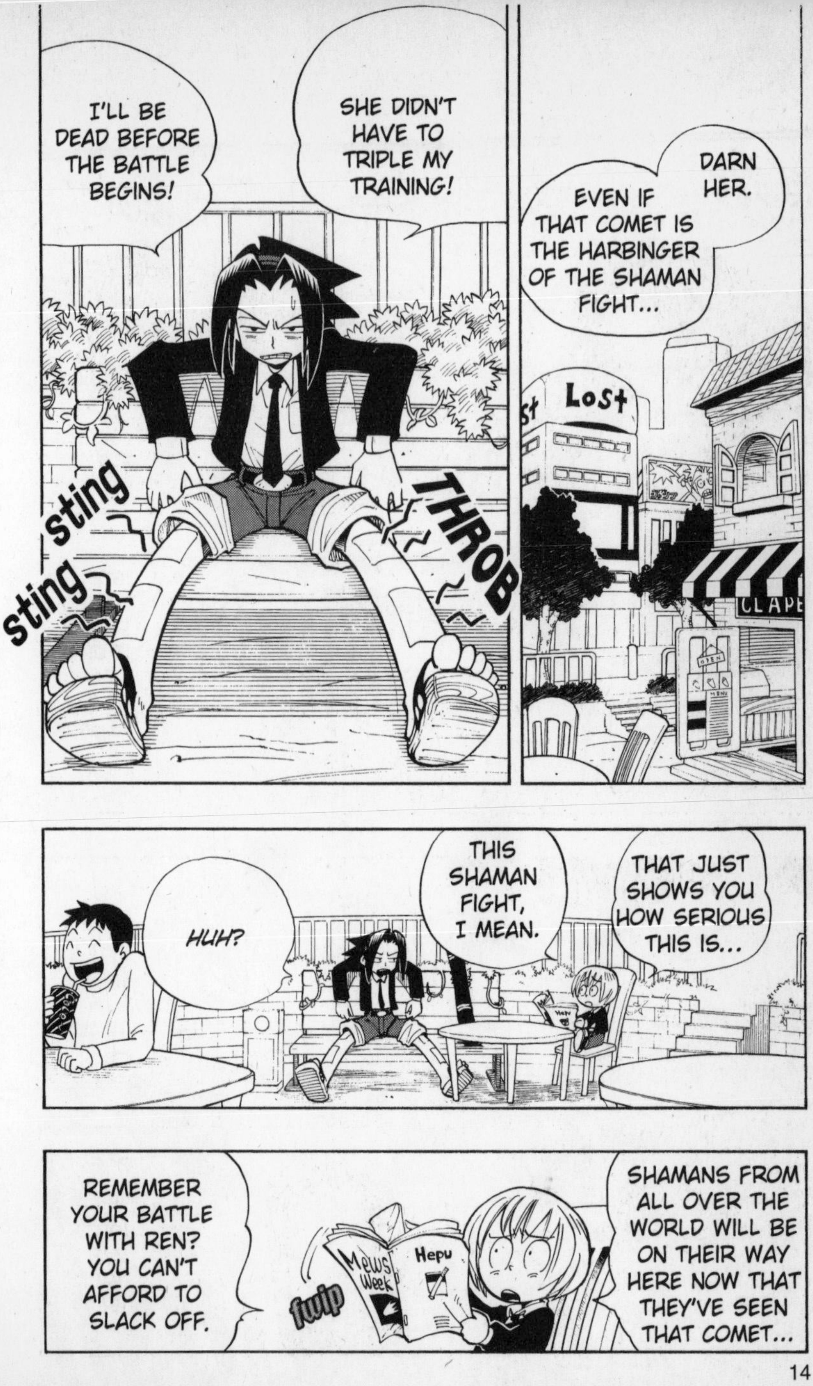
DARN HER.
EVEN IF THAT COMET IS THE HARBINGER OF THE SHAMAN FIGHT...
Lost
CLAPE
SHE DIDN'T HAVE TO TRIPLE MY TRAINING!
I'LL BE DEAD BEFORE THE BATTLE BEGINS!
THROB
sting sting
THAT JUST SHOWS YOU HOW SERIOUS THIS IS...
THIS SHAMAN FIGHT, I MEAN.
HUH?
SHAMANS FROM ALL OVER THE WORLD WILL BE ON THEIR WAY HERE NOW THAT THEY'VE SEEN THAT COMET...
Hepu
Mews Week
fwip
REMEMBER YOUR BATTLE WITH REN? YOU CAN'T AFFORD TO SLACK OFF.

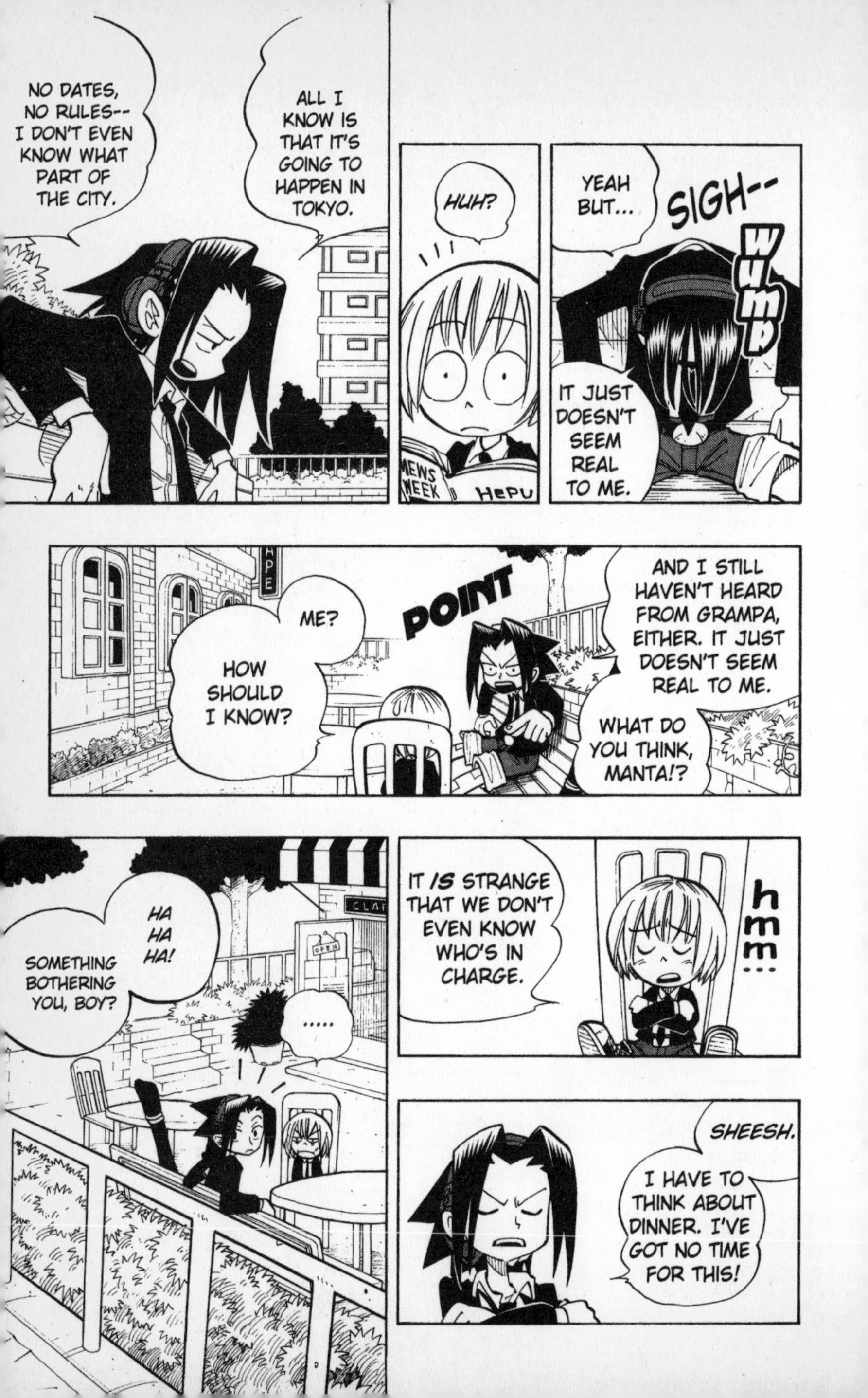
YEAH BUT...
SIGH--
WUMP
IT JUST DOESN'T SEEM REAL TO ME.
HUH?
NEWS WEEK
HEPU
ALL I KNOW IS THAT IT'S GOING TO HAPPEN IN TOKYO.
NO DATES, NO RULES-- I DON'T EVEN KNOW WHAT PART OF THE CITY.
AND I STILL HAVEN'T HEARD FROM GRAMPA, EITHER. IT JUST DOESN'T SEEM REAL TO ME.
WHAT DO YOU THINK, MANTA!?
POINT
ME?
HOW SHOULD I KNOW?
IT *IS* STRANGE THAT WE DON'T EVEN KNOW WHO'S IN CHARGE.
hmm...
SHEESH.
I HAVE TO THINK ABOUT DINNER. I'VE GOT NO TIME FOR THIS!
HA HA HA!
SOMETHING BOTHERING YOU, BOY?
.....

READ THIS WAY

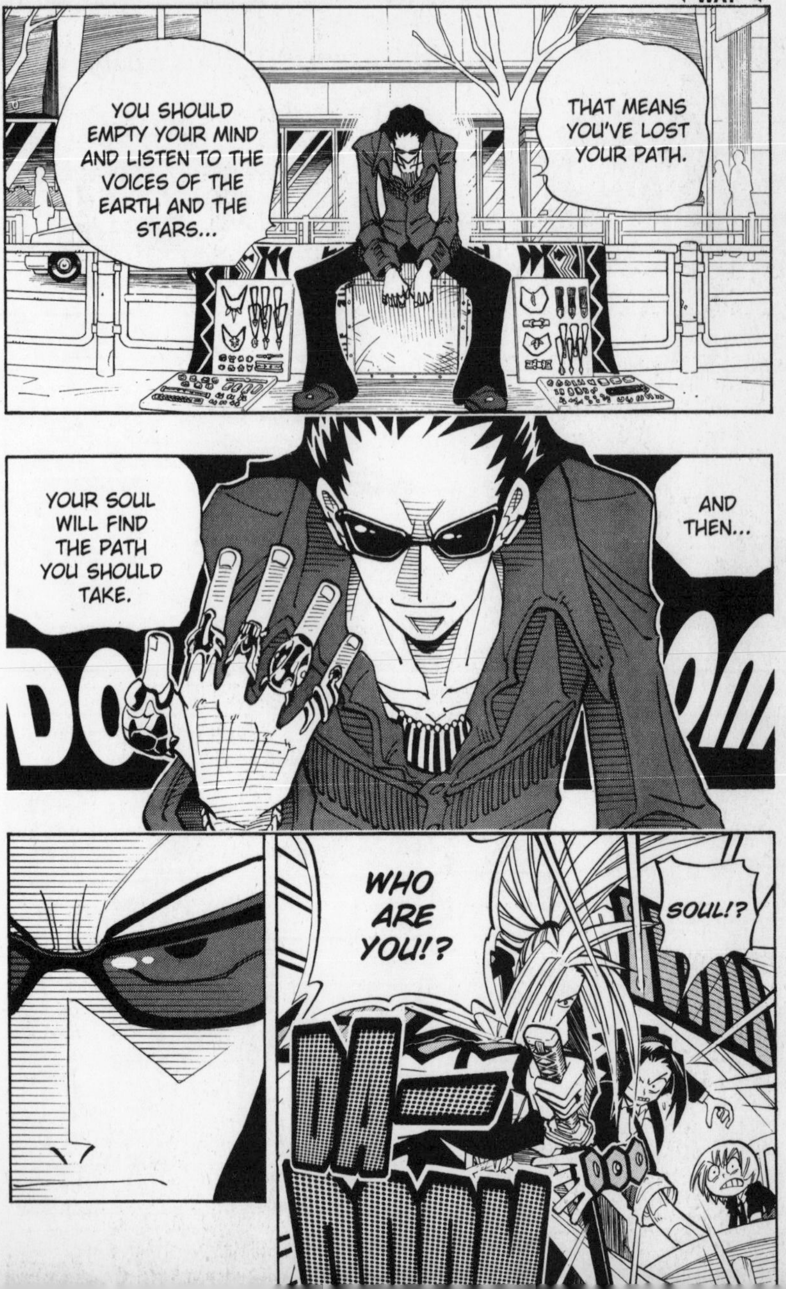
THAT MEANS YOU'VE LOST YOUR PATH.
YOU SHOULD EMPTY YOUR MIND AND LISTEN TO THE VOICES OF THE EARTH AND THE STARS...
AND THEN...
YOUR SOUL WILL FIND THE PATH YOU SHOULD TAKE.
SOUL!?
WHO ARE YOU!?
DA-

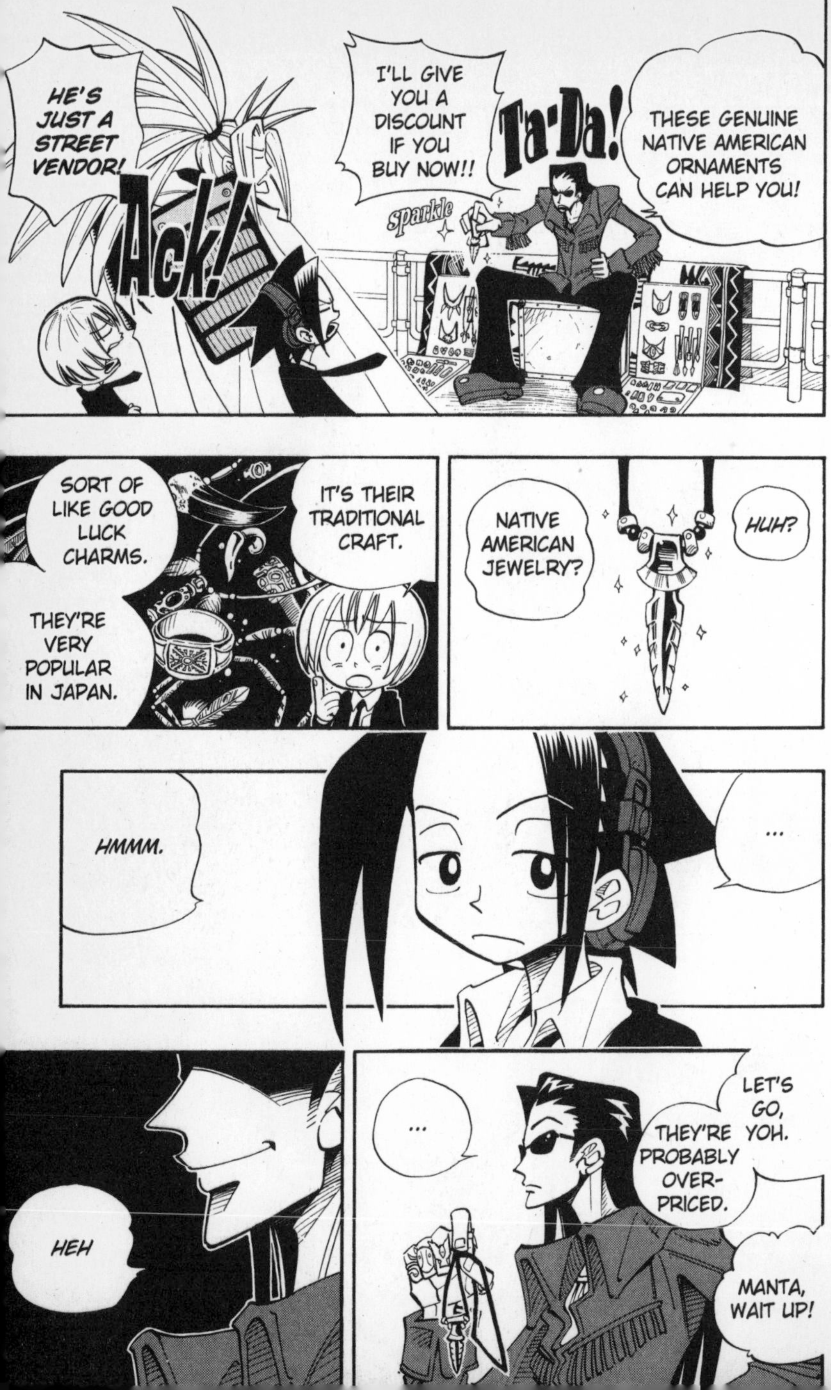
THESE GENUINE NATIVE AMERICAN ORNAMENTS CAN HELP YOU!
Ta-Da!
I'LL GIVE YOU A DISCOUNT IF YOU BUY NOW!!
sparkle
HE'S JUST A STREET VENDOR!
Ack!
HUH?
NATIVE AMERICAN JEWELRY?
IT'S THEIR TRADITIONAL CRAFT.
SORT OF LIKE GOOD LUCK CHARMS.
THEY'RE VERY POPULAR IN JAPAN.
...
HMMM.
LET'S GO, YOH.
THEY'RE PROBABLY OVER-PRICED.
...
MANTA, WAIT UP!
HEH

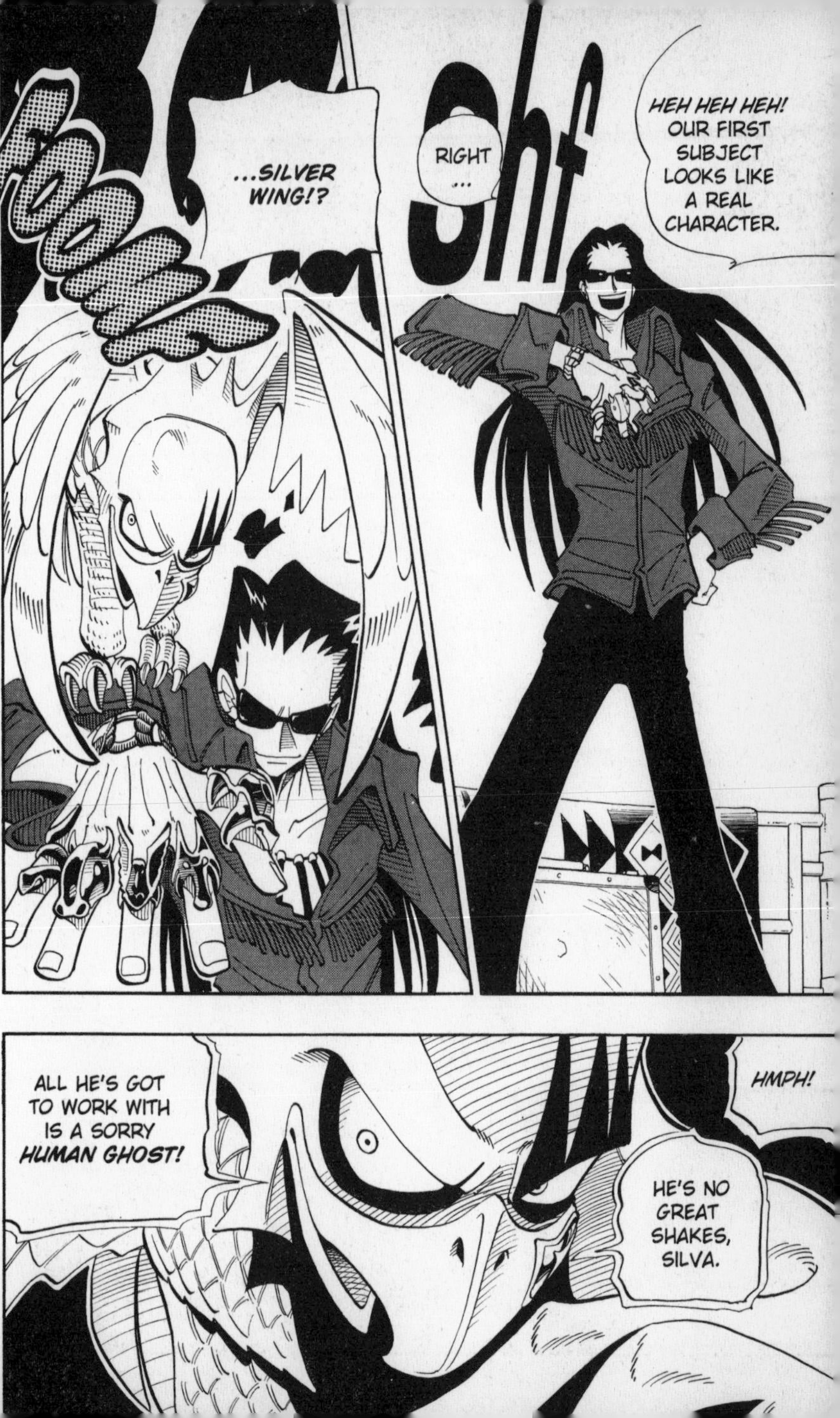
HEH HEH HEH! OUR FIRST SUBJECT LOOKS LIKE A REAL CHARACTER.
Shf
RIGHT ...
...SILVER WING!?
HMPH!
HE'S NO GREAT SHAKES, SILVA.
ALL HE'S GOT TO WORK WITH IS A SORRY HUMAN GHOST!

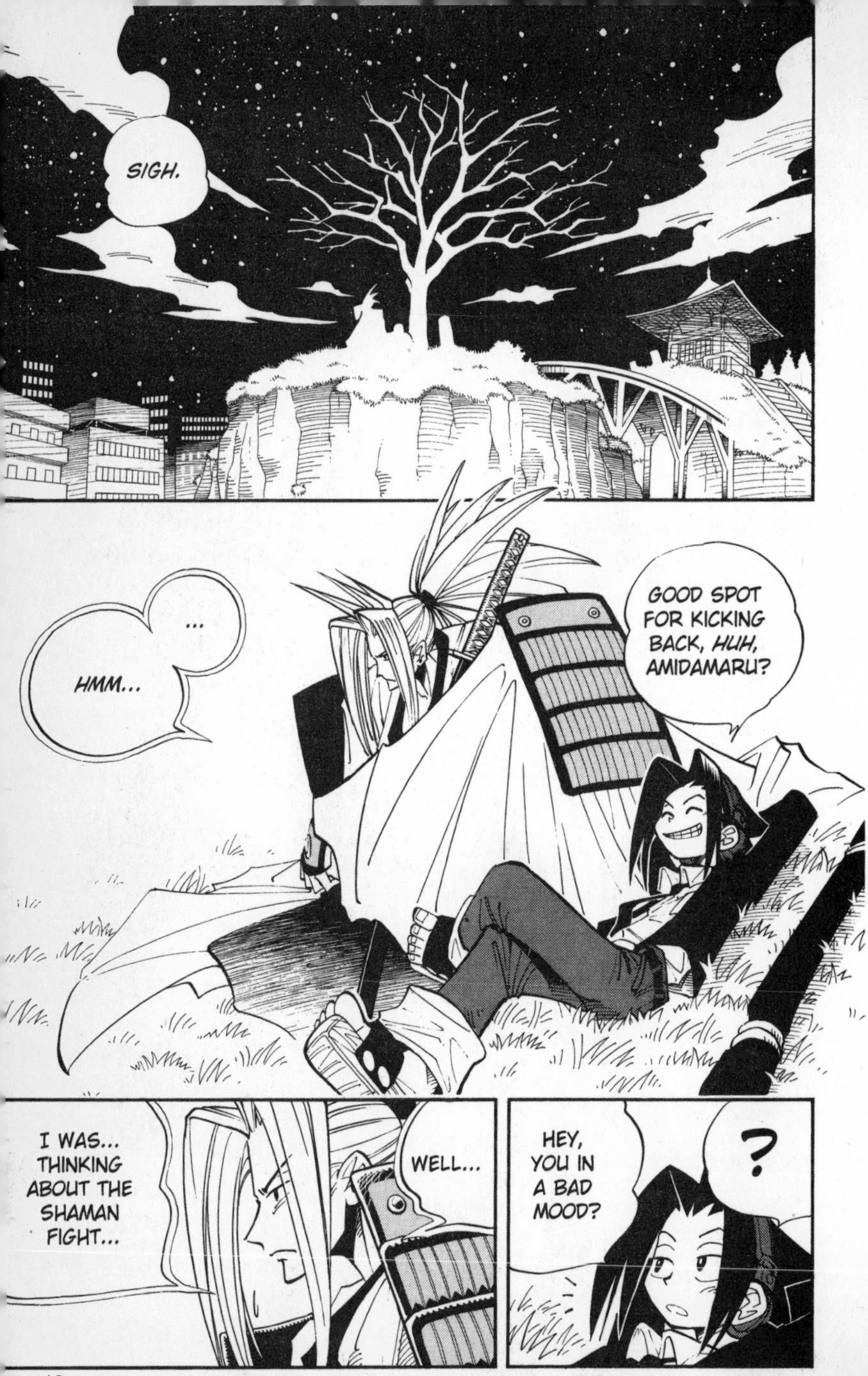
SIGH.
GOOD SPOT FOR KICKING BACK, *HUH*, AMIDAMARU?
...
HMM...
?
HEY, YOU IN A BAD MOOD?
WELL...
I WAS... THINKING ABOUT THE SHAMAN FIGHT...

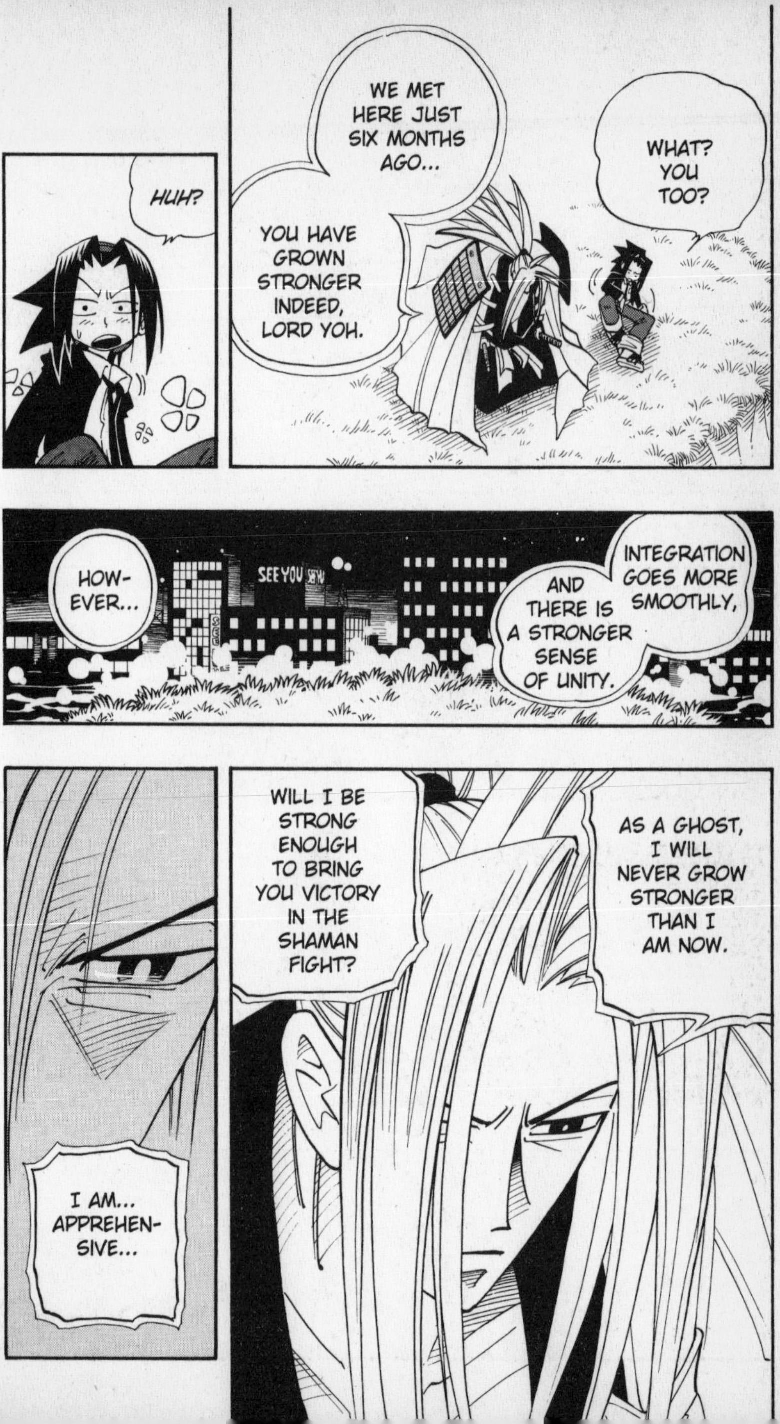
WE MET HERE JUST SIX MONTHS AGO...
YOU HAVE GROWN STRONGER INDEED, LORD YOH.
WHAT? YOU TOO?
HUH?
INTEGRATION GOES MORE SMOOTHLY,
AND THERE IS A STRONGER SENSE OF UNITY.
SEE YOU
HOW-EVER...
AS A GHOST, I WILL NEVER GROW STRONGER THAN I AM NOW.
WILL I BE STRONG ENOUGH TO BRING YOU VICTORY IN THE SHAMAN FIGHT?
I AM... APPREHEN-SIVE...

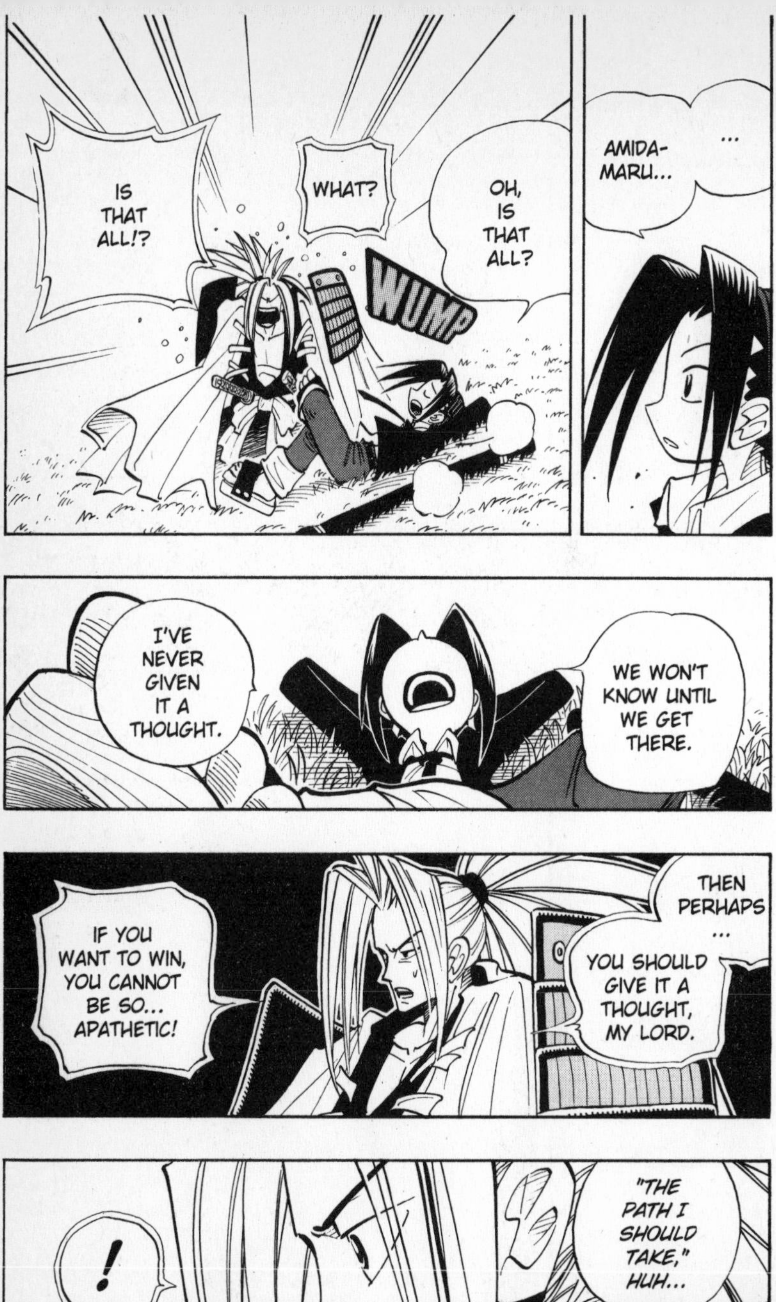
...
AMIDA-MARU...
OH, IS THAT ALL?
WHAT?
WUMP
IS THAT ALL!?
WE WON'T KNOW UNTIL WE GET THERE.
I'VE NEVER GIVEN IT A THOUGHT.
THEN PERHAPS... YOU SHOULD GIVE IT A THOUGHT, MY LORD.
IF YOU WANT TO WIN, YOU CANNOT BE SO... APATHETIC!
"THE PATH I SHOULD TAKE," HUH...
!

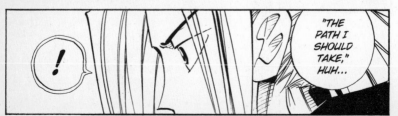

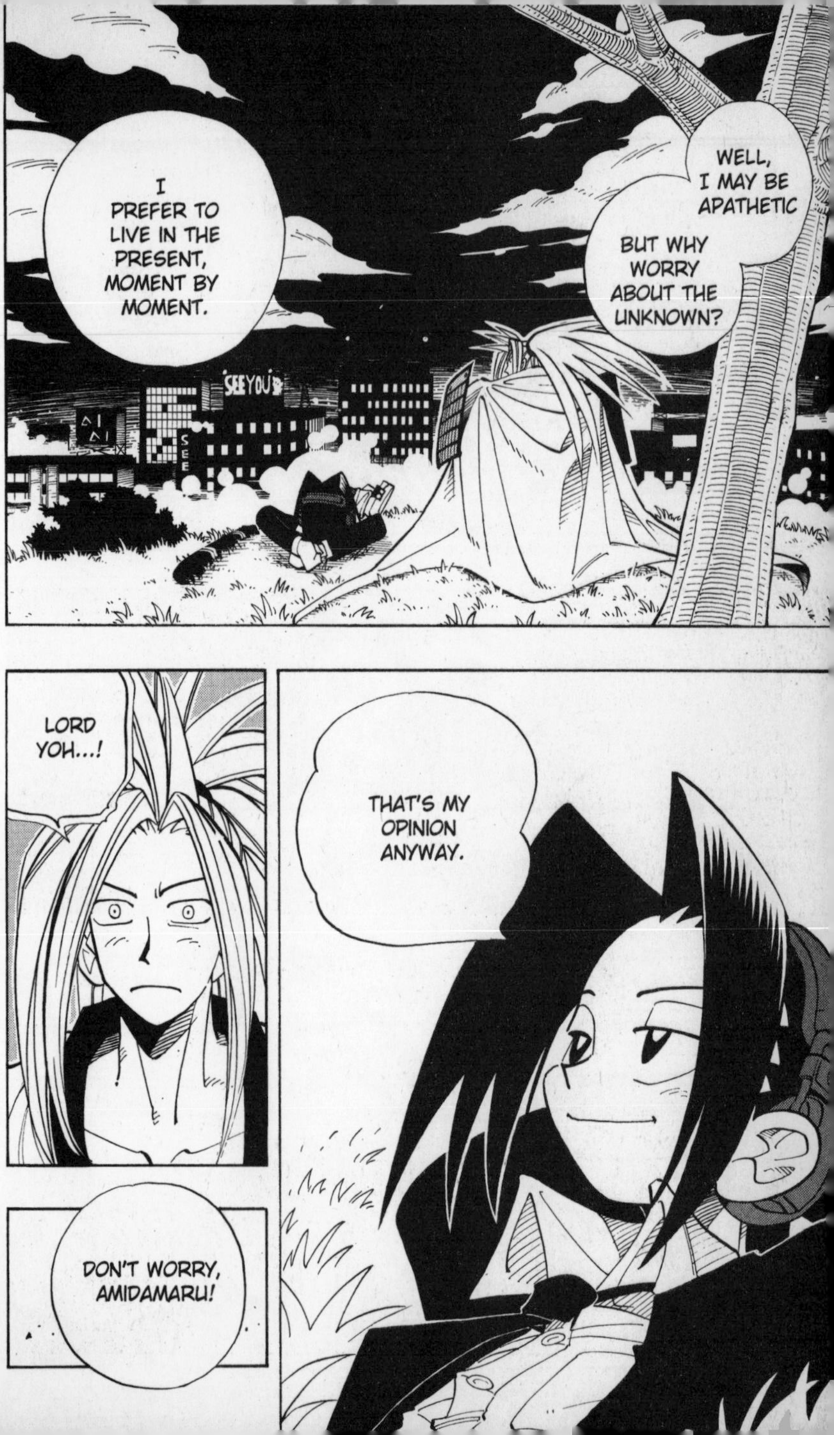
WELL, I MAY BE APATHETIC
BUT WHY WORRY ABOUT THE UNKNOWN?
I PREFER TO LIVE IN THE PRESENT, MOMENT BY MOMENT.
SEEYOU
THAT'S MY OPINION ANYWAY.
LORD YOH...!
DON'T WORRY, AMIDAMARU!

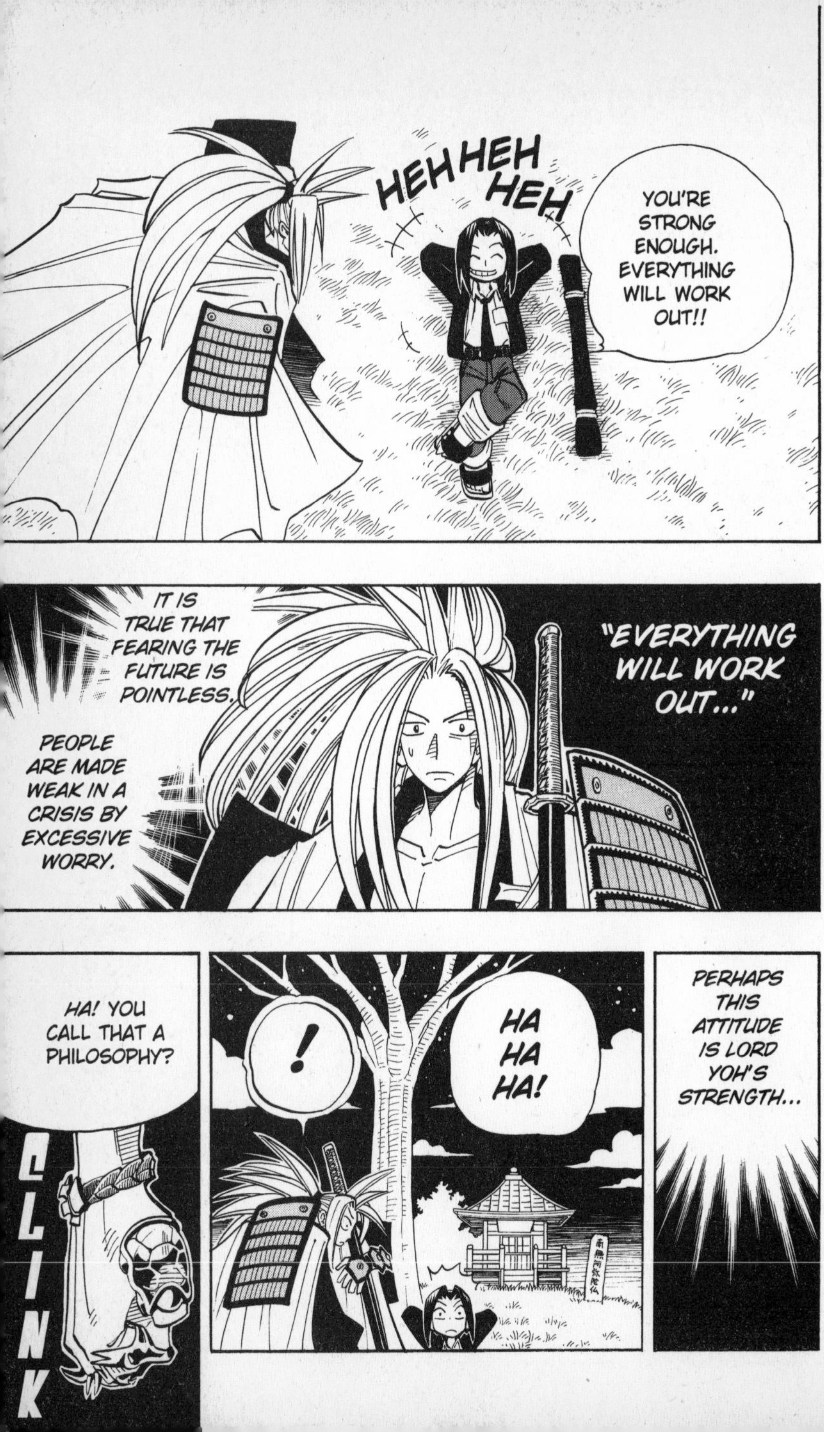
HEH HEH HEH
YOU'RE STRONG ENOUGH. EVERYTHING WILL WORK OUT!!
"EVERYTHING WILL WORK OUT..."
IT IS TRUE THAT FEARING THE FUTURE IS POINTLESS.
PEOPLE ARE MADE WEAK IN A CRISIS BY EXCESSIVE WORRY.
PERHAPS THIS ATTITUDE IS LORD YOH'S STRENGTH...
HA HA HA!
!
HA! YOU CALL THAT A PHILOSOPHY?
CLINK

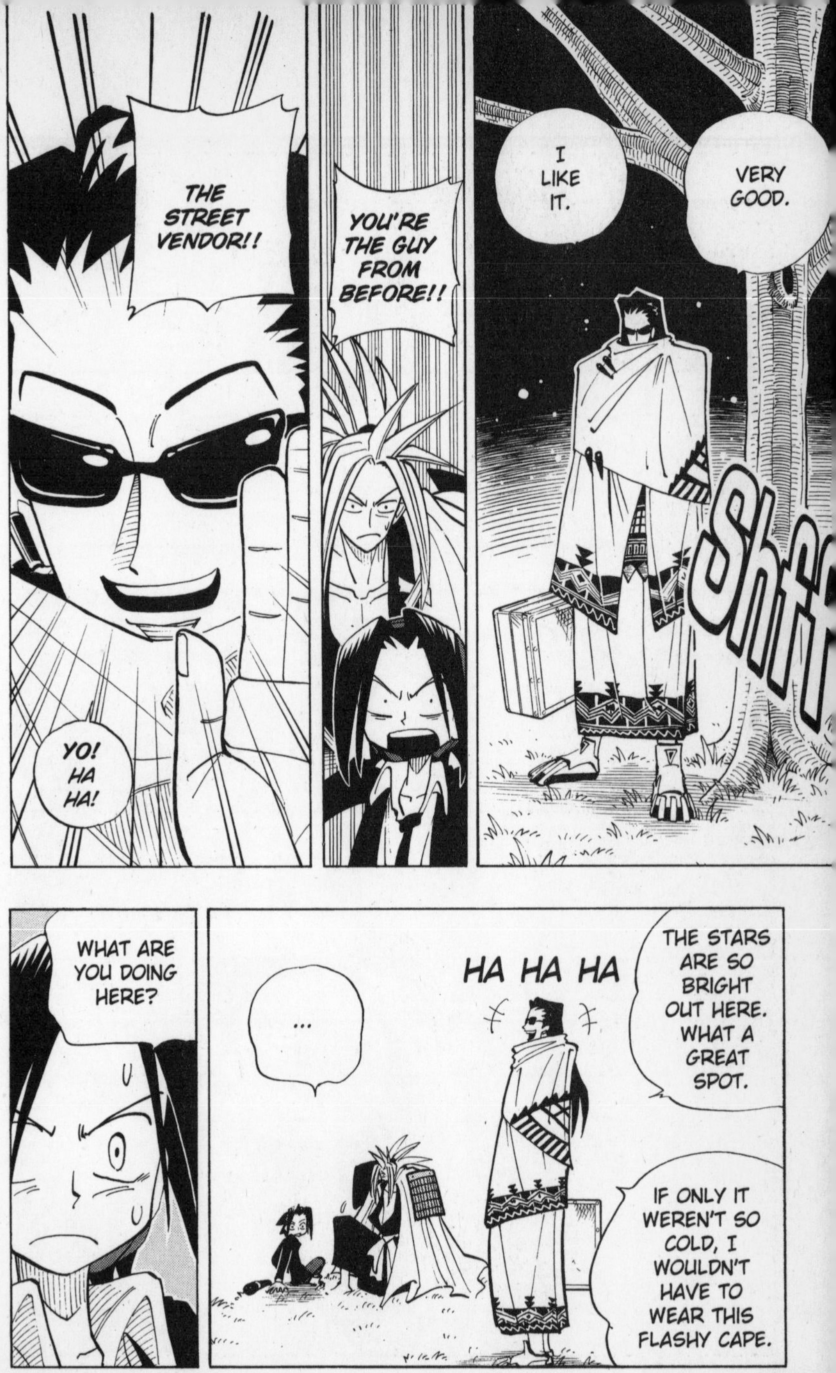
VERY GOOD.
I LIKE IT.
Shff
YOU'RE THE GUY FROM BEFORE!!
THE STREET VENDOR!!
YO! HA HA!
THE STARS ARE SO BRIGHT OUT HERE. WHAT A GREAT SPOT.
HA HA HA
...
IF ONLY IT WEREN'T SO COLD, I WOULDN'T HAVE TO WEAR THIS FLASHY CAPE.
WHAT ARE YOU DOING HERE?

READ THIS WAY

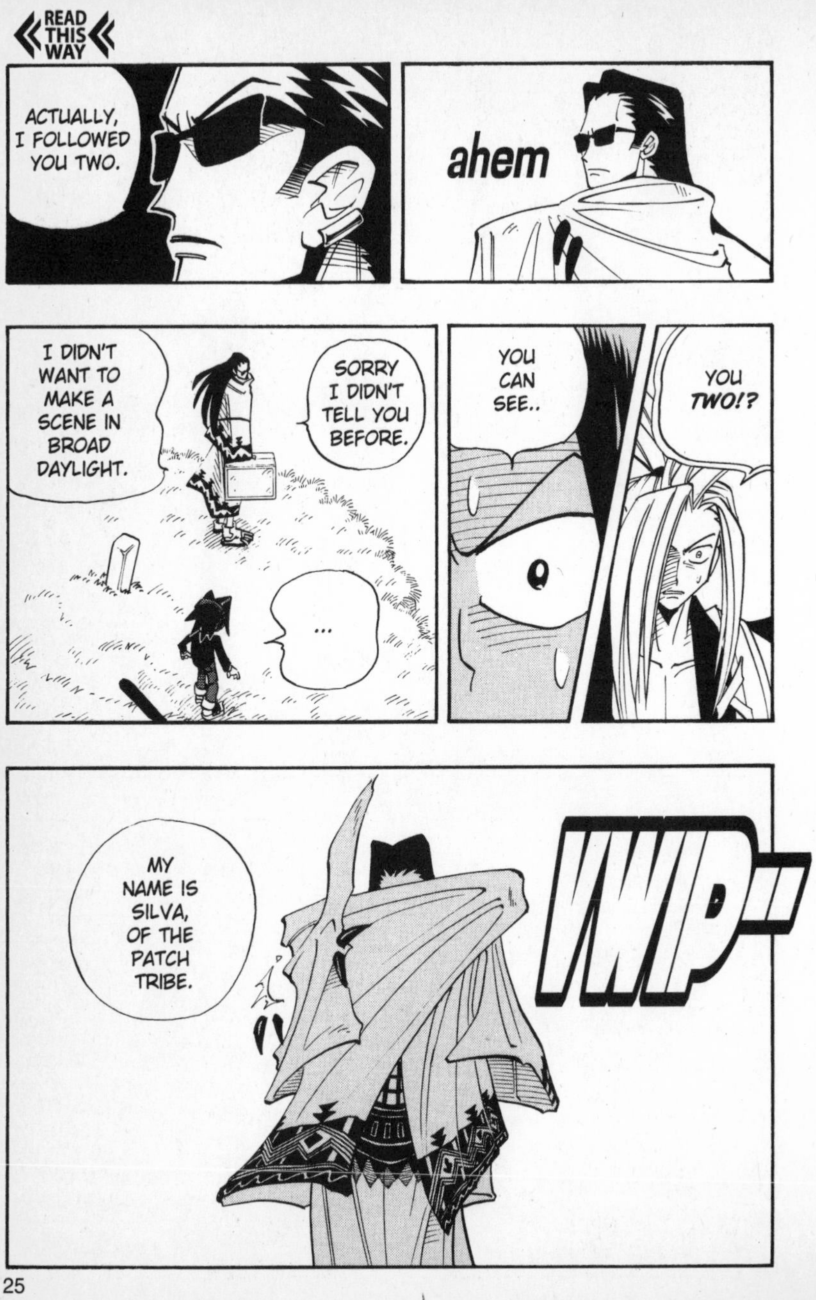
ahem
ACTUALLY, I FOLLOWED YOU TWO.
YOU *TWO!?*
YOU CAN SEE..
SORRY I DIDN'T TELL YOU BEFORE.
I DIDN'T WANT TO MAKE A SCENE IN BROAD DAYLIGHT.
...
VWIP-
MY NAME IS SILVA, OF THE PATCH TRIBE.

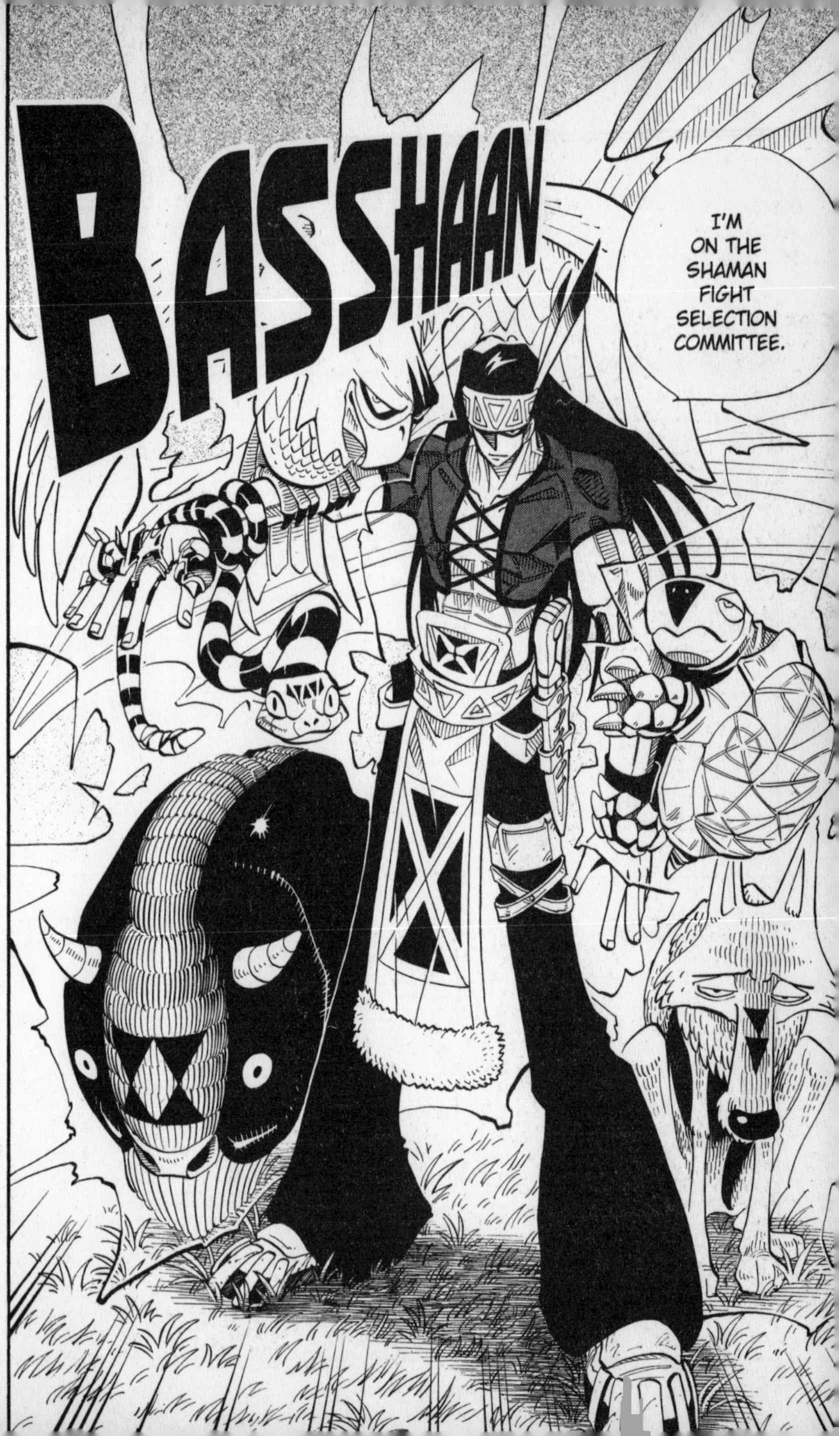
I'M ON THE SHAMAN FIGHT SELECTION COMMITTEE.
BASSHAAN

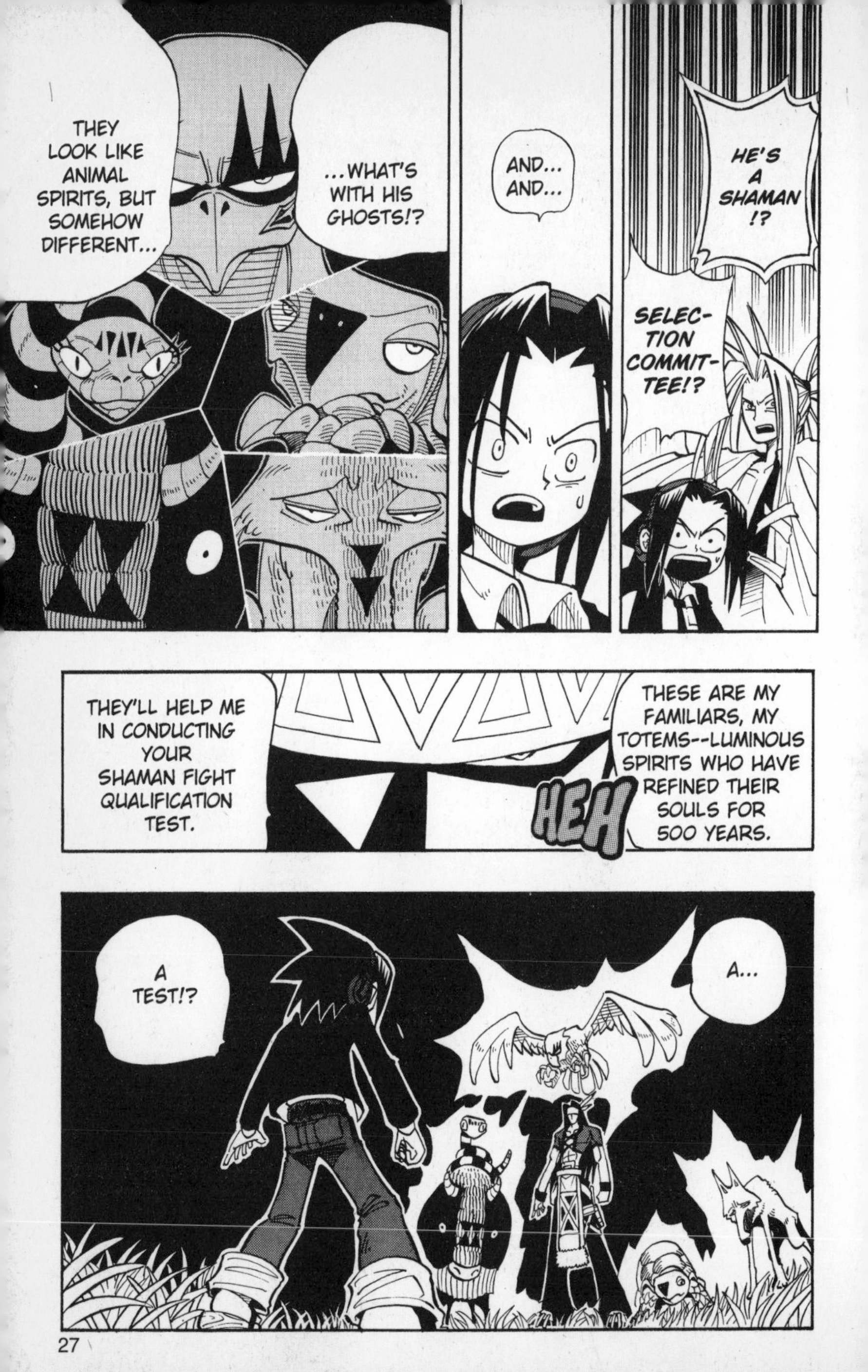
HE'S A SHAMAN !?
SELEC-TION COMMIT-TEE!?
AND... AND...
...WHAT'S WITH HIS GHOSTS!?
THEY LOOK LIKE ANIMAL SPIRITS, BUT SOMEHOW DIFFERENT...
THESE ARE MY FAMILIARS, MY TOTEMS--LUMINOUS SPIRITS WHO HAVE REFINED THEIR SOULS FOR 500 YEARS.
HEH
THEY'LL HELP ME IN CONDUCTING YOUR SHAMAN FIGHT QUALIFICATION TEST.
A...
A TEST!?

SHAMAN
KING
4

THE COMET
RAHU

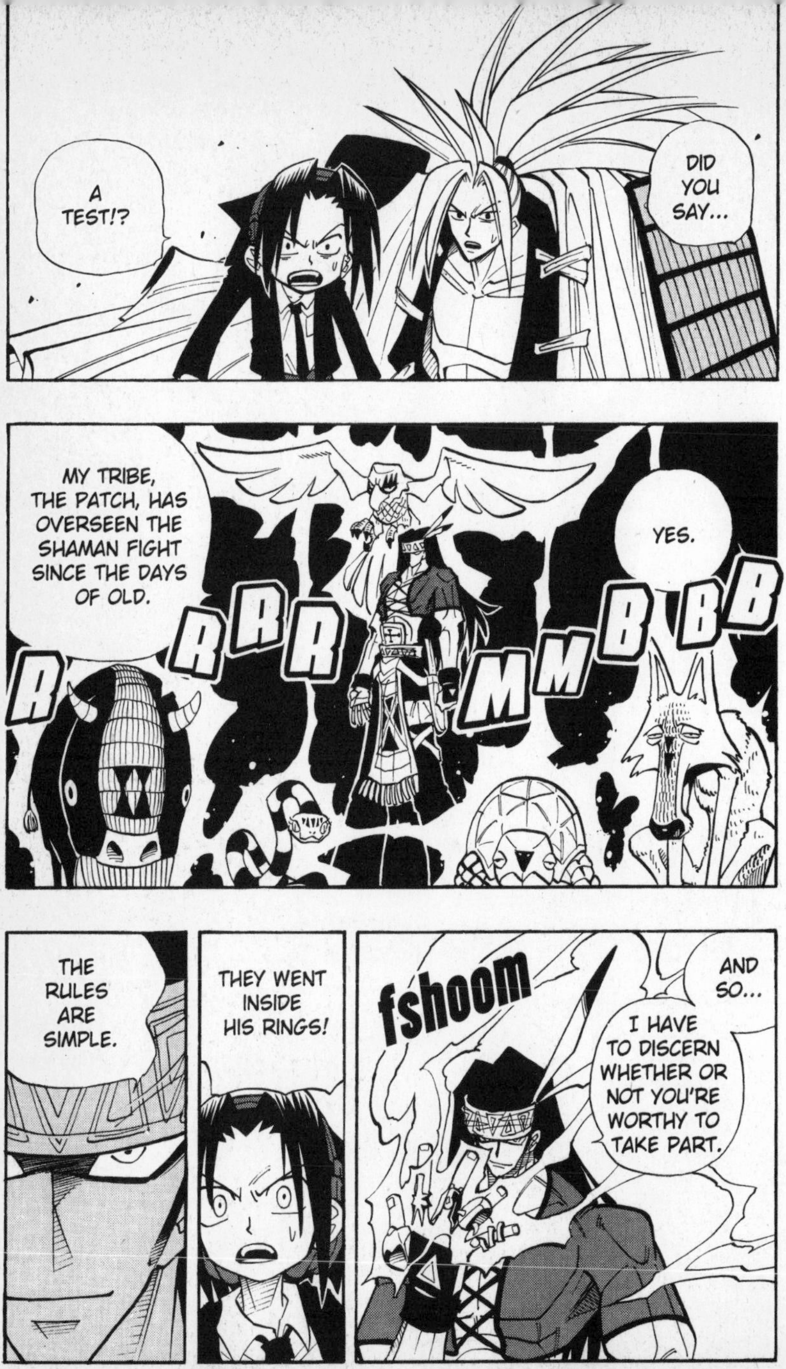
DID YOU SAY...
A TEST!?
YES.
MY TRIBE, THE PATCH, HAS OVERSEEN THE SHAMAN FIGHT SINCE THE DAYS OF OLD.
RRRRRMMMBBB
AND SO...
I HAVE TO DISCERN WHETHER OR NOT YOU'RE WORTHY TO TAKE PART.
fshoom
THEY WENT INSIDE HIS RINGS!
THE RULES ARE SIMPLE.

REINCARNATION 28: SILVA STYLE

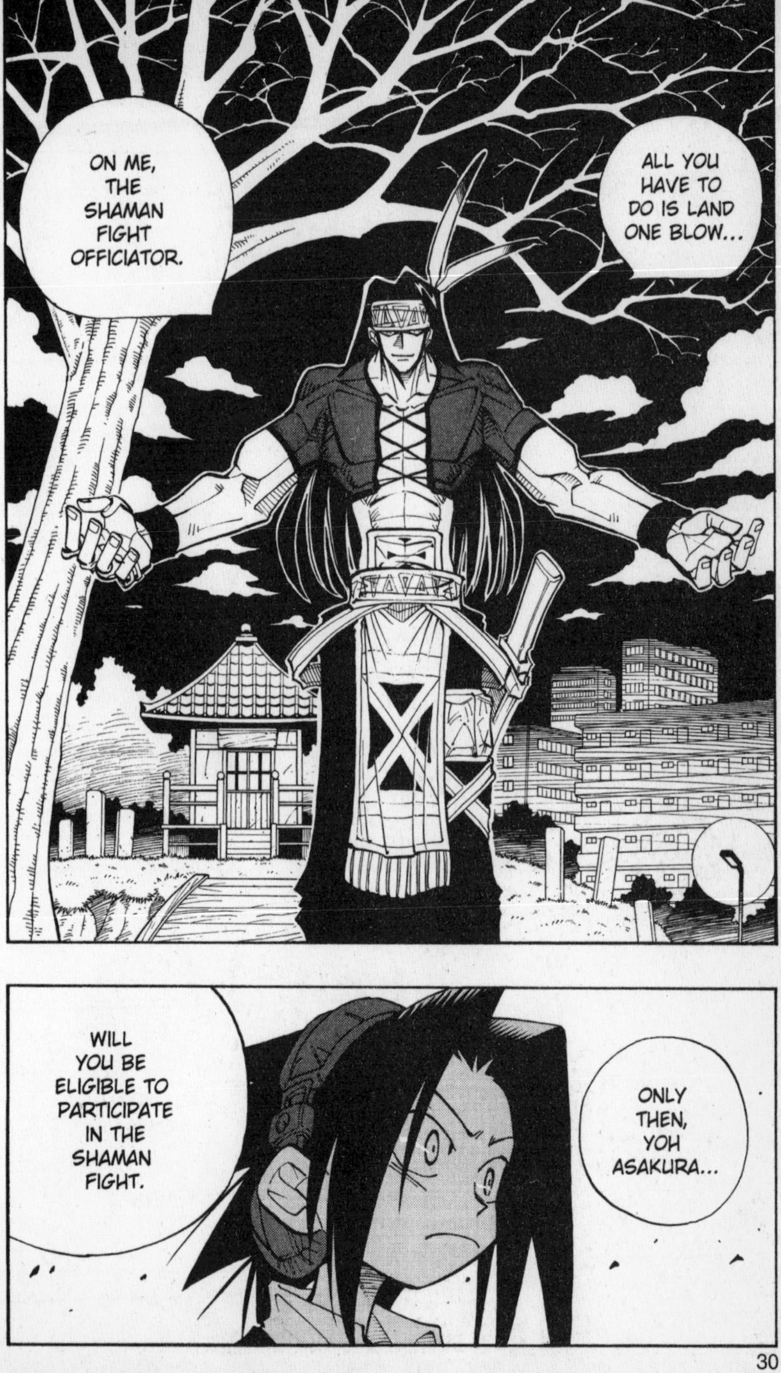
ALL YOU HAVE TO DO IS LAND ONE BLOW...
ON ME, THE SHAMAN FIGHT OFFICIATOR.
ONLY THEN, YOH ASAKURA...
WILL YOU BE ELIGIBLE TO PARTICIPATE IN THE SHAMAN FIGHT.

READ THIS WAY

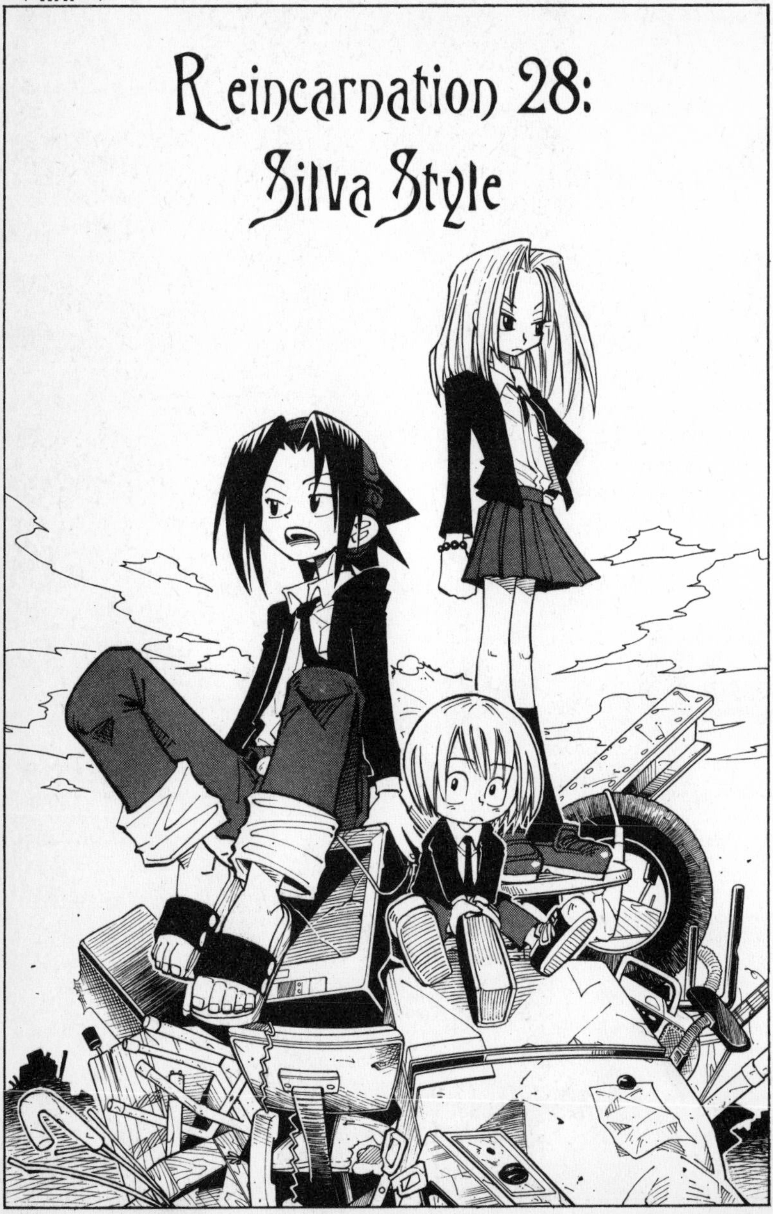
Reincarnation 28:
Silva Style

READ THIS WAY

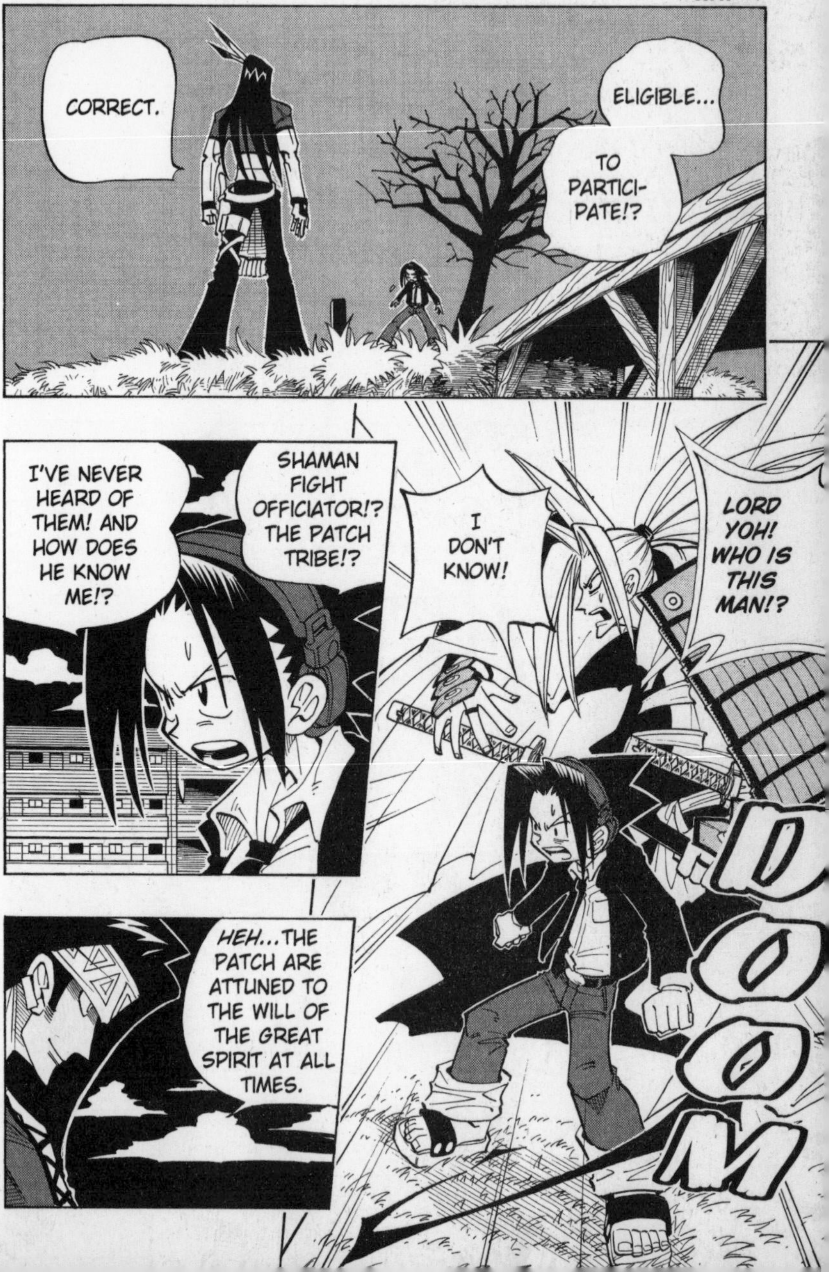
ELIGIBLE...
TO PARTICI-PATE!?
CORRECT.
LORD YOH! WHO IS THIS MAN!?
I DON'T KNOW!
DOOOM
SHAMAN FIGHT OFFICIATOR!? THE PATCH TRIBE!?
I'VE NEVER HEARD OF THEM! AND HOW DOES HE KNOW ME!?
HEH...THE PATCH ARE ATTUNED TO THE WILL OF THE GREAT SPIRIT AT ALL TIMES.

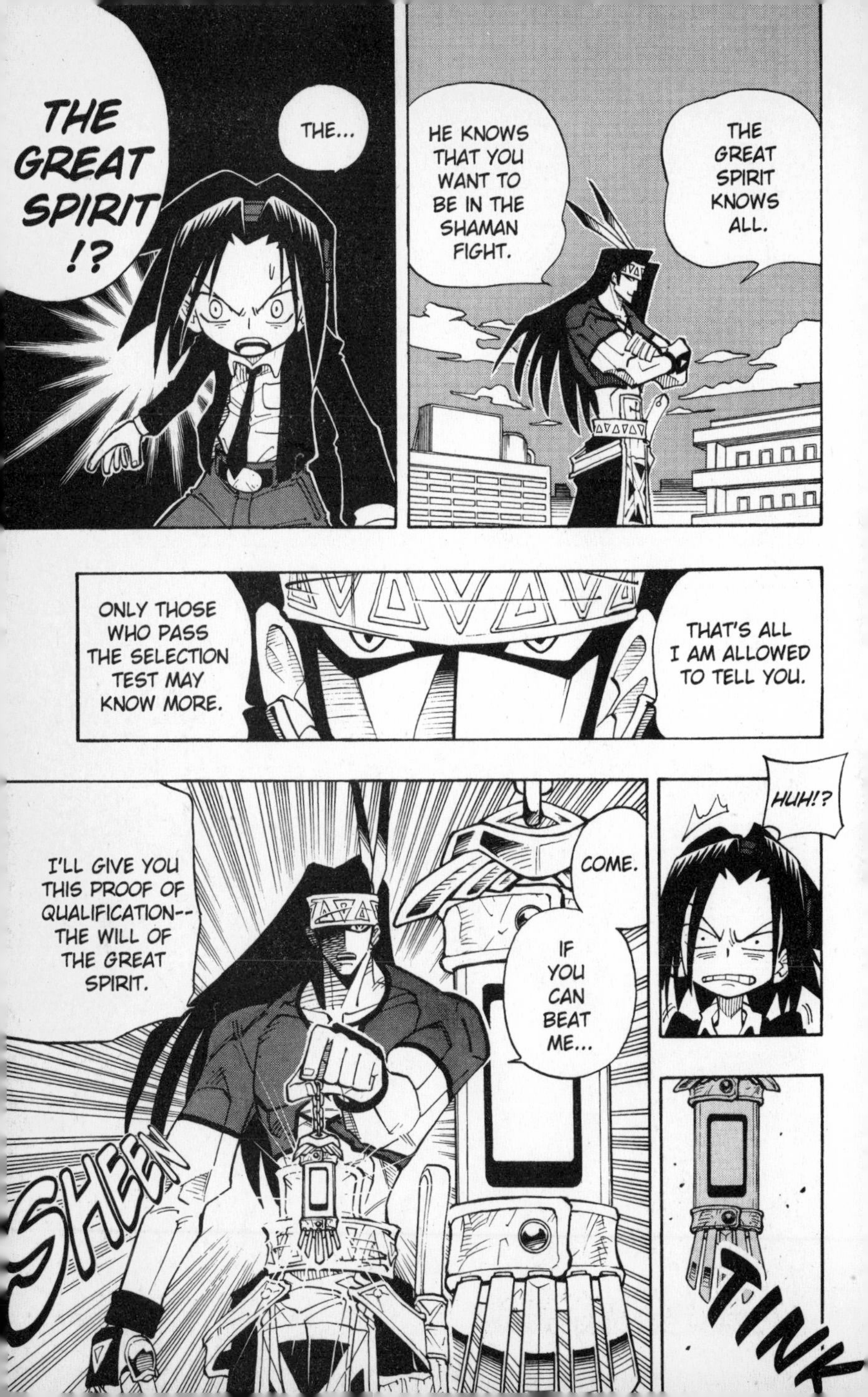
THE GREAT SPIRIT KNOWS ALL.
HE KNOWS THAT YOU WANT TO BE IN THE SHAMAN FIGHT.
THE...
THE GREAT SPIRIT !?
THAT'S ALL I AM ALLOWED TO TELL YOU.
ONLY THOSE WHO PASS THE SELECTION TEST MAY KNOW MORE.
HUH!?
TINK
COME.
IF YOU CAN BEAT ME...
I'LL GIVE YOU THIS PROOF OF QUALIFICATION-- THE WILL OF THE GREAT SPIRIT.
SHEEN

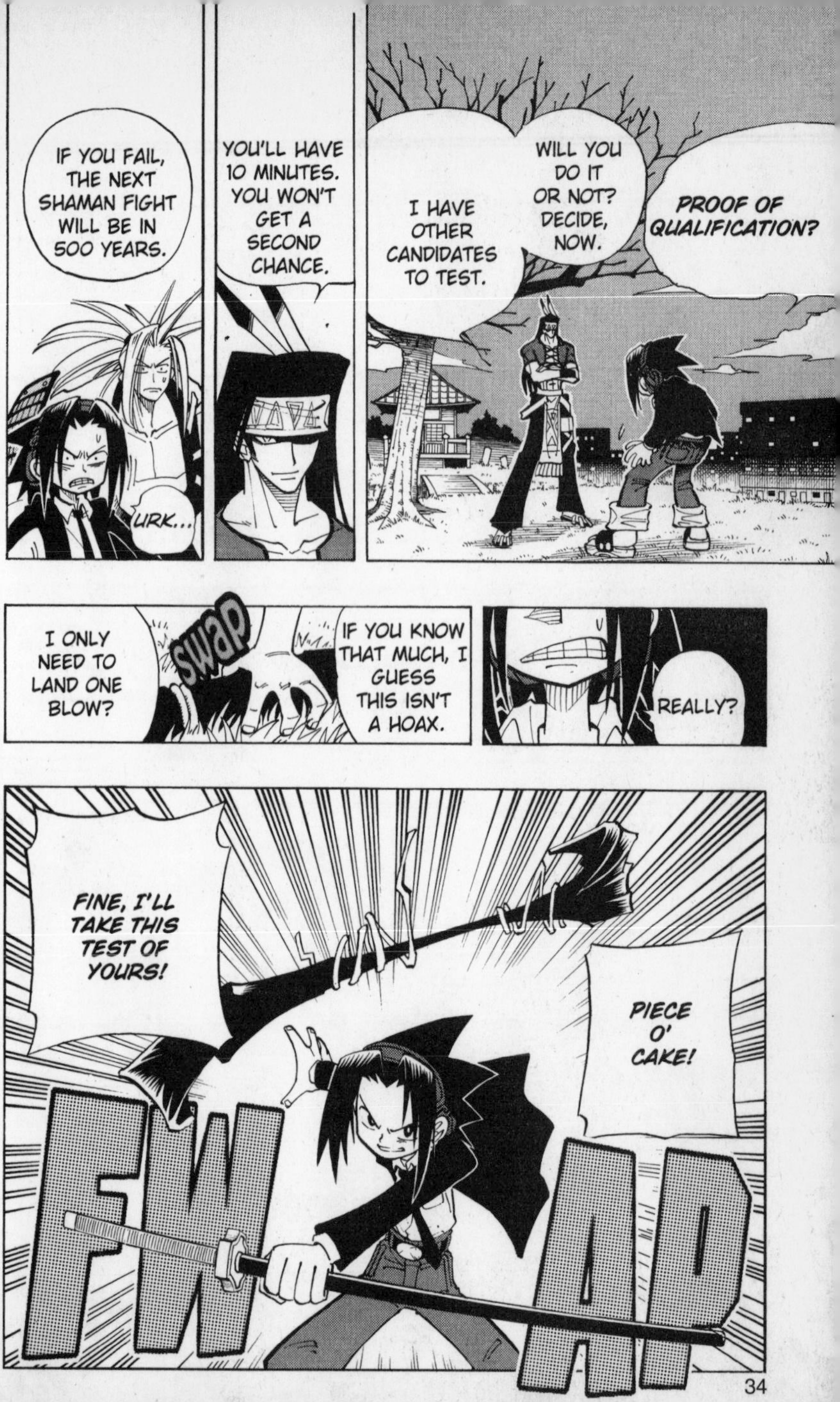
PROOF OF QUALIFICATION?
WILL YOU DO IT OR NOT? DECIDE, NOW.
I HAVE OTHER CANDIDATES TO TEST.
YOU'LL HAVE 10 MINUTES. YOU WON'T GET A SECOND CHANCE.
IF YOU FAIL, THE NEXT SHAMAN FIGHT WILL BE IN 500 YEARS.
URK...
REALLY?
IF YOU KNOW THAT MUCH, I GUESS THIS ISN'T A HOAX.
SWAP
I ONLY NEED TO LAND ONE BLOW?
PIECE O' CAKE!
FINE, I'LL TAKE THIS TEST OF YOURS!
FWAP

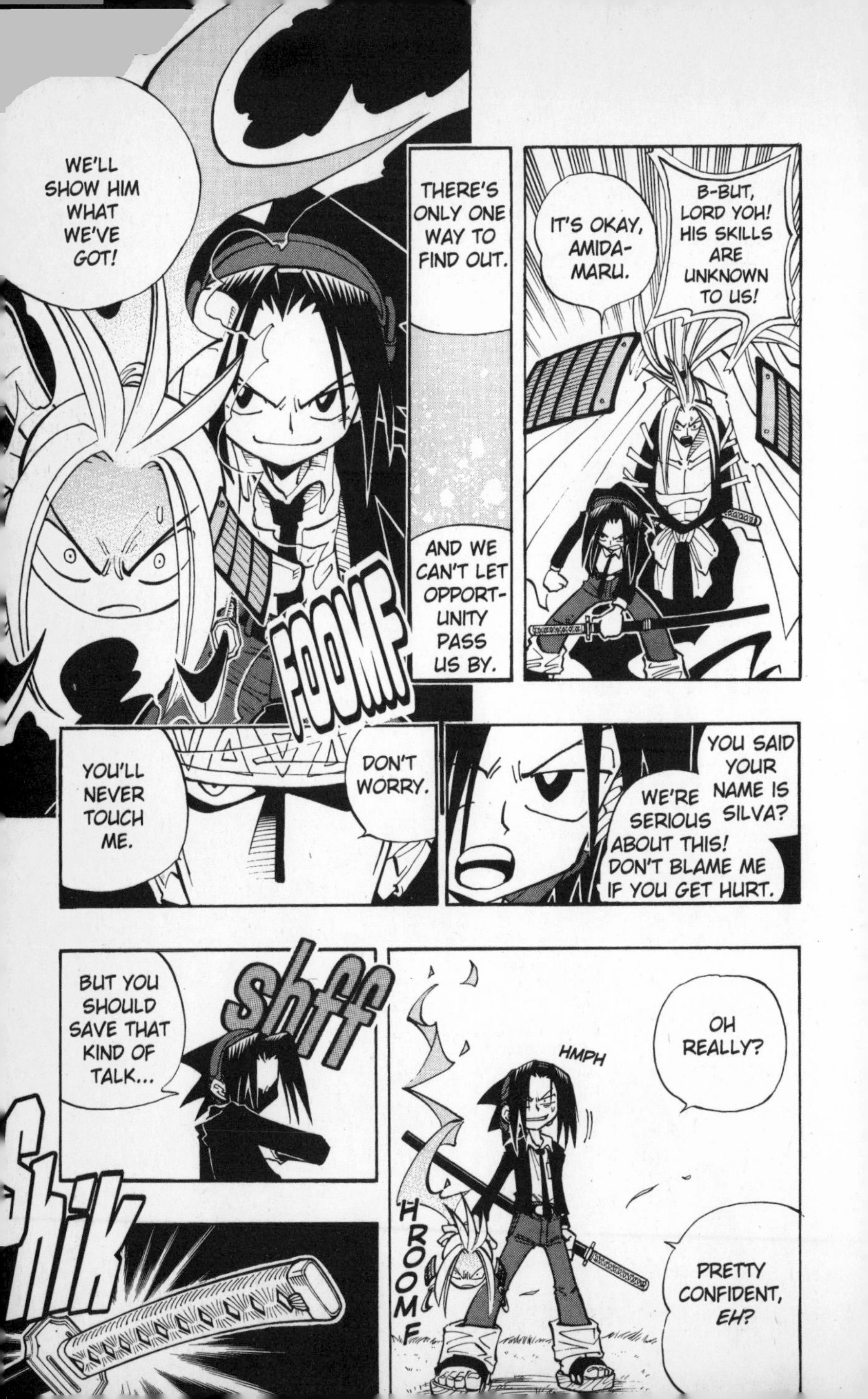
B-BUT, LORD YOH! HIS SKILLS ARE UNKNOWN TO US!
IT'S OKAY, AMIDA-MARU.
THERE'S ONLY ONE WAY TO FIND OUT.
AND WE CAN'T LET OPPORT-UNITY PASS US BY.
WE'LL SHOW HIM WHAT WE'VE GOT!
FOOMF
YOU SAID YOUR NAME IS SILVA?
WE'RE SERIOUS ABOUT THIS! DON'T BLAME ME IF YOU GET HURT.
DON'T WORRY.
YOU'LL NEVER TOUCH ME.
OH REALLY?
HMPH
HROOMF
PRETTY CONFIDENT, EH?
shff
BUT YOU SHOULD SAVE THAT KIND OF TALK...
Shik

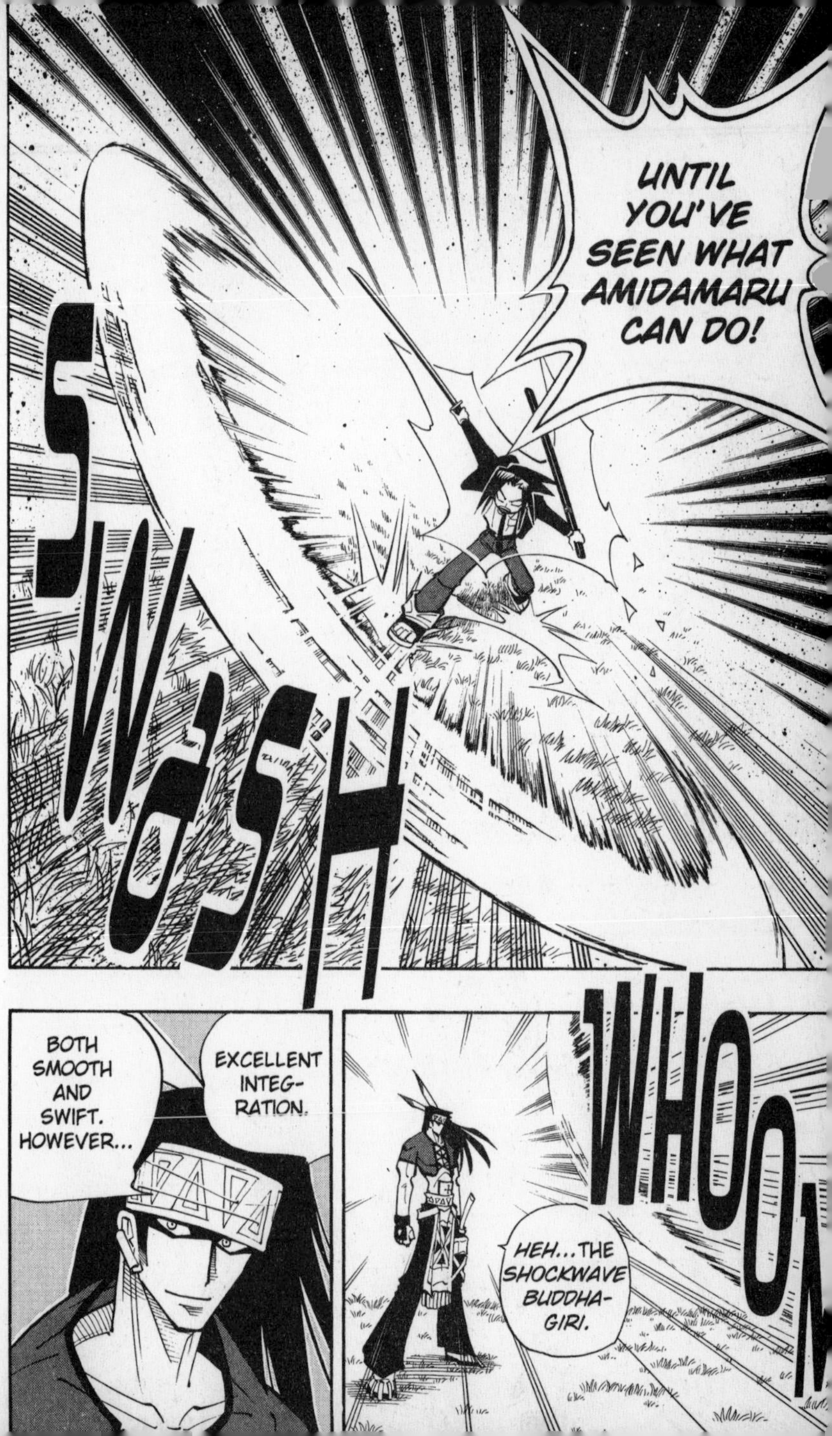
UNTIL YOU'VE SEEN WHAT AMIDAMARU CAN DO!
SWASH
WHOOM
HEH... THE SHOCKWAVE BUDDHA-GIRI.
EXCELLENT INTEG-RATION.
BOTH SMOOTH AND SWIFT. HOWEVER...

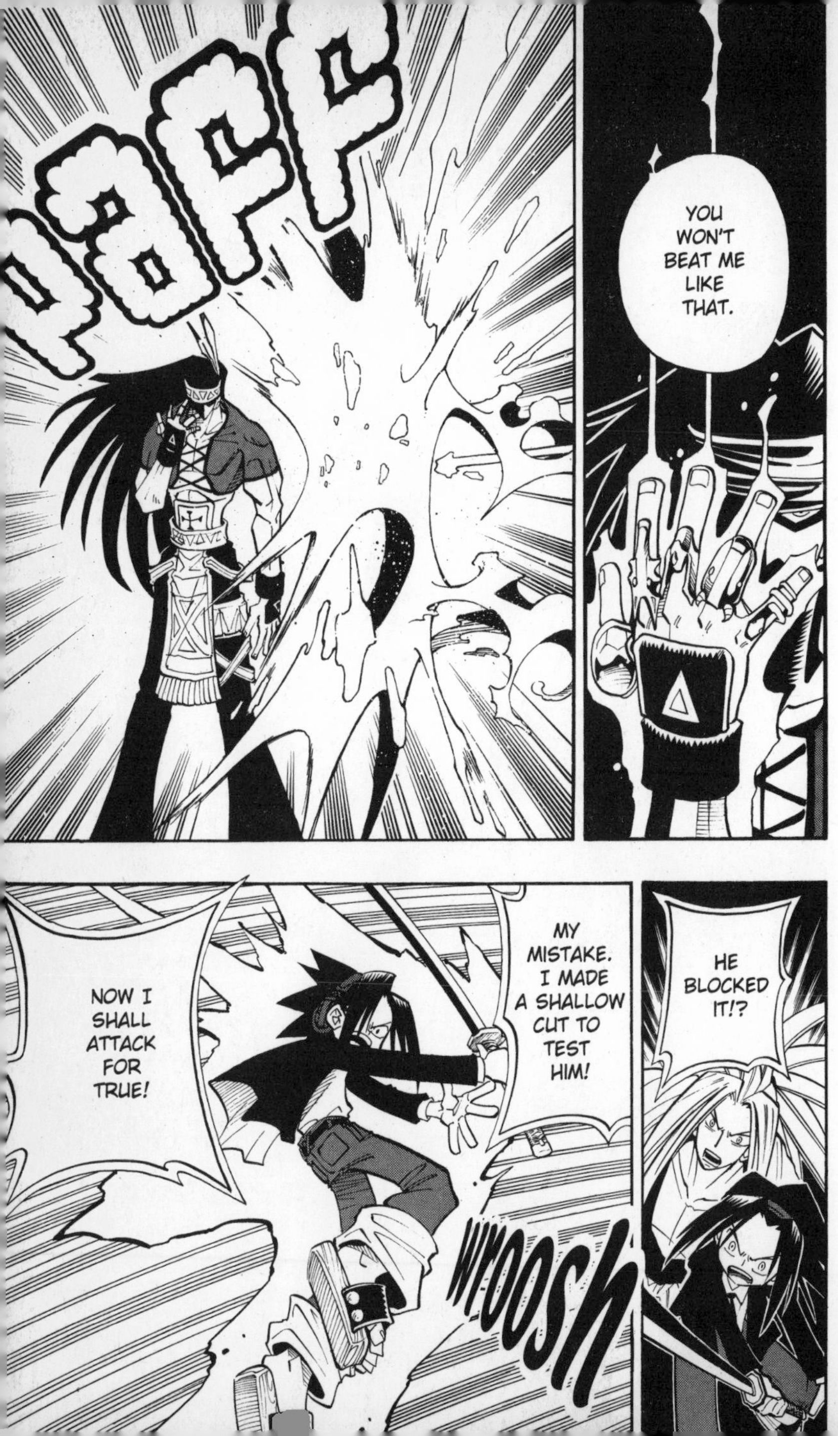
YOU WON'T BEAT ME LIKE THAT.
HE BLOCKED IT!?
MY MISTAKE. I MADE A SHALLOW CUT TO TEST HIM!
NOW I SHALL ATTACK FOR TRUE!
WROOSH

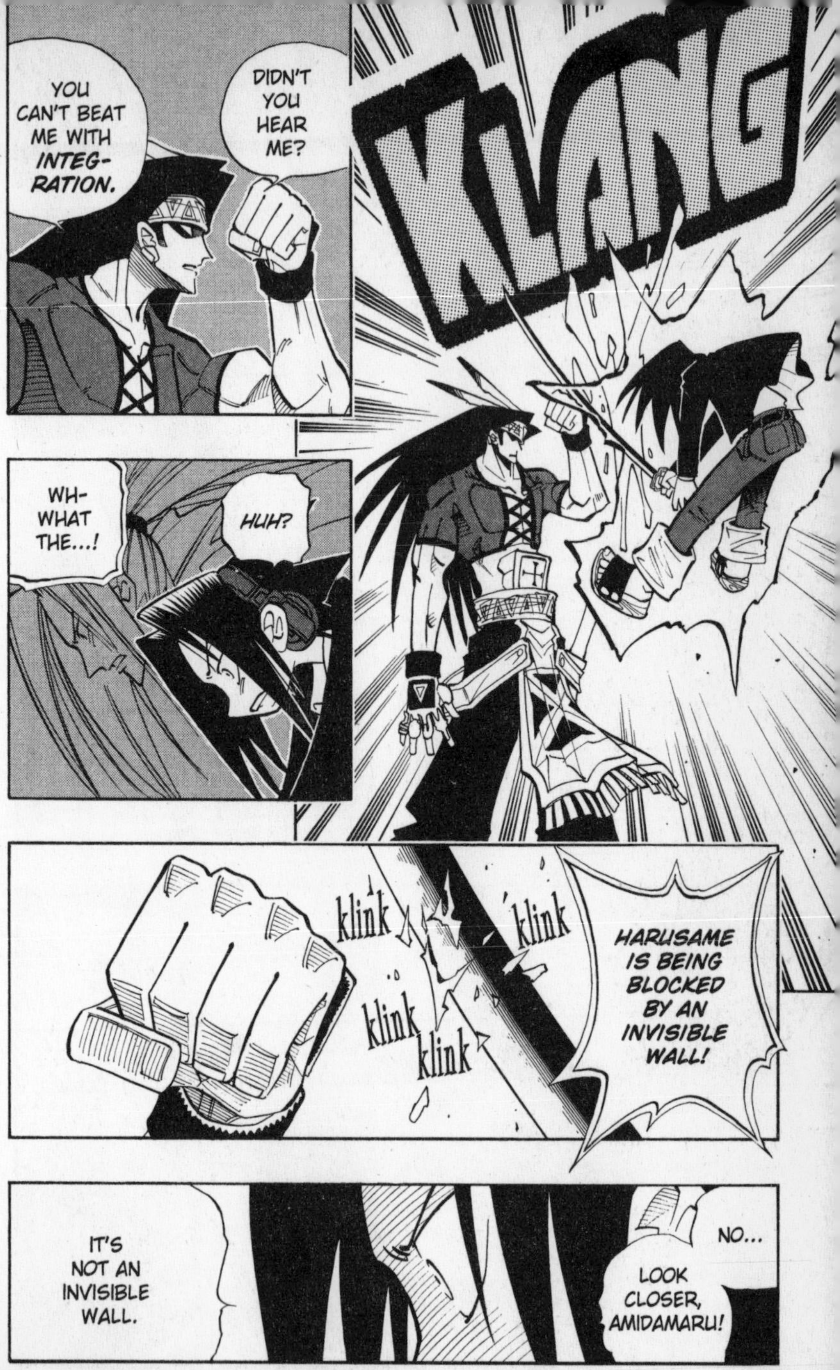
KLANG
DIDN'T YOU HEAR ME?
YOU CAN'T BEAT ME WITH *INTEGRATION.*
HUH?
WH-WHAT THE...!
HARUSAME IS BEING BLOCKED BY AN INVISIBLE WALL!
klink
klink
klink
klink
NO...
LOOK CLOSER, AMIDAMARU!
IT'S NOT AN INVISIBLE WALL.

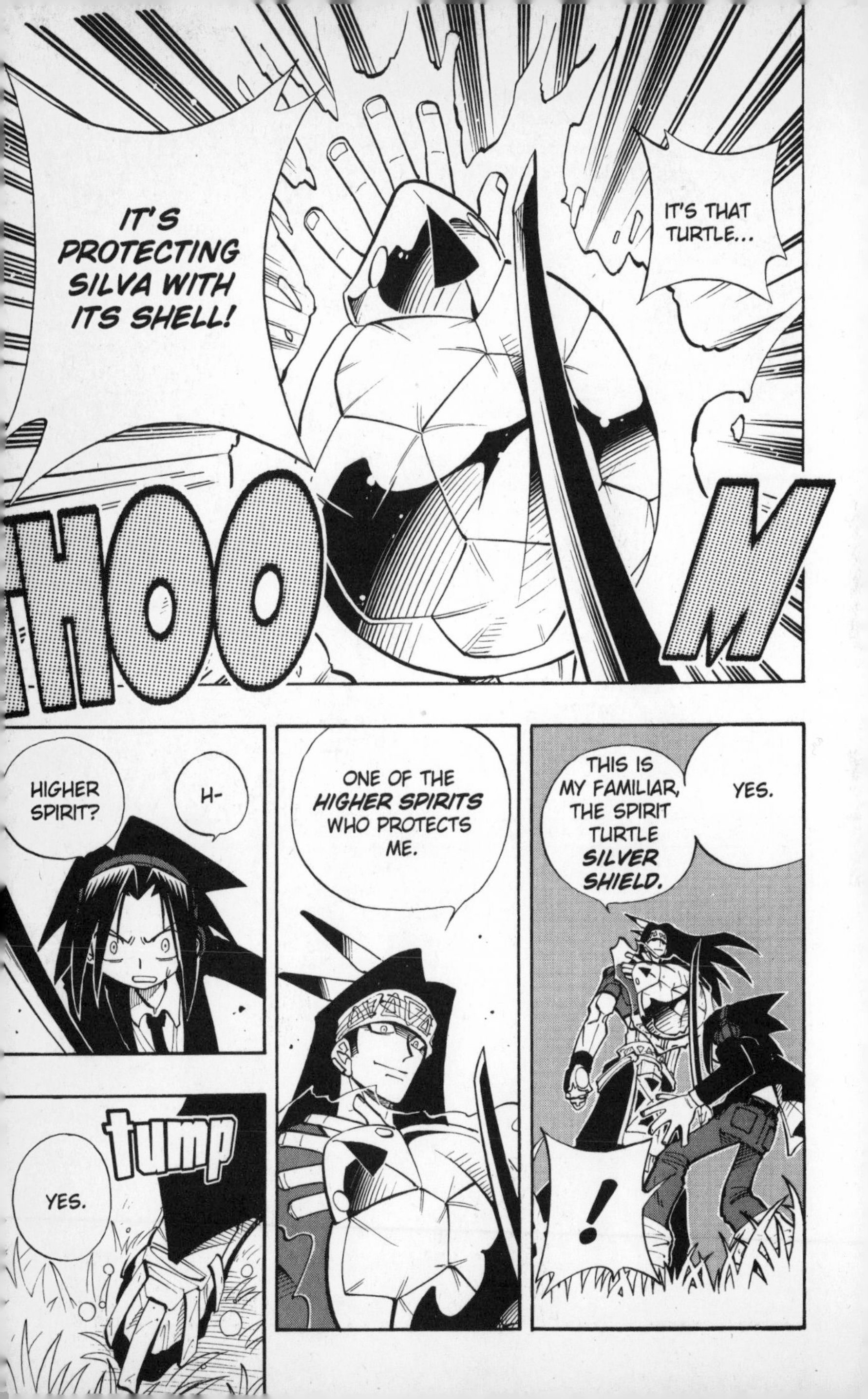
IT'S THAT TURTLE...
IT'S PROTECTING SILVA WITH ITS SHELL!
HOOM
YES.
THIS IS MY FAMILIAR, THE SPIRIT TURTLE *SILVER SHIELD.*
!
ONE OF THE *HIGHER SPIRITS* WHO PROTECTS ME.
H-
HIGHER SPIRIT?
tump
YES.

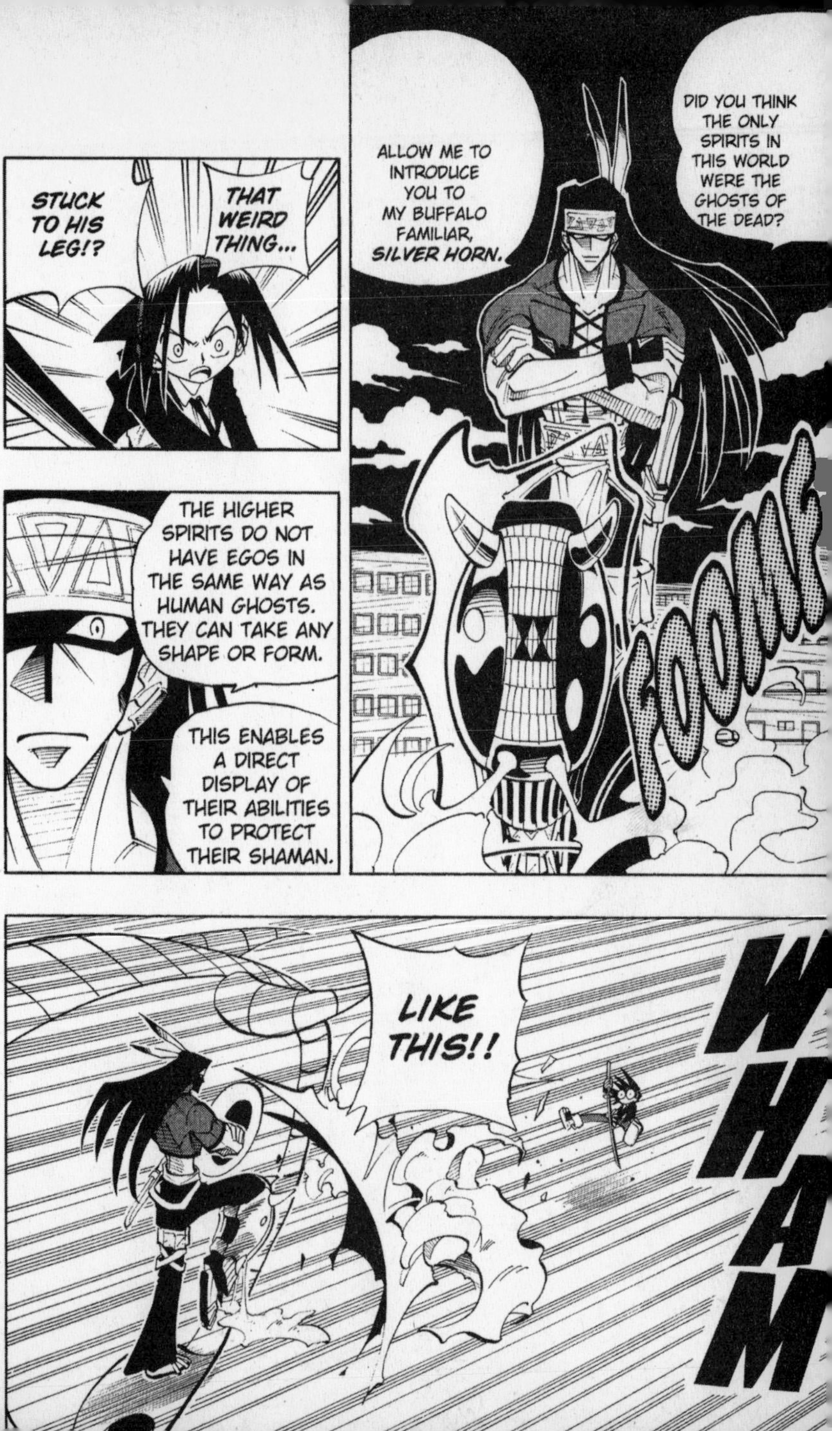
DID YOU THINK THE ONLY SPIRITS IN THIS WORLD WERE THE GHOSTS OF THE DEAD?
ALLOW ME TO INTRODUCE YOU TO MY BUFFALO FAMILIAR, SILVER HORN.
FOOM
THAT WEIRD THING...
STUCK TO HIS LEG!?
THE HIGHER SPIRITS DO NOT HAVE EGOS IN THE SAME WAY AS HUMAN GHOSTS. THEY CAN TAKE ANY SHAPE OR FORM.
THIS ENABLES A DIRECT DISPLAY OF THEIR ABILITIES TO PROTECT THEIR SHAMAN.
LIKE THIS!!
WHAM

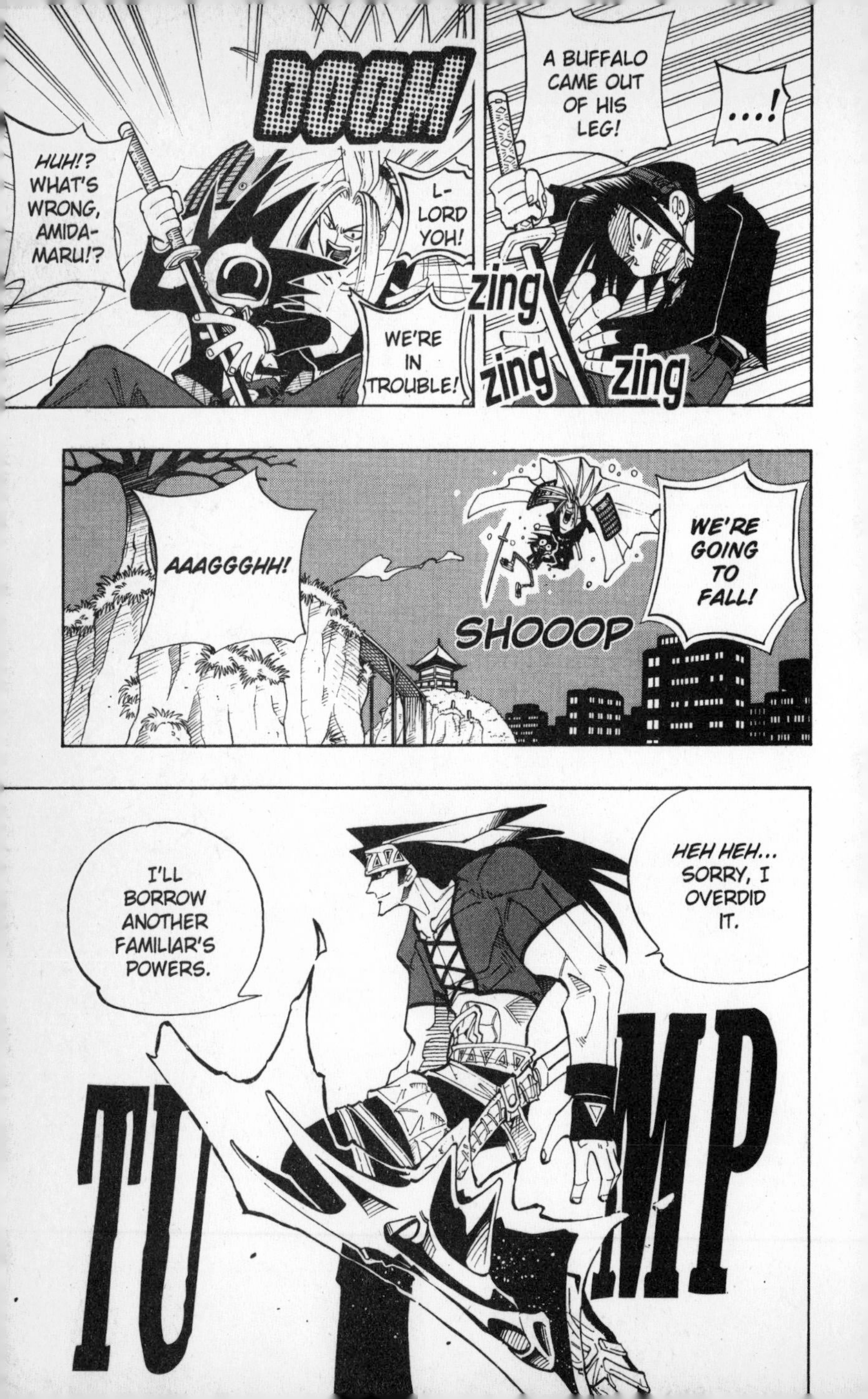
A BUFFALO CAME OUT OF HIS LEG!
...!
zing
zing
zing
DOOM
HUH!? WHAT'S WRONG, AMIDA-MARU!?
L-LORD YOH!
WE'RE IN TROUBLE!
WE'RE GOING TO FALL!
SHOOOP
AAAGGGHH!
HEH HEH... SORRY, I OVERDID IT.
I'LL BORROW ANOTHER FAMILIAR'S POWERS.
TU
MP

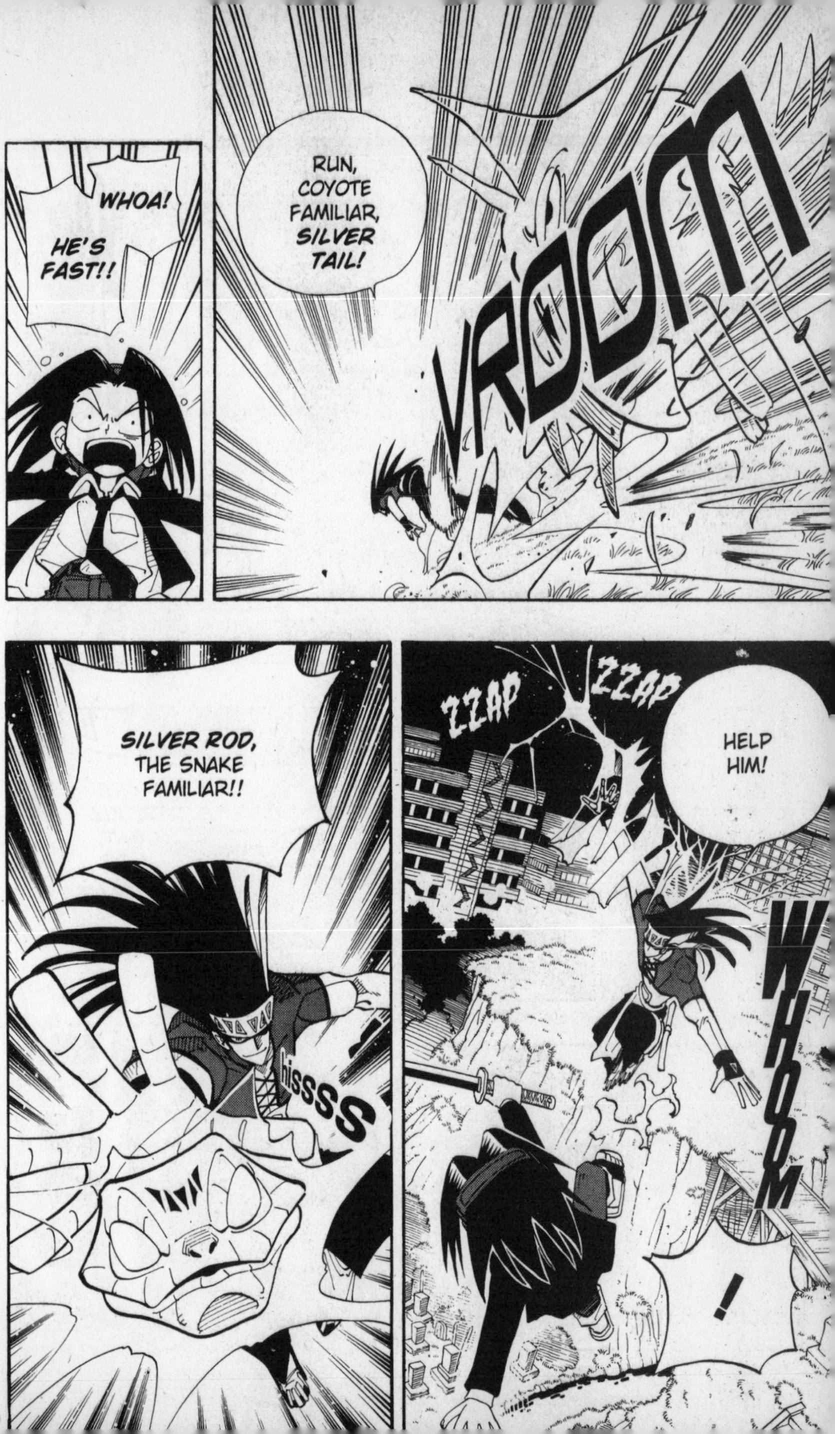
VROOM
RUN, COYOTE FAMILIAR, SILVER TAIL!
WHOA!
HE'S FAST!!
HELP HIM!
ZZAP
ZZAP
WHOOM
!
SILVER ROD, THE SNAKE FAMILIAR!!
hissss

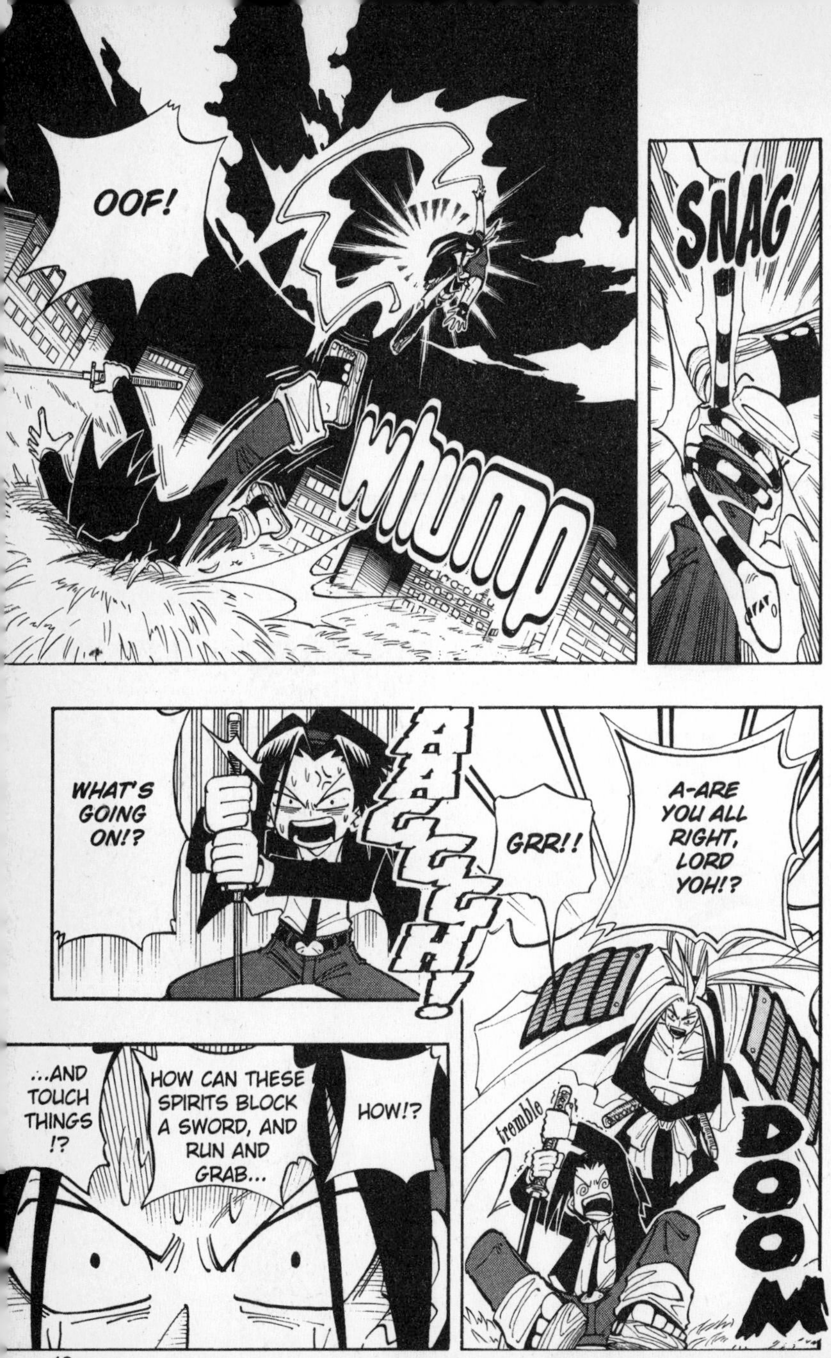
SNAG
OOF!
WHUMP
A-ARE YOU ALL RIGHT, LORD YOH!?
GRR!!
tremble
DOOM
AAUGHH!
WHAT'S GOING ON!?
HOW!?
HOW CAN THESE SPIRITS BLOCK A SWORD, AND RUN AND GRAB...
...AND TOUCH THINGS!?

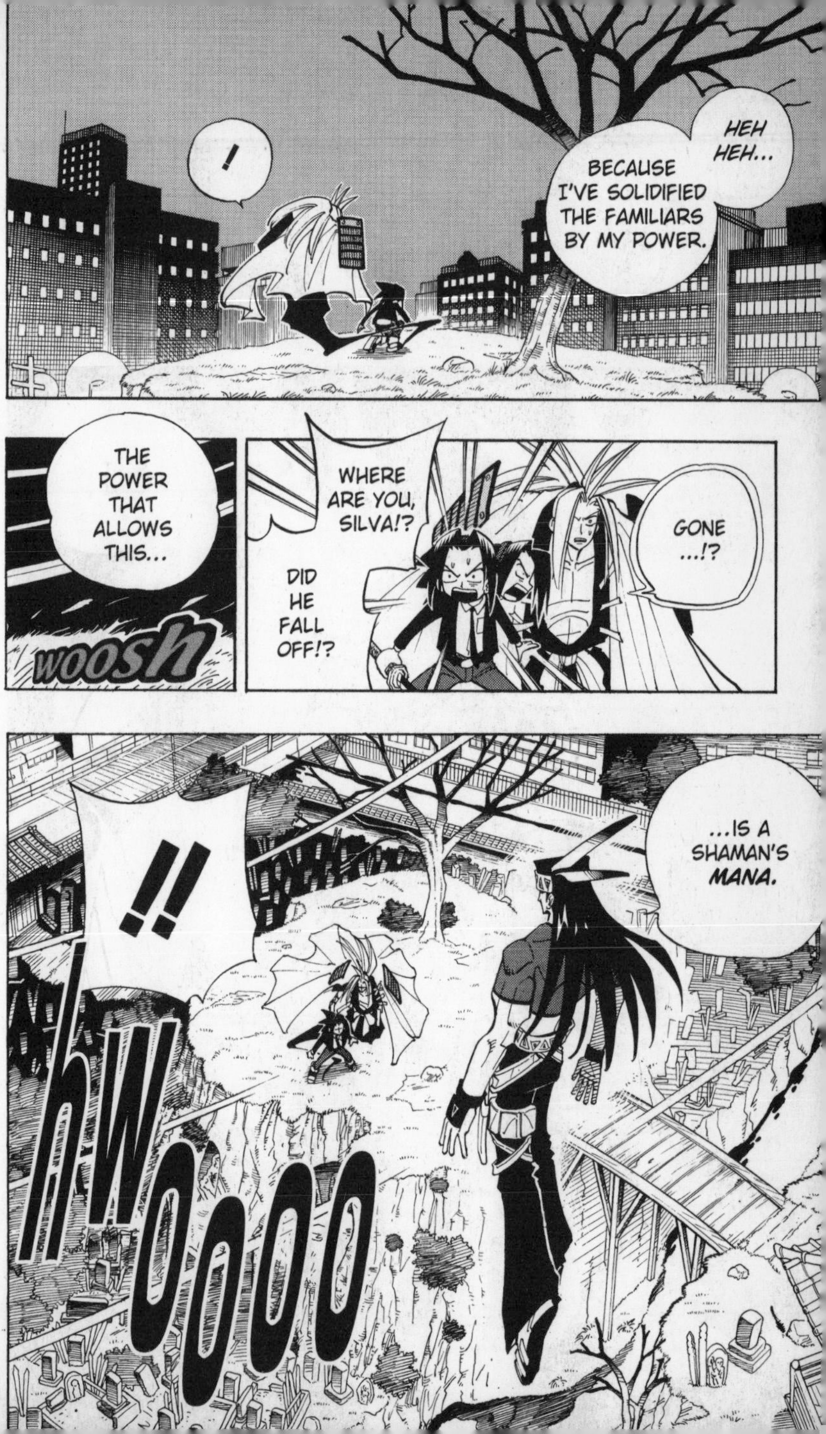
HEH HEH... BECAUSE I'VE SOLIDIFIED THE FAMILIARS BY MY POWER.
!
GONE ...!?
WHERE ARE YOU, SILVA!?
DID HE FALL OFF!?
THE POWER THAT ALLOWS THIS...
woosh
...IS A SHAMAN'S *MANA.*
!!
hWOOOOO

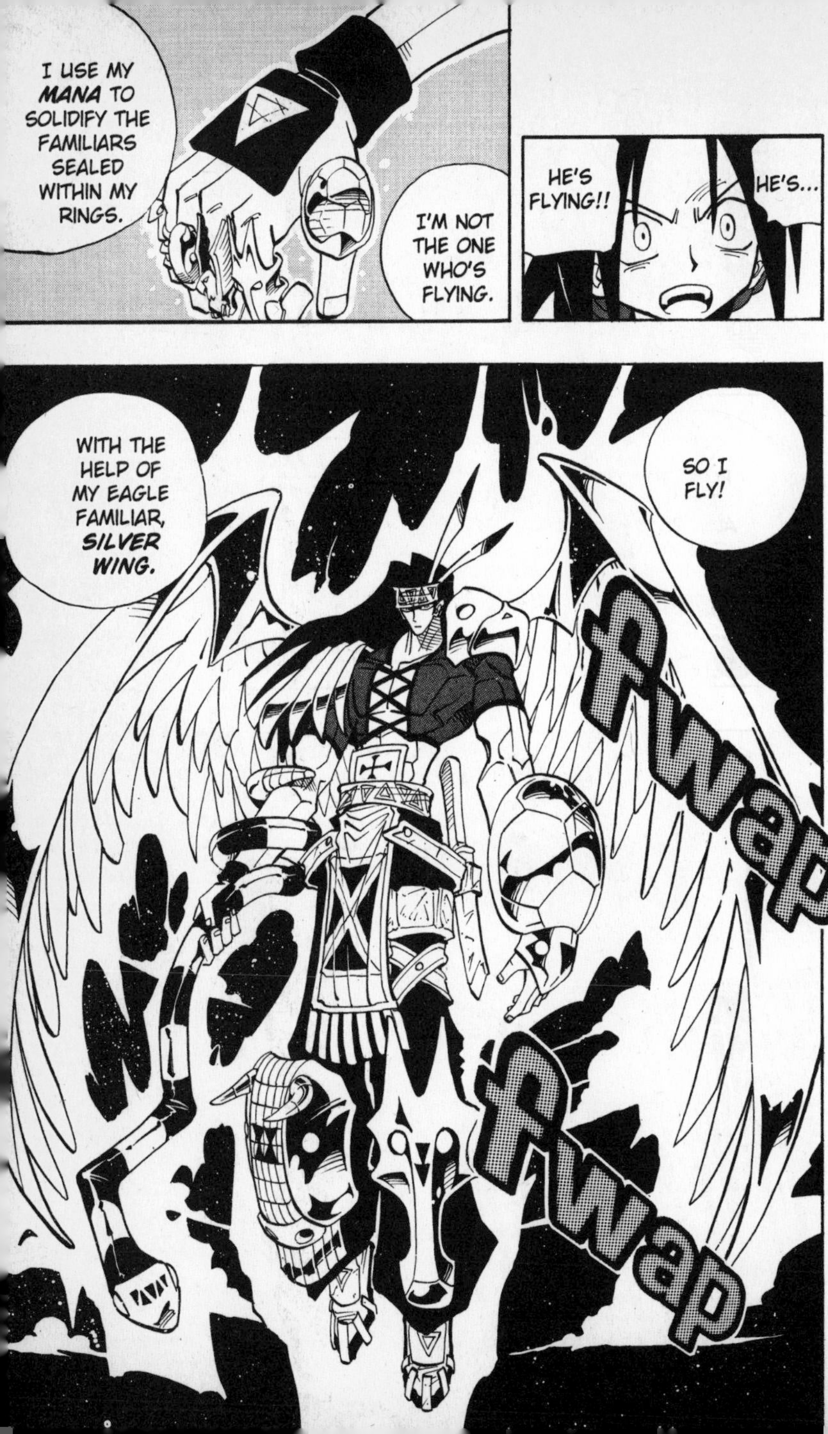
HE'S...
HE'S FLYING!!
I'M NOT THE ONE WHO'S FLYING.
I USE MY MANA TO SOLIDIFY THE FAMILIARS SEALED WITHIN MY RINGS.
SO I FLY!
WITH THE HELP OF MY EAGLE FAMILIAR, SILVER WING.
fwap
fwap

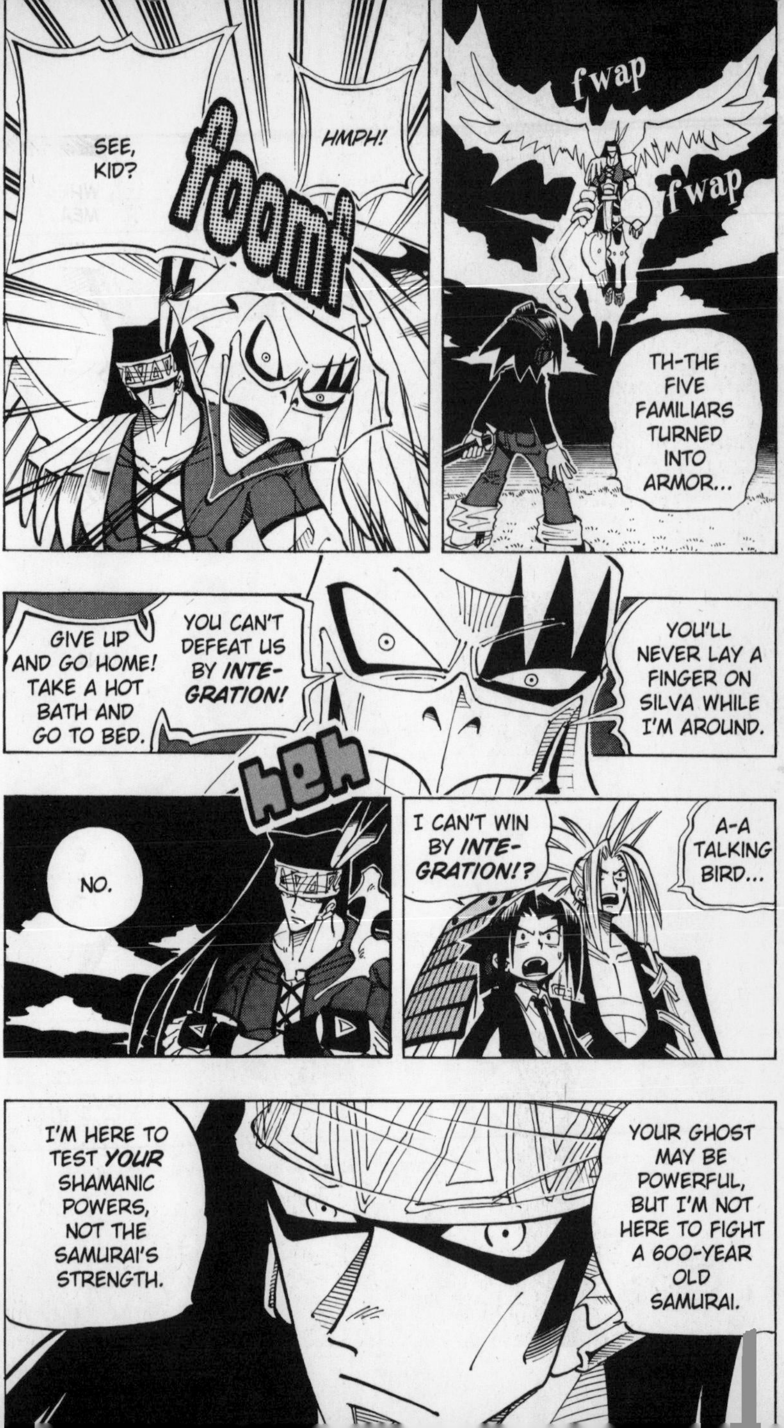
fwap
fwap
TH-THE FIVE FAMILIARS TURNED INTO ARMOR...
HMPH!
foom!
SEE, KID?
YOU'LL NEVER LAY A FINGER ON SILVA WHILE I'M AROUND.
YOU CAN'T DEFEAT US BY *INTE-GRATION!*
GIVE UP AND GO HOME! TAKE A HOT BATH AND GO TO BED.
heh
A-A TALKING BIRD...
I CAN'T WIN BY *INTE-GRATION!?*
NO.
YOUR GHOST MAY BE POWERFUL, BUT I'M NOT HERE TO FIGHT A 600-YEAR OLD SAMURAI.
I'M HERE TO TEST ***YOUR*** SHAMANIC POWERS, NOT THE SAMURAI'S STRENGTH.

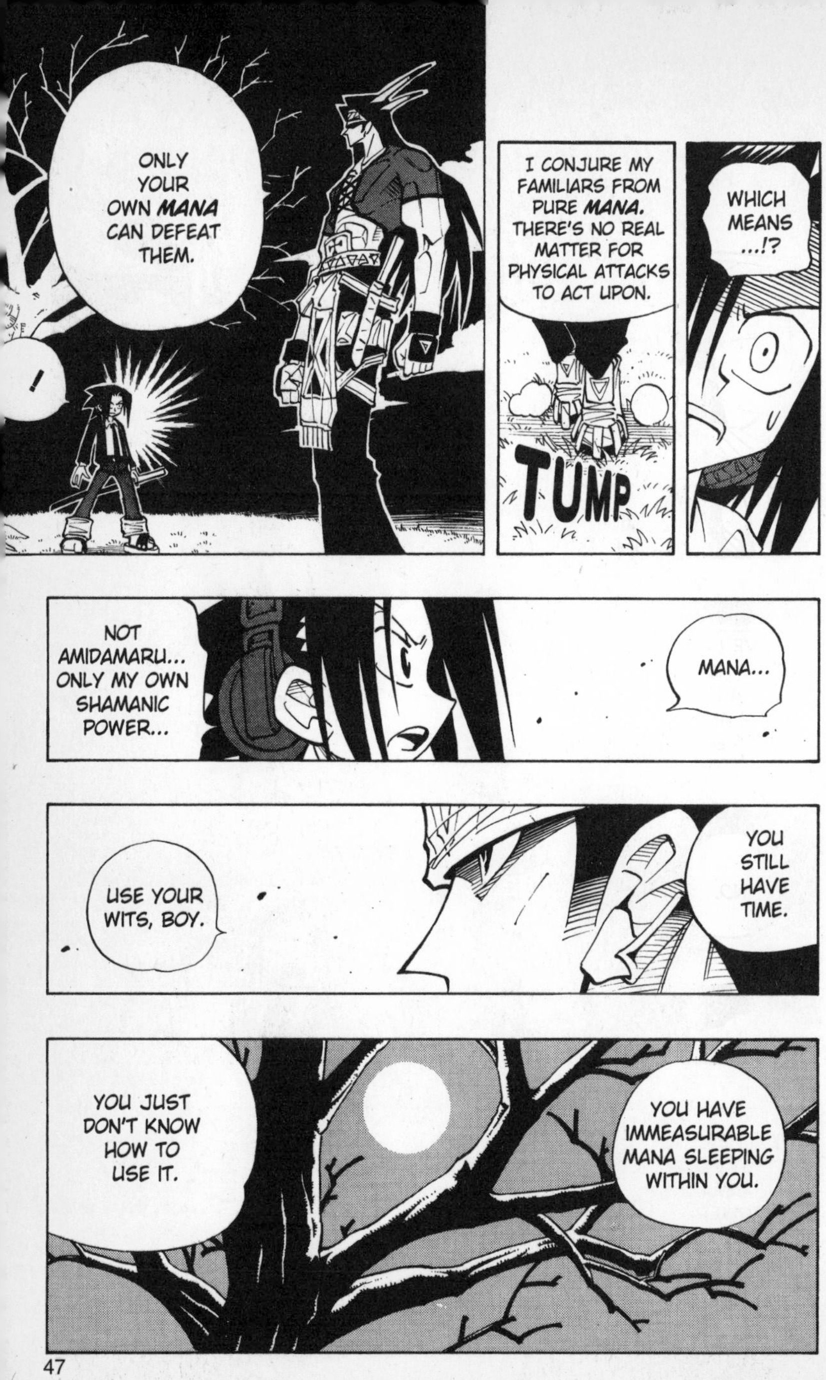
WHICH MEANS ...!?
I CONJURE MY FAMILIARS FROM PURE MANA. THERE'S NO REAL MATTER FOR PHYSICAL ATTACKS TO ACT UPON.
TUMP
ONLY YOUR OWN MANA CAN DEFEAT THEM.
!
MANA...
NOT AMIDAMARU... ONLY MY OWN SHAMANIC POWER...
YOU STILL HAVE TIME.
USE YOUR WITS, BOY.
YOU HAVE IMMEASURABLE MANA SLEEPING WITHIN YOU.
YOU JUST DON'T KNOW HOW TO USE IT.

SHAMAN KING CHARACTER FILE No.15

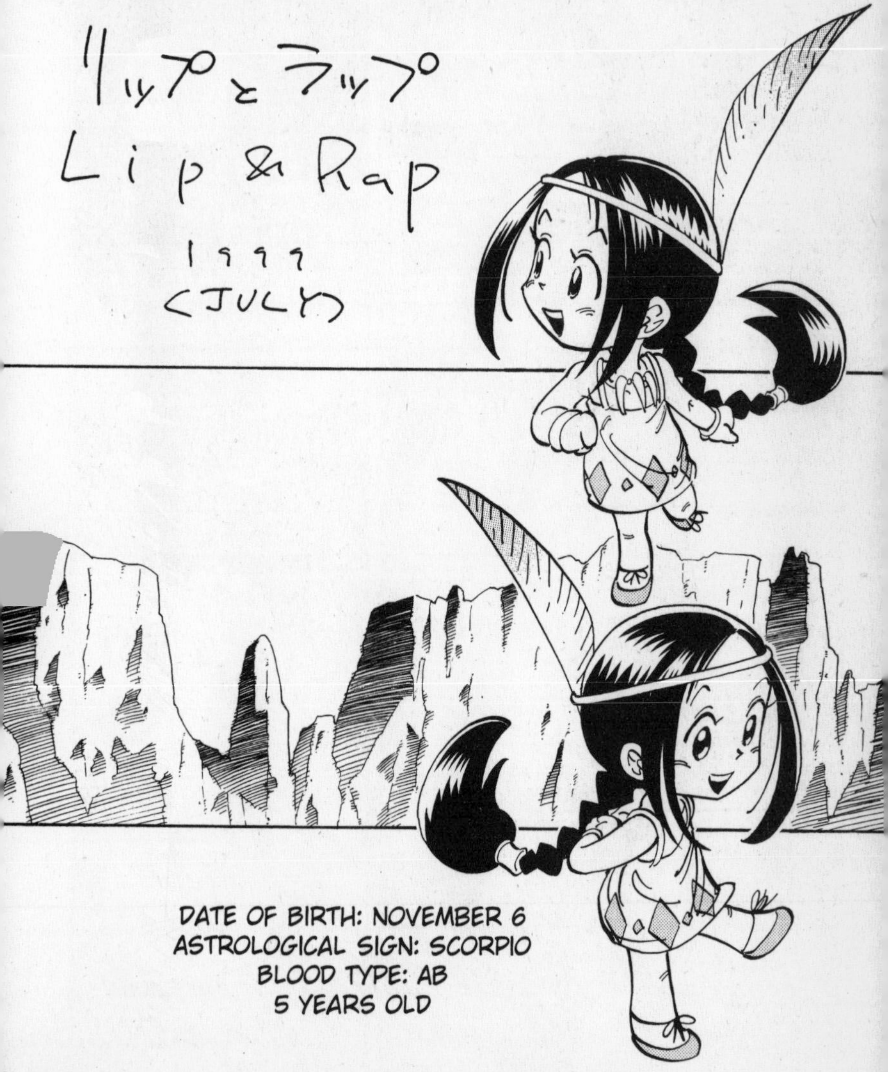
リップとラップ
Lip & Rap
1999
<JULY>

DATE OF BIRTH: NOVEMBER 6
ASTROLOGICAL SIGN: SCORPIO
BLOOD TYPE: AB
5 YEARS OLD

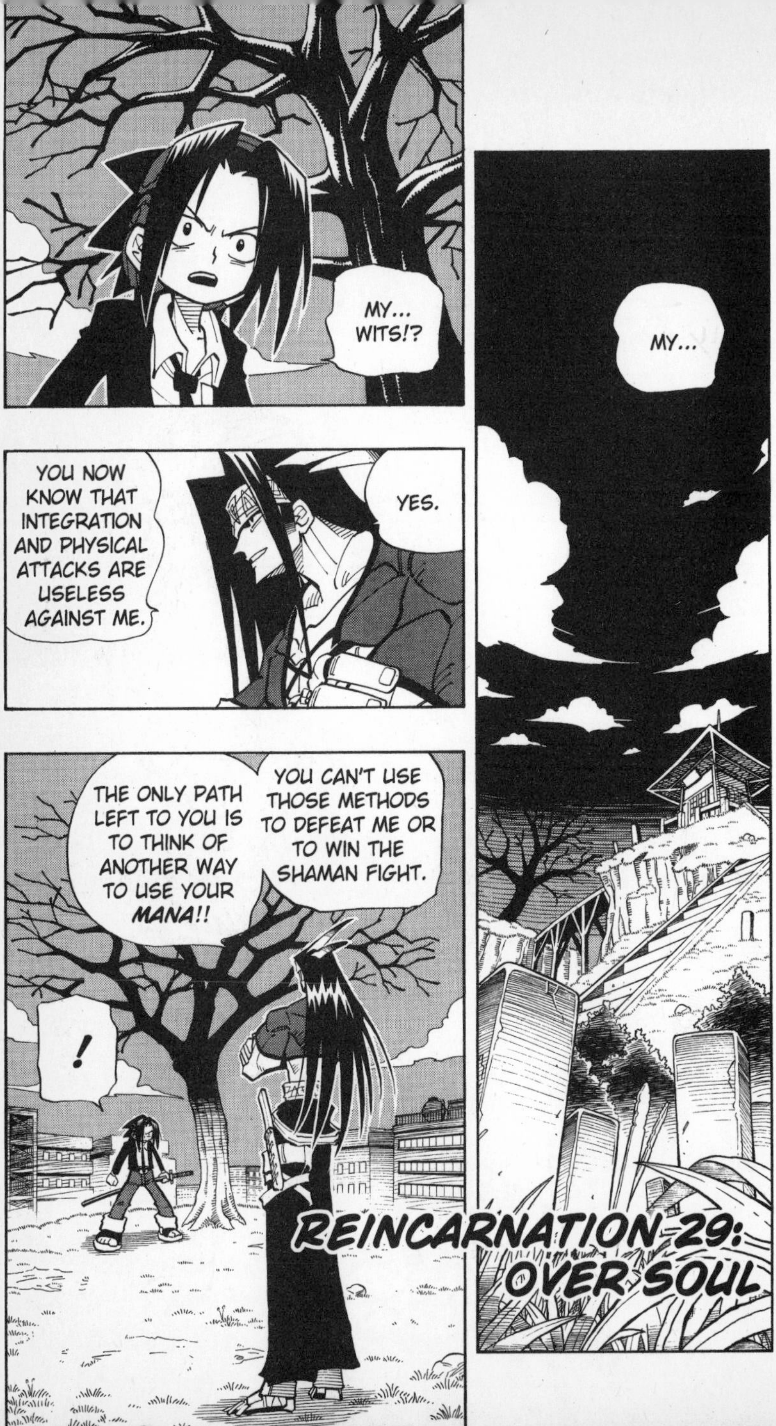
MY...
REINCARNATION 29: OVER SOUL
MY... WITS!?
YES.
YOU NOW KNOW THAT INTEGRATION AND PHYSICAL ATTACKS ARE USELESS AGAINST ME.
YOU CAN'T USE THOSE METHODS TO DEFEAT ME OR TO WIN THE SHAMAN FIGHT.
THE ONLY PATH LEFT TO YOU IS TO THINK OF ANOTHER WAY TO USE YOUR *MANA*!!
!

READ THIS WAY

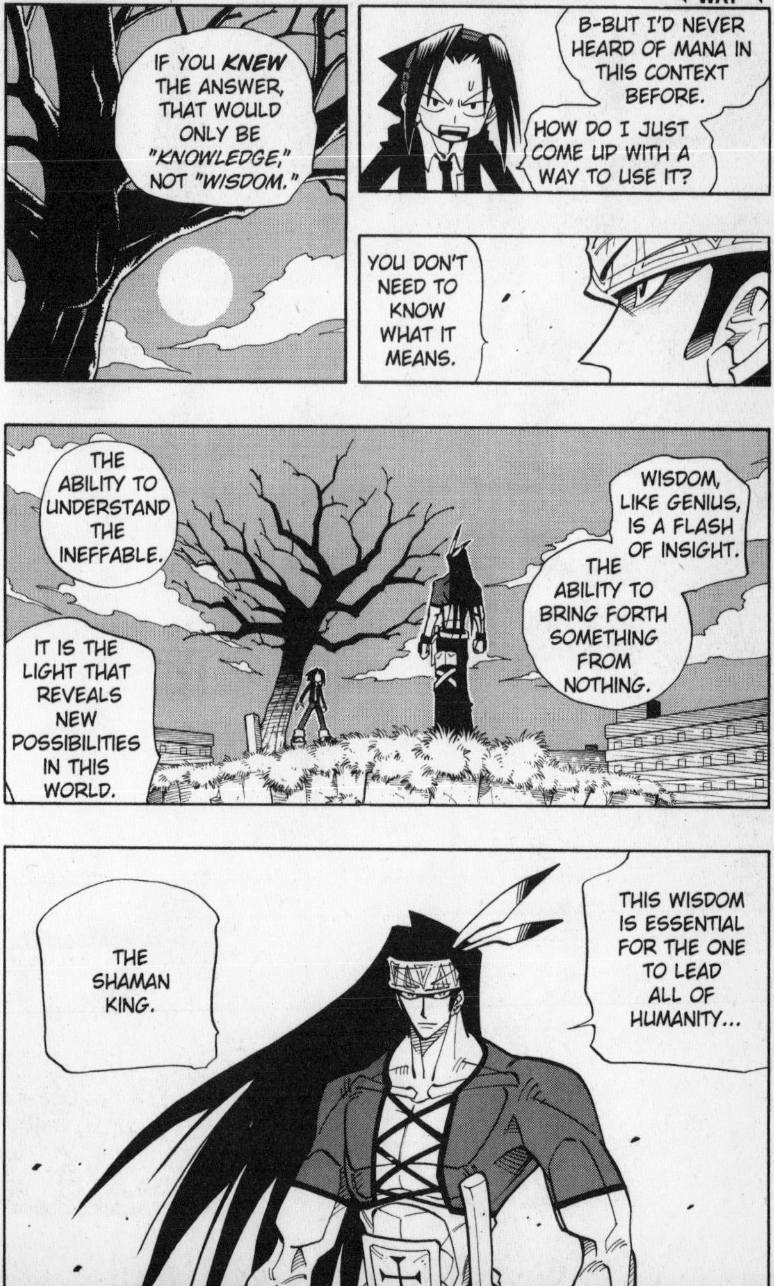

B-BUT I'D NEVER HEARD OF MANA IN THIS CONTEXT BEFORE.
HOW DO I JUST COME UP WITH A WAY TO USE IT?
YOU DON'T NEED TO KNOW WHAT IT MEANS.
IF YOU *KNEW* THE ANSWER, THAT WOULD ONLY BE "KNOWLEDGE," NOT "WISDOM."
WISDOM, LIKE GENIUS, IS A FLASH OF INSIGHT.
THE ABILITY TO BRING FORTH SOMETHING FROM NOTHING.
THE ABILITY TO UNDERSTAND THE INEFFABLE.
IT IS THE LIGHT THAT REVEALS NEW POSSIBILITIES IN THIS WORLD.
THIS WISDOM IS ESSENTIAL FOR THE ONE TO LEAD ALL OF HUMANITY...
THE SHAMAN KING.

«READ THIS WAY«

SHAMAN KING

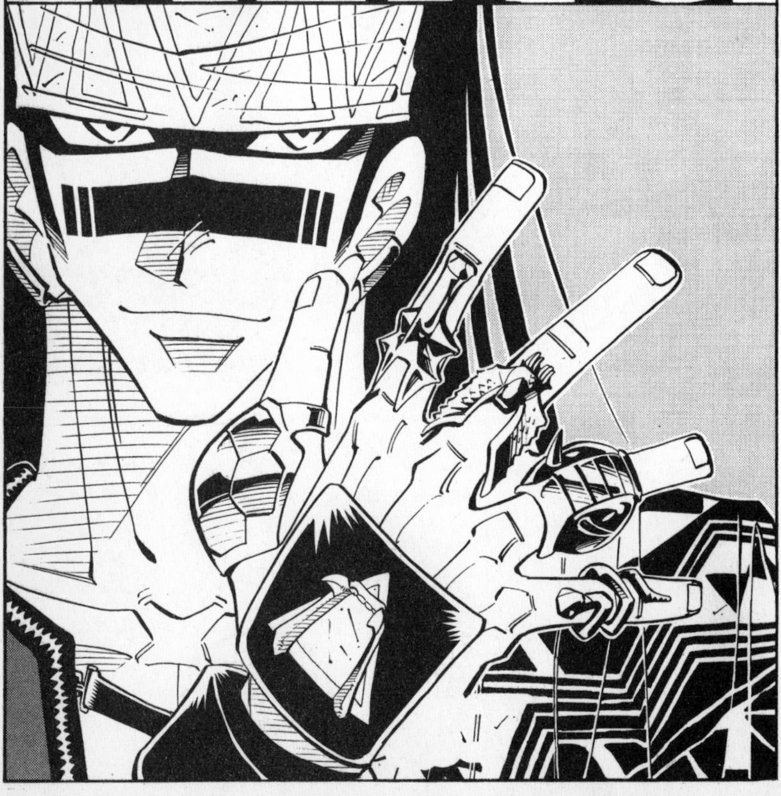

Reincarnation 29: Over Soul

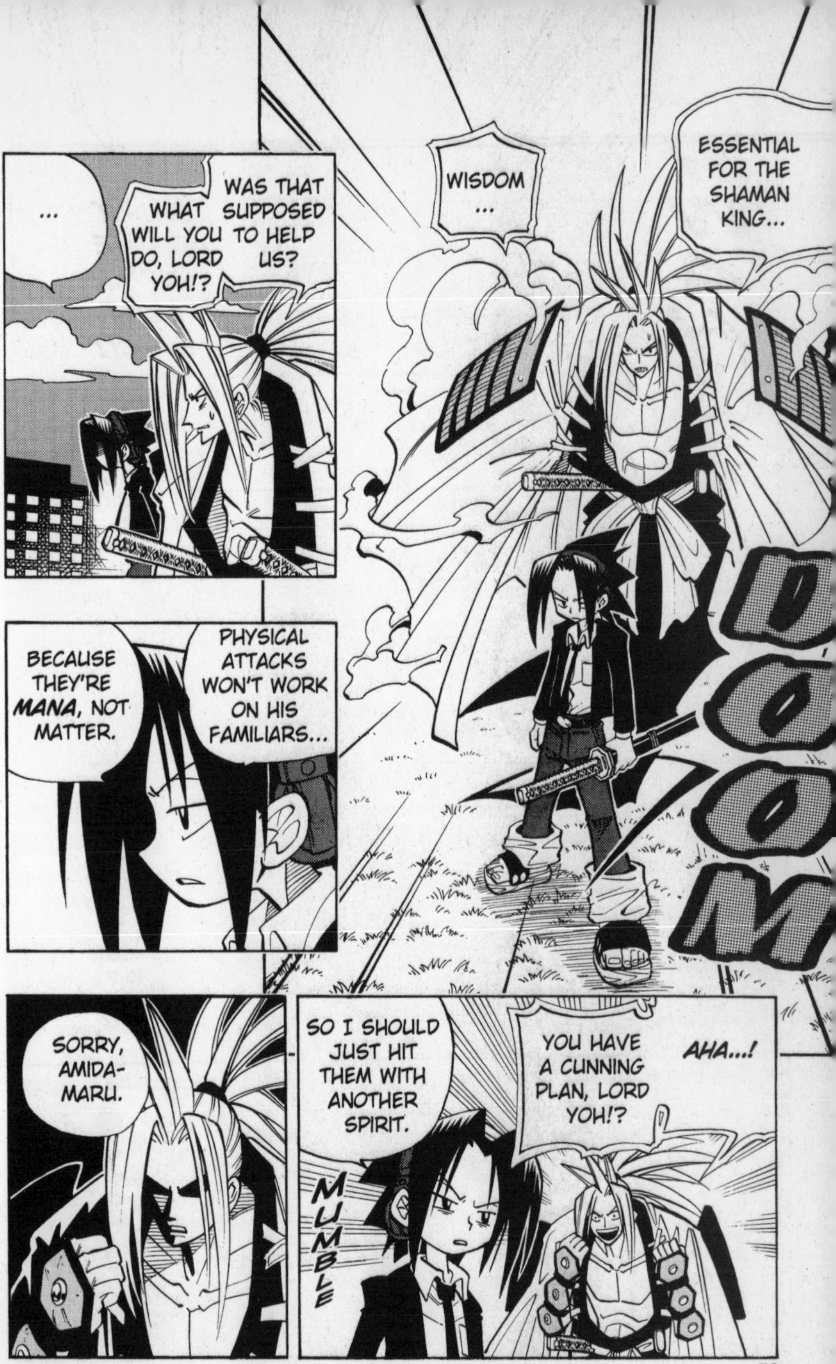
ESSENTIAL FOR THE SHAMAN KING...
WISDOM ...
DOOOM
WAS THAT SUPPOSED TO HELP US?
WHAT WILL YOU DO, LORD YOH!?
...
PHYSICAL ATTACKS WON'T WORK ON HIS FAMILIARS...
BECAUSE THEY'RE *MANA*, NOT MATTER.
AHA...!
YOU HAVE A CUNNING PLAN, LORD YOH!?
SO I SHOULD JUST HIT THEM WITH ANOTHER SPIRIT.
MUMBLE
SORRY, AMIDA-MARU.

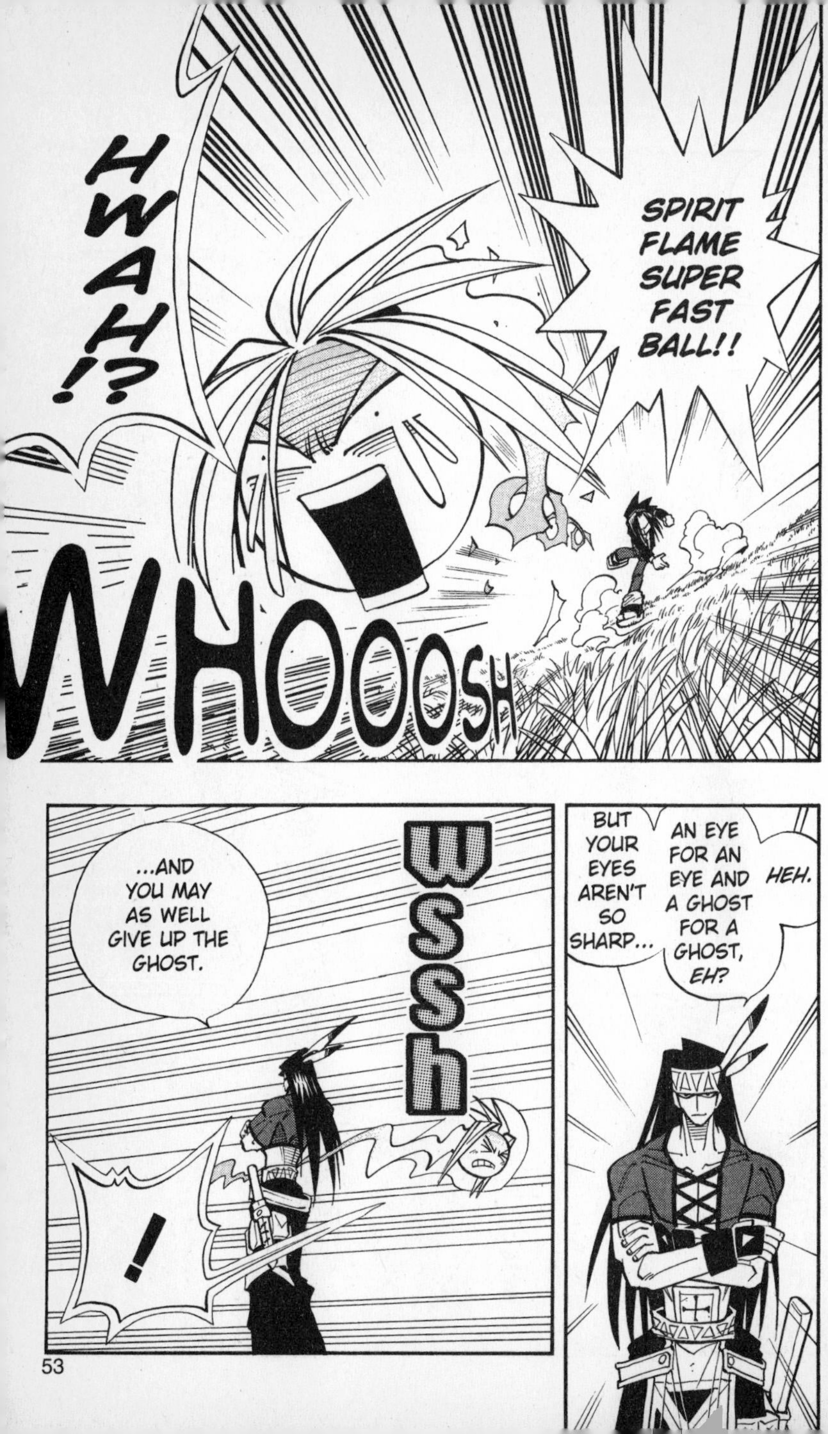
SPIRIT FLAME SUPER FAST BALL!!
HWAH!?
WHOOOSH
HEH.
AN EYE FOR AN EYE AND A GHOST FOR A GHOST, EH?
BUT YOUR EYES AREN'T SO SHARP...
WSSH
...AND YOU MAY AS WELL GIVE UP THE GHOST.
!

READ THIS WAY

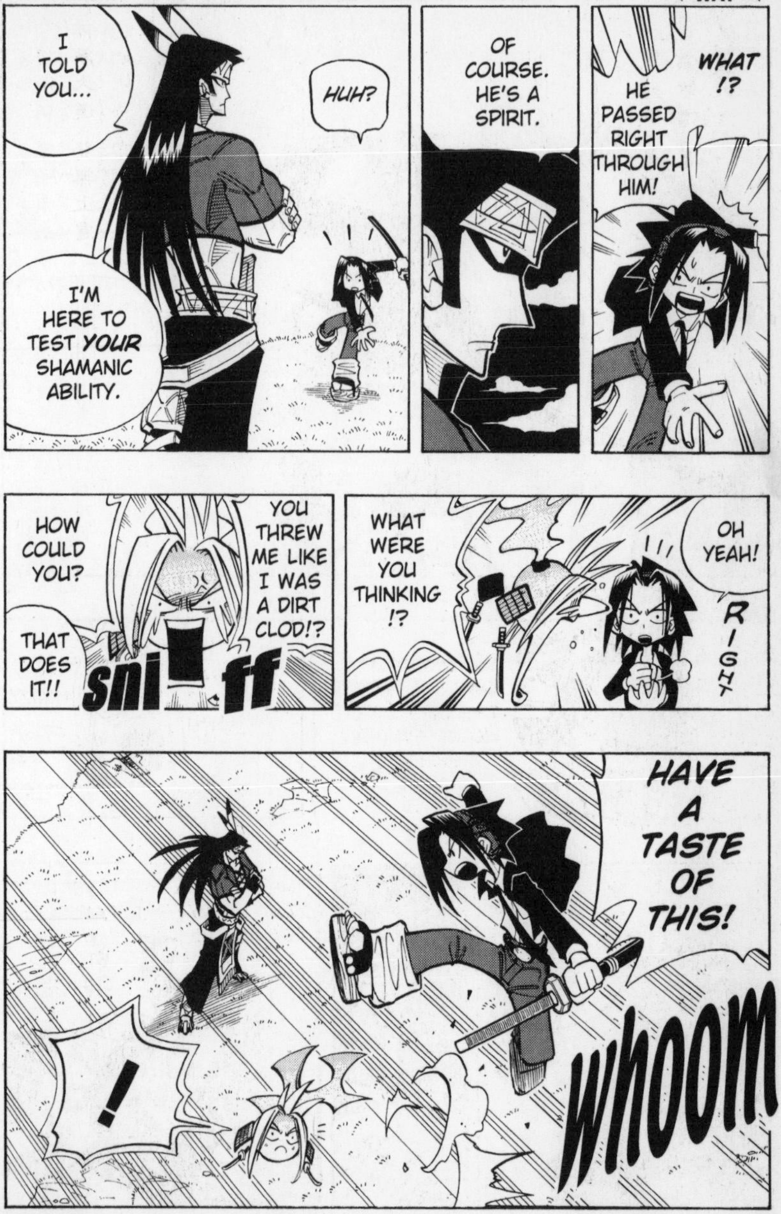

WHAT !?
HE PASSED RIGHT THROUGH HIM!
OF COURSE. HE'S A SPIRIT.
I TOLD YOU...
HUH?
I'M HERE TO TEST *YOUR* SHAMANIC ABILITY.
OH YEAH!
RIGHT
WHAT WERE YOU THINKING !?
YOU THREW ME LIKE I WAS A DIRT CLOD!?
HOW COULD YOU?
THAT DOES IT!!
sniff
HAVE A TASTE OF THIS!
!
whoom

READ THIS WAY

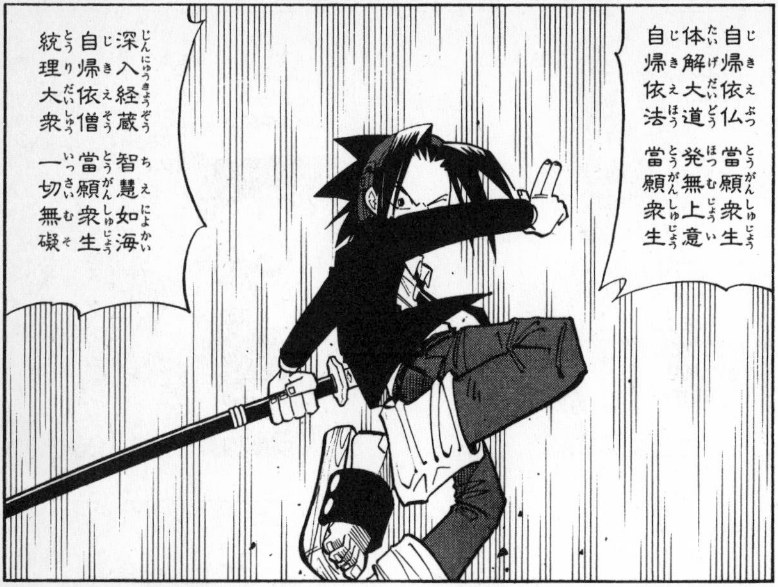

自帰依仏　當願衆生
体解大道　発無上意
自帰依法　當願衆生
深入経蔵　智慧如海
自帰依僧　當願衆生
統理大衆　一切無礙

* A BUDDHIST EXORCISM CHANT

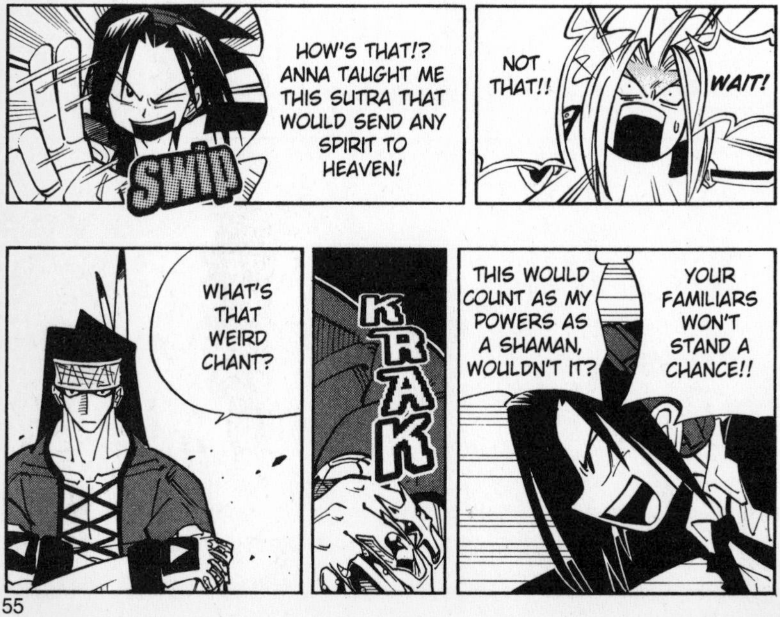

WAIT!
NOT THAT!!
HOW'S THAT!? ANNA TAUGHT ME THIS SUTRA THAT WOULD SEND ANY SPIRIT TO HEAVEN!
SWIP
YOUR FAMILIARS WON'T STAND A CHANCE!!
THIS WOULD COUNT AS MY POWERS AS A SHAMAN, WOULDN'T IT?
KRAK
WHAT'S THAT WEIRD CHANT?

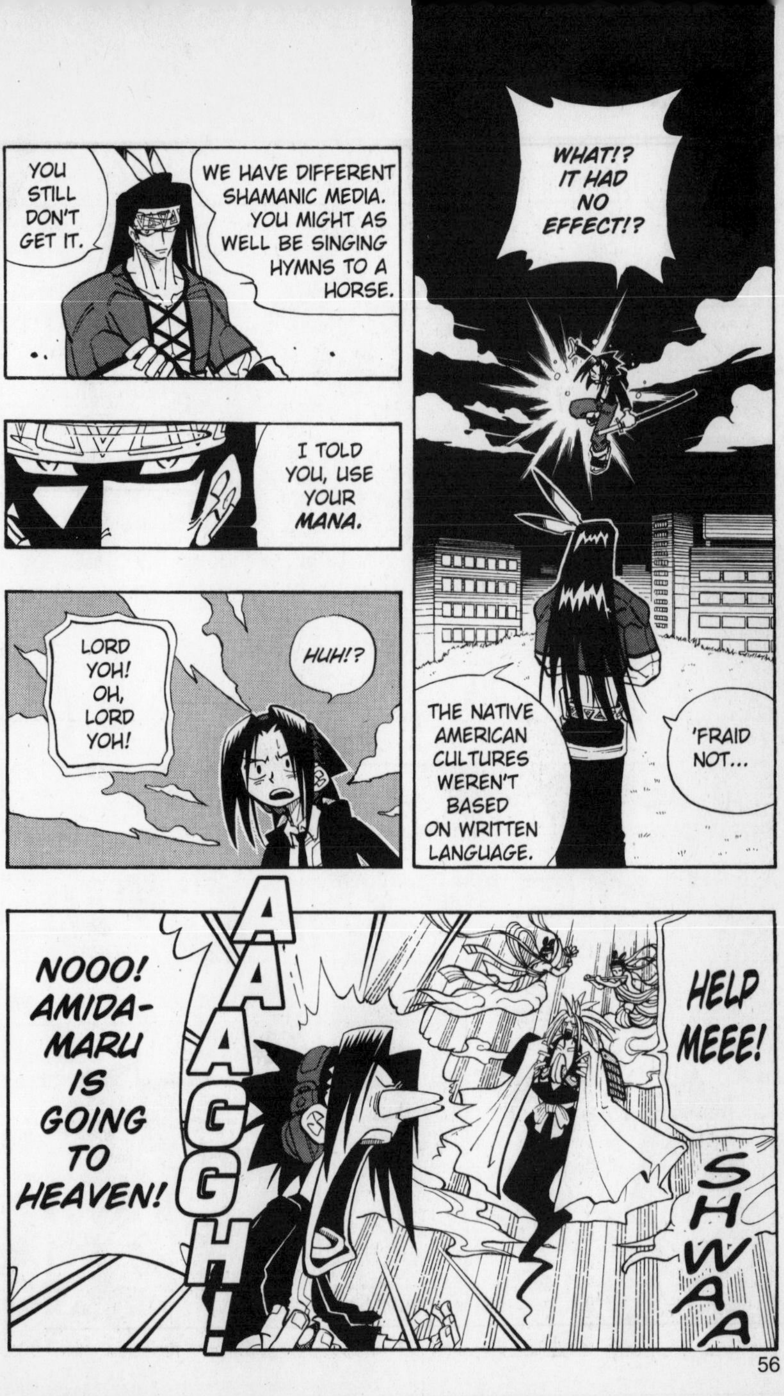
WHAT!? IT HAD NO EFFECT!?
'FRAID NOT...
THE NATIVE AMERICAN CULTURES WEREN'T BASED ON WRITTEN LANGUAGE.
WE HAVE DIFFERENT SHAMANIC MEDIA. YOU MIGHT AS WELL BE SINGING HYMNS TO A HORSE.
YOU STILL DON'T GET IT.
I TOLD YOU, USE YOUR *MANA.*
HUH!?
LORD YOH! OH, LORD YOH!
HELP MEEE!
SHWAA
AAAGGH!
NOOO! AMIDA-MARU IS GOING TO HEAVEN!

READ THIS WAY

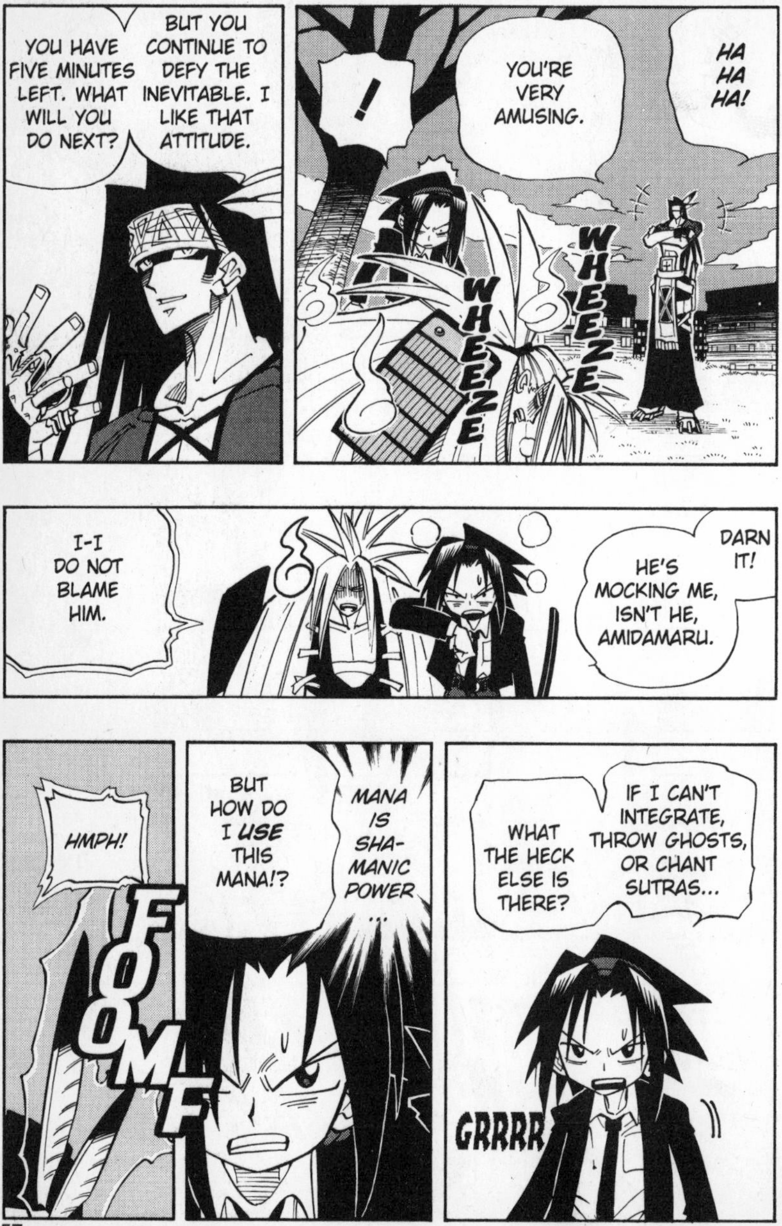
HA HA HA!
YOU'RE VERY AMUSING.
!
WHEEZE
WHEEZE
BUT YOU CONTINUE TO DEFY THE INEVITABLE. I LIKE THAT ATTITUDE.
YOU HAVE FIVE MINUTES LEFT. WHAT WILL YOU DO NEXT?
DARN IT!
HE'S MOCKING ME, ISN'T HE, AMIDAMARU.
I-I DO NOT BLAME HIM.
IF I CAN'T INTEGRATE, THROW GHOSTS, OR CHANT SUTRAS...
WHAT THE HECK ELSE IS THERE?
GRRRR
MANA IS SHA-MANIC POWER...
BUT HOW DO I USE THIS MANA!?
FOOMF
HMPH!

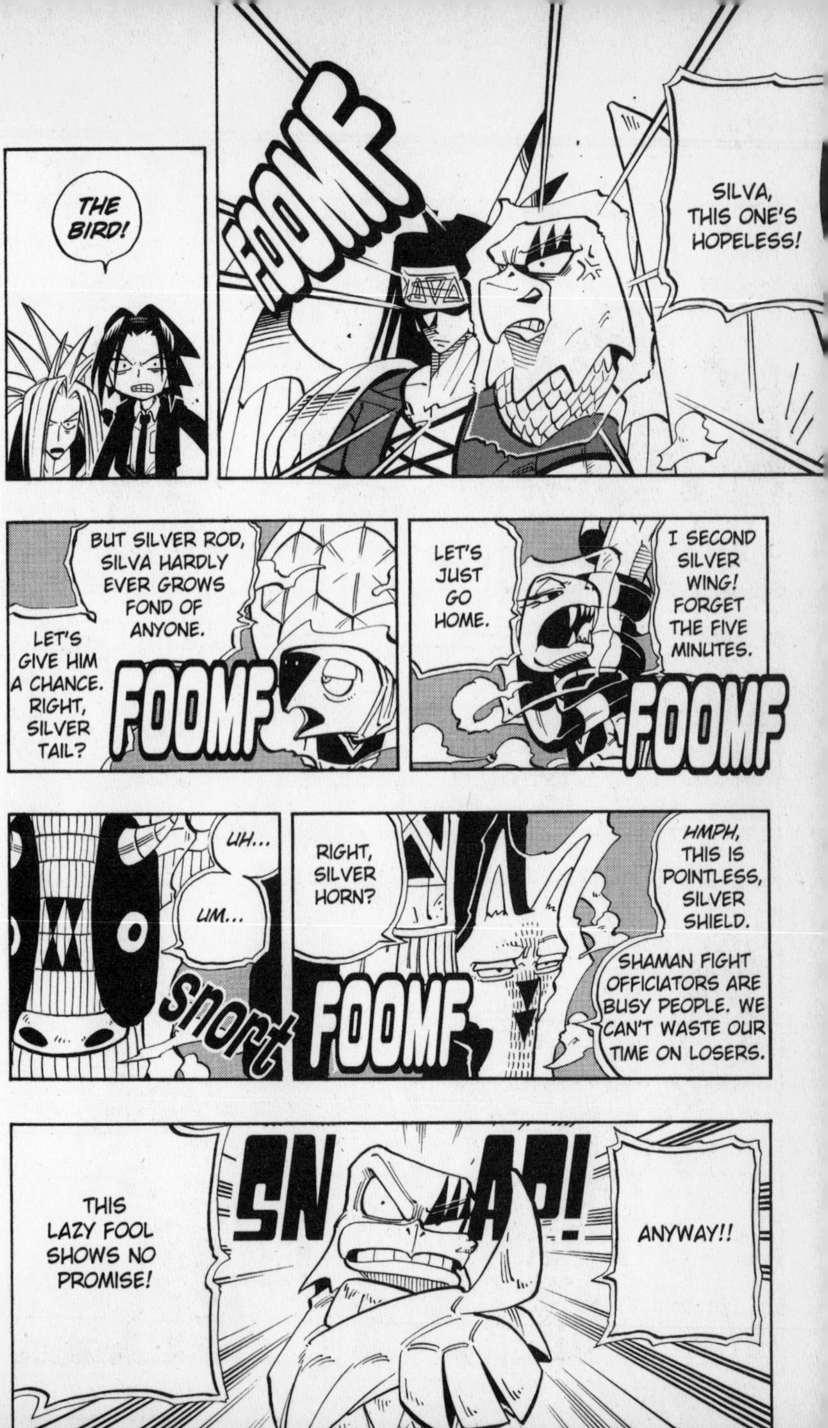
SILVA, THIS ONE'S HOPELESS!
FOOMF
THE BIRD!
I SECOND SILVER WING! FORGET THE FIVE MINUTES.
LET'S JUST GO HOME.
FOOMF
BUT SILVER ROD, SILVA HARDLY EVER GROWS FOND OF ANYONE.
LET'S GIVE HIM A CHANCE. RIGHT, SILVER TAIL?
FOOMF
HMPH, THIS IS POINTLESS, SILVER SHIELD.
SHAMAN FIGHT OFFICIATORS ARE BUSY PEOPLE. WE CAN'T WASTE OUR TIME ON LOSERS.
RIGHT, SILVER HORN?
FOOMF
UH...
UM...
Snort
ANYWAY!!
SNAP!
THIS LAZY FOOL SHOWS NO PROMISE!

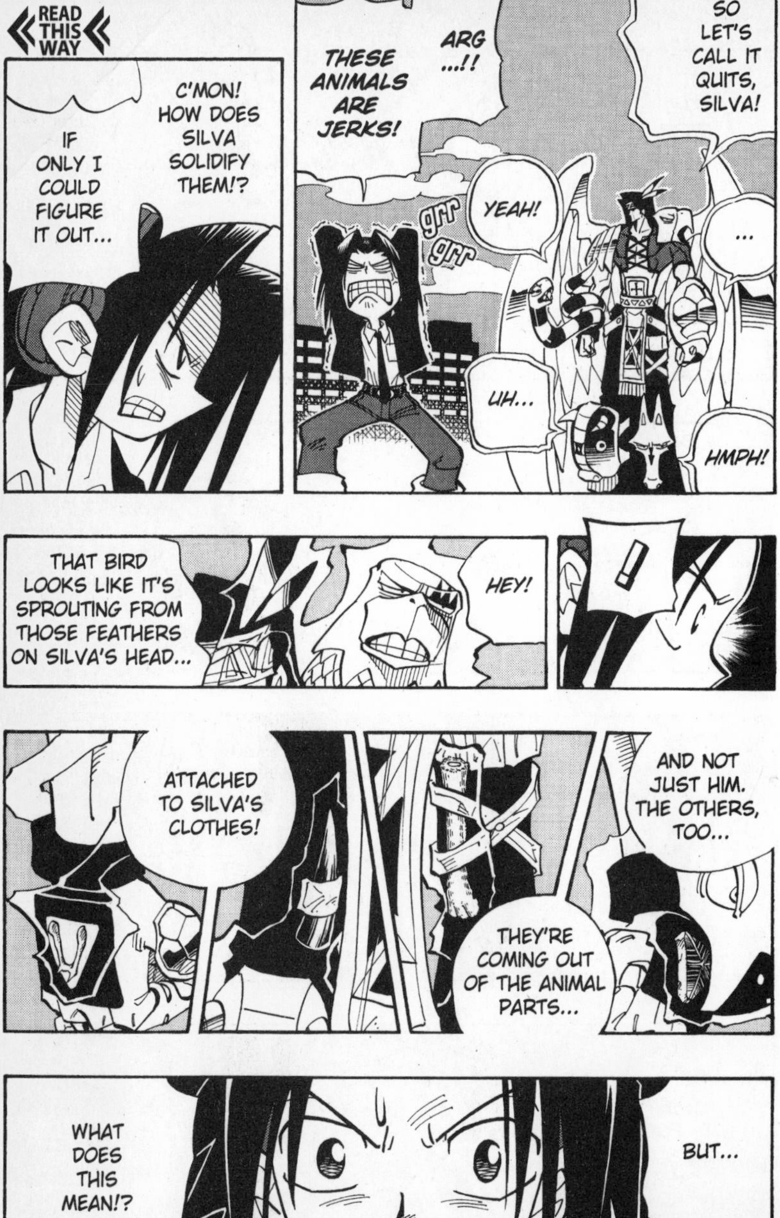
READ THIS WAY
SO LET'S CALL IT QUITS, SILVA!
ARG ...!!
THESE ANIMALS ARE JERKS!
...
YEAH!
grr grr
UH...
HMPH!
C'MON! HOW DOES SILVA SOLIDIFY THEM!?
IF ONLY I COULD FIGURE IT OUT...
!
HEY!
THAT BIRD LOOKS LIKE IT'S SPROUTING FROM THOSE FEATHERS ON SILVA'S HEAD...
AND NOT JUST HIM. THE OTHERS, TOO...
THEY'RE COMING OUT OF THE ANIMAL PARTS...
ATTACHED TO SILVA'S CLOTHES!
BUT...
WHAT DOES THIS MEAN!?

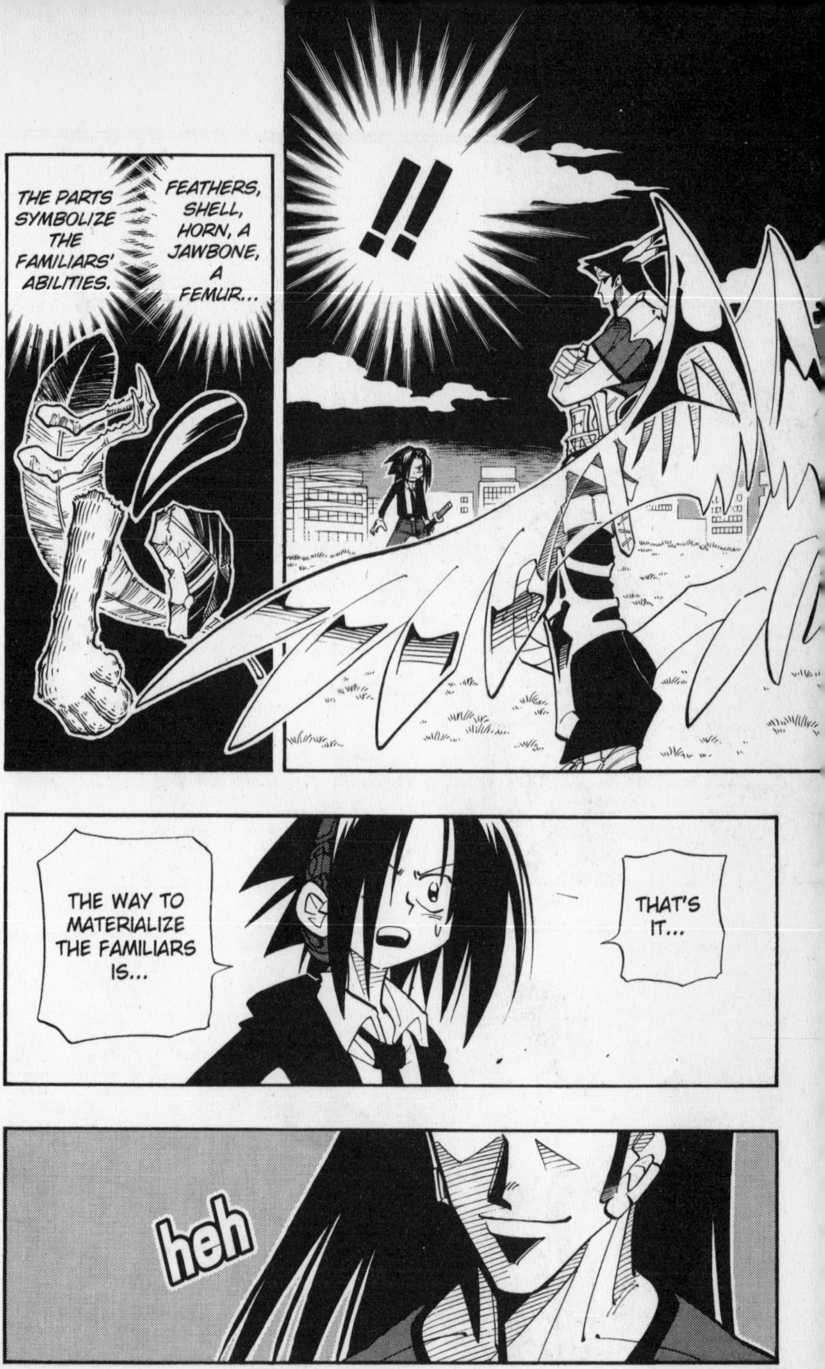
!!
FEATHERS, SHELL, HORN, A JAWBONE, A FEMUR...
THE PARTS SYMBOLIZE THE FAMILIARS' ABILITIES.
THAT'S IT...
THE WAY TO MATERIALIZE THE FAMILIARS IS...
heh

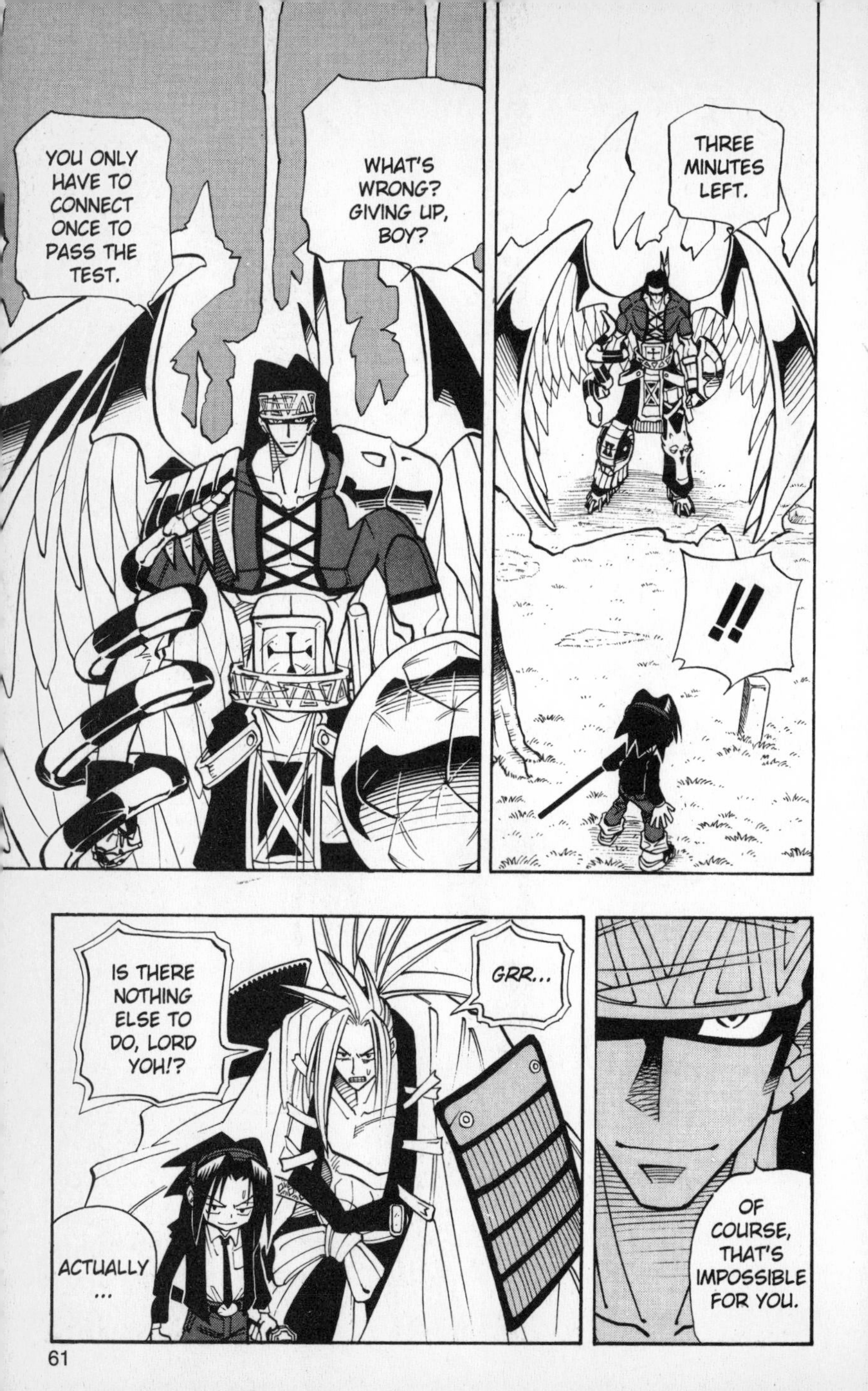
THREE MINUTES LEFT.
!!
WHAT'S WRONG? GIVING UP, BOY?
YOU ONLY HAVE TO CONNECT ONCE TO PASS THE TEST.
OF COURSE, THAT'S IMPOSSIBLE FOR YOU.
GRR...
IS THERE NOTHING ELSE TO DO, LORD YOH!?
ACTUALLY ...

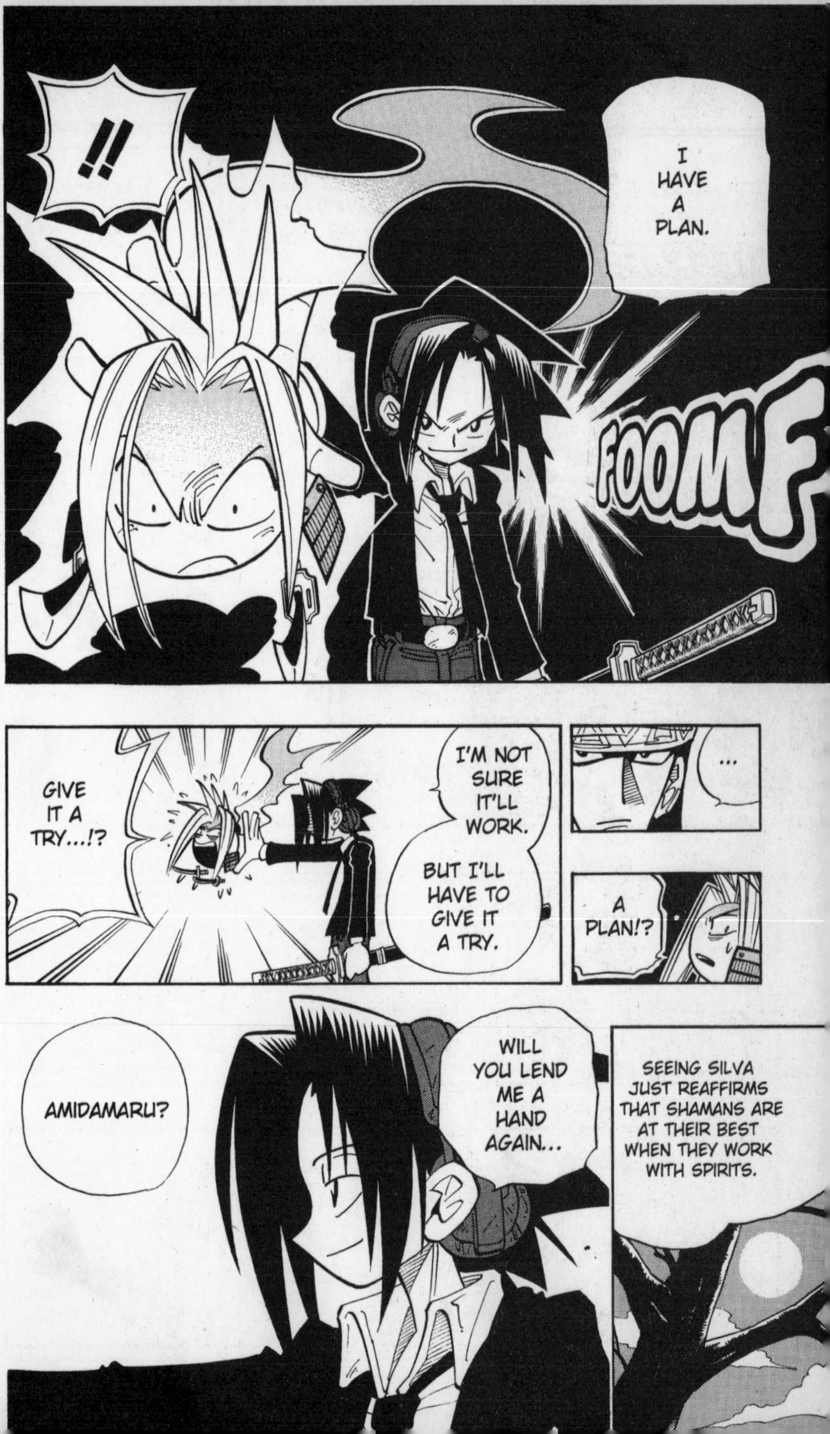
I HAVE A PLAN.
FOOMF
!!
...
A PLAN!?
I'M NOT SURE IT'LL WORK.
BUT I'LL HAVE TO GIVE IT A TRY.
GIVE IT A TRY...!?
SEEING SILVA JUST REAFFIRMS THAT SHAMANS ARE AT THEIR BEST WHEN THEY WORK WITH SPIRITS.
WILL YOU LEND ME A HAND AGAIN...
AMIDAMARU?

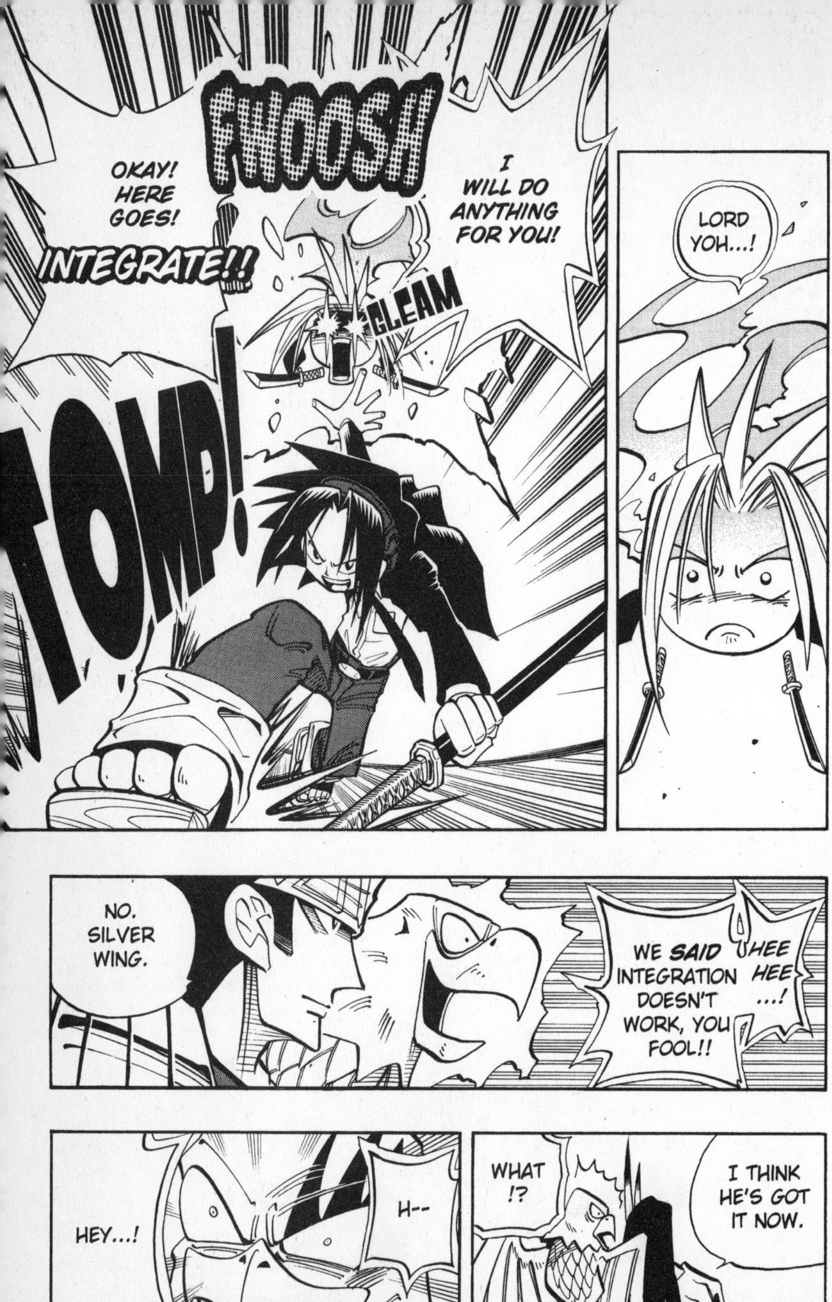
LORD YOH...!
I WILL DO ANYTHING FOR YOU!
FWOOSH
GLEAM
OKAY! HERE GOES!
INTEGRATE!!
TOMP!
HEE HEE ...!
WE SAID INTEGRATION DOESN'T WORK, YOU FOOL!!
NO. SILVER WING.
I THINK HE'S GOT IT NOW.
WHAT !?
H--
HEY...!

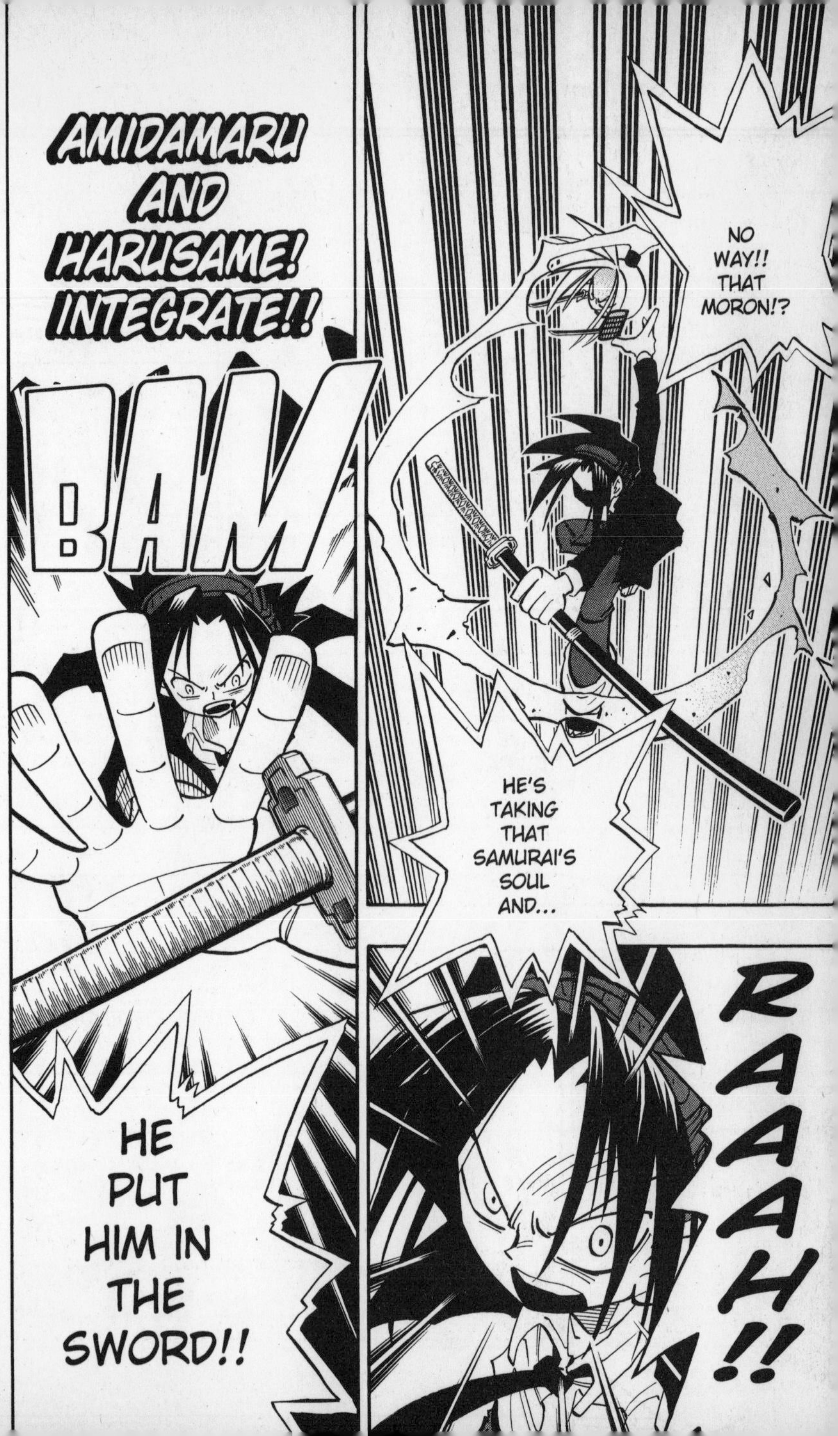
NO WAY!! THAT MORON!?
HE'S TAKING THAT SAMURAI'S SOUL AND...
RAAAH!!
AMIDAMARU AND HARUSAME! INTEGRATE!!
BAM
HE PUT HIM IN THE SWORD!!

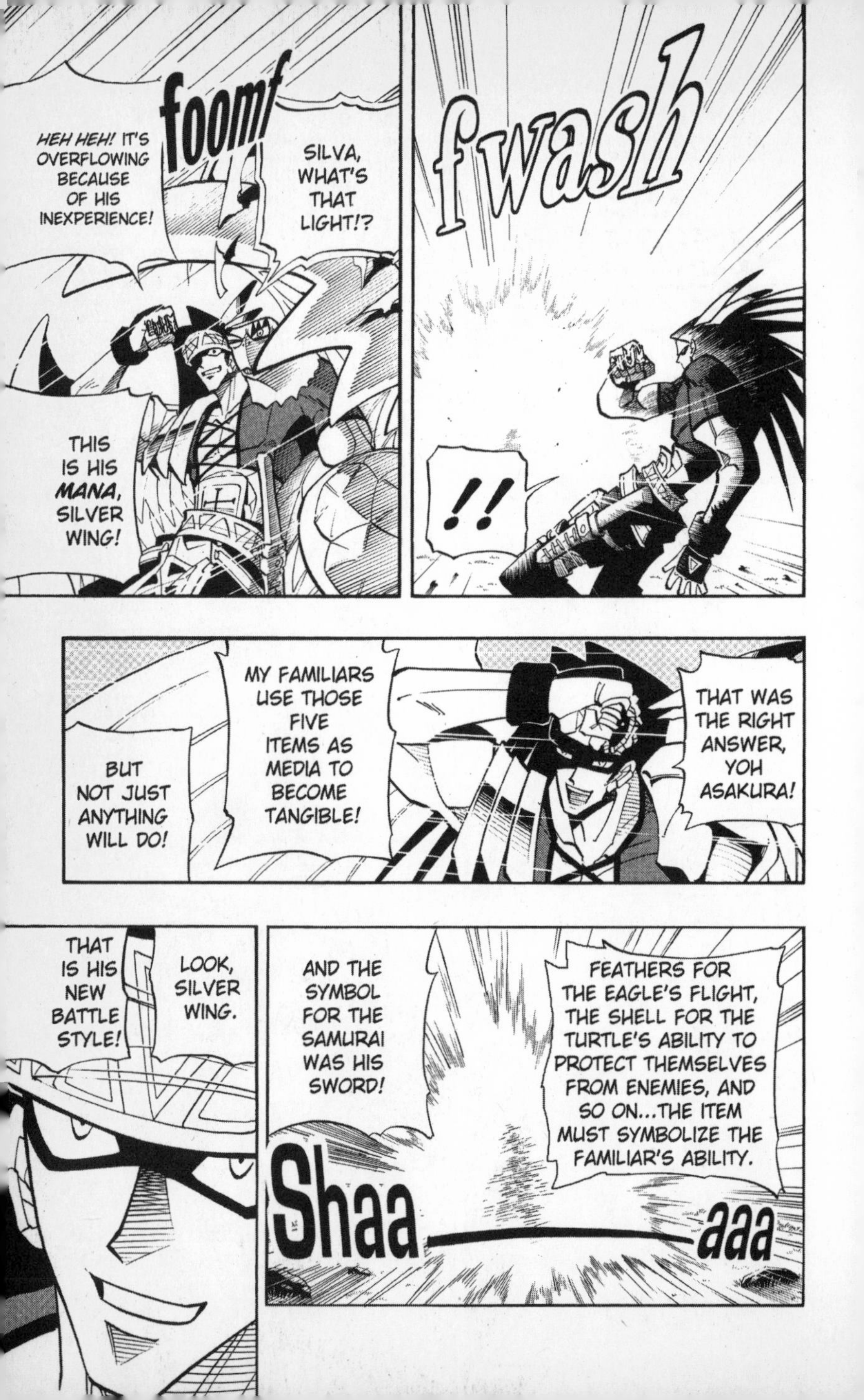
fwash
!!
SILVA, WHAT'S THAT LIGHT!?
foomf
HEH HEH! IT'S OVERFLOWING BECAUSE OF HIS INEXPERIENCE!
THIS IS HIS *MANA*, SILVER WING!
THAT WAS THE RIGHT ANSWER, YOH ASAKURA!
MY FAMILIARS USE THOSE FIVE ITEMS AS MEDIA TO BECOME TANGIBLE!
BUT NOT JUST ANYTHING WILL DO!
FEATHERS FOR THE EAGLE'S FLIGHT, THE SHELL FOR THE TURTLE'S ABILITY TO PROTECT THEMSELVES FROM ENEMIES, AND SO ON...THE ITEM MUST SYMBOLIZE THE FAMILIAR'S ABILITY.
AND THE SYMBOL FOR THE SAMURAI WAS HIS SWORD!
Shaa——aaa
LOOK, SILVER WING.
THAT IS HIS NEW BATTLE STYLE!

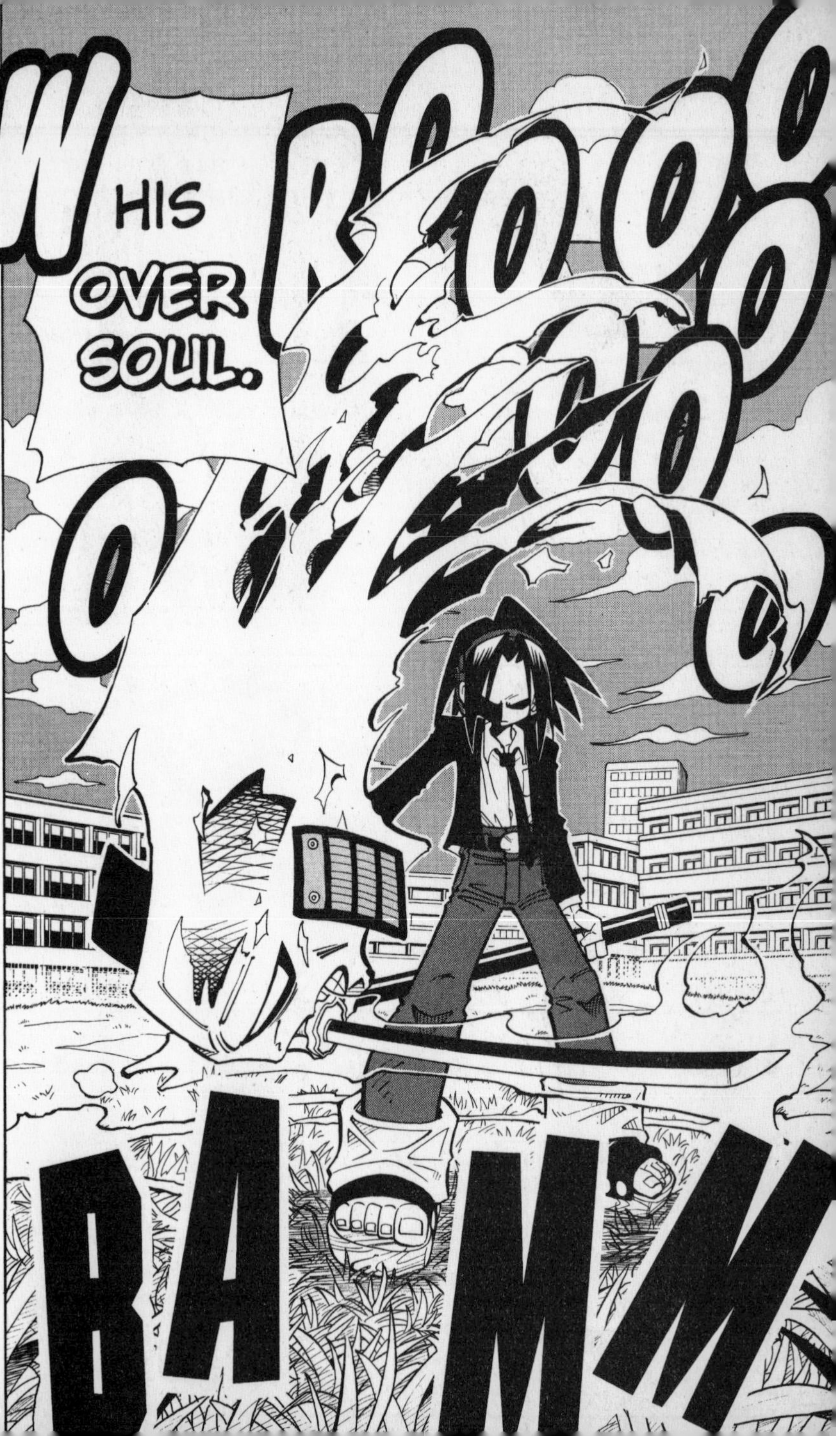
HIS OVER SOUL.
WROOOOOOOOO
BAMM

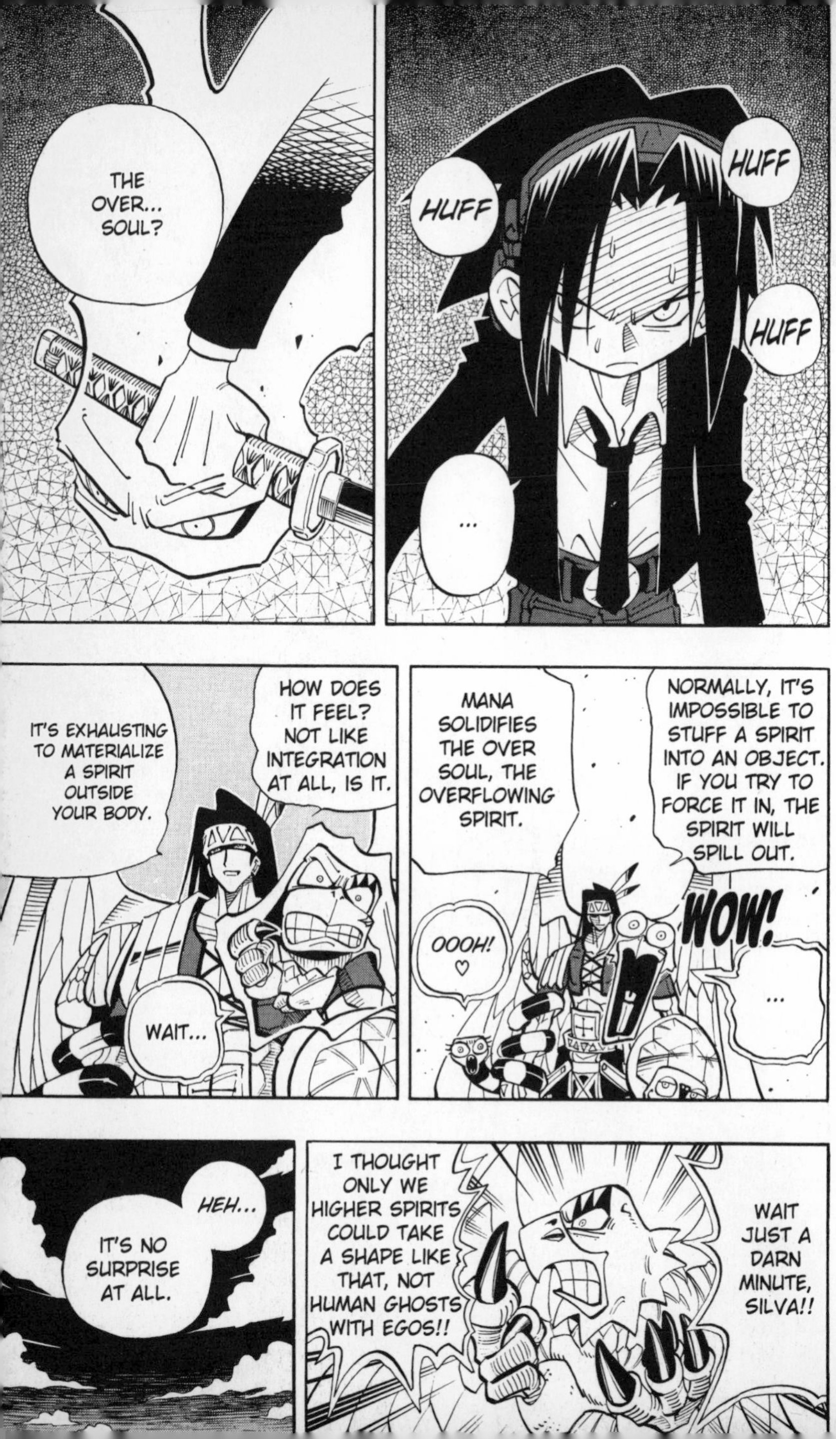
HUFF
HUFF
HUFF
...
THE OVER... SOUL?
NORMALLY, IT'S IMPOSSIBLE TO STUFF A SPIRIT INTO AN OBJECT. IF YOU TRY TO FORCE IT IN, THE SPIRIT WILL SPILL OUT.
MANA SOLIDIFIES THE OVER SOUL, THE OVERFLOWING SPIRIT.
WOW!
OOOH! ♡
...
HOW DOES IT FEEL? NOT LIKE INTEGRATION AT ALL, IS IT.
IT'S EXHAUSTING TO MATERIALIZE A SPIRIT OUTSIDE YOUR BODY.
WAIT...
WAIT JUST A DARN MINUTE, SILVA!!
I THOUGHT ONLY WE HIGHER SPIRITS COULD TAKE A SHAPE LIKE THAT, NOT HUMAN GHOSTS WITH EGOS!!
HEH...
IT'S NO SURPRISE AT ALL.

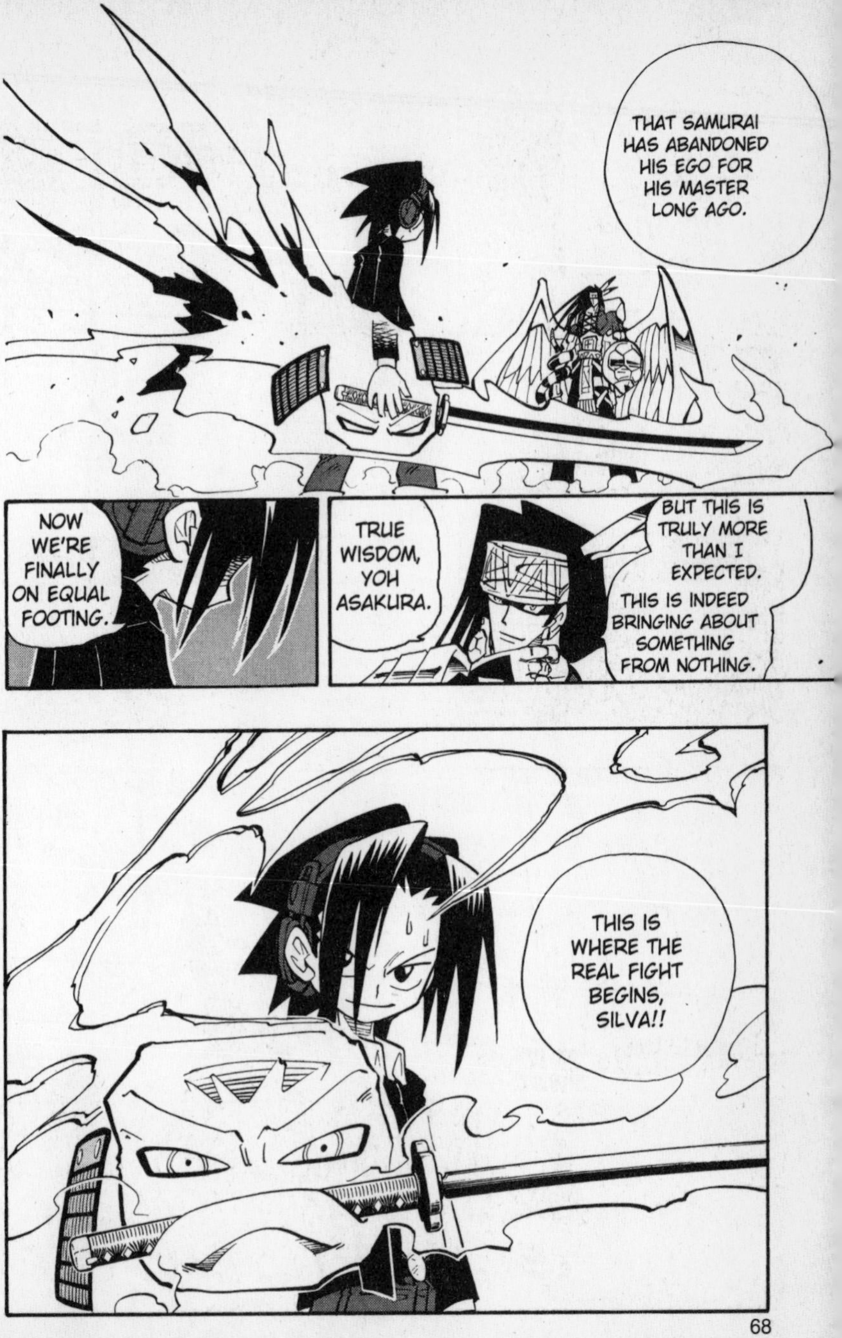
THAT SAMURAI HAS ABANDONED HIS EGO FOR HIS MASTER LONG AGO.
TRUE WISDOM, YOH ASAKURA.
BUT THIS IS TRULY MORE THAN I EXPECTED.
THIS IS INDEED BRINGING ABOUT SOMETHING FROM NOTHING.
NOW WE'RE FINALLY ON EQUAL FOOTING.
THIS IS WHERE THE REAL FIGHT BEGINS, SILVA!!

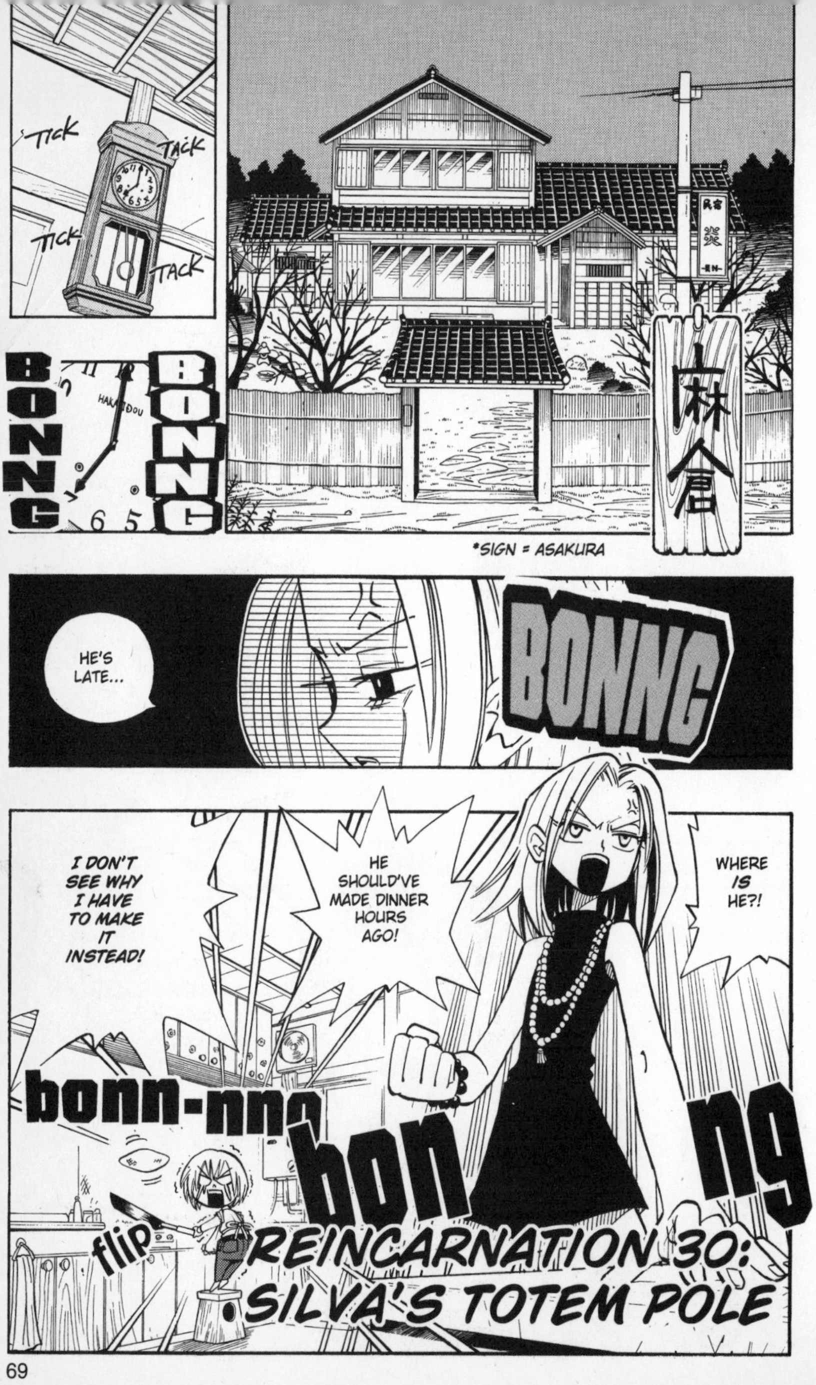

民宿
炎
-EN-
麻倉
*SIGN = ASAKURA
TICK
TACK
TICK
TACK
BONNG
HAKAIDOU
BONNG
BONNG
HE'S LATE...
WHERE IS HE?!
HE SHOULD'VE MADE DINNER HOURS AGO!
I DON'T SEE WHY I HAVE TO MAKE IT INSTEAD!
bonn-nng
bon
ng
flip
REINCARNATION 30: SILVA'S TOTEM POLE

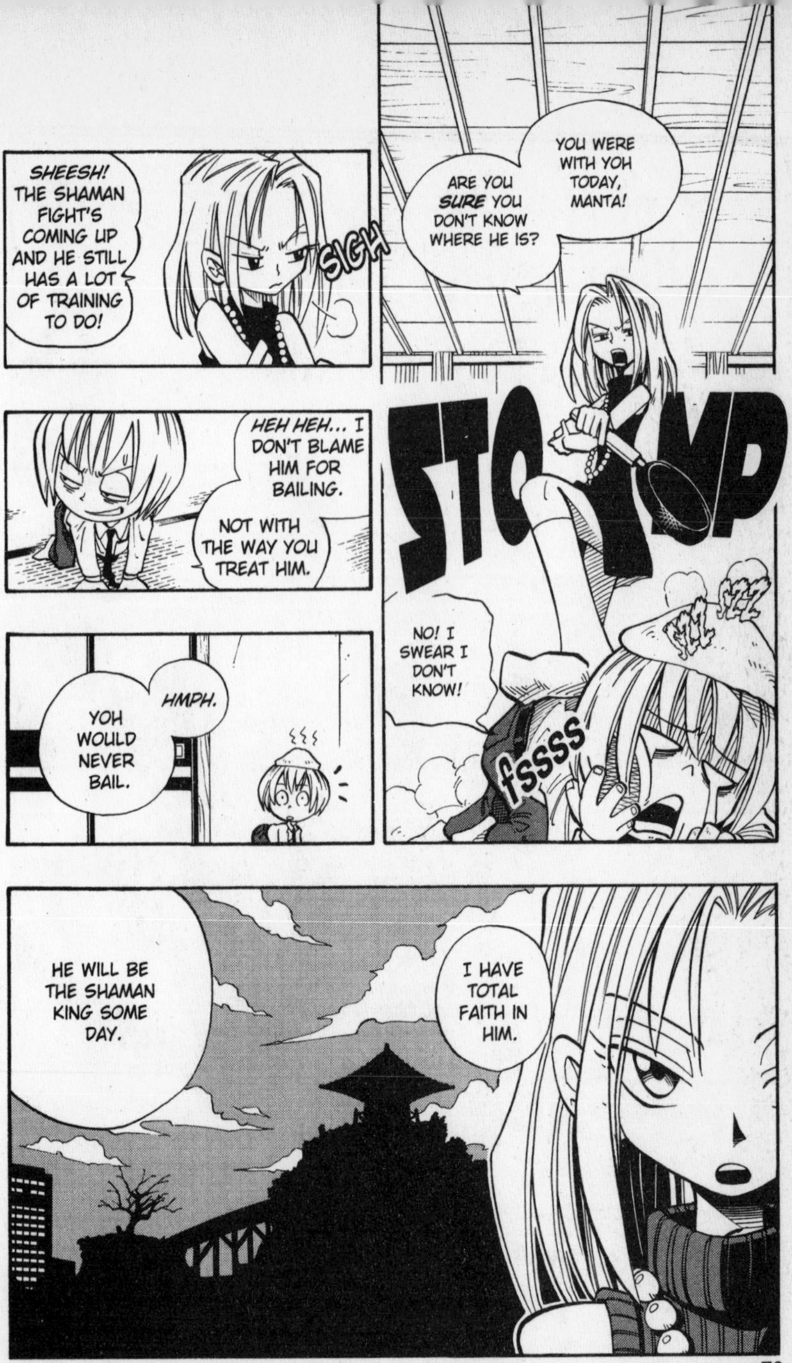
YOU WERE WITH YOH TODAY, MANTA!
ARE YOU *SURE* YOU DON'T KNOW WHERE HE IS?
STOMP
NO! I SWEAR I DON'T KNOW!
fssss
SHEESH! THE SHAMAN FIGHT'S COMING UP AND HE STILL HAS A LOT OF TRAINING TO DO!
SIGH
HEH HEH... I DON'T BLAME HIM FOR BAILING.
NOT WITH THE WAY YOU TREAT HIM.
HMPH.
YOH WOULD NEVER BAIL.
I HAVE TOTAL FAITH IN HIM.
HE WILL BE THE SHAMAN KING SOME DAY.

READ THIS WAY

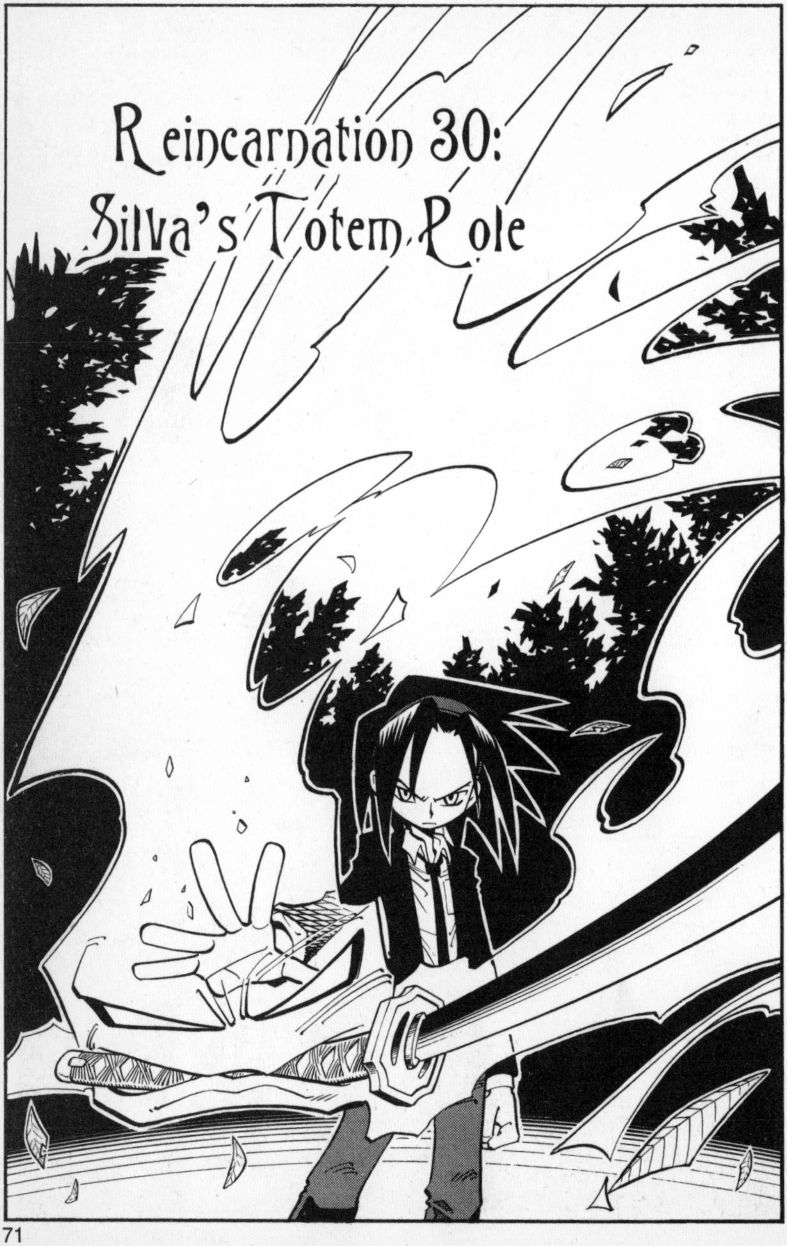
Reincarnation 30:
Silva's Totem Pole

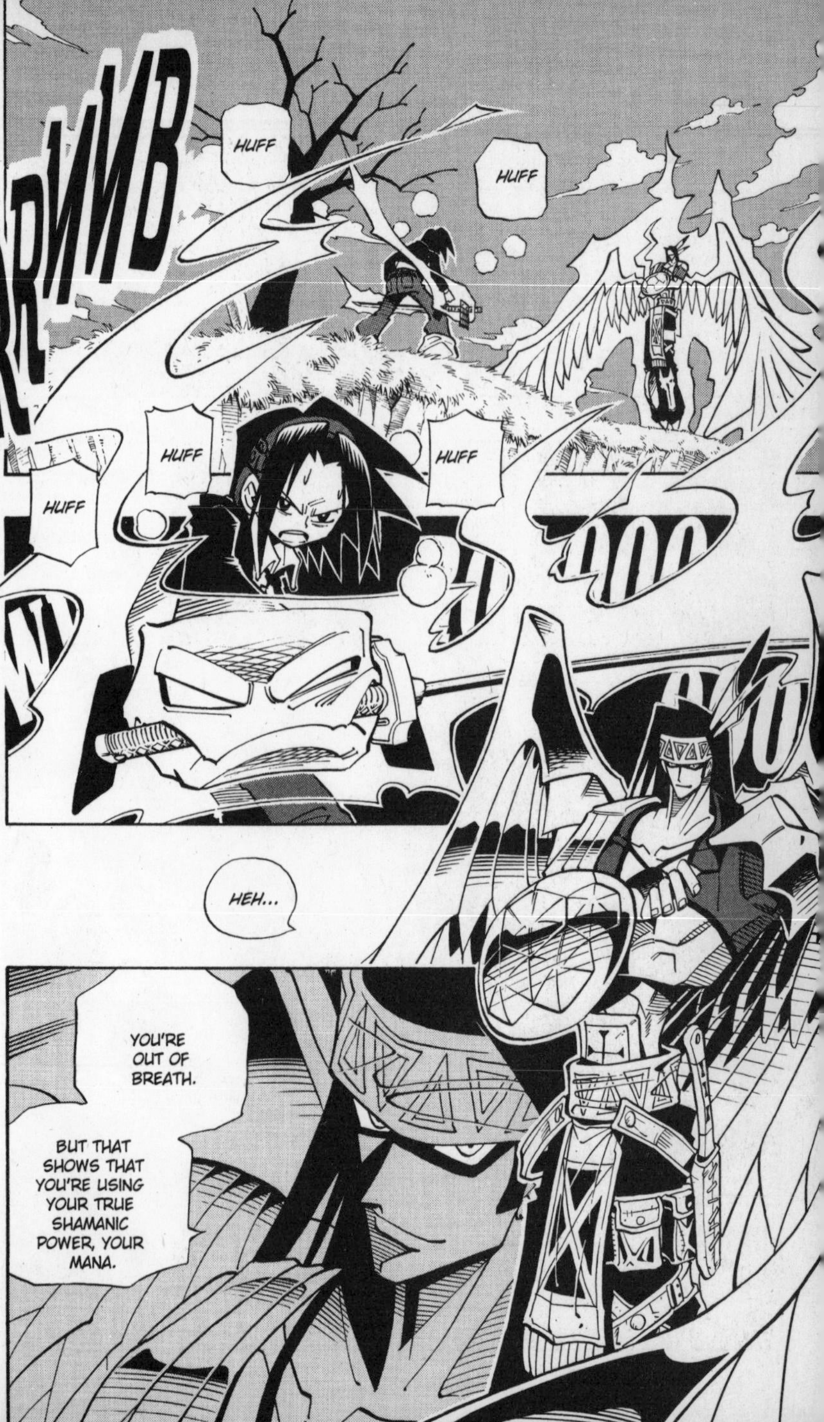
RRUMB
HUFF
HUFF
HUFF
HUFF
HUFF
HEH...
YOU'RE OUT OF BREATH.
BUT THAT SHOWS THAT YOU'RE USING YOUR TRUE SHAMANIC POWER, YOUR MANA.

READ THIS WAY

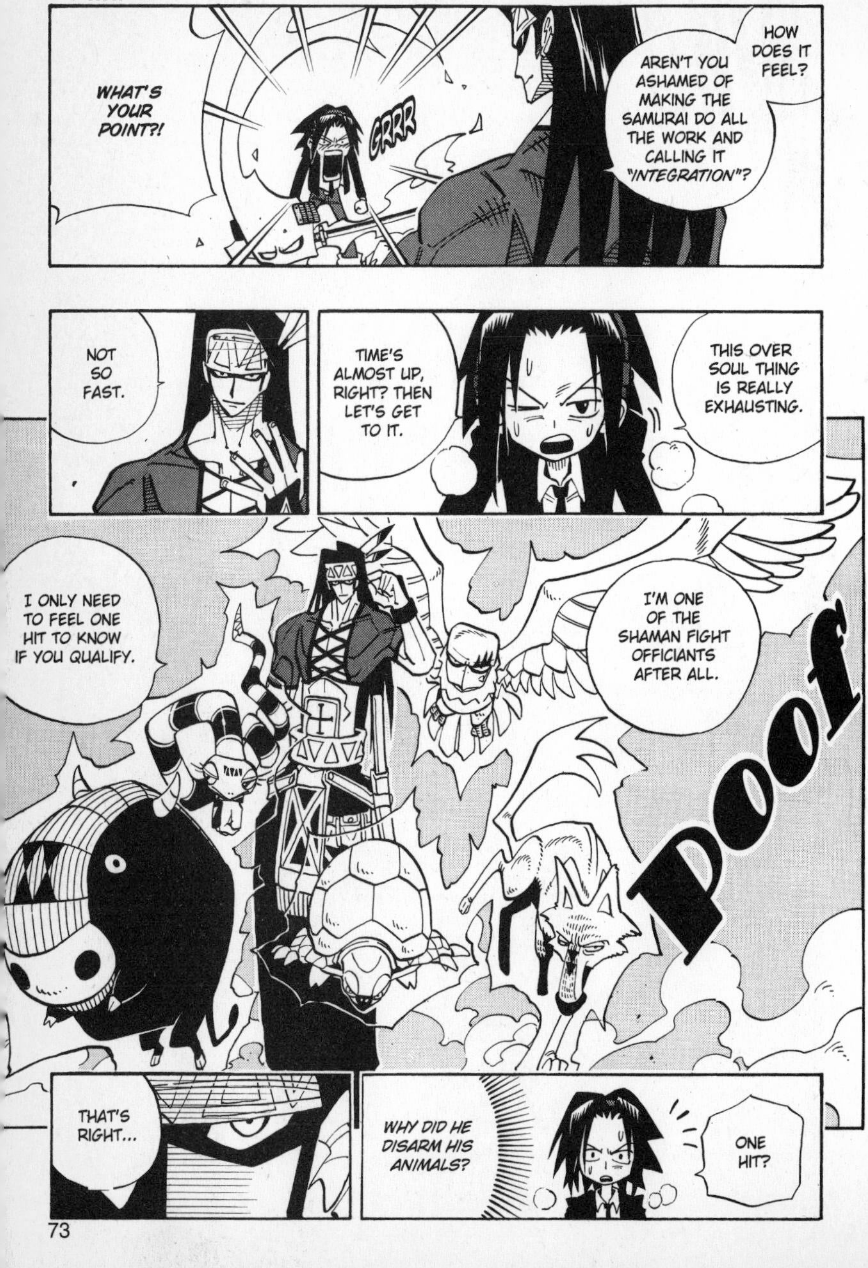
HOW DOES IT FEEL?
AREN'T YOU ASHAMED OF MAKING THE SAMURAI DO ALL THE WORK AND CALLING IT "INTEGRATION"?
GRRR
WHAT'S YOUR POINT?!
THIS OVER SOUL THING IS REALLY EXHAUSTING.
TIME'S ALMOST UP, RIGHT? THEN LET'S GET TO IT.
NOT SO FAST.
I'M ONE OF THE SHAMAN FIGHT OFFICIANTS AFTER ALL.
Poof
I ONLY NEED TO FEEL ONE HIT TO KNOW IF YOU QUALIFY.
ONE HIT?
WHY DID HE DISARM HIS ANIMALS?
THAT'S RIGHT...

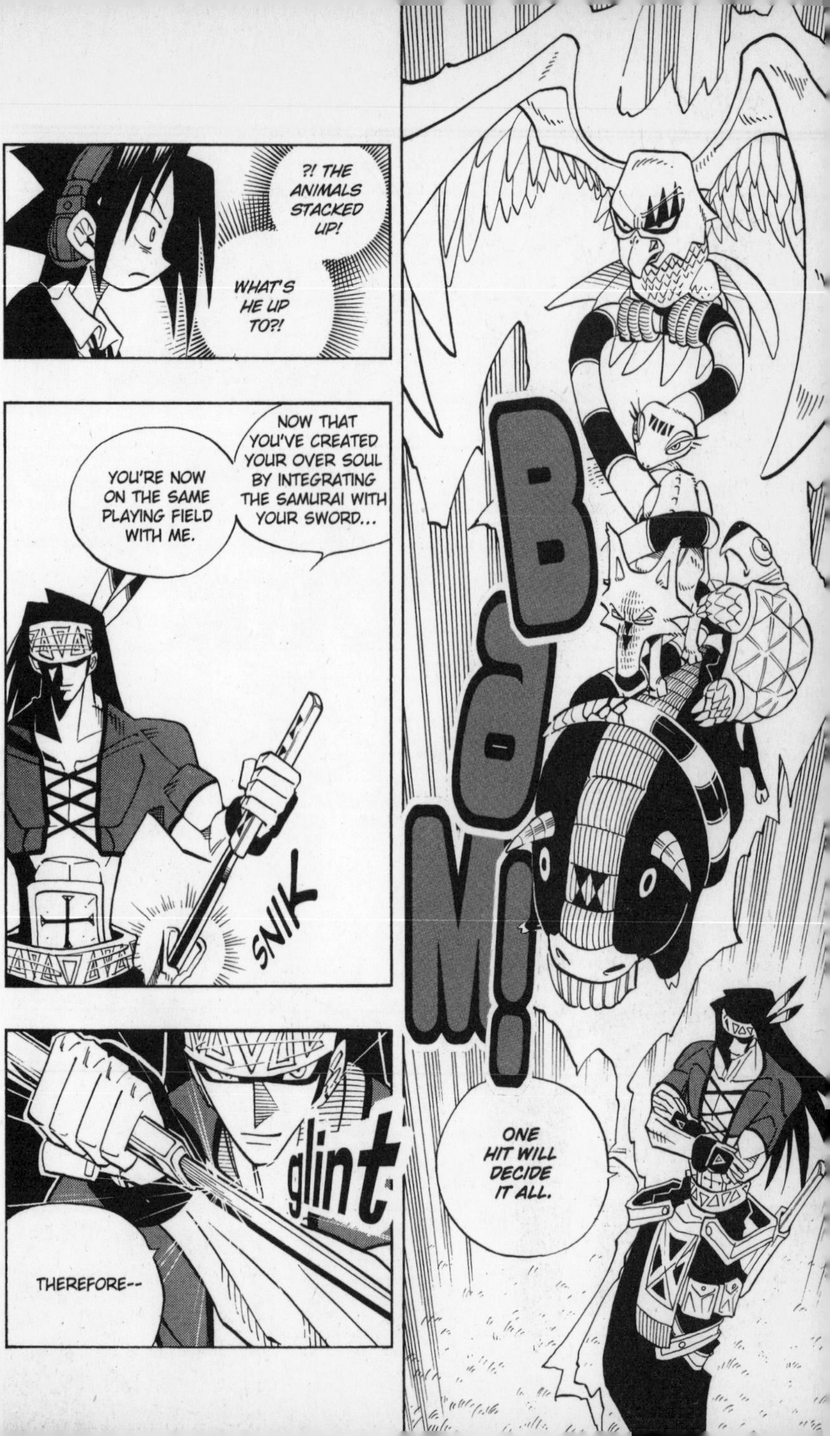

?! THE ANIMALS STACKED UP!
WHAT'S HE UP TO?!
NOW THAT YOU'VE CREATED YOUR OVER SOUL BY INTEGRATING THE SAMURAI WITH YOUR SWORD...
YOU'RE NOW ON THE SAME PLAYING FIELD WITH ME.
SNIK
THEREFORE--
glint
BOOM!
ONE HIT WILL DECIDE IT ALL.

READ THIS WAY

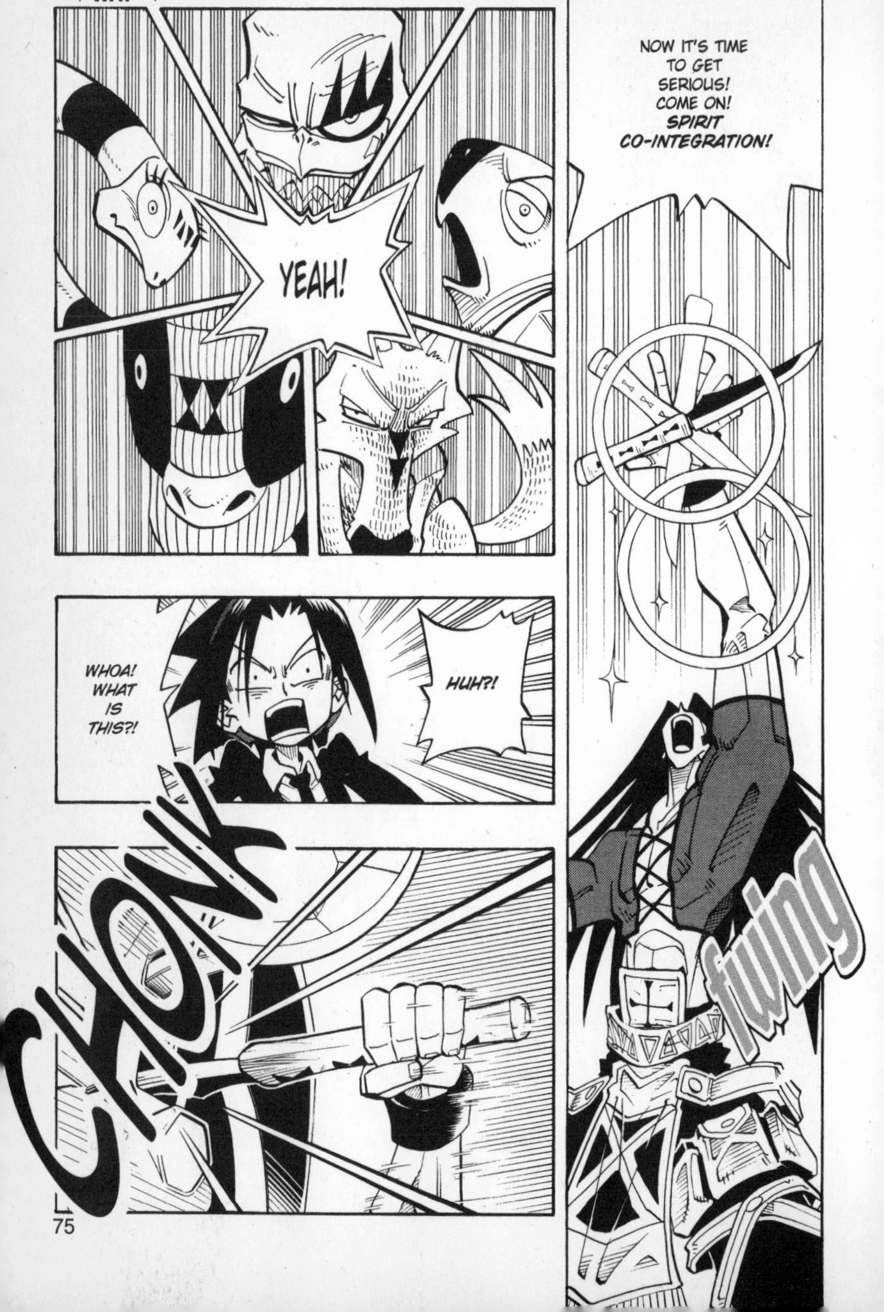

NOW IT'S TIME TO GET SERIOUS! COME ON! SPIRIT CO-INTEGRATION!
FWING
YEAH!
HUH?!
WHOA! WHAT IS THIS?!
CHONK

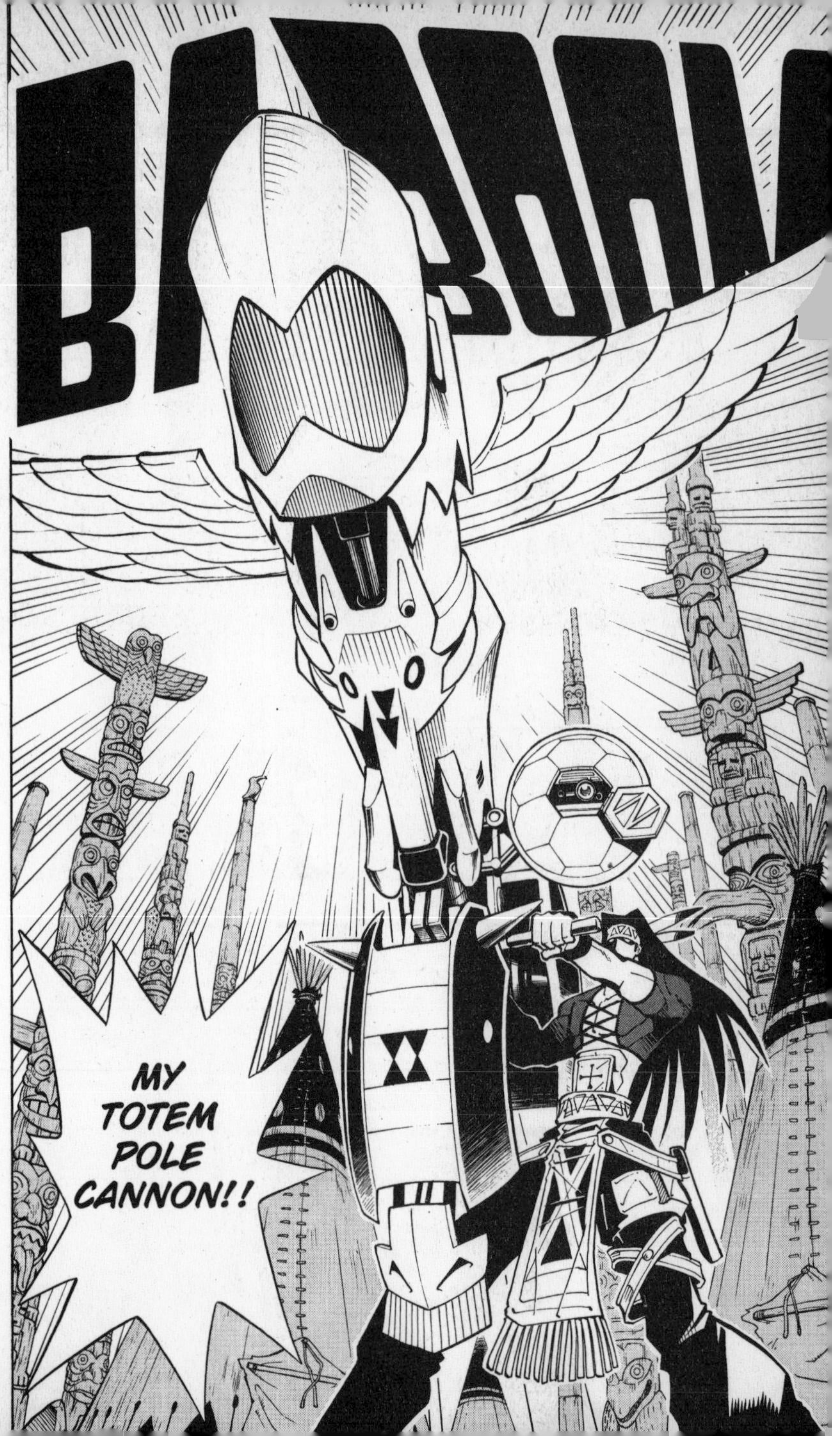
MY TOTEM POLE CANNON!!

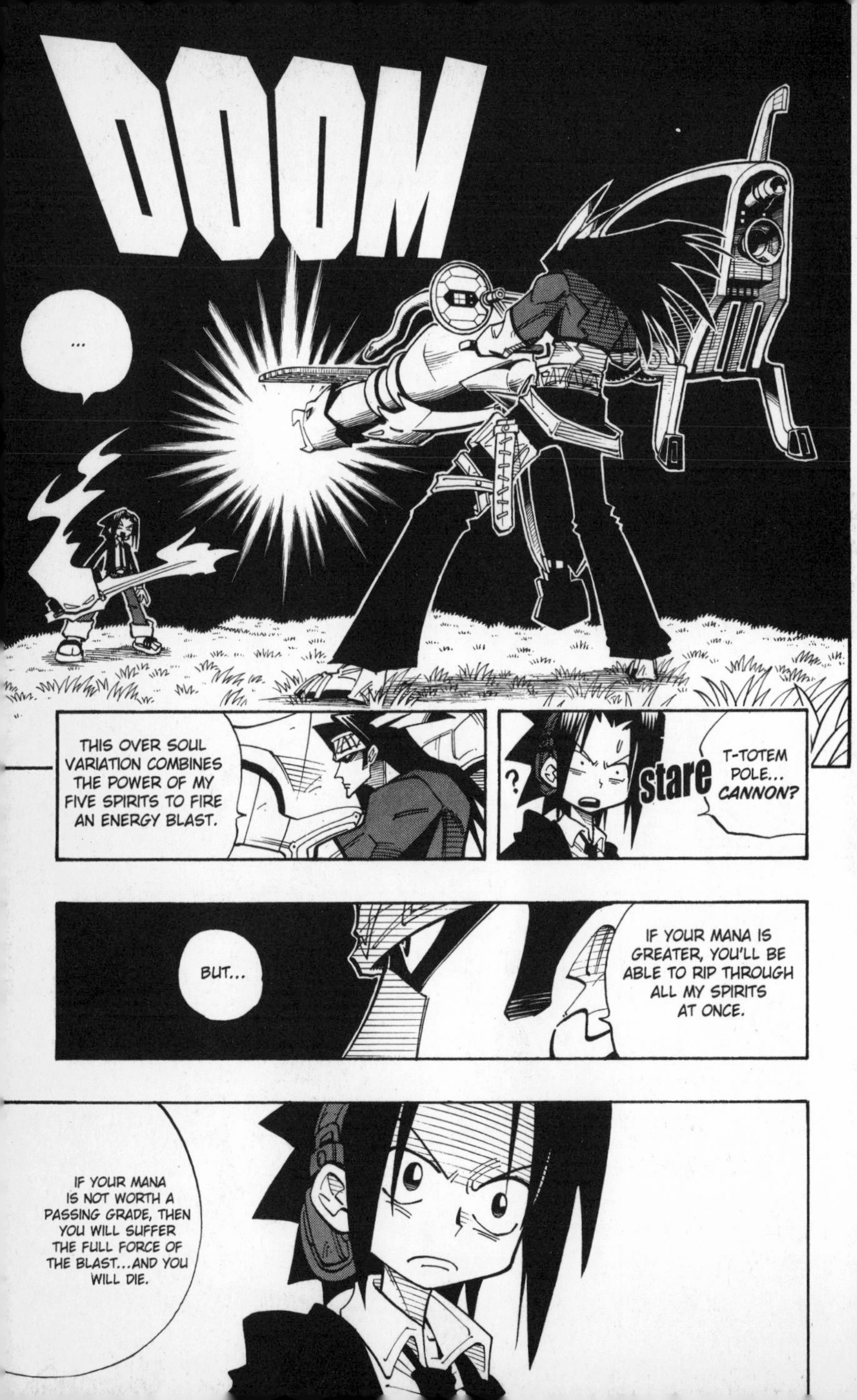
DOOM
...
T-TOTEM POLE... CANNON?
stare
?
THIS OVER SOUL VARIATION COMBINES THE POWER OF MY FIVE SPIRITS TO FIRE AN ENERGY BLAST.
IF YOUR MANA IS GREATER, YOU'LL BE ABLE TO RIP THROUGH ALL MY SPIRITS AT ONCE.
BUT...
IF YOUR MANA IS NOT WORTH A PASSING GRADE, THEN YOU WILL SUFFER THE FULL FORCE OF THE BLAST...AND YOU WILL DIE.

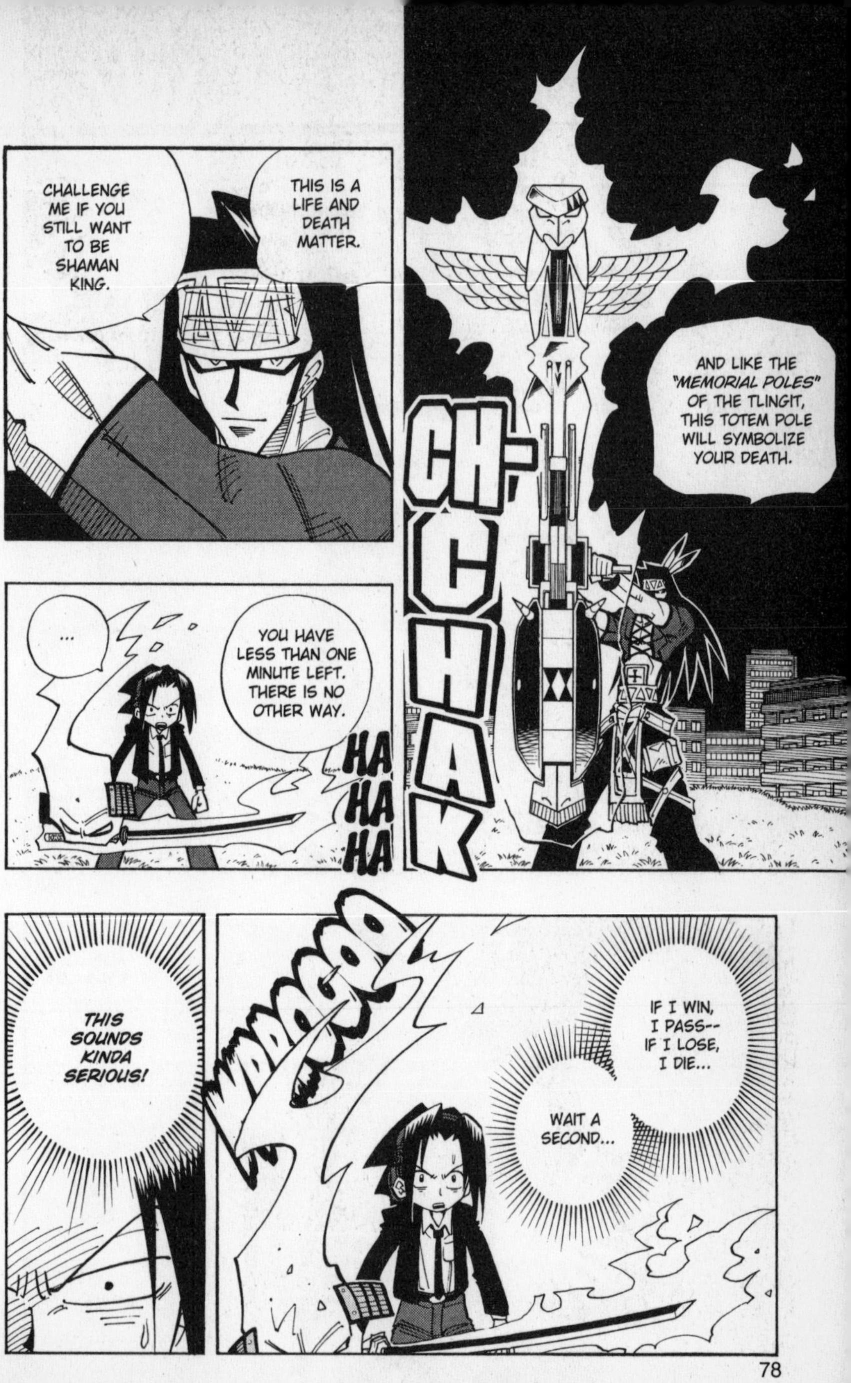

AND LIKE THE *"MEMORIAL POLES"* OF THE TLINGIT, THIS TOTEM POLE WILL SYMBOLIZE YOUR DEATH.
CH-CHAK
THIS IS A LIFE AND DEATH MATTER.
CHALLENGE ME IF YOU STILL WANT TO BE SHAMAN KING.
YOU HAVE LESS THAN ONE MINUTE LEFT. THERE IS NO OTHER WAY.
...
HA HA HA
IF I WIN, I PASS-- IF I LOSE, I DIE...
WAIT A SECOND...
THIS SOUNDS KINDA SERIOUS!

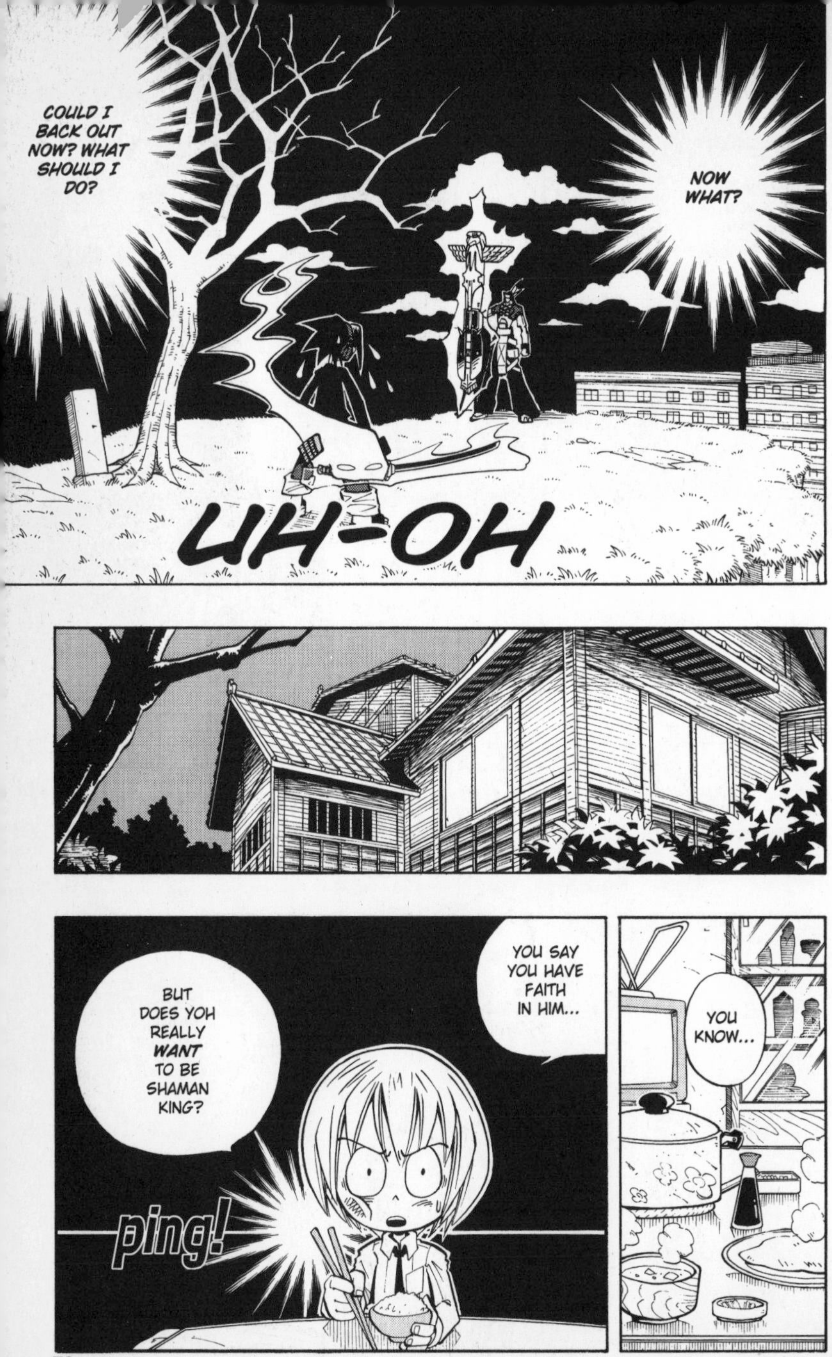
NOW WHAT?
COULD I BACK OUT NOW? WHAT SHOULD I DO?
UH-OH
YOU KNOW...
YOU SAY YOU HAVE FAITH IN HIM...
BUT DOES YOH REALLY *WANT* TO BE SHAMAN KING?
ping!

READ THIS WAY

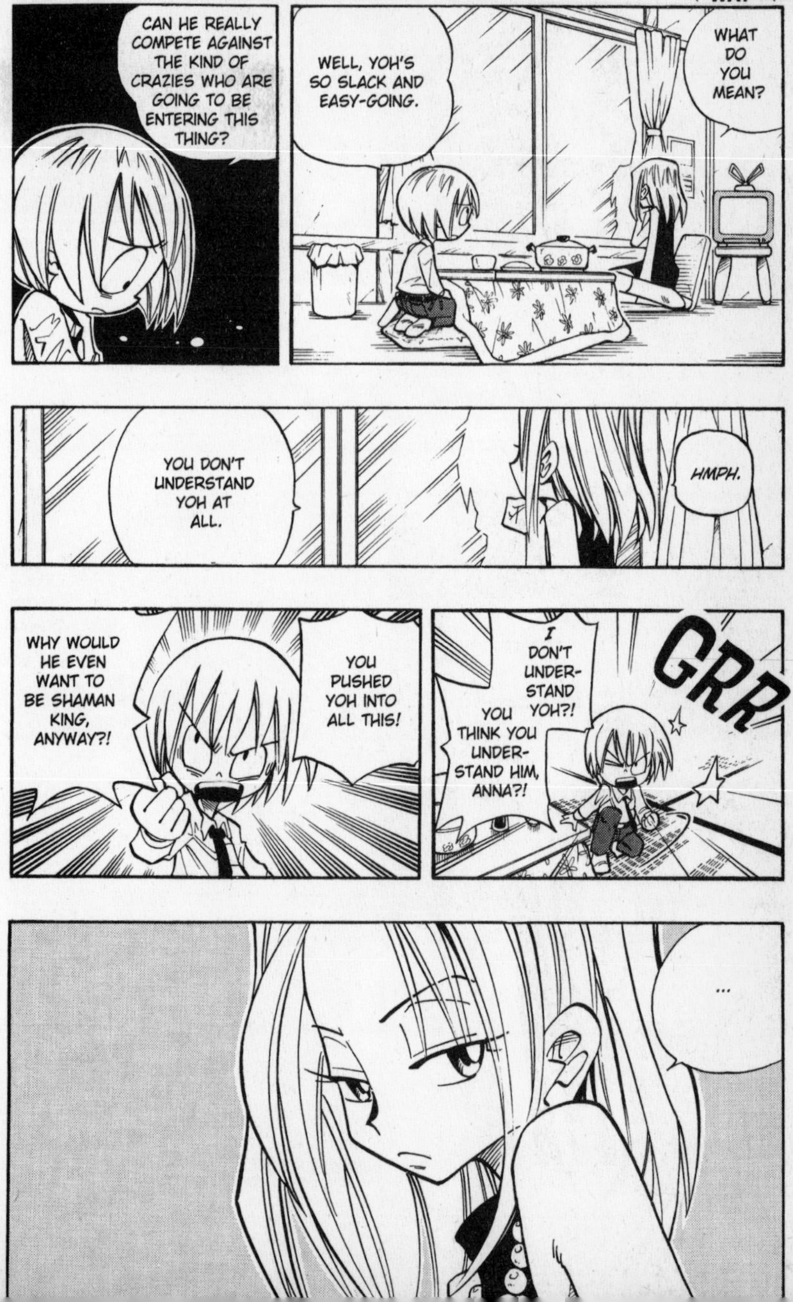
WHAT DO YOU MEAN?
WELL, YOH'S SO SLACK AND EASY-GOING.
CAN HE REALLY COMPETE AGAINST THE KIND OF CRAZIES WHO ARE GOING TO BE ENTERING THIS THING?
HMPH.
YOU DON'T UNDERSTAND YOH AT ALL.
GRR
I DON'T UNDER-STAND YOH?!
YOU THINK YOU UNDER-STAND HIM, ANNA?!
YOU PUSHED YOH INTO ALL THIS!
WHY WOULD HE EVEN WANT TO BE SHAMAN KING, ANYWAY?!
...

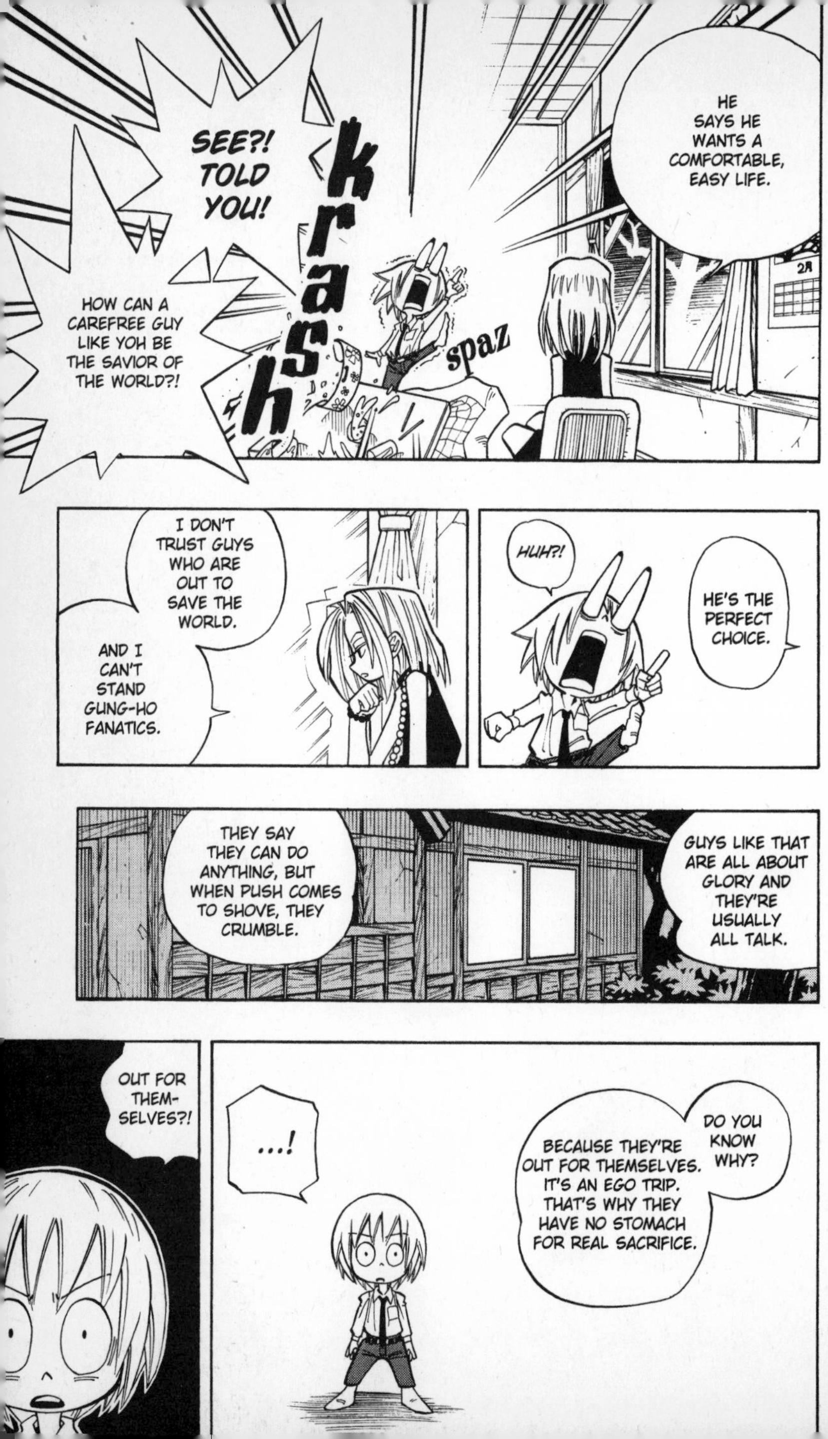
HE SAYS HE WANTS A COMFORTABLE, EASY LIFE.
SEE?! TOLD YOU!
krash
spaz
HOW CAN A CAREFREE GUY LIKE YOH BE THE SAVIOR OF THE WORLD?!
HE'S THE PERFECT CHOICE.
HUH?!
I DON'T TRUST GUYS WHO ARE OUT TO SAVE THE WORLD.
AND I CAN'T STAND GUNG-HO FANATICS.
GUYS LIKE THAT ARE ALL ABOUT GLORY AND THEY'RE USUALLY ALL TALK.
THEY SAY THEY CAN DO ANYTHING, BUT WHEN PUSH COMES TO SHOVE, THEY CRUMBLE.
DO YOU KNOW WHY?
BECAUSE THEY'RE OUT FOR THEMSELVES. IT'S AN EGO TRIP. THAT'S WHY THEY HAVE NO STOMACH FOR REAL SACRIFICE.
...!
OUT FOR THEM-SELVES?!

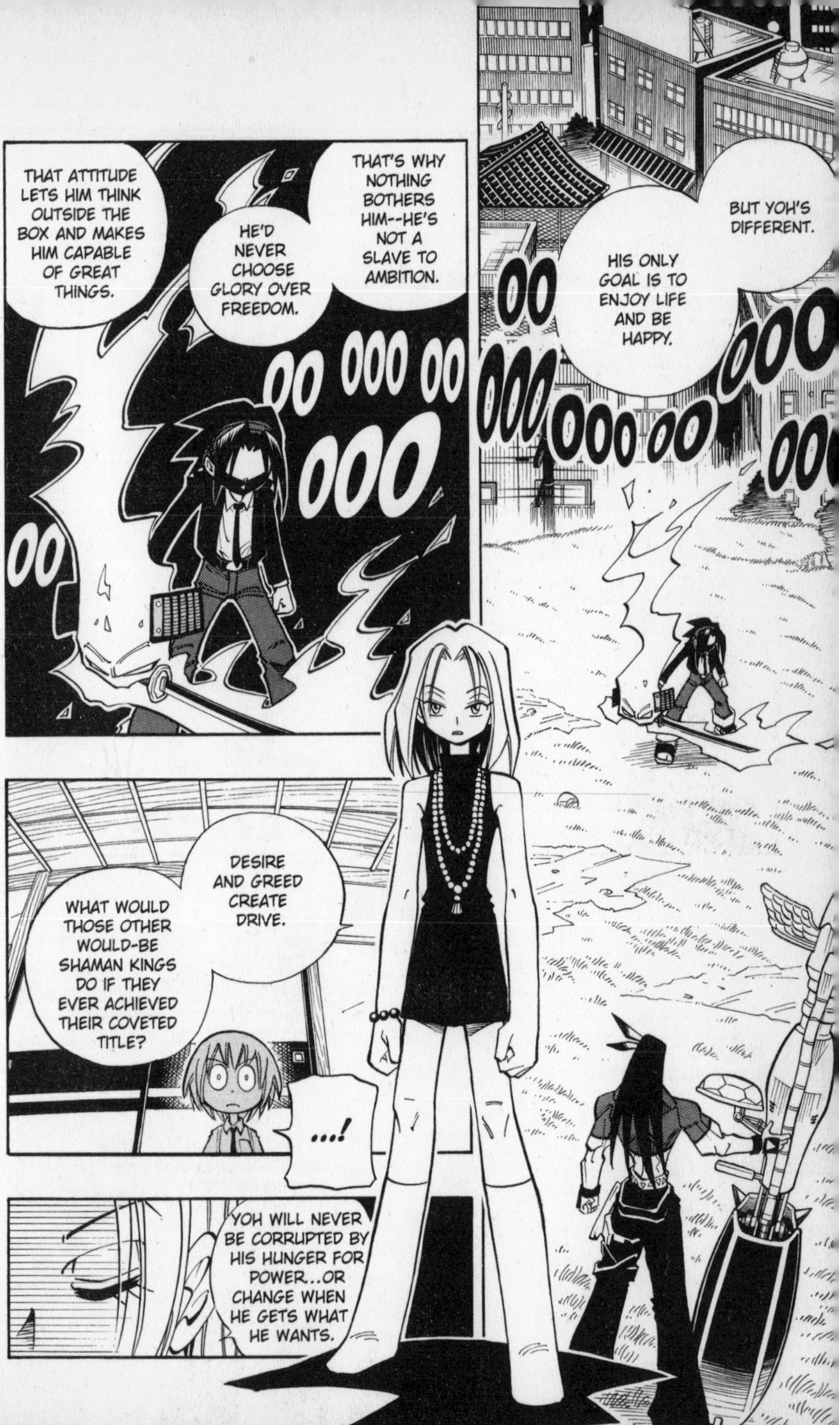
BUT YOH'S DIFFERENT.
HIS ONLY GOAL IS TO ENJOY LIFE AND BE HAPPY.
OO OOO OOO OO OOO OO
THAT'S WHY NOTHING BOTHERS HIM--HE'S NOT A SLAVE TO AMBITION.
HE'D NEVER CHOOSE GLORY OVER FREEDOM.
THAT ATTITUDE LETS HIM THINK OUTSIDE THE BOX AND MAKES HIM CAPABLE OF GREAT THINGS.
OO OOO OO OOO OO
DESIRE AND GREED CREATE DRIVE.
WHAT WOULD THOSE OTHER WOULD-BE SHAMAN KINGS DO IF THEY EVER ACHIEVED THEIR COVETED TITLE?
...!
YOH WILL NEVER BE CORRUPTED BY HIS HUNGER FOR POWER...OR CHANGE WHEN HE GETS WHAT HE WANTS.

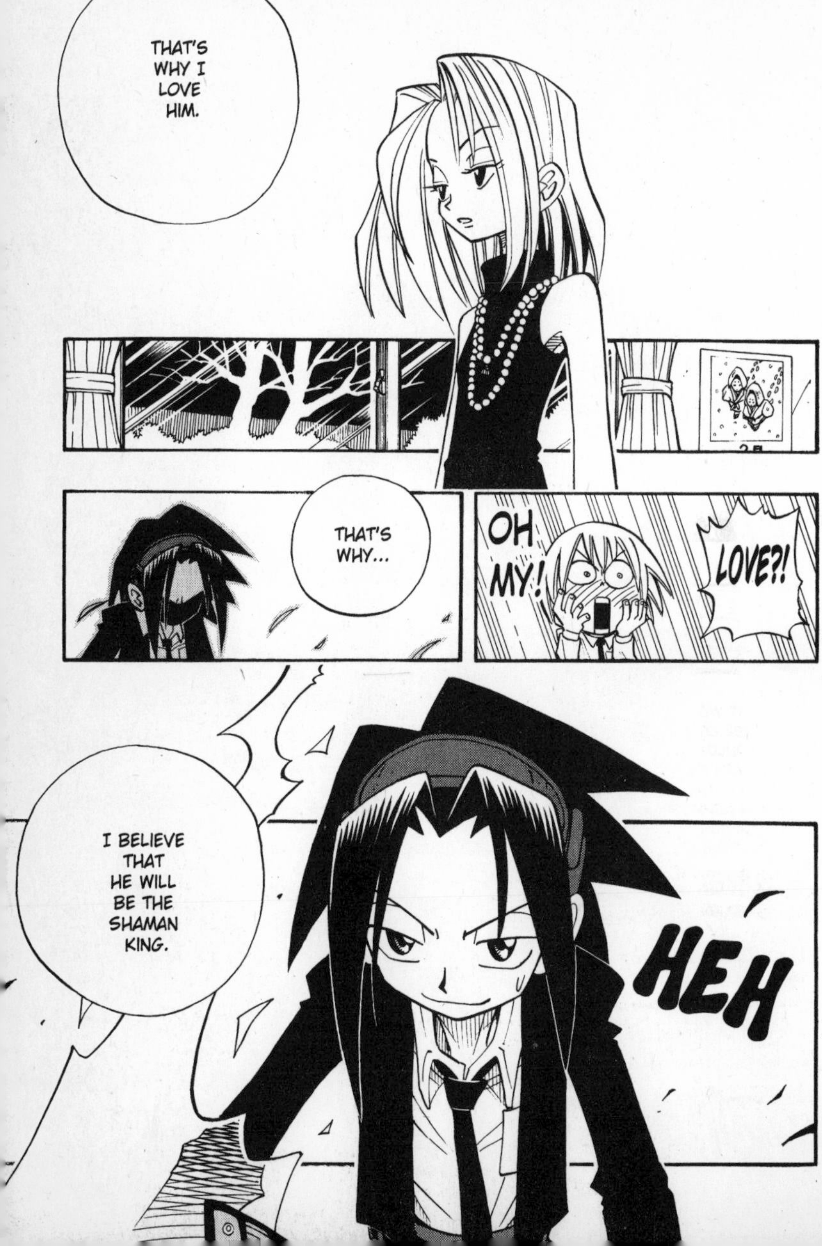
THAT'S WHY I LOVE HIM.
LOVE?!
OH MY!
THAT'S WHY...
I BELIEVE THAT HE WILL BE THE SHAMAN KING.
HEH

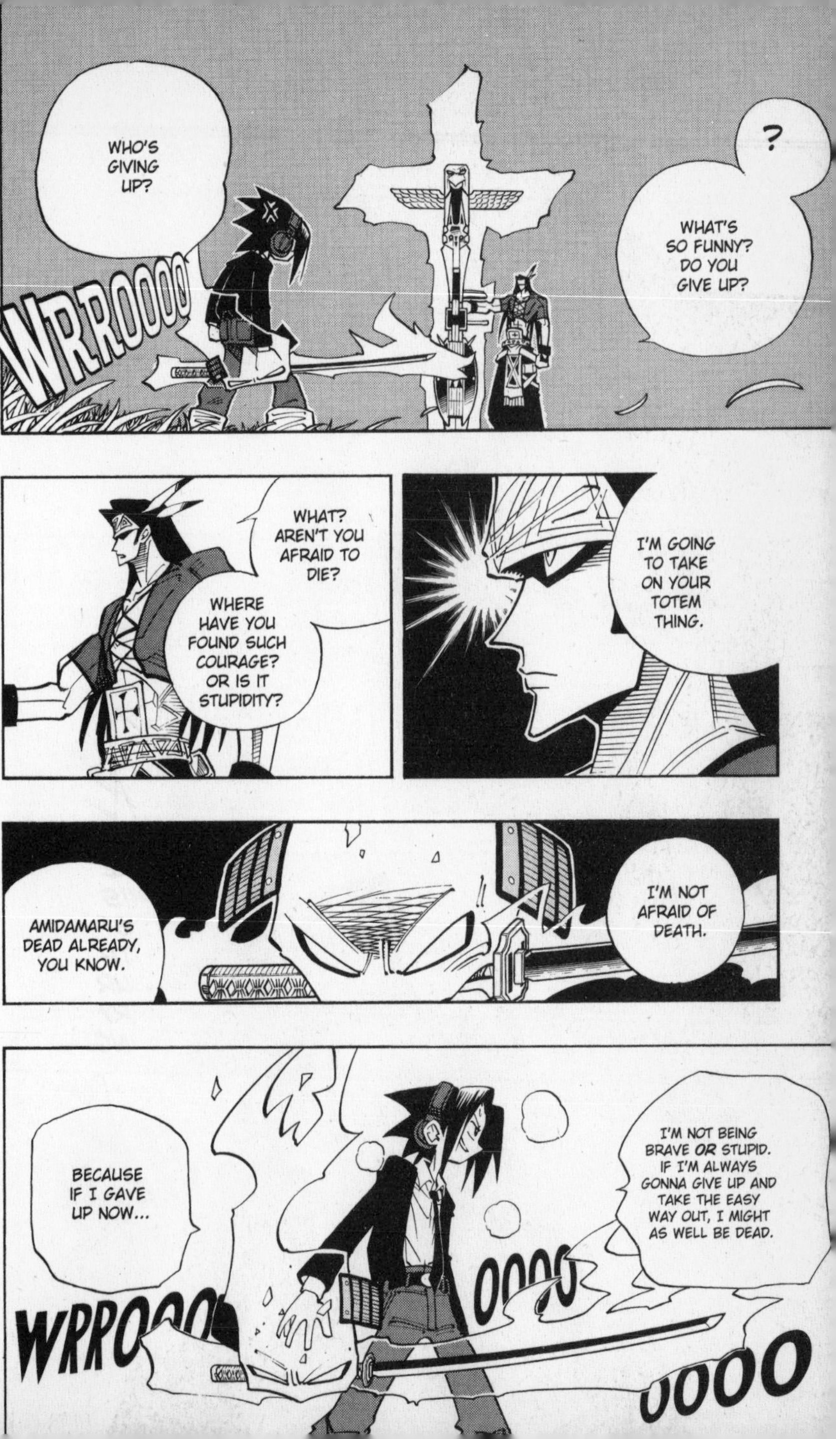
?
WHAT'S SO FUNNY? DO YOU GIVE UP?
WHO'S GIVING UP?
WRROOOO
I'M GOING TO TAKE ON YOUR TOTEM THING.
WHAT? AREN'T YOU AFRAID TO DIE?
WHERE HAVE YOU FOUND SUCH COURAGE? OR IS IT STUPIDITY?
I'M NOT AFRAID OF DEATH.
AMIDAMARU'S DEAD ALREADY, YOU KNOW.
I'M NOT BEING BRAVE *OR* STUPID. IF I'M ALWAYS GONNA GIVE UP AND TAKE THE EASY WAY OUT, I MIGHT AS WELL BE DEAD.
BECAUSE IF I GAVE UP NOW...
WRROOOOOOOOOO

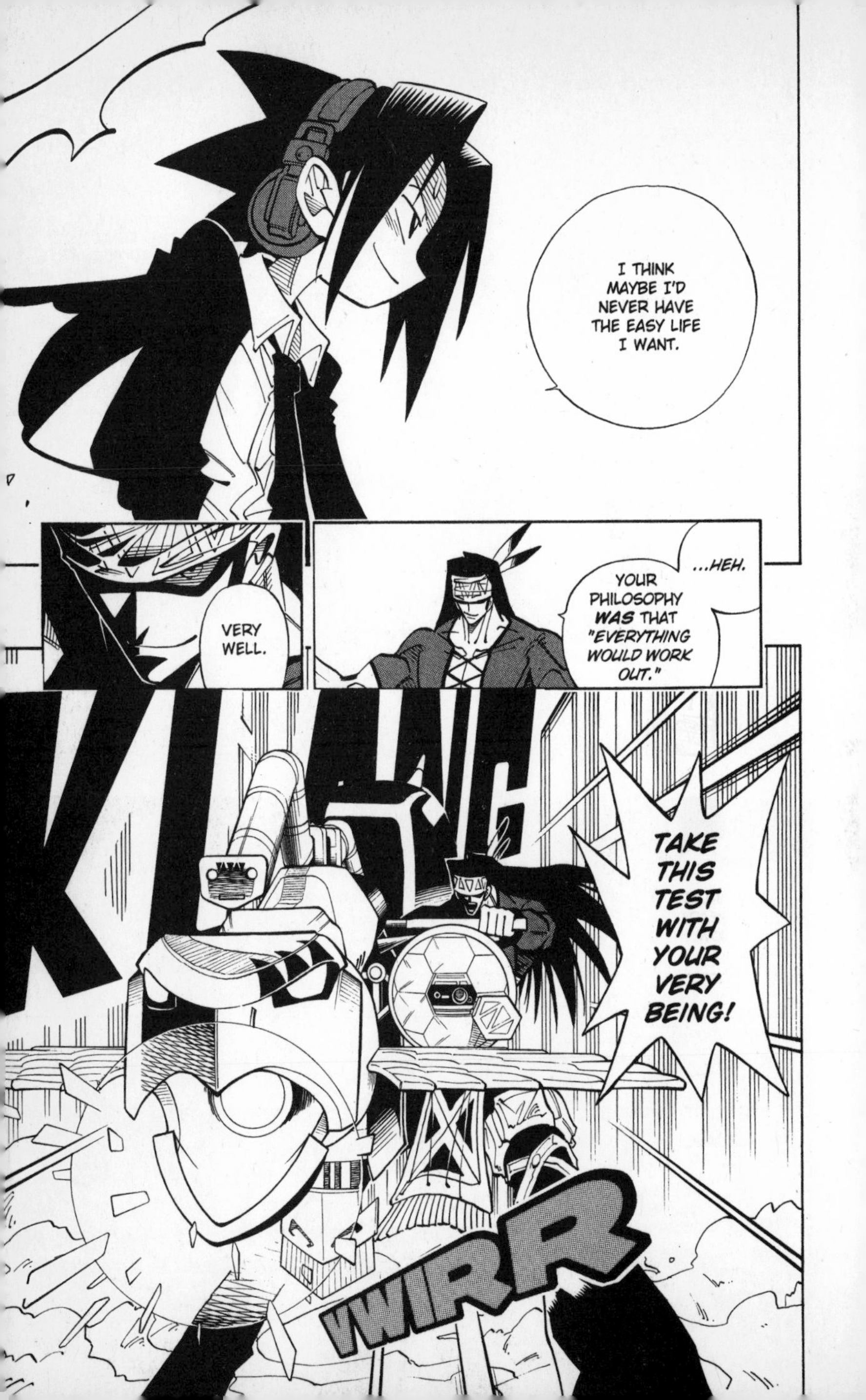
I THINK MAYBE I'D NEVER HAVE THE EASY LIFE I WANT.
...HEH.
YOUR PHILOSOPHY WAS THAT "EVERYTHING WOULD WORK OUT."
VERY WELL.
TAKE THIS TEST WITH YOUR VERY BEING!
VWIRR

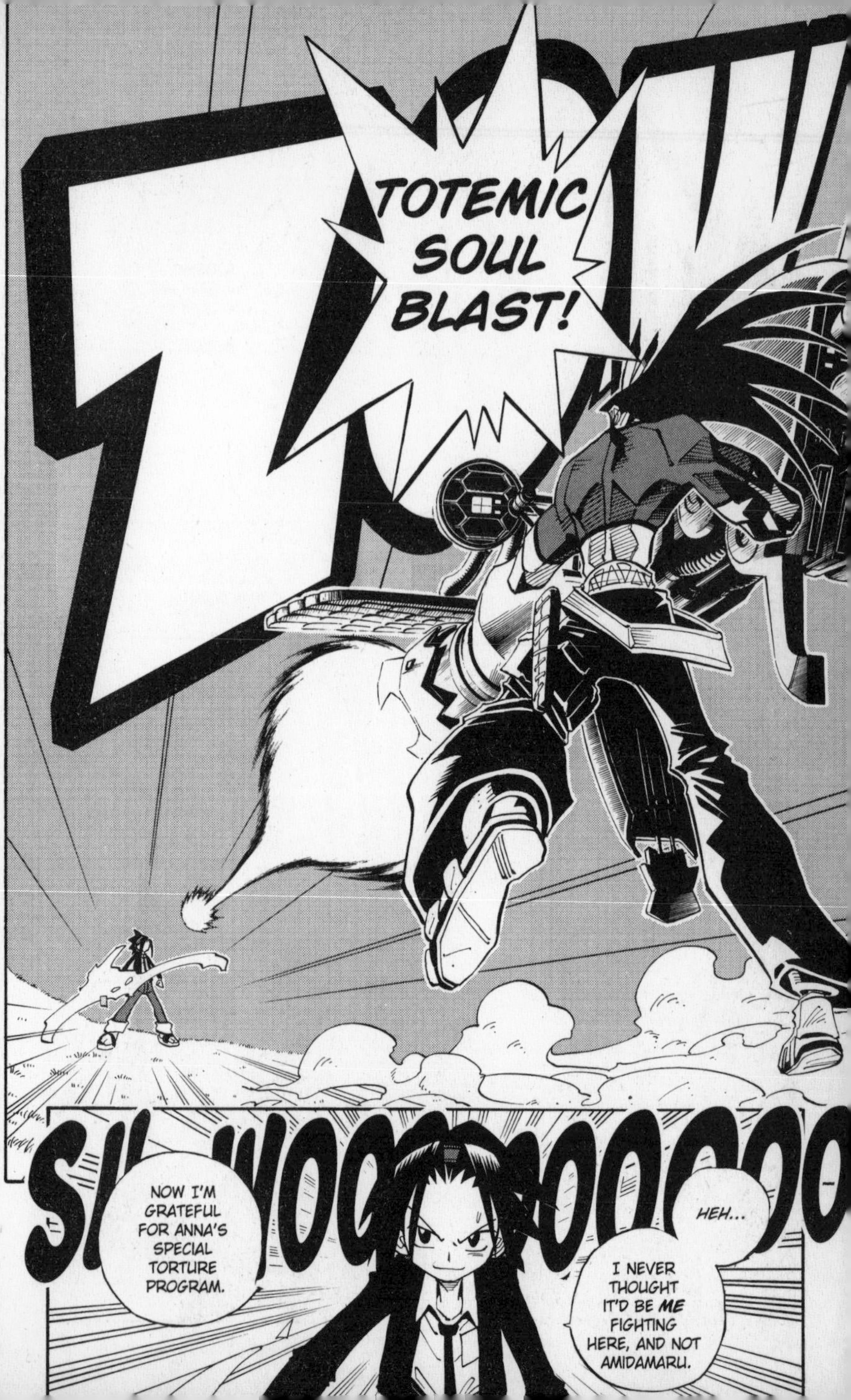
TOTEMIC SOUL BLAST!
HEH...
I NEVER THOUGHT IT'D BE *ME* FIGHTING HERE, AND NOT AMIDAMARU.
NOW I'M GRATEFUL FOR ANNA'S SPECIAL TORTURE PROGRAM.

READ THIS WAY

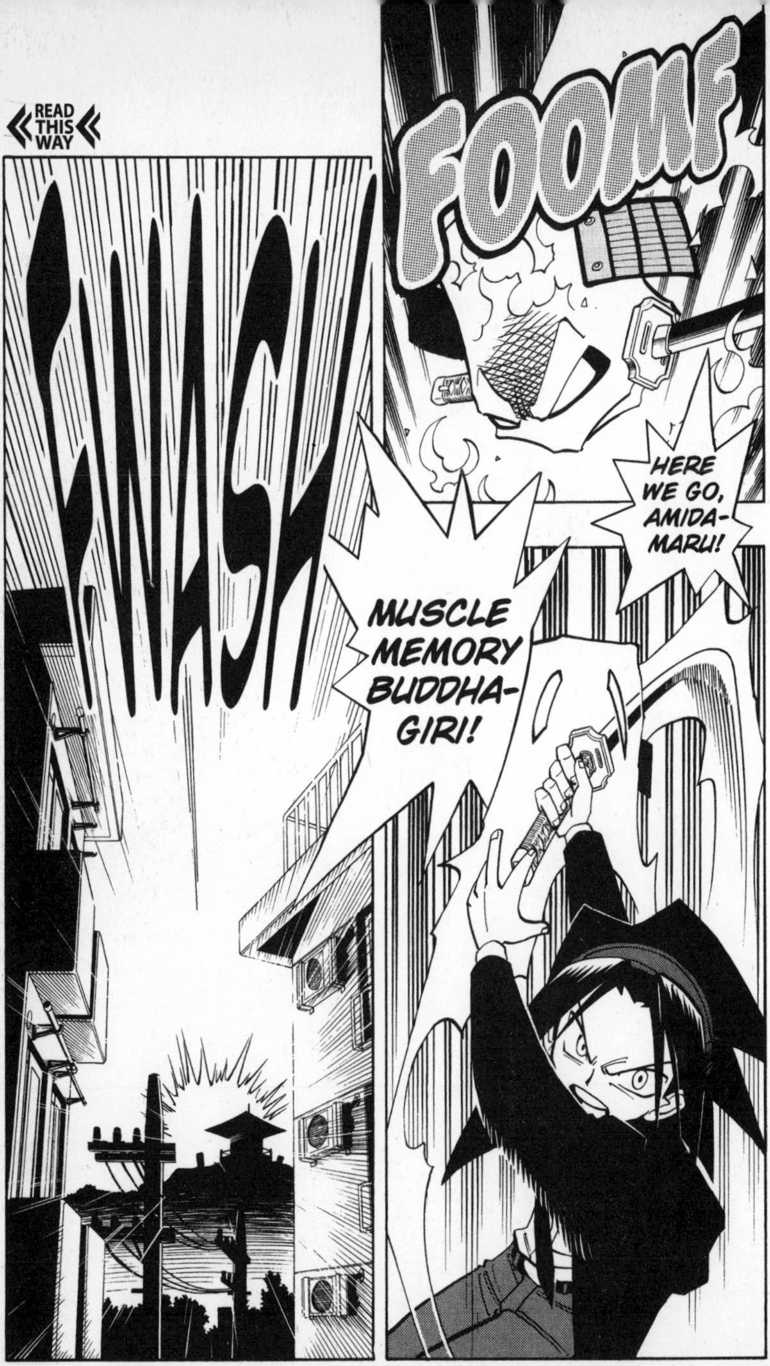
FOOMF
HERE WE GO, AMIDA-MARU!
MUSCLE MEMORY BUDDHA-GIRI!
FWASH

SHAMAN
KING
4

THE ORACLE
PAGER

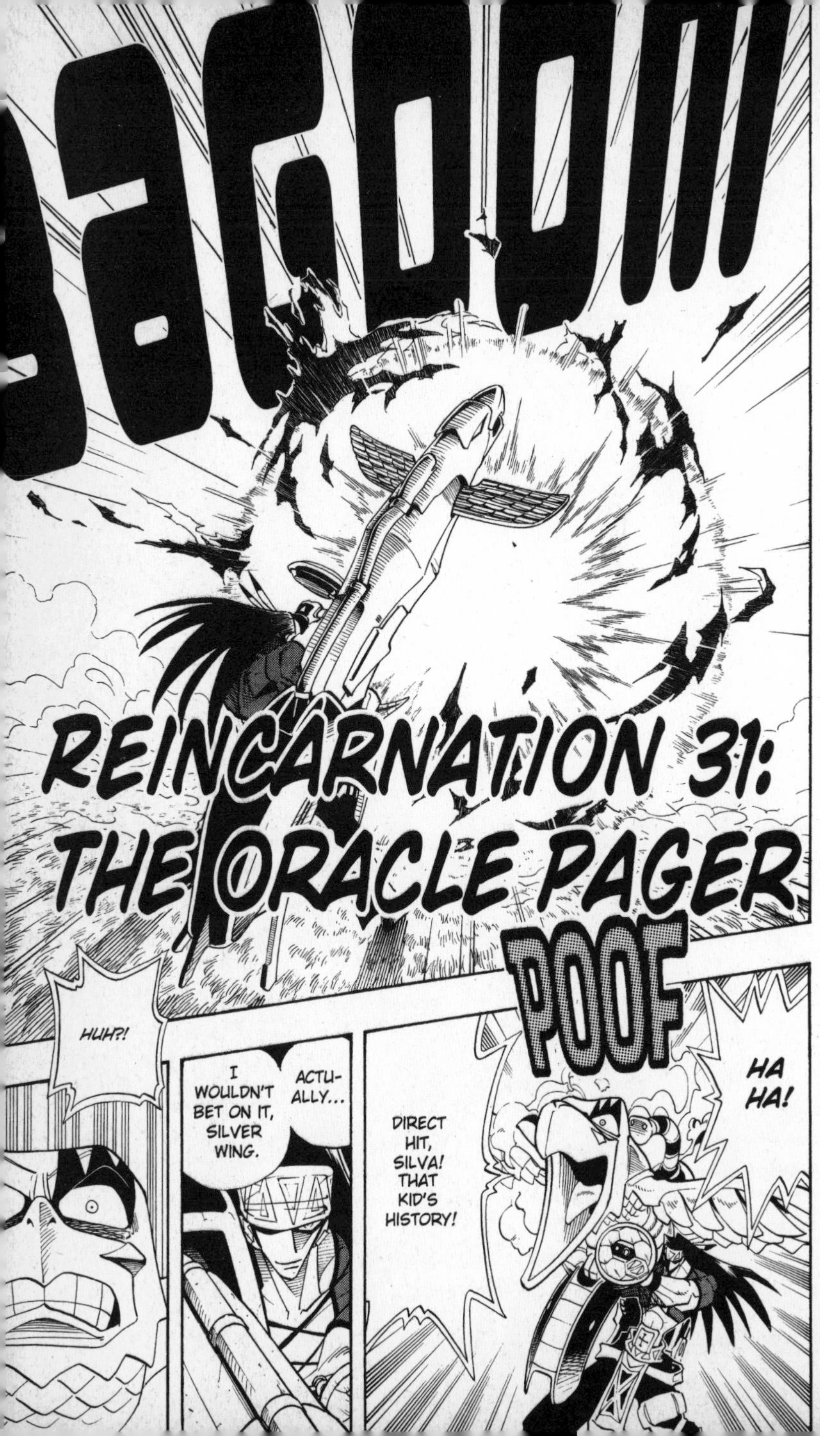
REINCARNATION 31: THE ORACLE PAGER
POOF
HA HA!
DIRECT HIT, SILVA! THAT KID'S HISTORY!
ACTU-ALLY...
I WOULDN'T BET ON IT, SILVER WING.
HUH?!

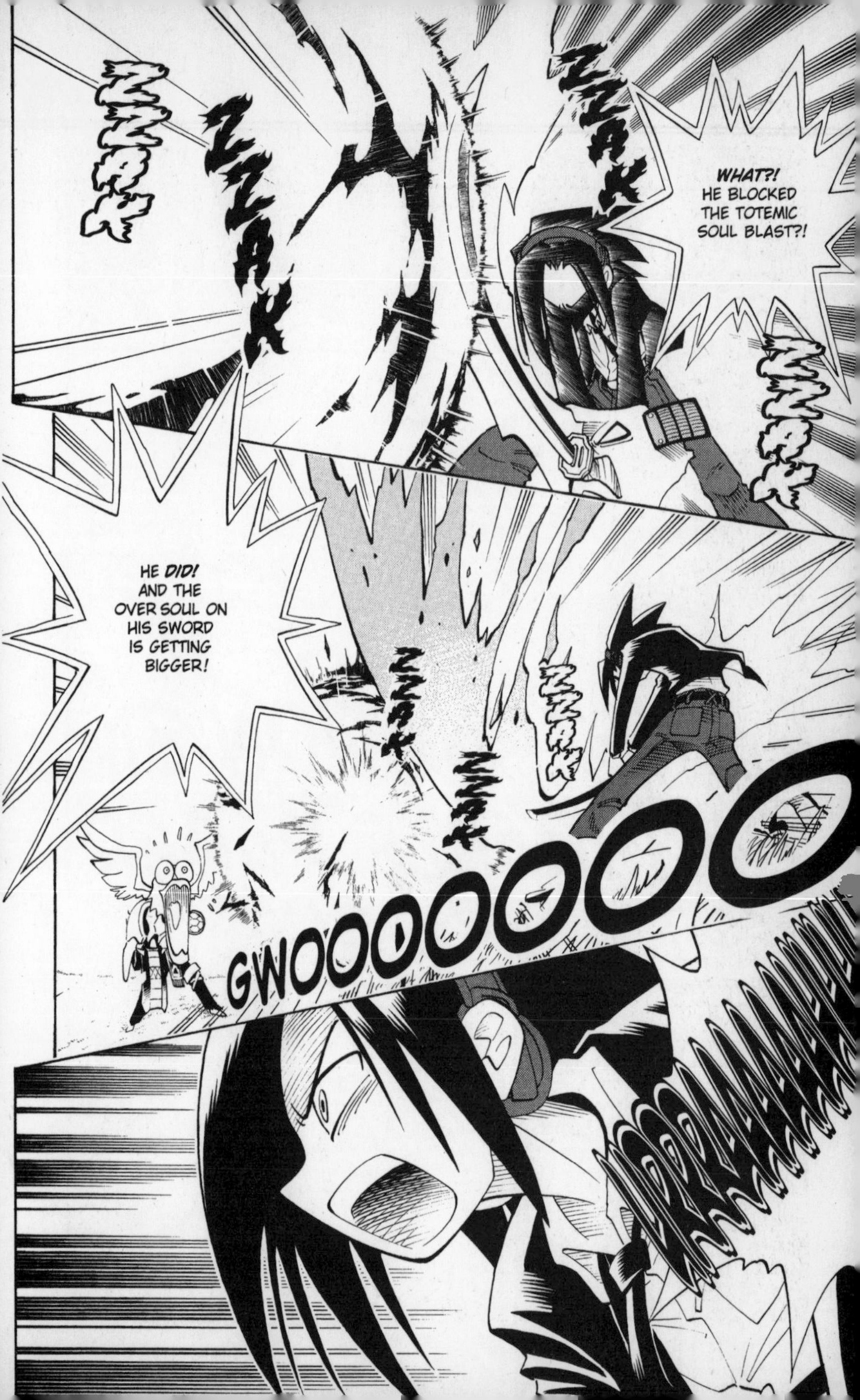
WHAT?! HE BLOCKED THE TOTEMIC SOUL BLAST?!
HE DID! AND THE OVER SOUL ON HIS SWORD IS GETTING BIGGER!
GWOOOOOOOOO

READ THIS WAY

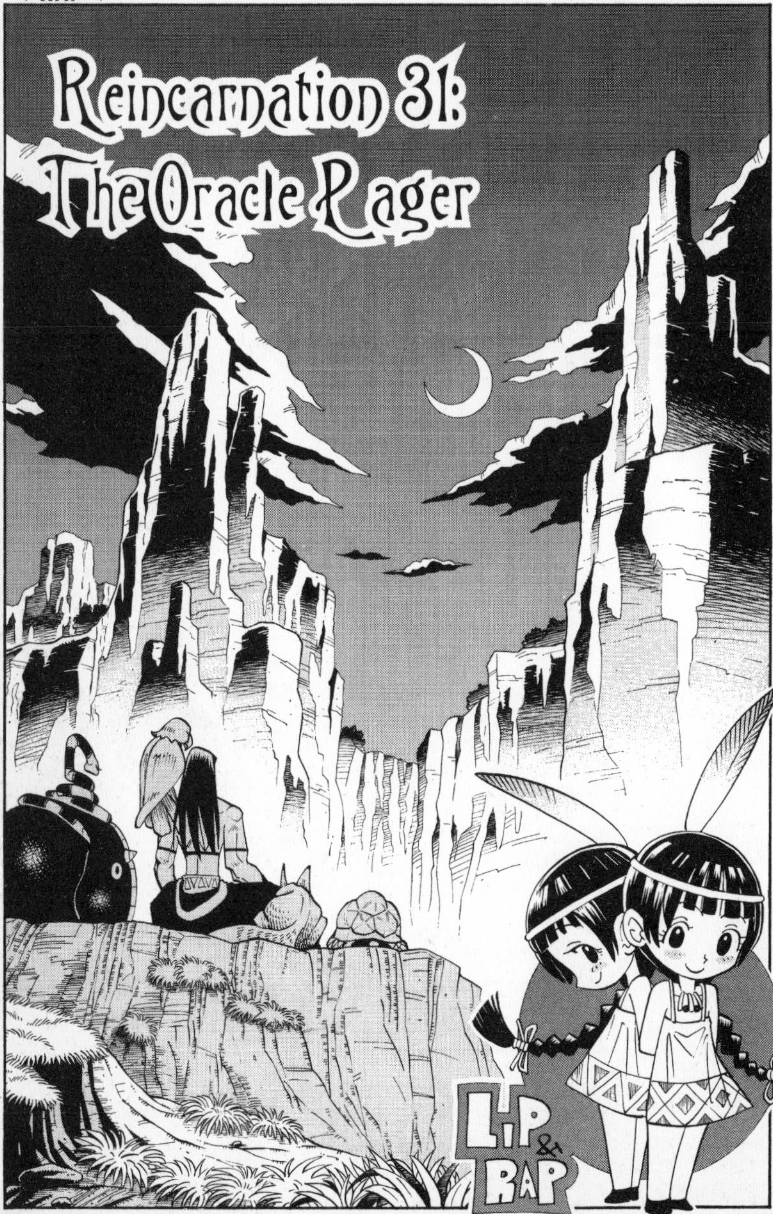

Reincarnation 31: The Oracle Rager
Lip & Rap

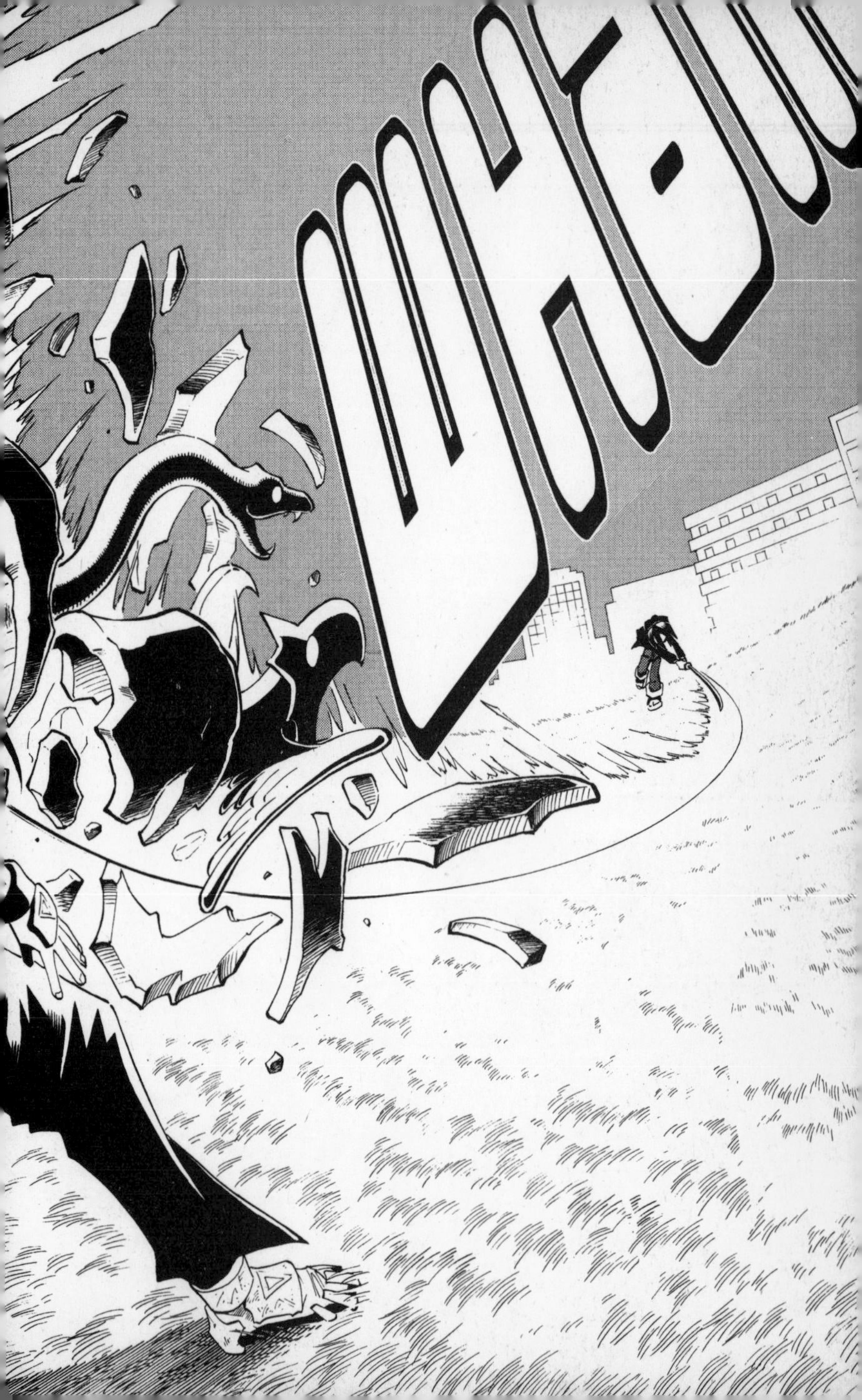

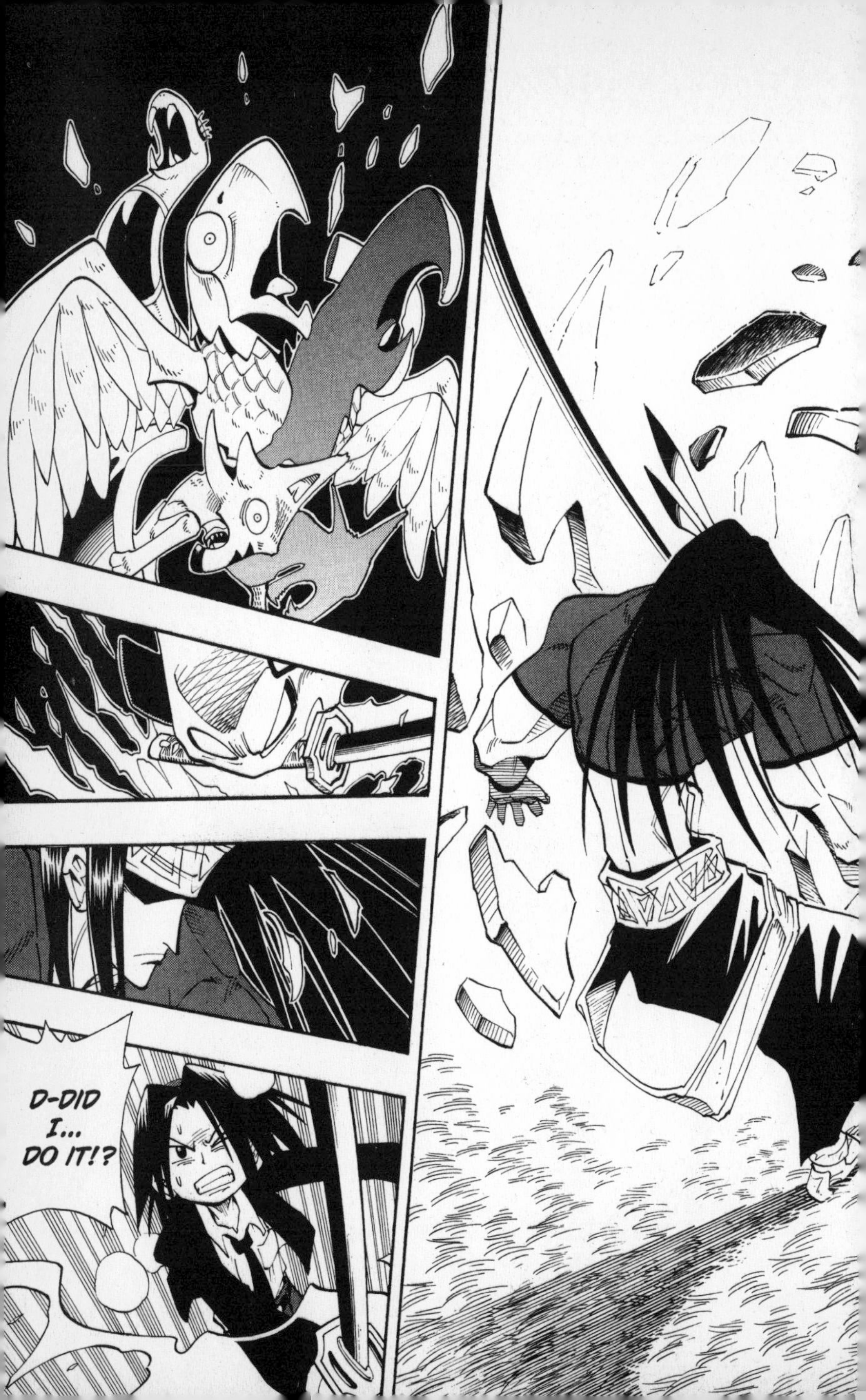
D-DID I... DO IT!?

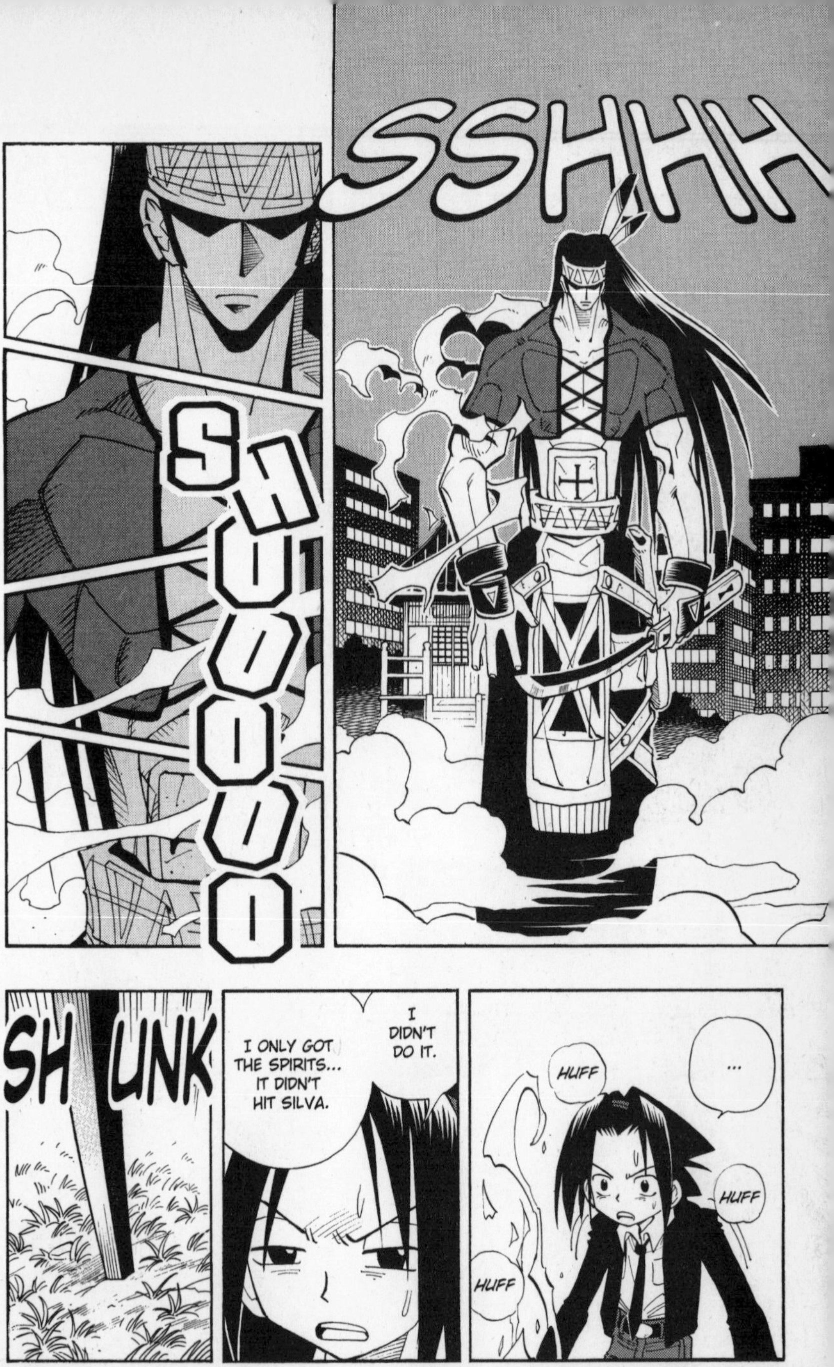
SSHHH
SHOOOOOO
...
HUFF
HUFF
HUFF
I DIDN'T DO IT.
I ONLY GOT THE SPIRITS... IT DIDN'T HIT SILVA.
SHUNK

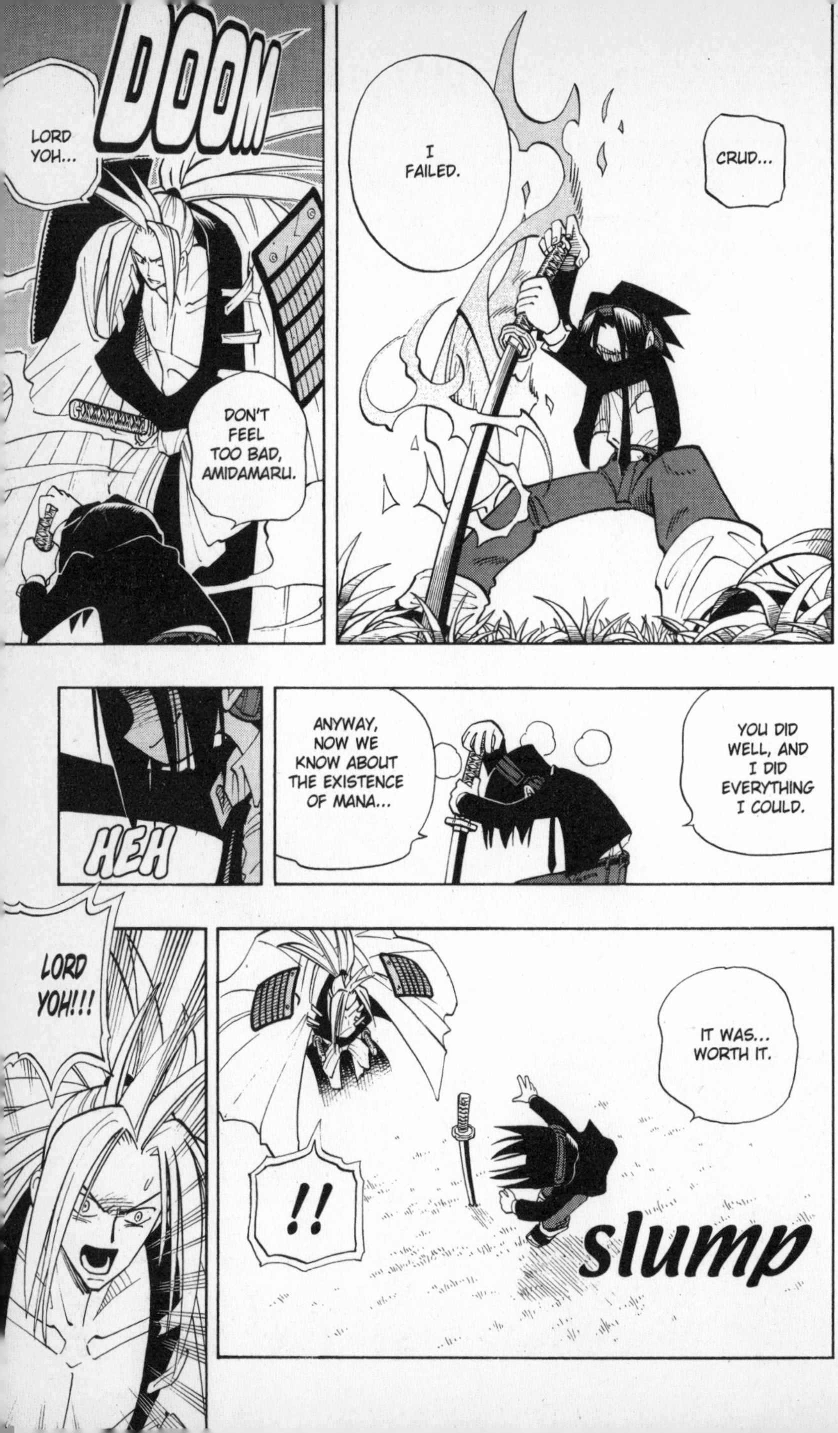
CRUD...
I FAILED.
DOOM
LORD YOH...
DON'T FEEL TOO BAD, AMIDAMARU.
YOU DID WELL, AND I DID EVERYTHING I COULD.
ANYWAY, NOW WE KNOW ABOUT THE EXISTENCE OF MANA...
HEH
IT WAS... WORTH IT.
!!
slump
LORD YOH!!!

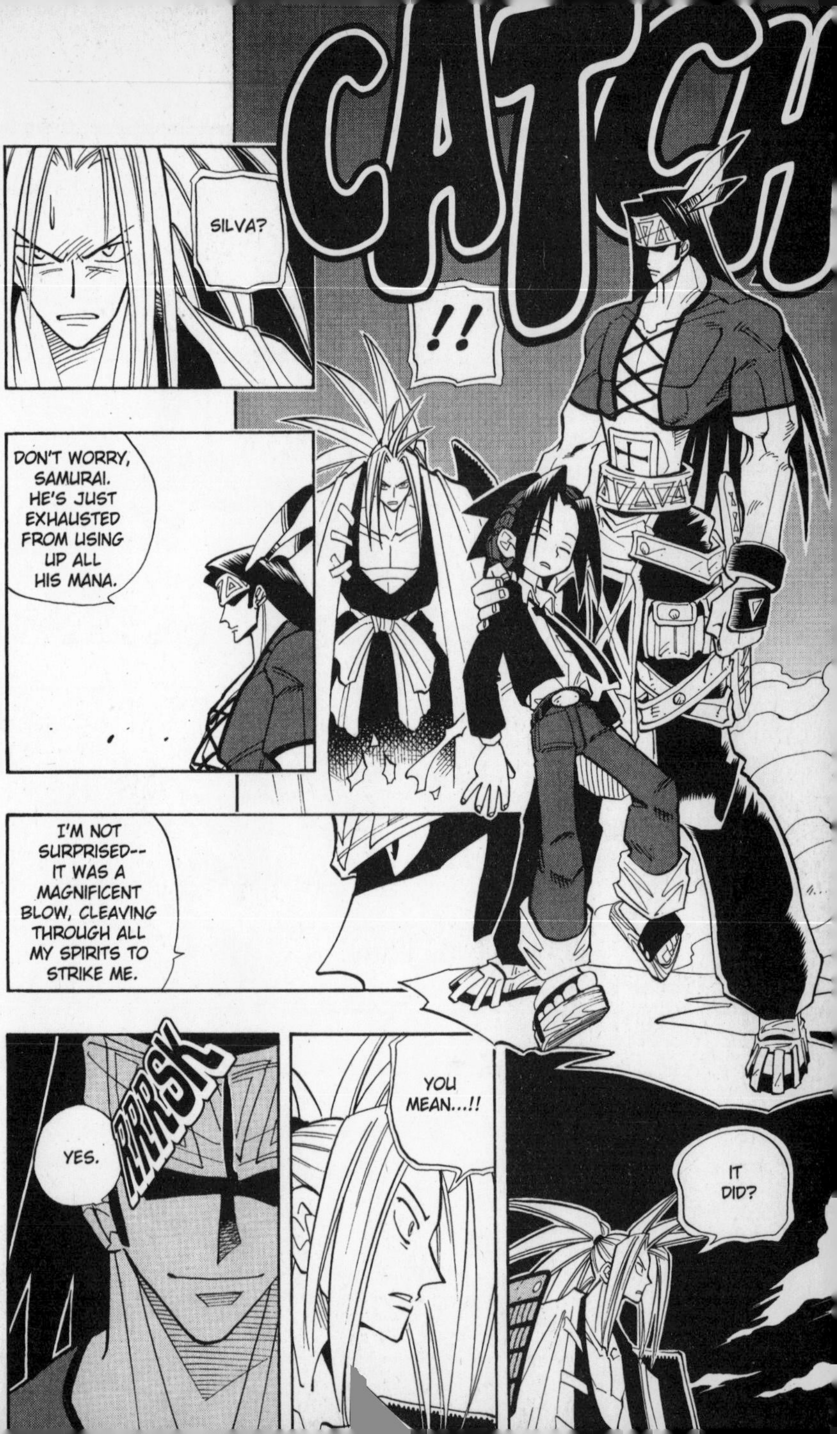
CATCH
!!
SILVA?
DON'T WORRY, SAMURAI. HE'S JUST EXHAUSTED FROM USING UP ALL HIS MANA.
I'M NOT SURPRISED-- IT WAS A MAGNIFICENT BLOW, CLEAVING THROUGH ALL MY SPIRITS TO STRIKE ME.
IT DID?
YOU MEAN...!!
YES.
RRRSK

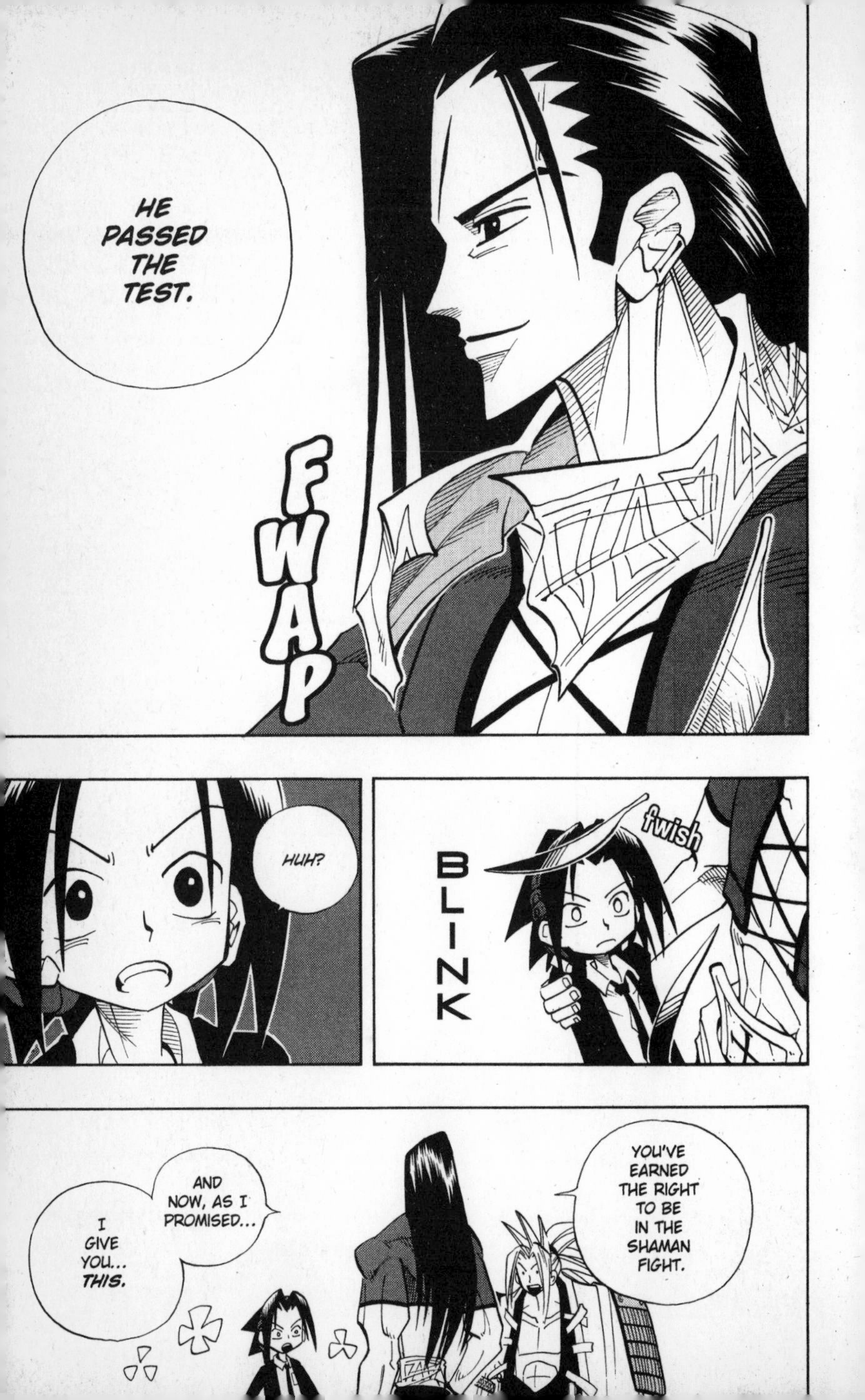
HE PASSED THE TEST.
FWAP
fwish
BLINK
HUH?
YOU'VE EARNED THE RIGHT TO BE IN THE SHAMAN FIGHT.
AND NOW, AS I PROMISED...
I GIVE YOU... THIS.

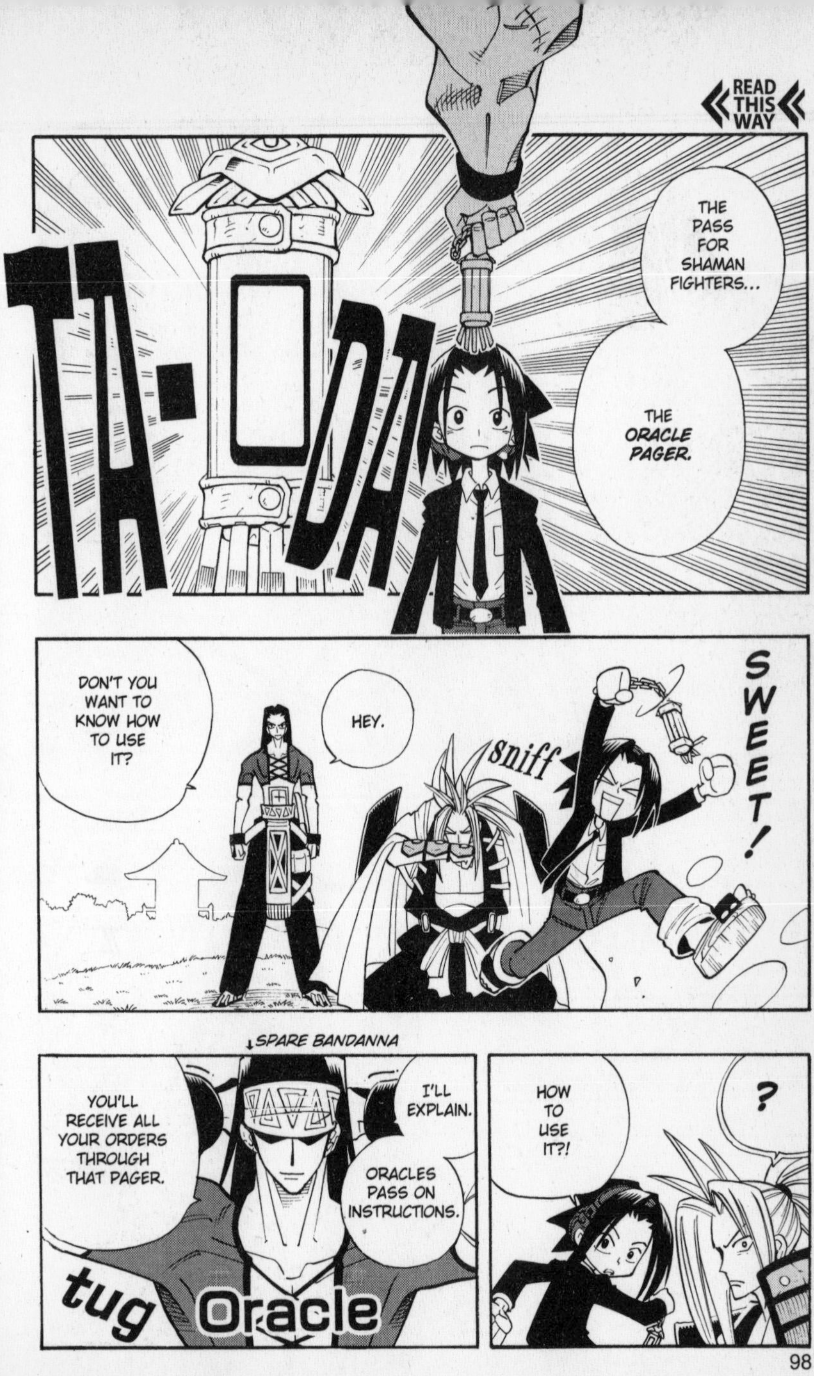
READ THIS WAY
TA-DA
THE PASS FOR SHAMAN FIGHTERS...
THE ORACLE PAGER.
SWEET!
sniff
HEY.
DON'T YOU WANT TO KNOW HOW TO USE IT?
?
HOW TO USE IT?!
SPARE BANDANNA
I'LL EXPLAIN.
ORACLES PASS ON INSTRUCTIONS.
YOU'LL RECEIVE ALL YOUR ORDERS THROUGH THAT PAGER.
tug
Oracle

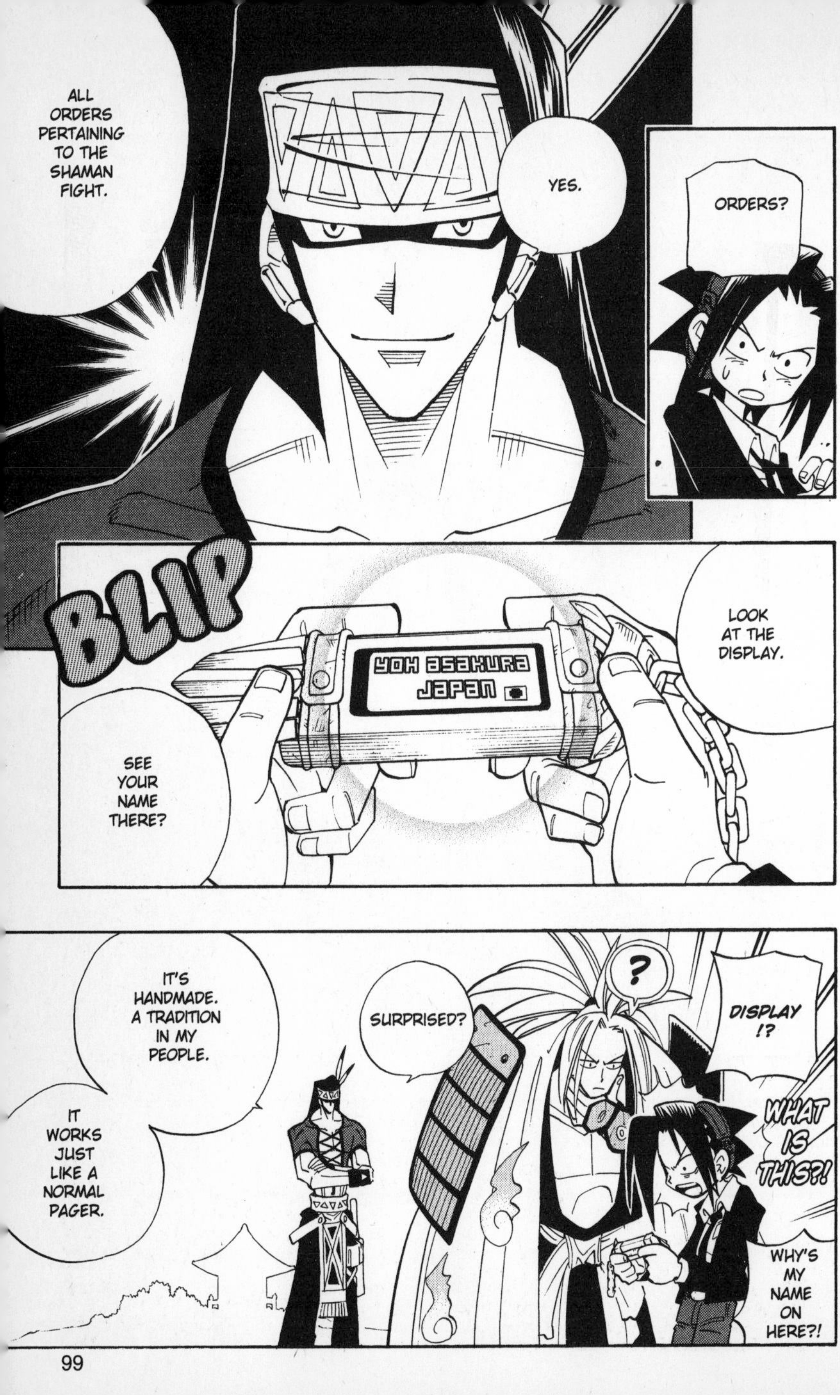

ORDERS?
YES.
ALL ORDERS PERTAINING TO THE SHAMAN FIGHT.
LOOK AT THE DISPLAY.
BLIP
YOH ASAKURA
JAPAN
SEE YOUR NAME THERE?
DISPLAY !?
WHAT IS THIS?!
?
WHY'S MY NAME ON HERE?!
SURPRISED?
IT'S HANDMADE. A TRADITION IN MY PEOPLE.
IT WORKS JUST LIKE A NORMAL PAGER.

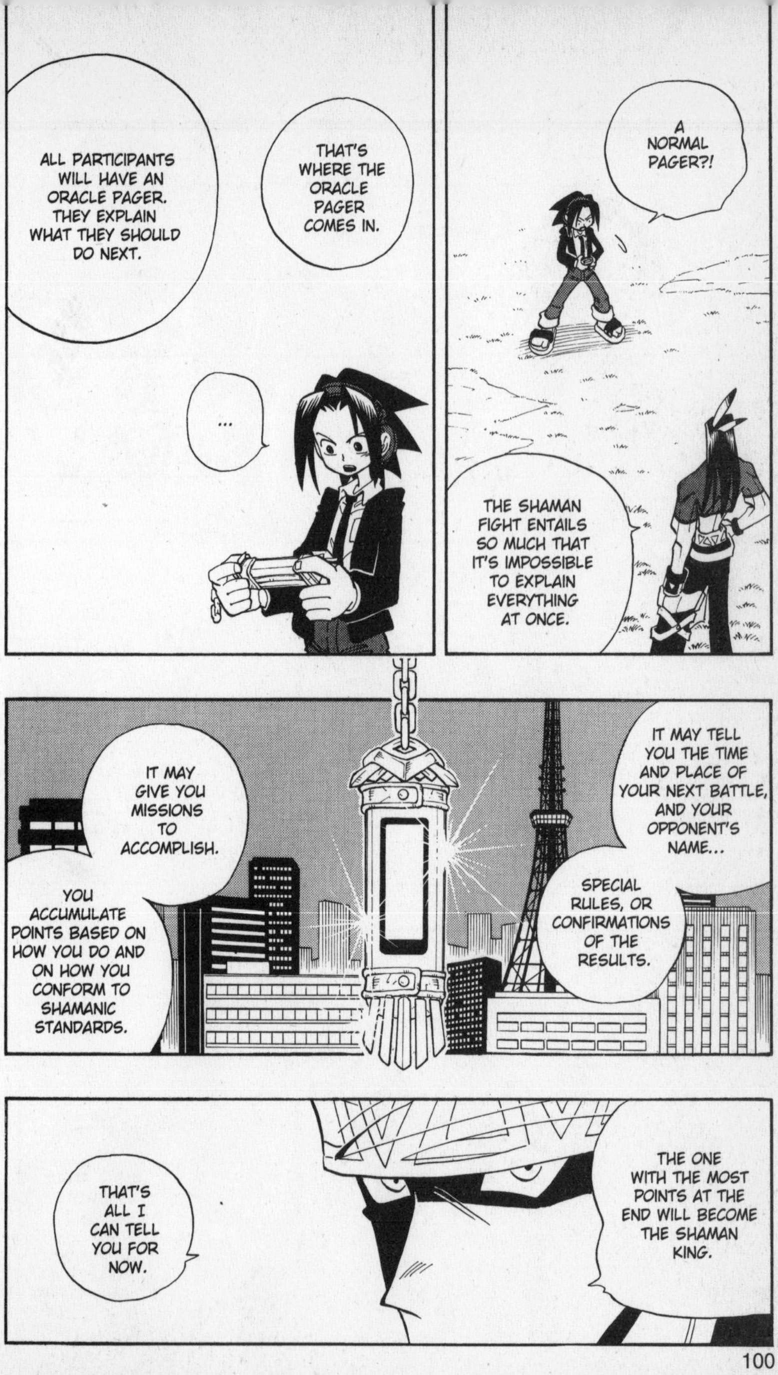
A NORMAL PAGER?!
THE SHAMAN FIGHT ENTAILS SO MUCH THAT IT'S IMPOSSIBLE TO EXPLAIN EVERYTHING AT ONCE.
THAT'S WHERE THE ORACLE PAGER COMES IN.
ALL PARTICIPANTS WILL HAVE AN ORACLE PAGER. THEY EXPLAIN WHAT THEY SHOULD DO NEXT.
...
IT MAY TELL YOU THE TIME AND PLACE OF YOUR NEXT BATTLE, AND YOUR OPPONENT'S NAME...
SPECIAL RULES, OR CONFIRMATIONS OF THE RESULTS.
IT MAY GIVE YOU MISSIONS TO ACCOMPLISH.
YOU ACCUMULATE POINTS BASED ON HOW YOU DO AND ON HOW YOU CONFORM TO SHAMANIC STANDARDS.
THE ONE WITH THE MOST POINTS AT THE END WILL BECOME THE SHAMAN KING.
THAT'S ALL I CAN TELL YOU FOR NOW.

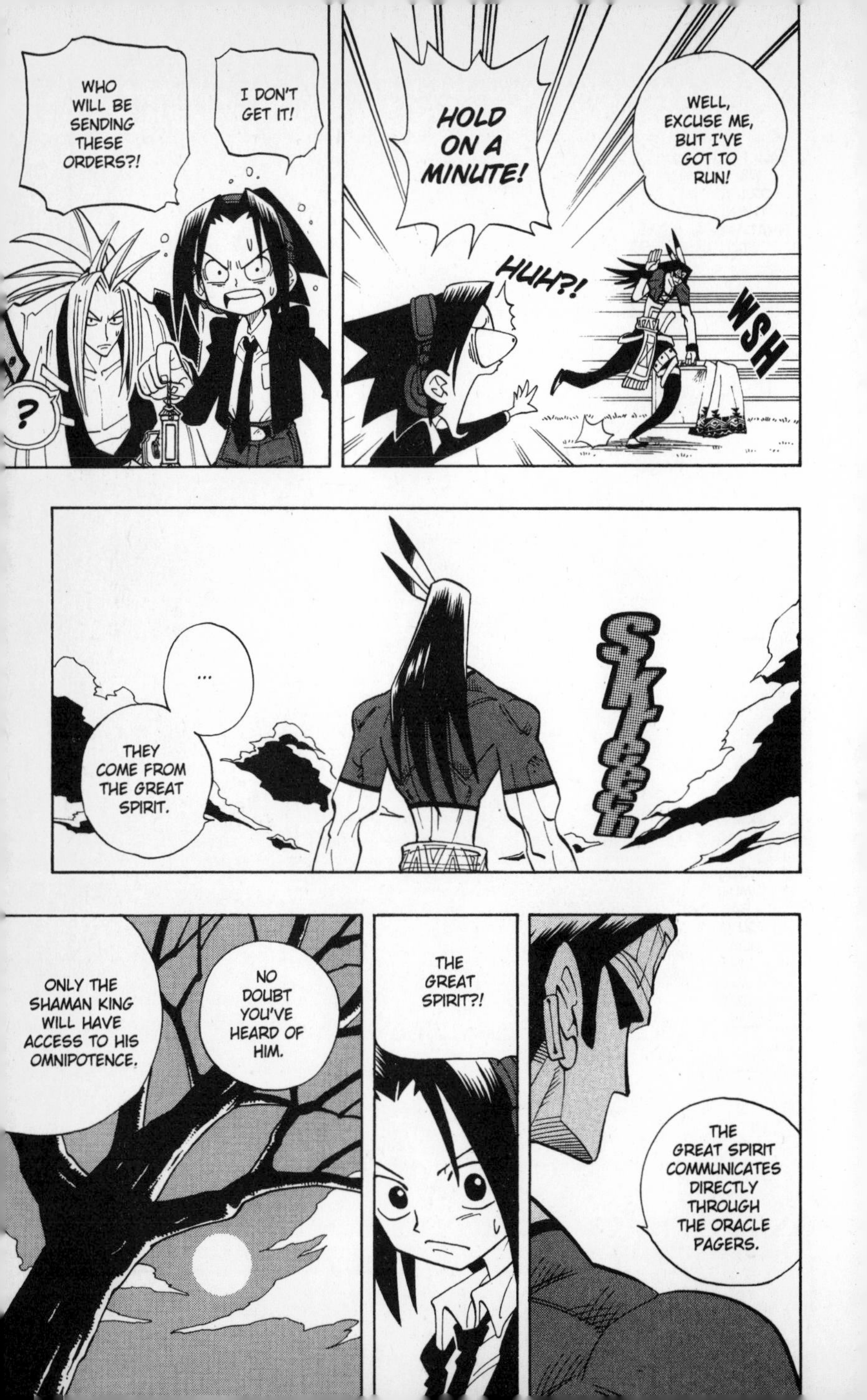
WELL, EXCUSE ME, BUT I'VE GOT TO RUN!
HOLD ON A MINUTE!
HUH?!
WSH
I DON'T GET IT!
WHO WILL BE SENDING THESE ORDERS?!
?
...
THEY COME FROM THE GREAT SPIRIT.
THE GREAT SPIRIT COMMUNICATES DIRECTLY THROUGH THE ORACLE PAGERS.
THE GREAT SPIRIT?!
NO DOUBT YOU'VE HEARD OF HIM.
ONLY THE SHAMAN KING WILL HAVE ACCESS TO HIS OMNIPOTENCE.

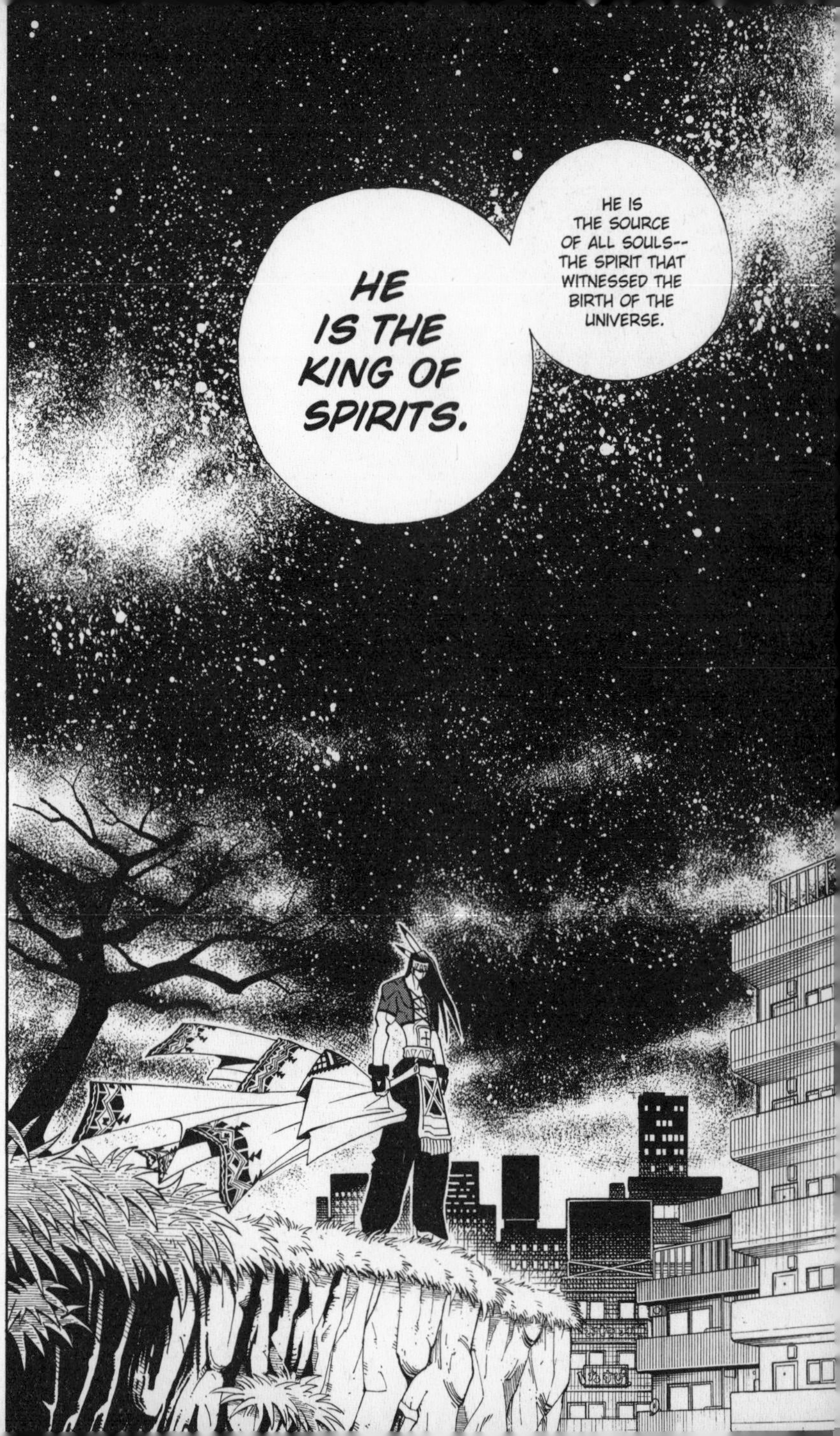
HE IS THE SOURCE OF ALL SOULS-- THE SPIRIT THAT WITNESSED THE BIRTH OF THE UNIVERSE.
HE IS THE KING OF SPIRITS.

READ THIS WAY

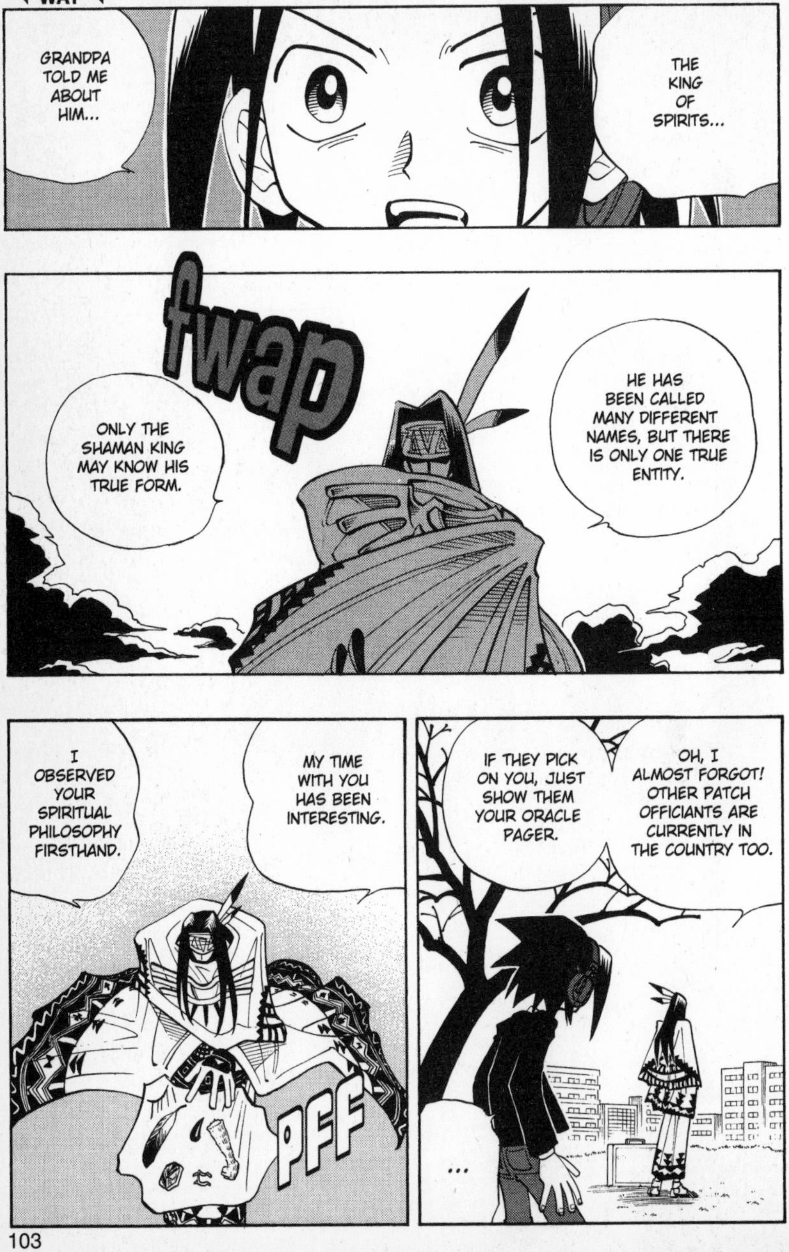
THE KING OF SPIRITS...
GRANDPA TOLD ME ABOUT HIM...
HE HAS BEEN CALLED MANY DIFFERENT NAMES, BUT THERE IS ONLY ONE TRUE ENTITY.
fwap
ONLY THE SHAMAN KING MAY KNOW HIS TRUE FORM.
OH, I ALMOST FORGOT! OTHER PATCH OFFICIANTS ARE CURRENTLY IN THE COUNTRY TOO.
IF THEY PICK ON YOU, JUST SHOW THEM YOUR ORACLE PAGER.
...
MY TIME WITH YOU HAS BEEN INTERESTING.
I OBSERVED YOUR SPIRITUAL PHILOSOPHY FIRSTHAND.
PFF

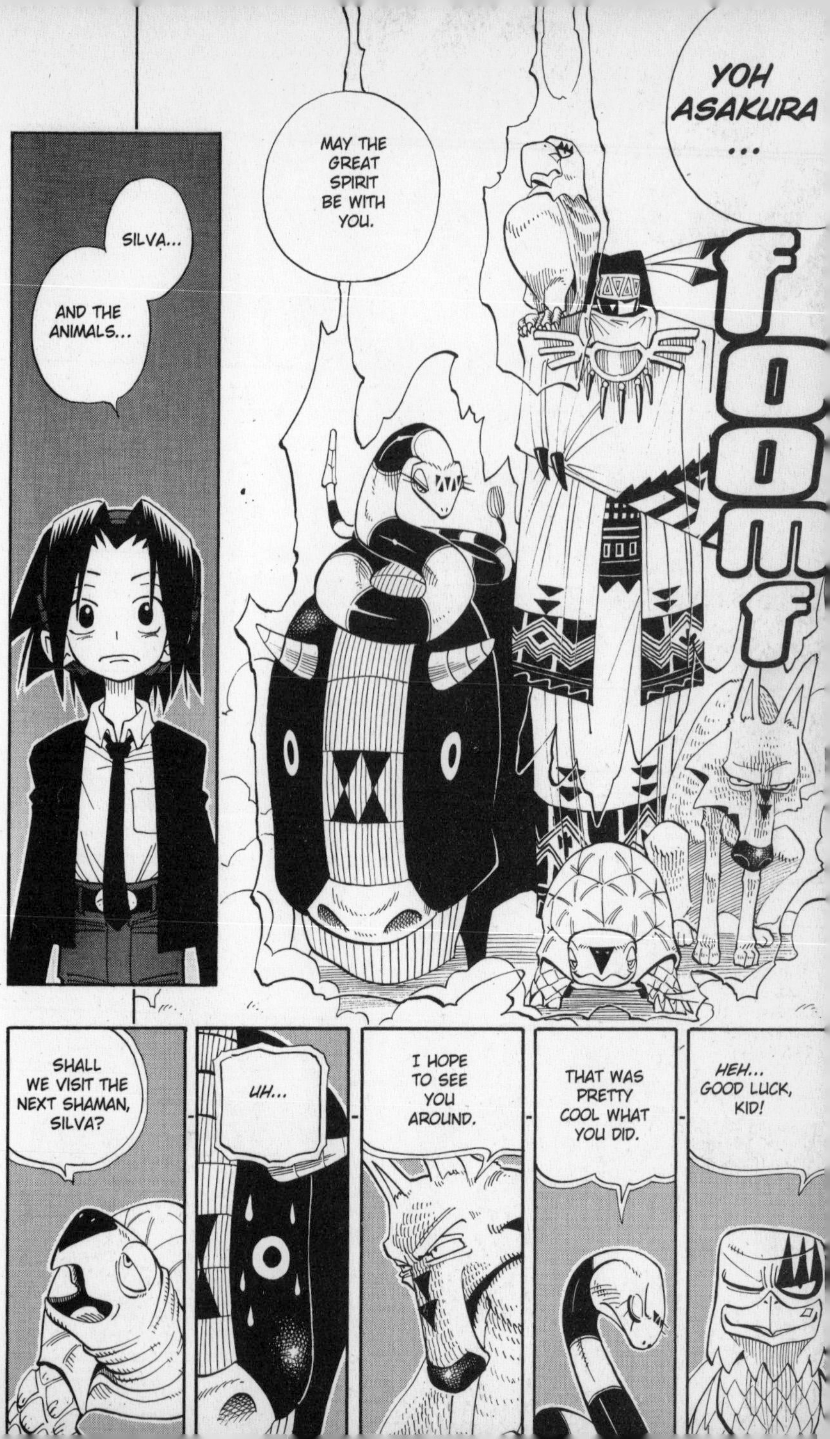
YOH ASAKURA...
FOOMF
MAY THE GREAT SPIRIT BE WITH YOU.
SILVA...
AND THE ANIMALS...
HEH... GOOD LUCK, KID!
THAT WAS PRETTY COOL WHAT YOU DID.
I HOPE TO SEE YOU AROUND.
UH...
SHALL WE VISIT THE NEXT SHAMAN, SILVA?

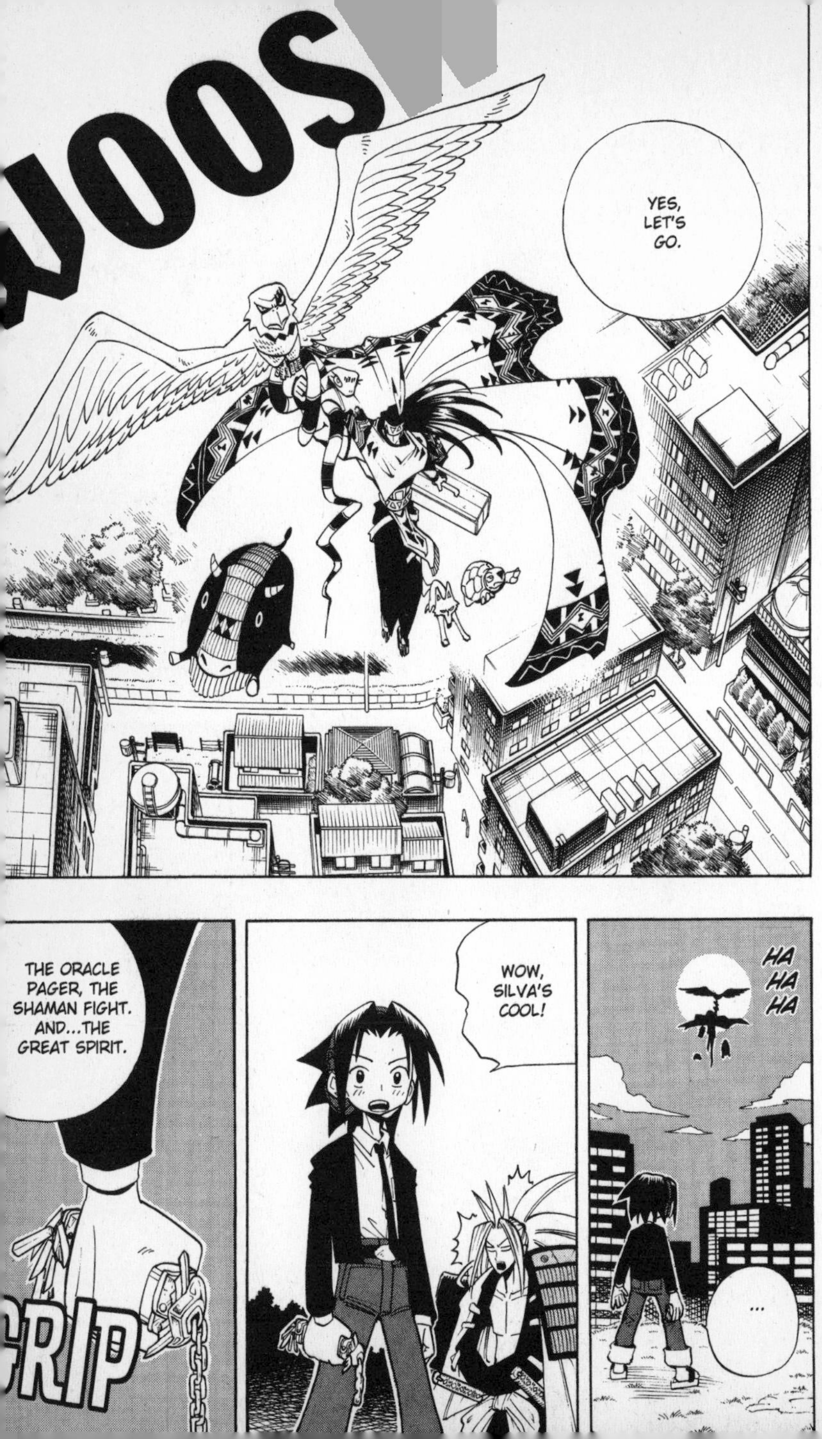
WOOS
YES, LET'S GO.
HA HA HA
...
WOW, SILVA'S COOL!
THE ORACLE PAGER, THE SHAMAN FIGHT. AND...THE GREAT SPIRIT.
GRIP

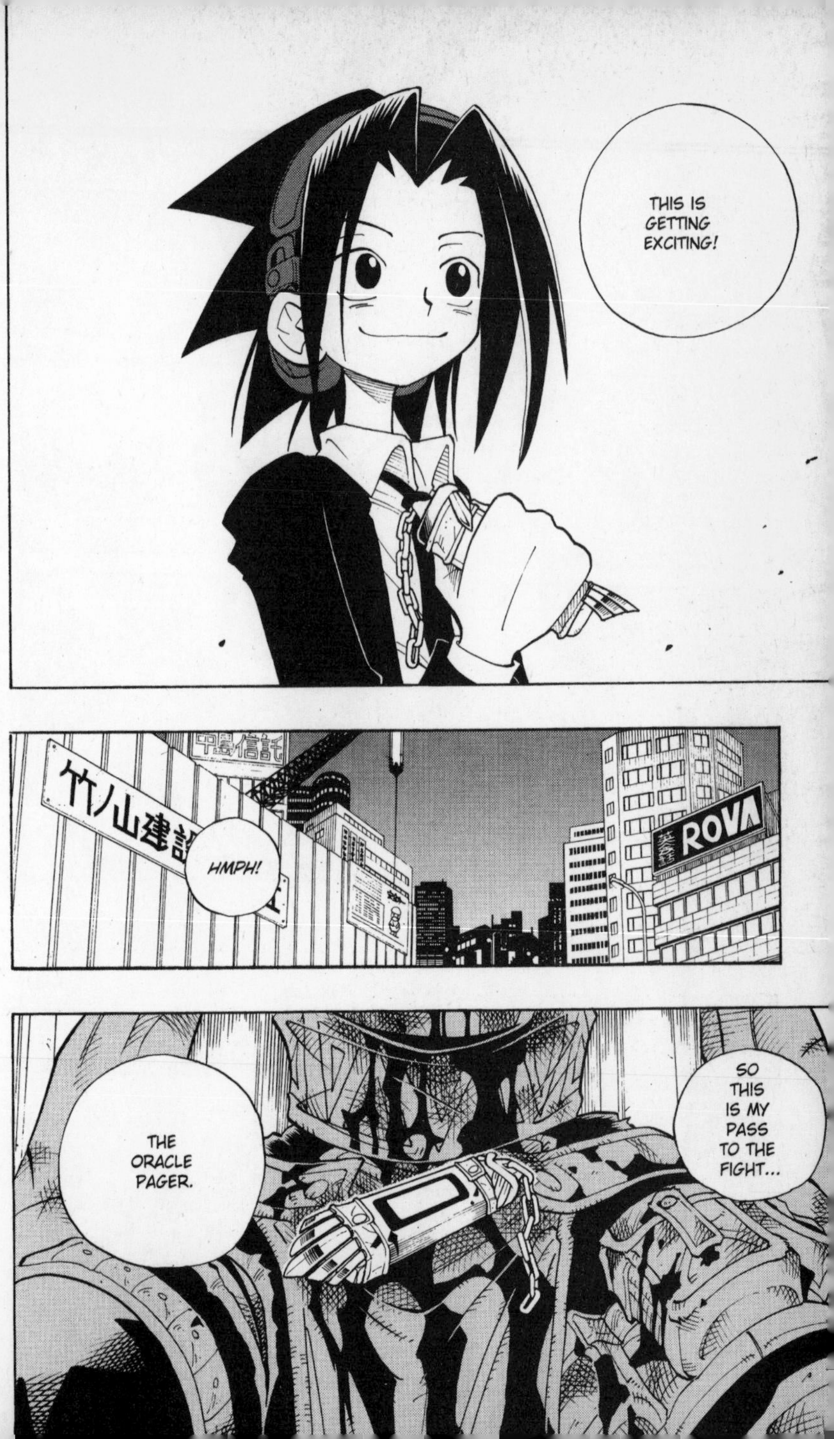
THIS IS GETTING EXCITING!
ROVA
HMPH!
SO THIS IS MY PASS TO THE FIGHT...
THE ORACLE PAGER.

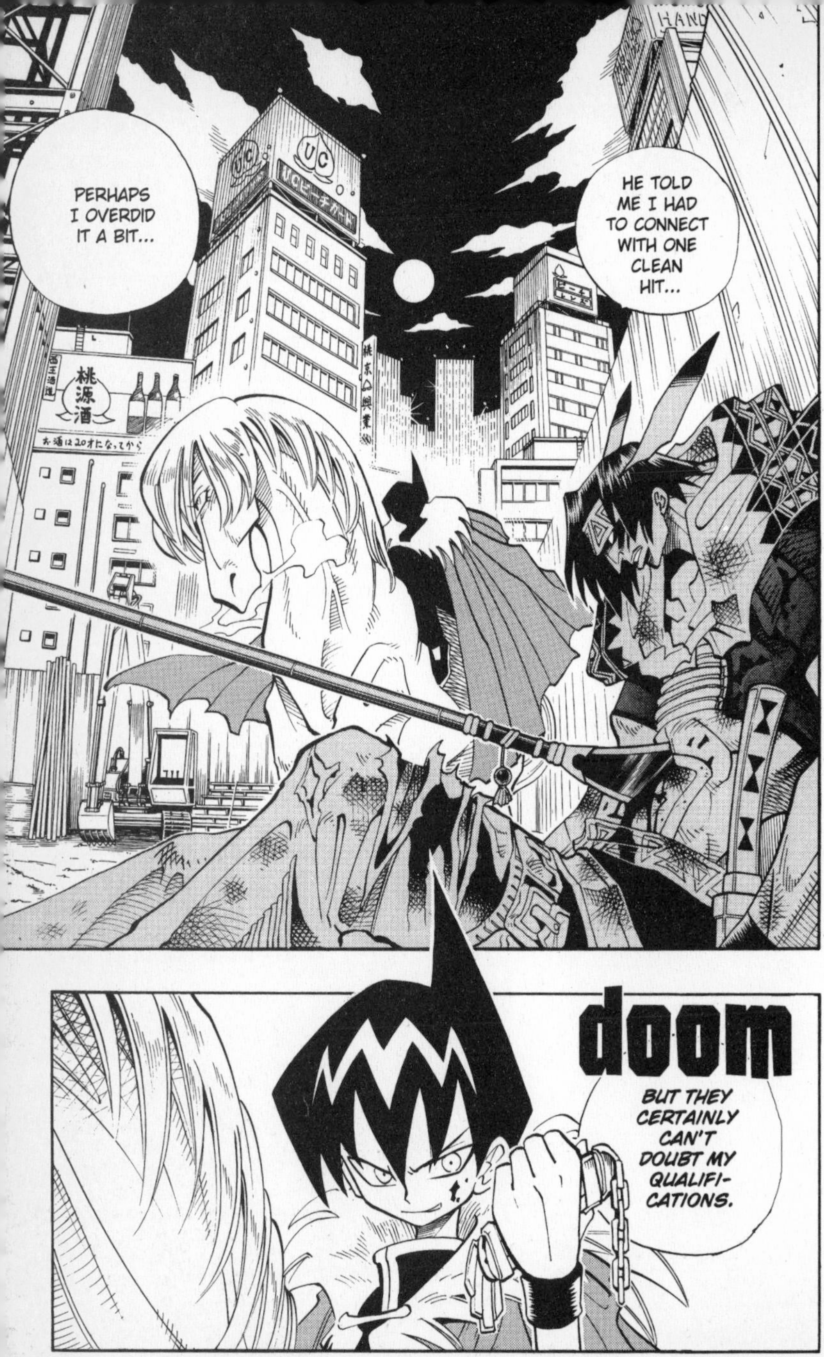
HE TOLD ME I HAD TO CONNECT WITH ONE CLEAN HIT...
PERHAPS I OVERDID IT A BIT...
doom
BUT THEY CERTAINLY CAN'T DOUBT MY QUALIFI-CATIONS.

SHAMAN KING CHARACTER FILE No.16

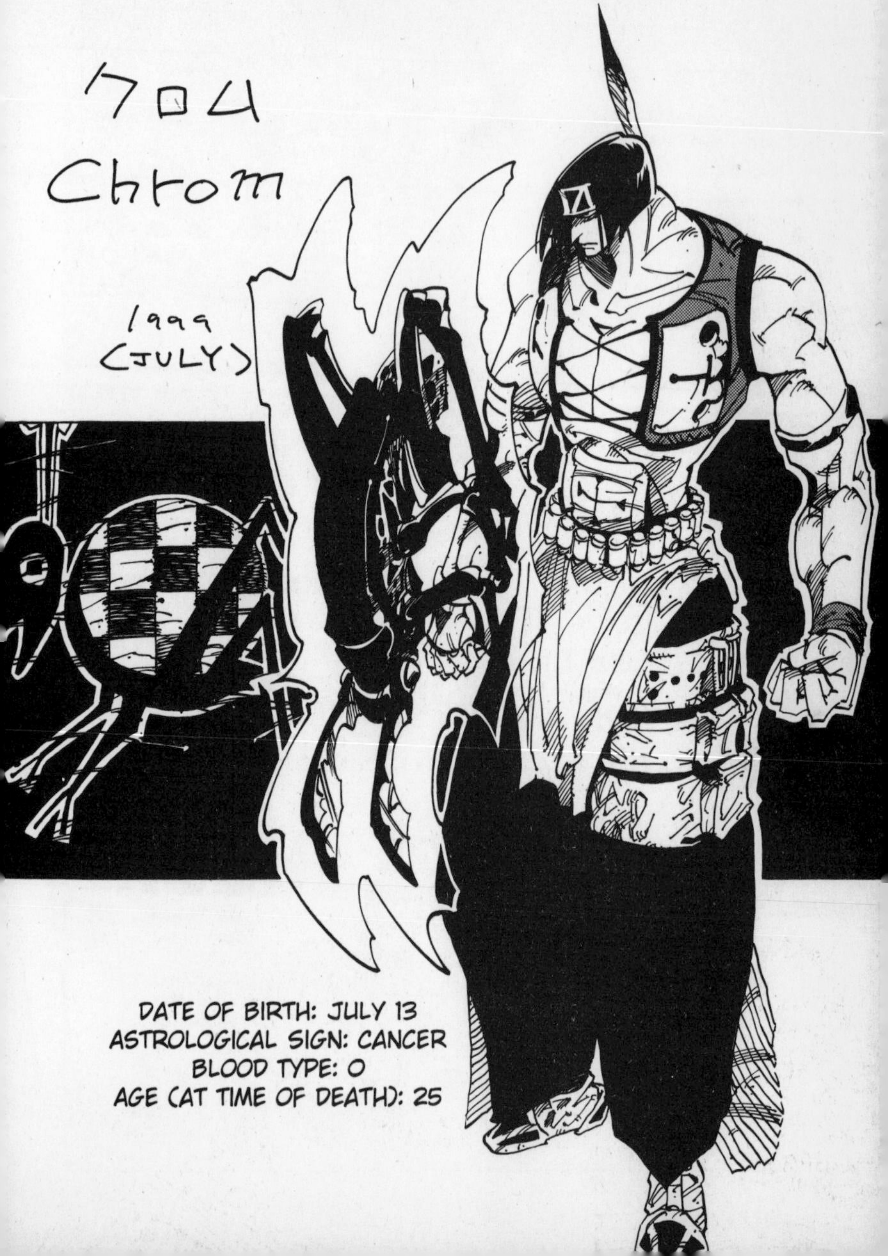
クロム
Chrom
1999
(JULY)

DATE OF BIRTH: JULY 13
ASTROLOGICAL SIGN: CANCER
BLOOD TYPE: O
AGE (AT TIME OF DEATH): 25

REINCARNATION 32: THE WAY OF THE PATCH

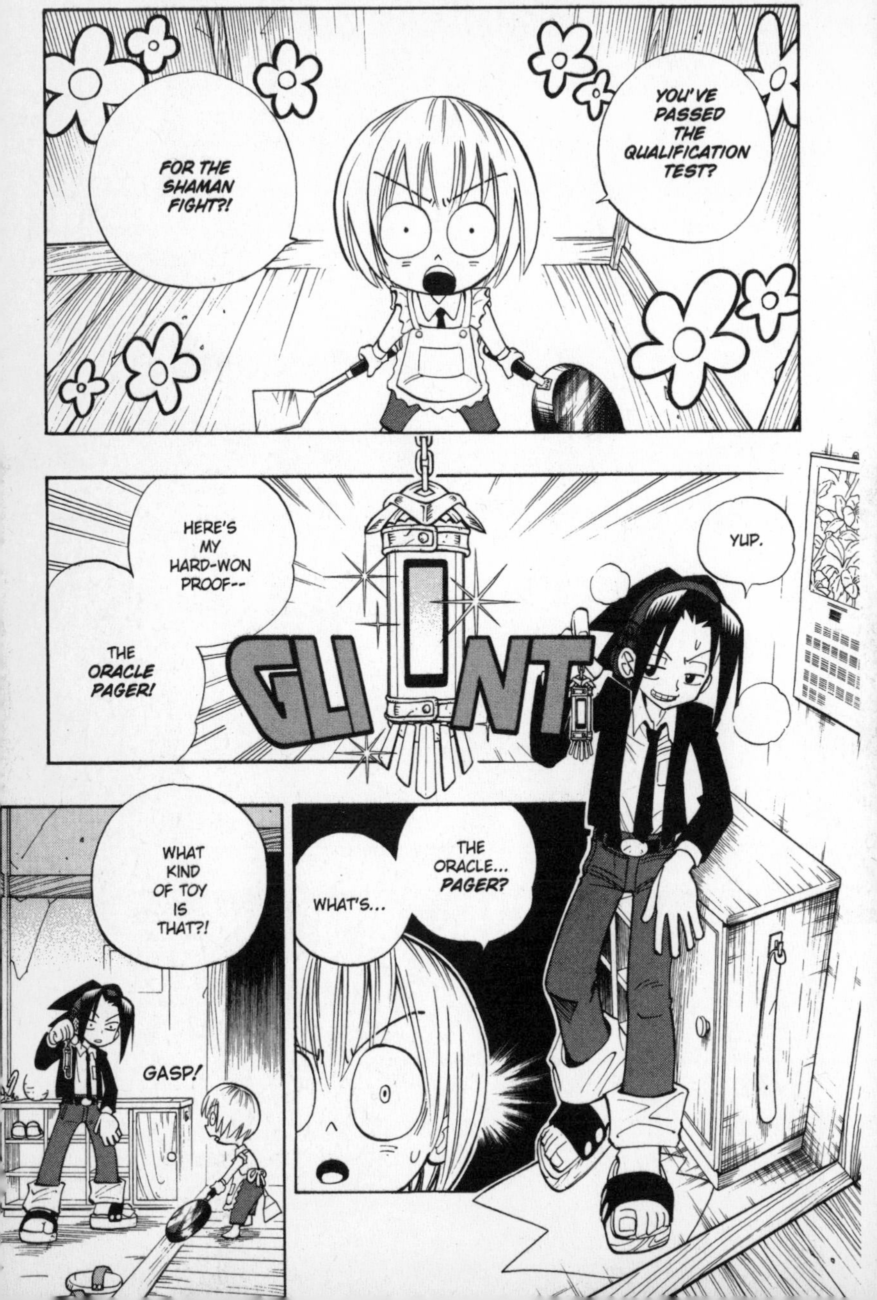

YOU'VE PASSED THE QUALIFICATION TEST?
FOR THE SHAMAN FIGHT?!
YUP.
HERE'S MY HARD-WON PROOF--
THE ORACLE PAGER!
GLINT
THE ORACLE... PAGER?
WHAT'S...
WHAT KIND OF TOY IS THAT?!
GASP!

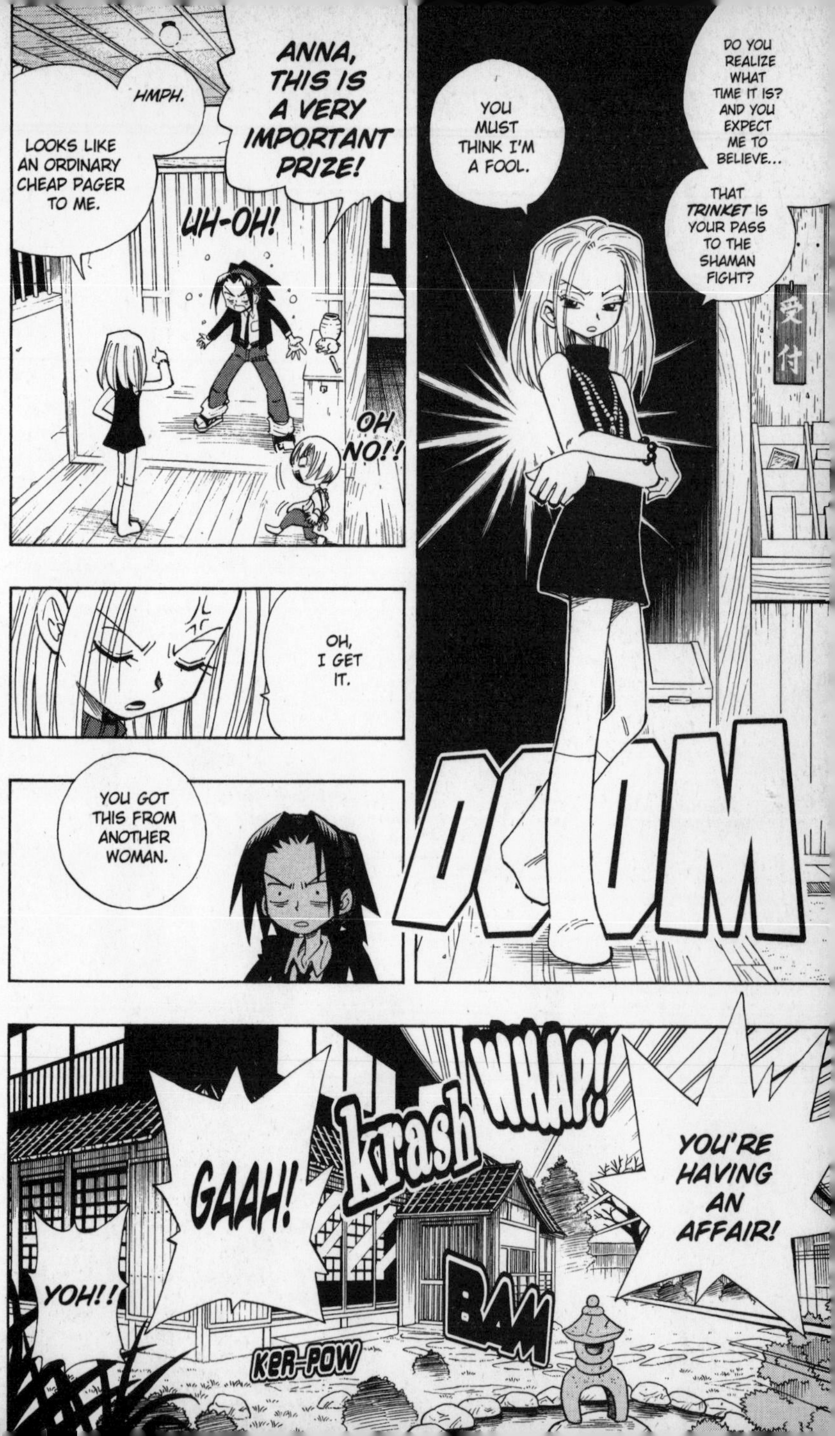
DO YOU REALIZE WHAT TIME IT IS? AND YOU EXPECT ME TO BELIEVE...
THAT *TRINKET* IS YOUR PASS TO THE SHAMAN FIGHT?
YOU MUST THINK I'M A FOOL.
受付
DOOM
ANNA, THIS IS A VERY IMPORTANT PRIZE!
HMPH.
LOOKS LIKE AN ORDINARY CHEAP PAGER TO ME.
UH-OH!
OH NO!!
OH, I GET IT.
YOU GOT THIS FROM ANOTHER WOMAN.
YOU'RE HAVING AN AFFAIR!
WHAP!
krash
GAAH!
BAM
YOH!!
KER-POW

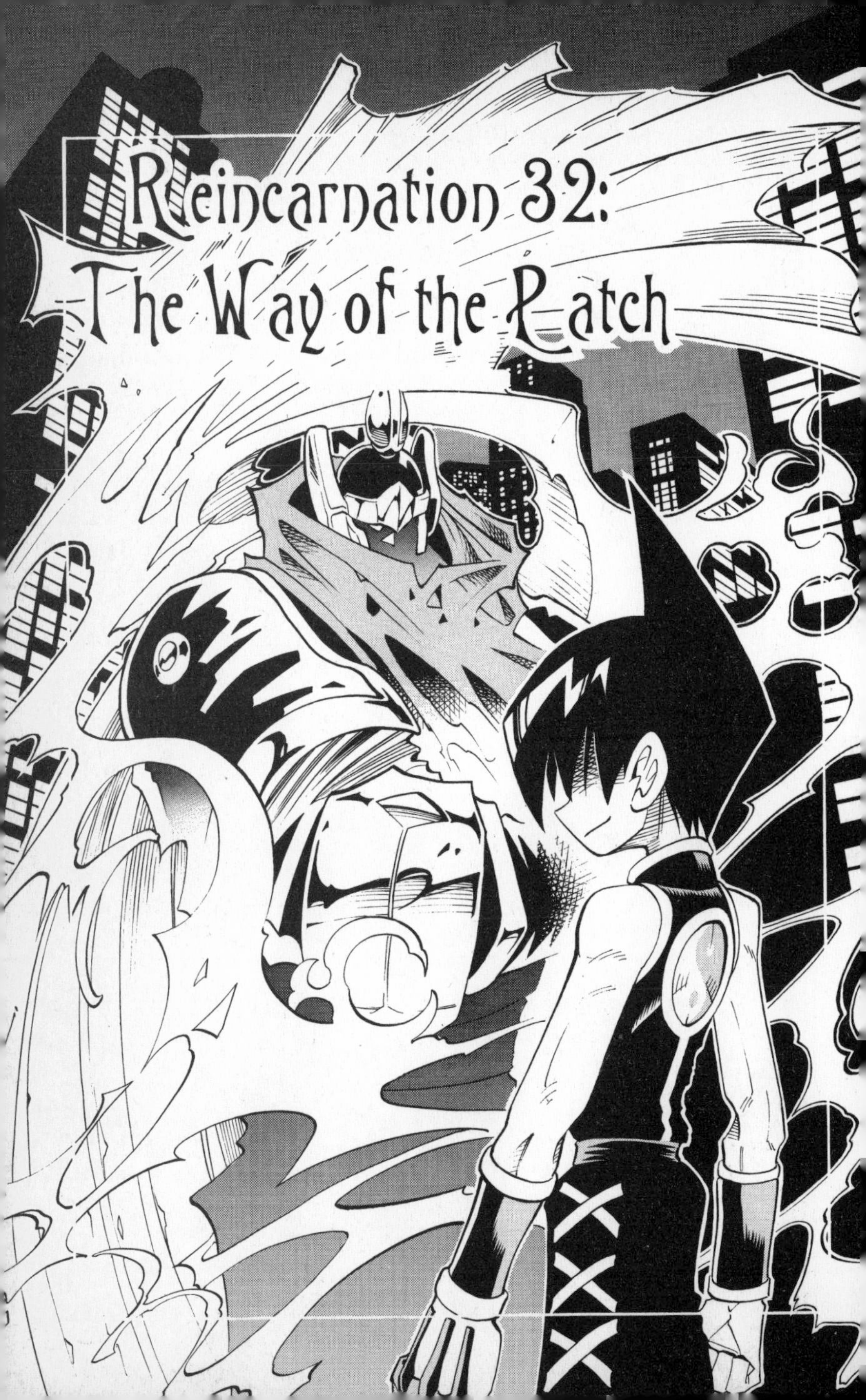
Reincarnation 32:
The Way of the Patch

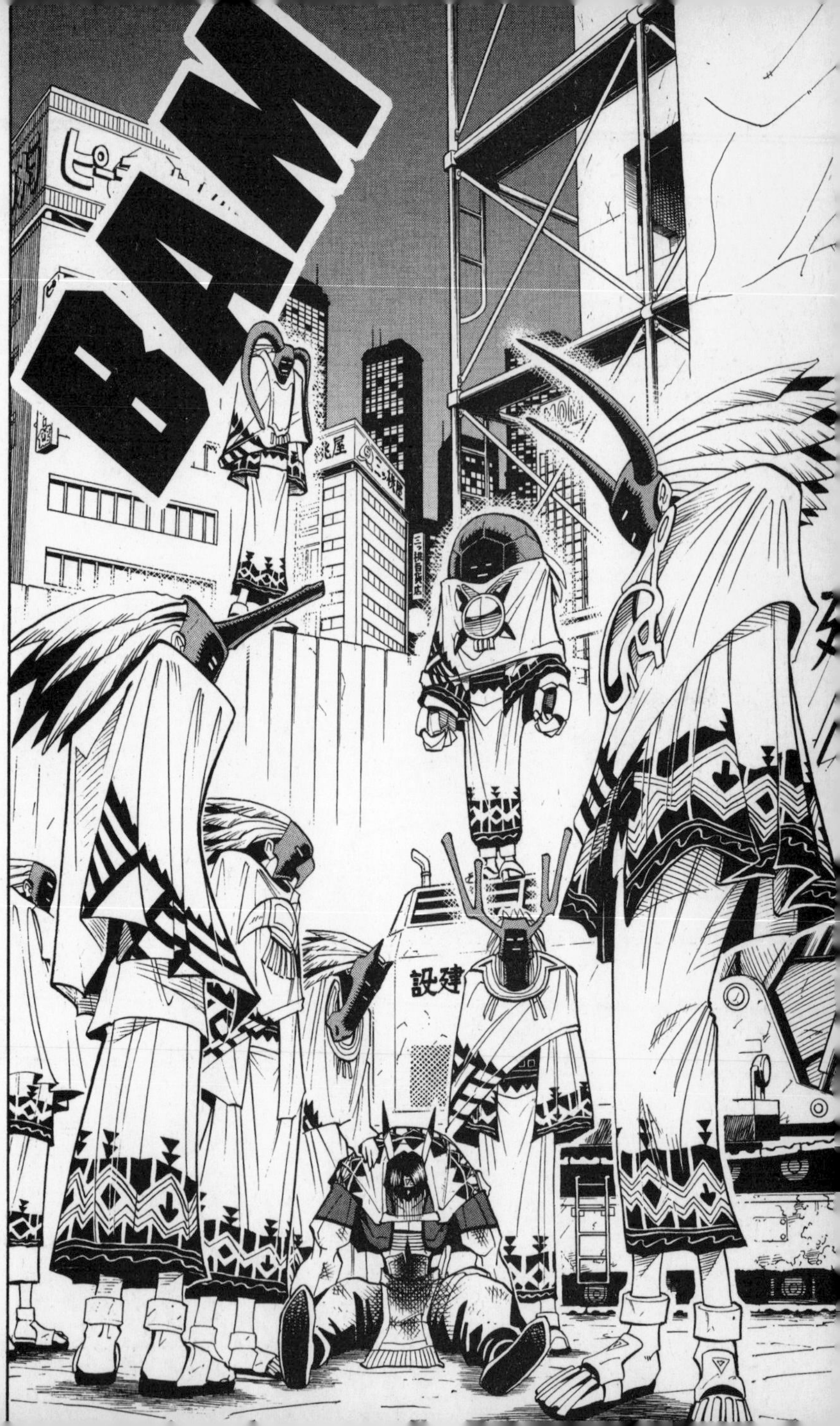
BAM

READ THIS WAY

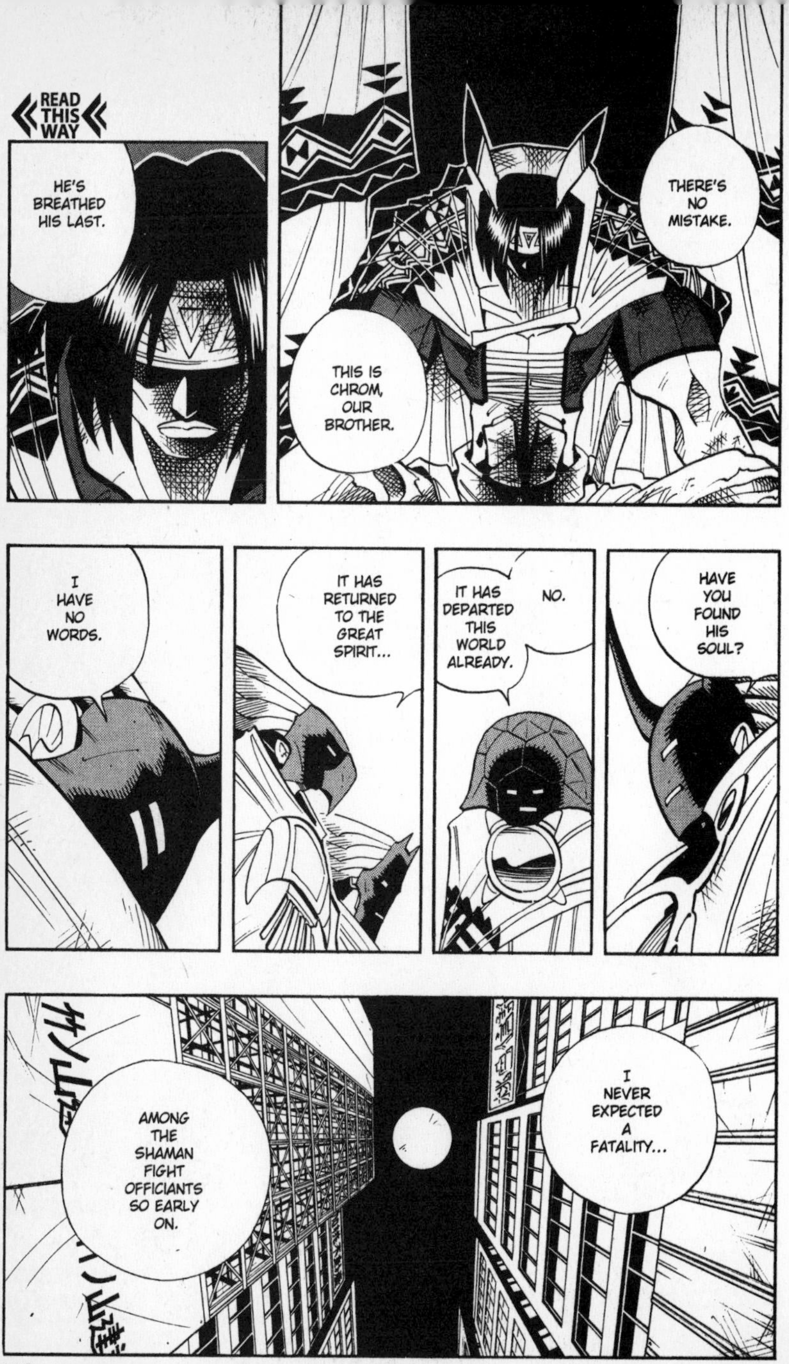
THERE'S NO MISTAKE.
THIS IS CHROM, OUR BROTHER.
HE'S BREATHED HIS LAST.
HAVE YOU FOUND HIS SOUL?
NO.
IT HAS DEPARTED THIS WORLD ALREADY.
IT HAS RETURNED TO THE GREAT SPIRIT...
I HAVE NO WORDS.
I NEVER EXPECTED A FATALITY...
AMONG THE SHAMAN FIGHT OFFICIANTS SO EARLY ON.

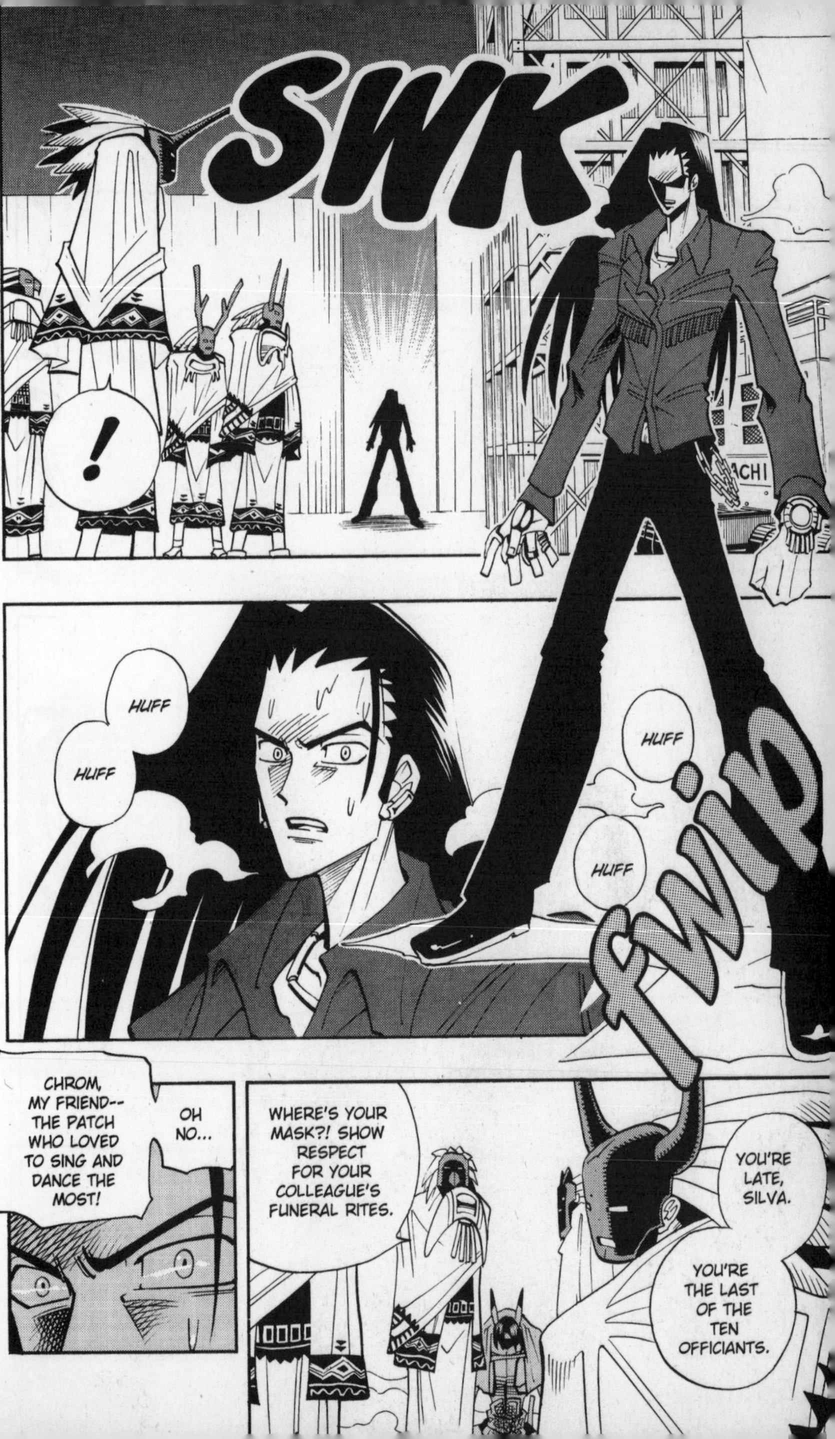
SWK
!
fwip
HUFF
HUFF
HUFF
HUFF
YOU'RE LATE, SILVA.
YOU'RE THE LAST OF THE TEN OFFICIANTS.
WHERE'S YOUR MASK?! SHOW RESPECT FOR YOUR COLLEAGUE'S FUNERAL RITES.
OH NO...
CHROM, MY FRIEND-- THE PATCH WHO LOVED TO SING AND DANCE THE MOST!

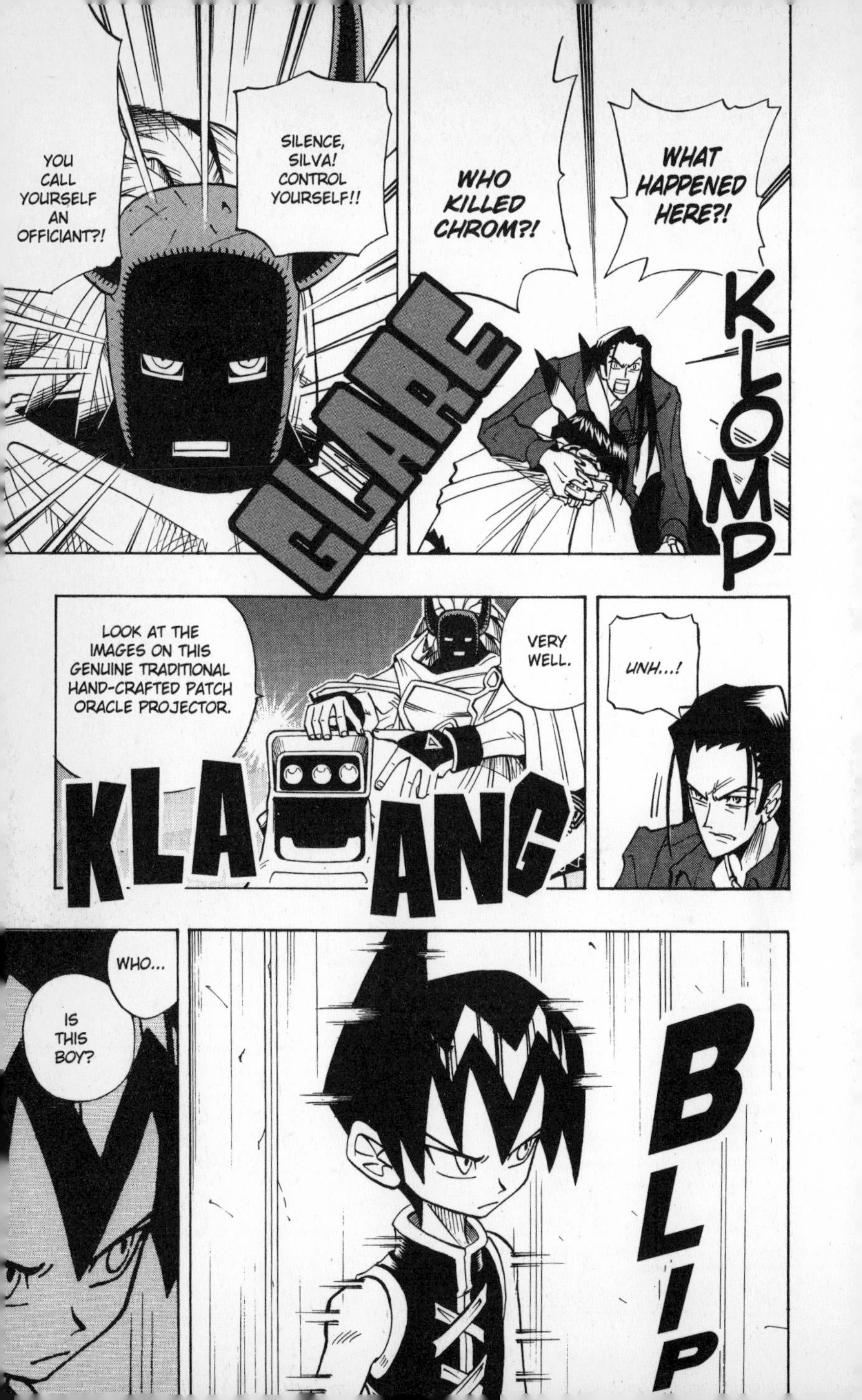
WHAT HAPPENED HERE?!
WHO KILLED CHROM?!
KLOMP
SILENCE, SILVA! CONTROL YOURSELF!!
YOU CALL YOURSELF AN OFFICIANT?!
GLARE
UNH...!
VERY WELL.
LOOK AT THE IMAGES ON THIS GENUINE TRADITIONAL HAND-CRAFTED PATCH ORACLE PROJECTOR.
KLA-ANG
BLIP
WHO...
IS THIS BOY?

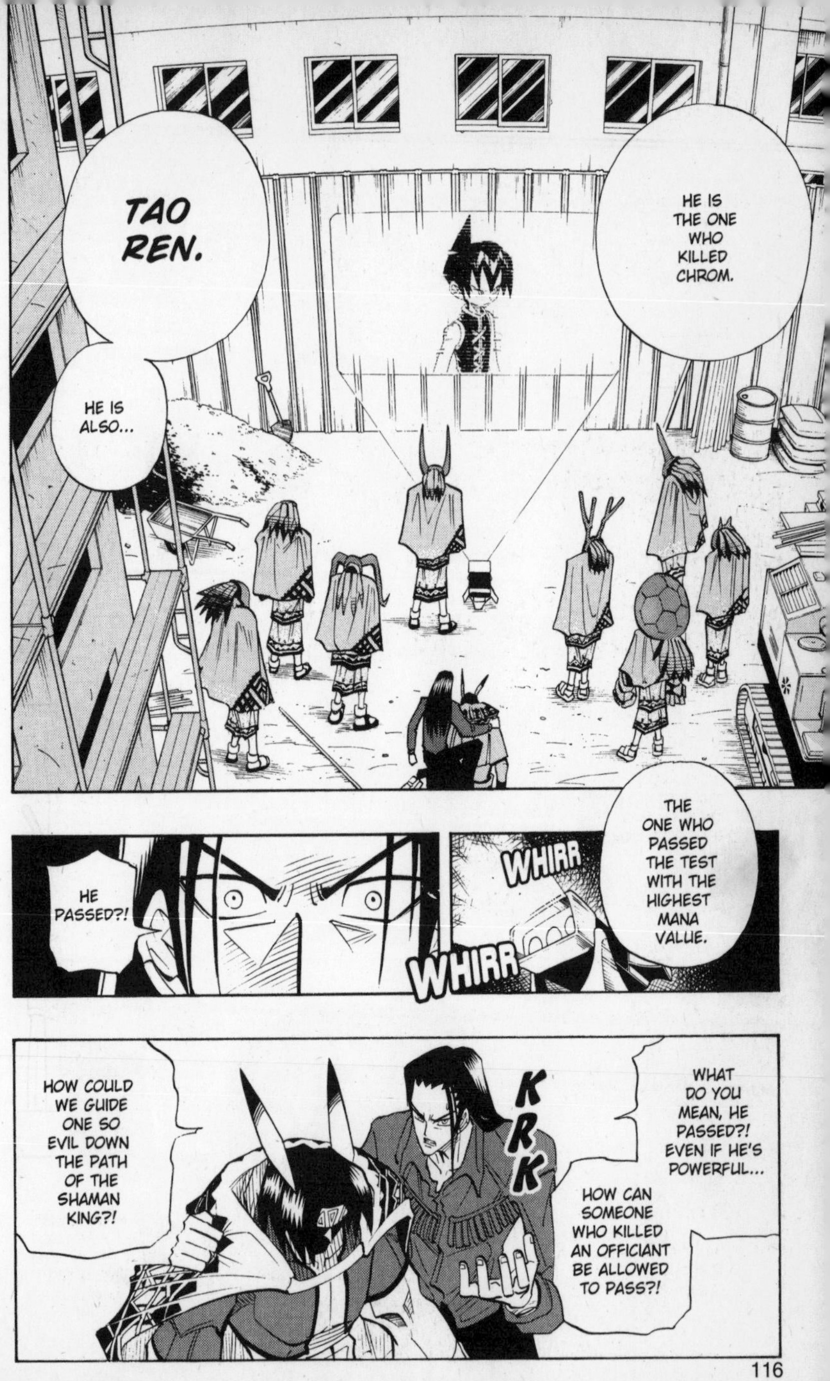
HE IS THE ONE WHO KILLED CHROM.
TAO REN.
HE IS ALSO...
THE ONE WHO PASSED THE TEST WITH THE HIGHEST MANA VALUE.
WHIRR
WHIRR
HE PASSED?!
WHAT DO YOU MEAN, HE PASSED?! EVEN IF HE'S POWERFUL...
KRK
HOW CAN SOMEONE WHO KILLED AN OFFICIANT BE ALLOWED TO PASS?!
HOW COULD WE GUIDE ONE SO EVIL DOWN THE PATH OF THE SHAMAN KING?!

READ THIS WAY

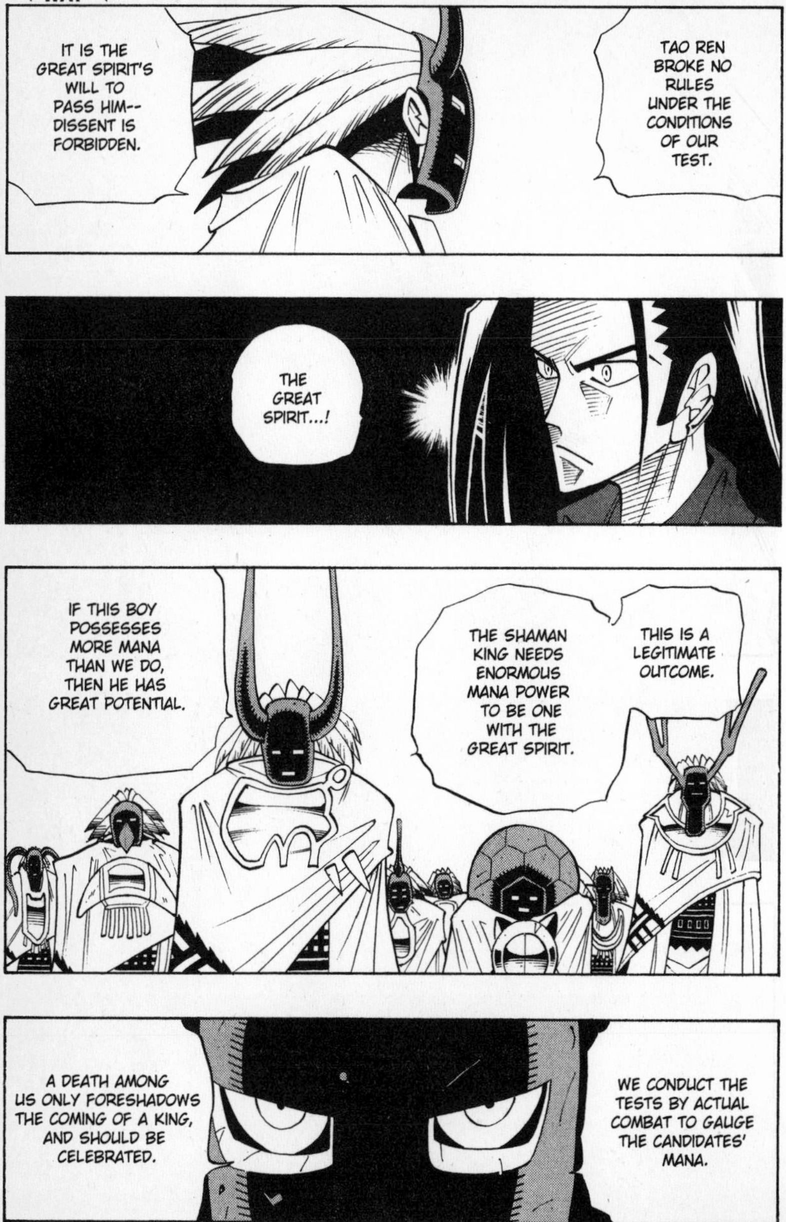
TAO REN BROKE NO RULES UNDER THE CONDITIONS OF OUR TEST.
IT IS THE GREAT SPIRIT'S WILL TO PASS HIM-- DISSENT IS FORBIDDEN.
THE GREAT SPIRIT...!
THIS IS A LEGITIMATE OUTCOME.
THE SHAMAN KING NEEDS ENORMOUS MANA POWER TO BE ONE WITH THE GREAT SPIRIT.
IF THIS BOY POSSESSES MORE MANA THAN WE DO, THEN HE HAS GREAT POTENTIAL.
WE CONDUCT THE TESTS BY ACTUAL COMBAT TO GAUGE THE CANDIDATES' MANA.
A DEATH AMONG US ONLY FORESHADOWS THE COMING OF A KING, AND SHOULD BE CELEBRATED.

READ THIS WAY

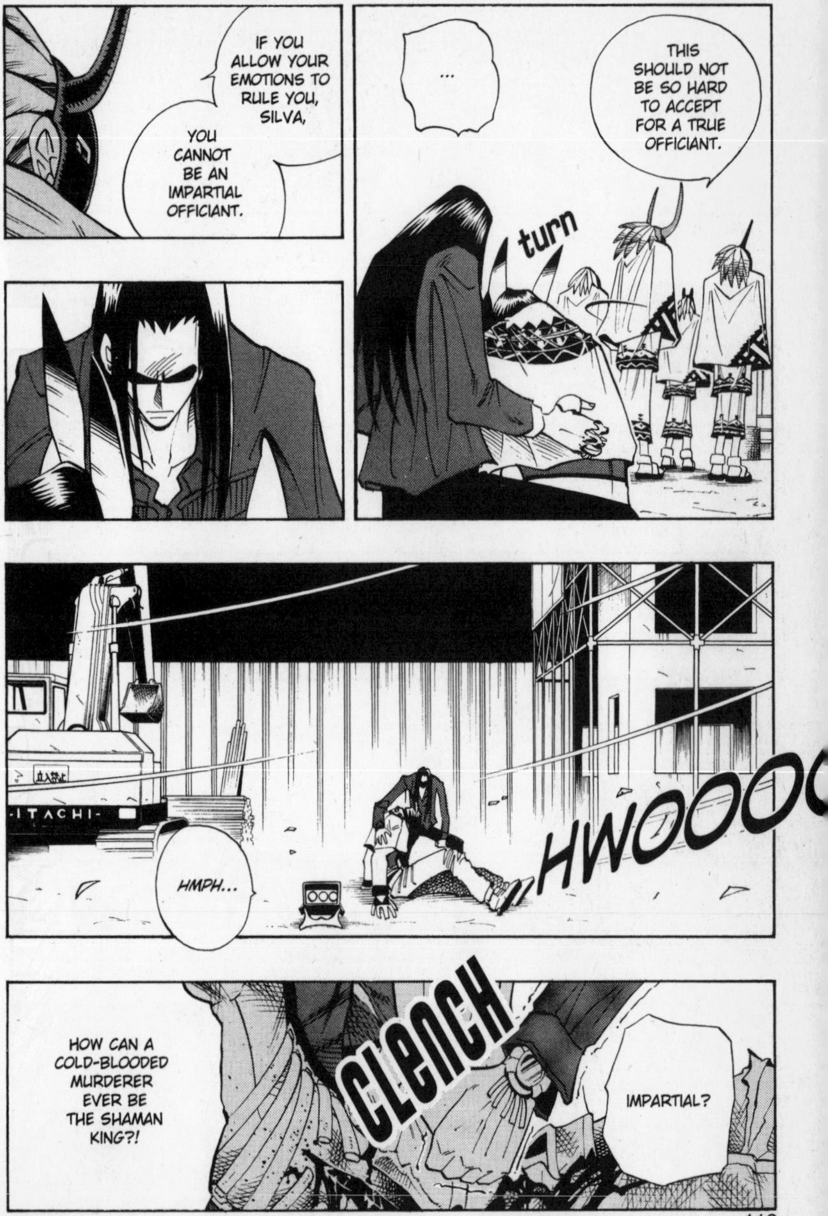
THIS SHOULD NOT BE SO HARD TO ACCEPT FOR A TRUE OFFICIANT.
...
IF YOU ALLOW YOUR EMOTIONS TO RULE YOU, SILVA,
YOU CANNOT BE AN IMPARTIAL OFFICIANT.
turn
HWOOOO
HMPH...
IMPARTIAL?
CLENCH
HOW CAN A COLD-BLOODED MURDERER EVER BE THE SHAMAN KING?!

READ THIS WAY

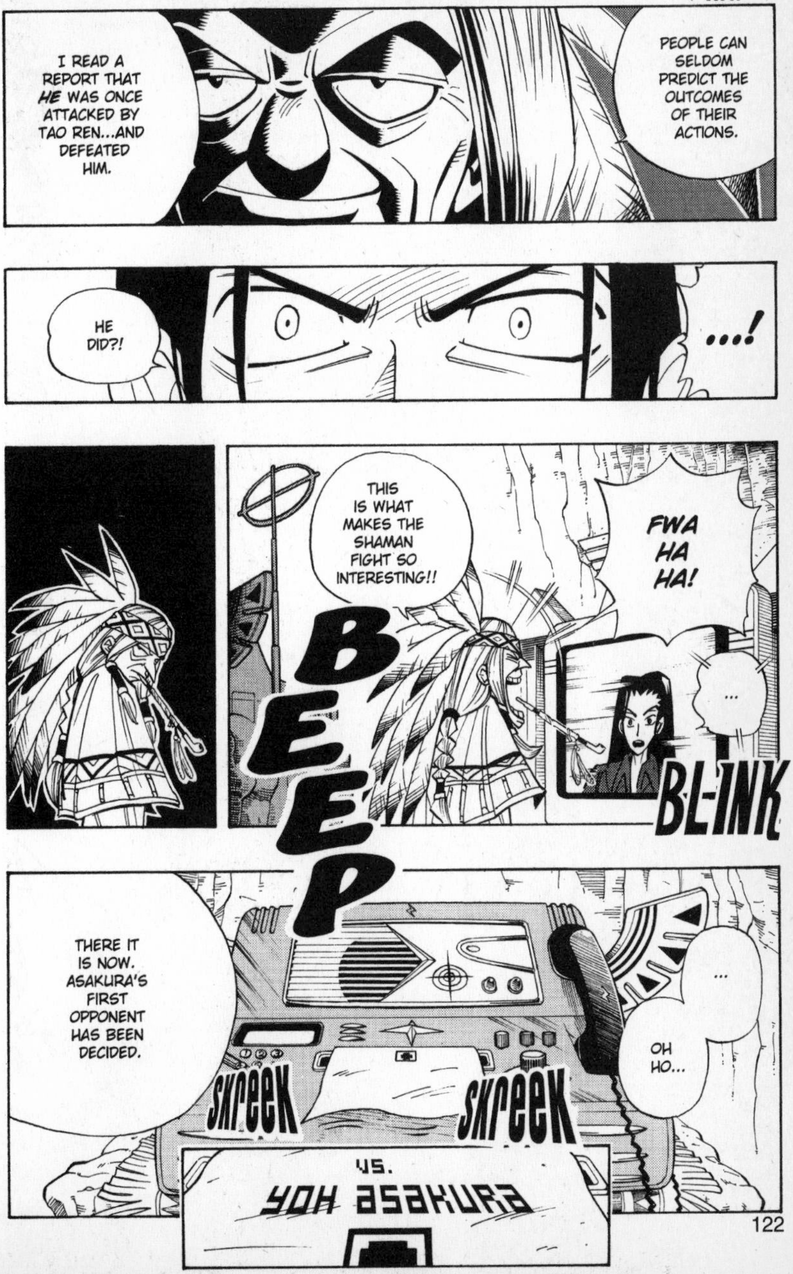
PEOPLE CAN SELDOM PREDICT THE OUTCOMES OF THEIR ACTIONS.
I READ A REPORT THAT *HE* WAS ONCE ATTACKED BY TAO REN...AND DEFEATED HIM.
...!
HE DID?!
FWA HA HA!
...
THIS IS WHAT MAKES THE SHAMAN FIGHT SO INTERESTING!!
B-L-INK
BEEP
...
OH HO...
THERE IT IS NOW. ASAKURA'S FIRST OPPONENT HAS BEEN DECIDED.
SKREEK
SKREEK
VS.
YOH ASAKURA

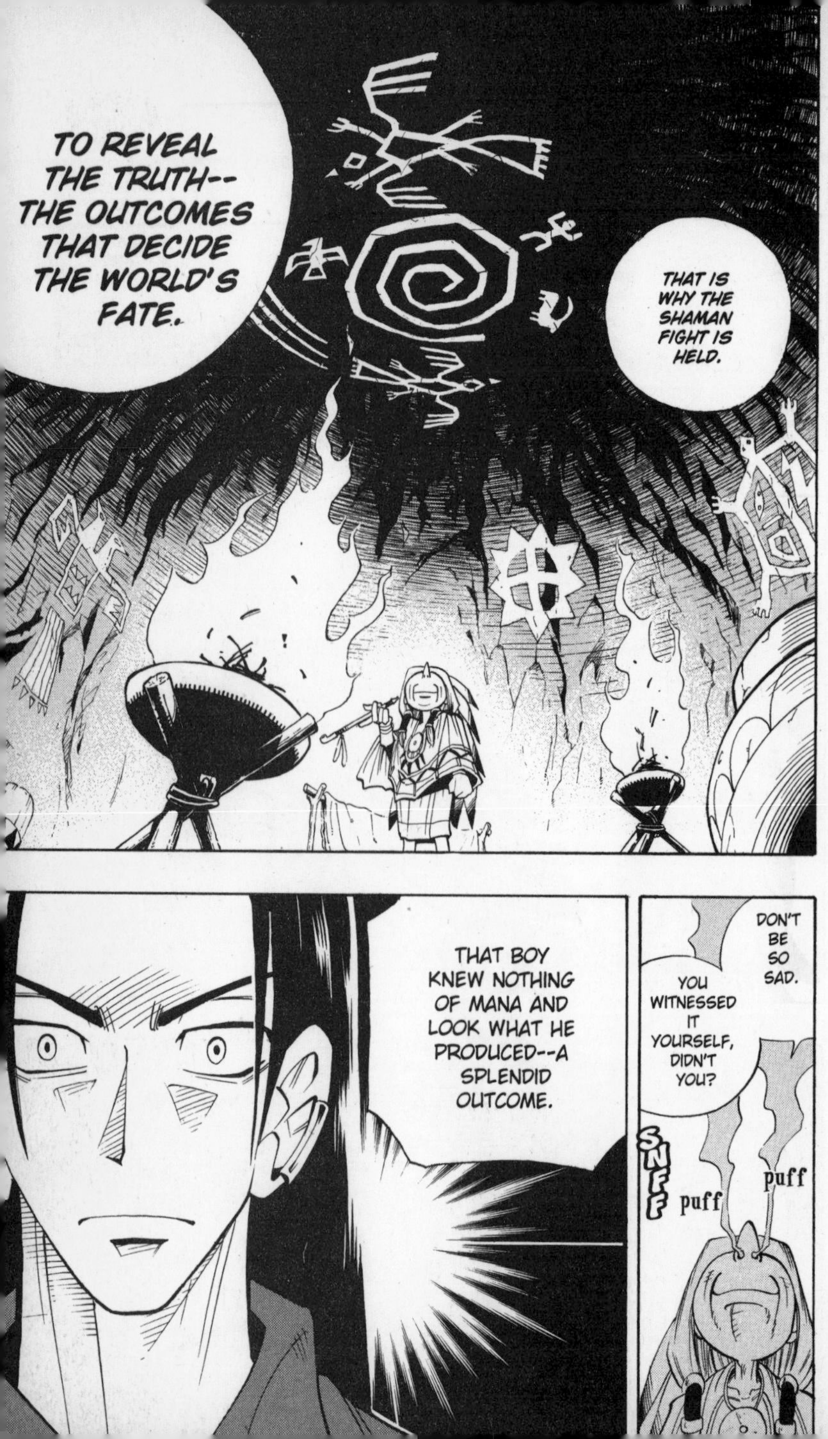
TO REVEAL THE TRUTH-- THE OUTCOMES THAT DECIDE THE WORLD'S FATE.
THAT IS WHY THE SHAMAN FIGHT IS HELD.
DON'T BE SO SAD.
YOU WITNESSED IT YOURSELF, DIDN'T YOU?
SNFF
puff
puff
THAT BOY KNEW NOTHING OF MANA AND LOOK WHAT HE PRODUCED--A SPLENDID OUTCOME.

READ THIS WAY

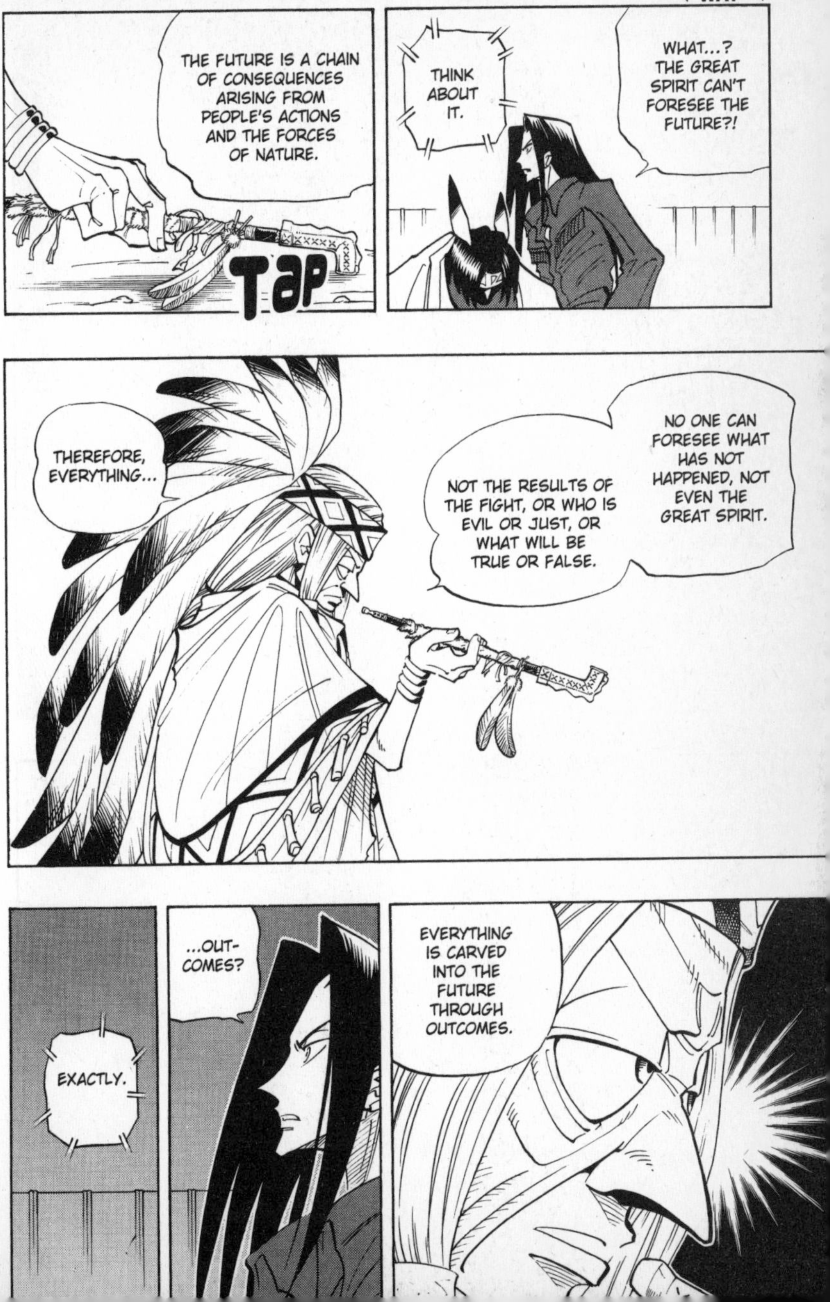
WHAT...? THE GREAT SPIRIT CAN'T FORESEE THE FUTURE?!
THINK ABOUT IT.
THE FUTURE IS A CHAIN OF CONSEQUENCES ARISING FROM PEOPLE'S ACTIONS AND THE FORCES OF NATURE.
TAP
NO ONE CAN FORESEE WHAT HAS NOT HAPPENED, NOT EVEN THE GREAT SPIRIT.
NOT THE RESULTS OF THE FIGHT, OR WHO IS EVIL OR JUST, OR WHAT WILL BE TRUE OR FALSE.
THEREFORE, EVERYTHING...
EVERYTHING IS CARVED INTO THE FUTURE THROUGH OUTCOMES.
...OUT-COMES?
EXACTLY.

READ THIS WAY

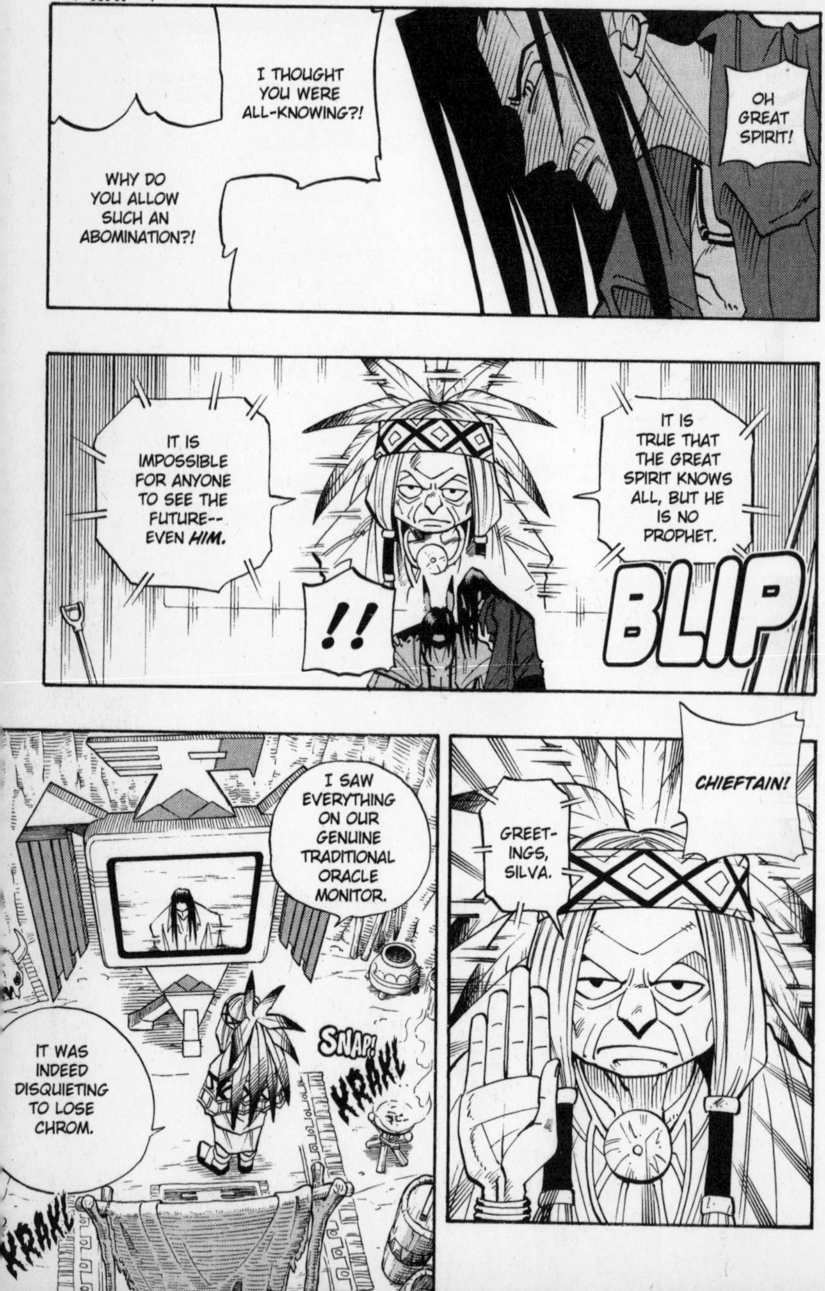

OH GREAT SPIRIT!
I THOUGHT YOU WERE ALL-KNOWING?!
WHY DO YOU ALLOW SUCH AN ABOMINATION?!
IT IS TRUE THAT THE GREAT SPIRIT KNOWS ALL, BUT HE IS NO PROPHET.
BLIP
!!
IT IS IMPOSSIBLE FOR ANYONE TO SEE THE FUTURE-- EVEN *HIM*.
CHIEFTAIN!
GREET- INGS, SILVA.
I SAW EVERYTHING ON OUR GENUINE TRADITIONAL ORACLE MONITOR.
SNAP!
KRAK!
IT WAS INDEED DISQUIETING TO LOSE CHROM.
KRAK!

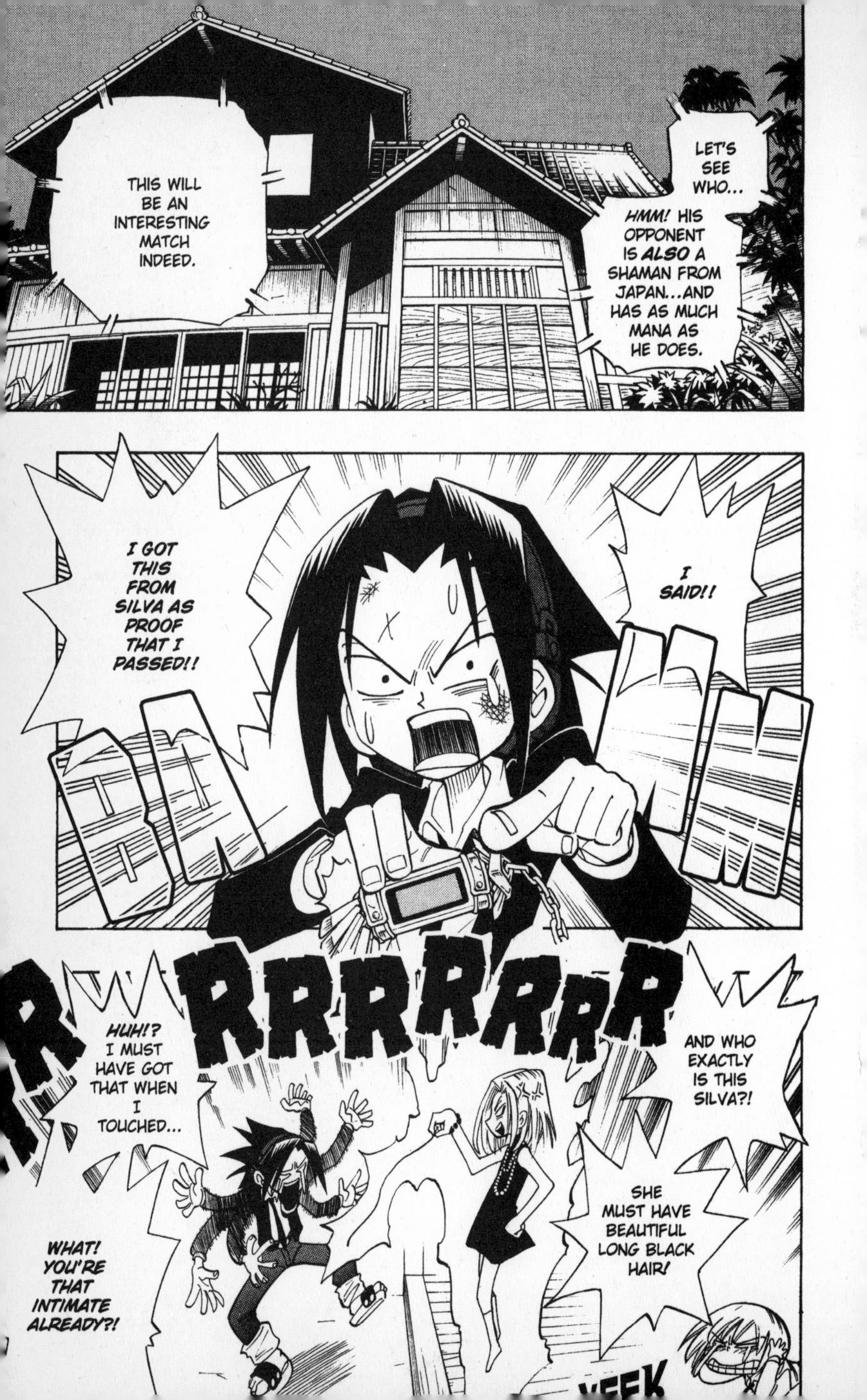
LET'S SEE WHO... HMM! HIS OPPONENT IS ALSO A SHAMAN FROM JAPAN...AND HAS AS MUCH MANA AS HE DOES.
THIS WILL BE AN INTERESTING MATCH INDEED.
I SAID!!
I GOT THIS FROM SILVA AS PROOF THAT I PASSED!!
RRRRRRR
AND WHO EXACTLY IS THIS SILVA?!
SHE MUST HAVE BEAUTIFUL LONG BLACK HAIR!
HUH!? I MUST HAVE GOT THAT WHEN I TOUCHED...
WHAT! YOU'RE THAT INTIMATE ALREADY?!
YEEK

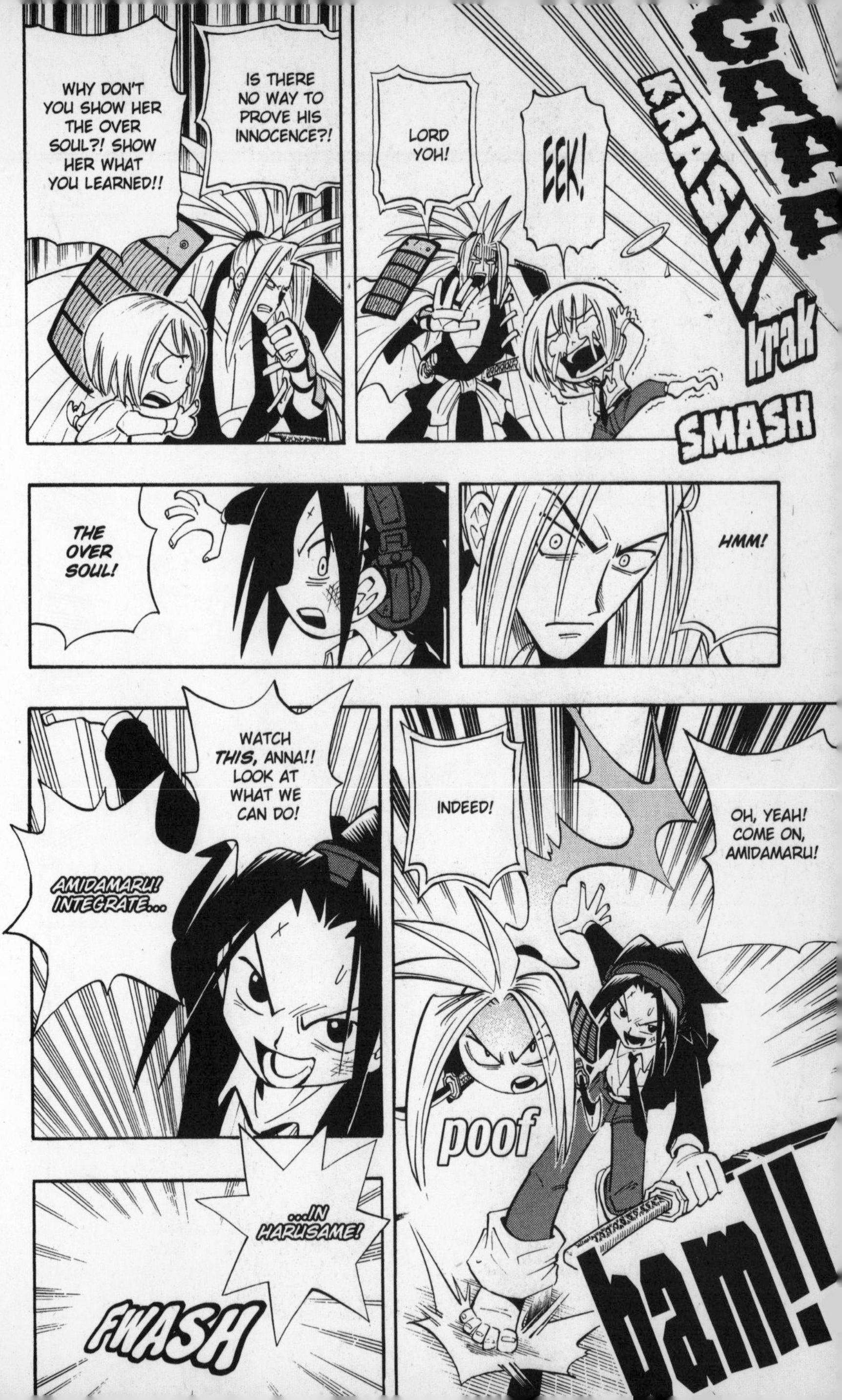
LORD YOH!
EEK!
KRASH
krak
SMASH
IS THERE NO WAY TO PROVE HIS INNOCENCE?!
WHY DON'T YOU SHOW HER THE OVER SOUL?! SHOW HER WHAT YOU LEARNED!!
HMM!
THE OVER SOUL!
OH, YEAH! COME ON, AMIDAMARU!
INDEED!
poof
bam!!
WATCH THIS, ANNA!! LOOK AT WHAT WE CAN DO!
AMIDAMARU! INTEGRATE...
...IN HARUSAME!
FWASH

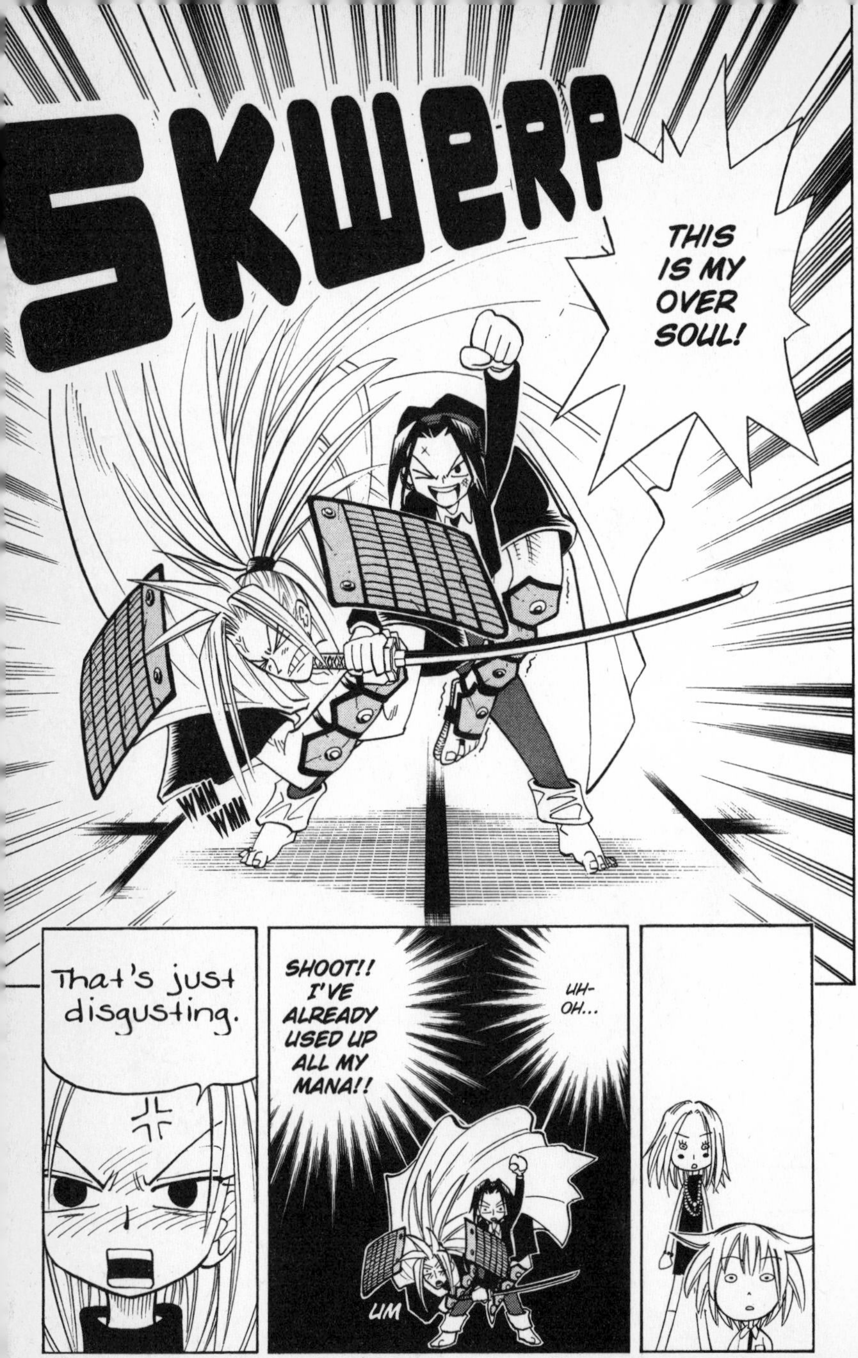
SKWERP
THIS IS MY OVER SOUL!
WMM WMM
UH-OH...
SHOOT!! I'VE ALREADY USED UP ALL MY MANA!!
UM
That's just disgusting.

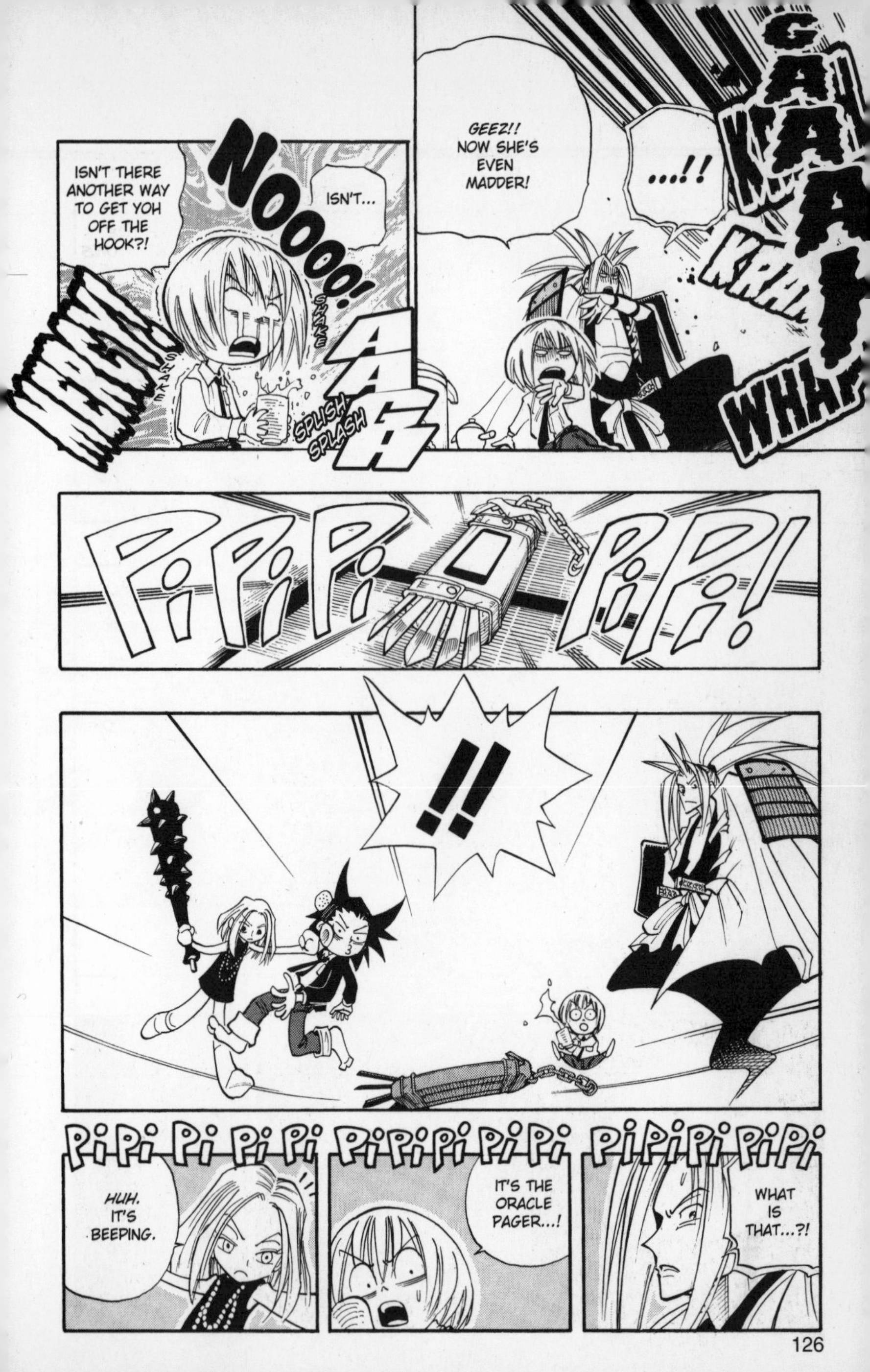
...!!
GEEZ!! NOW SHE'S EVEN MADDER!
ISN'T...
NOOOOO!
ISN'T THERE ANOTHER WAY TO GET YOH OFF THE HOOK?!
SHAKE
SHAKE
AAAH
SPLISH SPLASH
PiPiPi PiPiPi!
!!
PiPi Pi Pi Pi PiPiPiPiPi PiPiPiPiPiPi
WHAT IS THAT...?!
IT'S THE ORACLE PAGER...!
HUH. IT'S BEEPING.

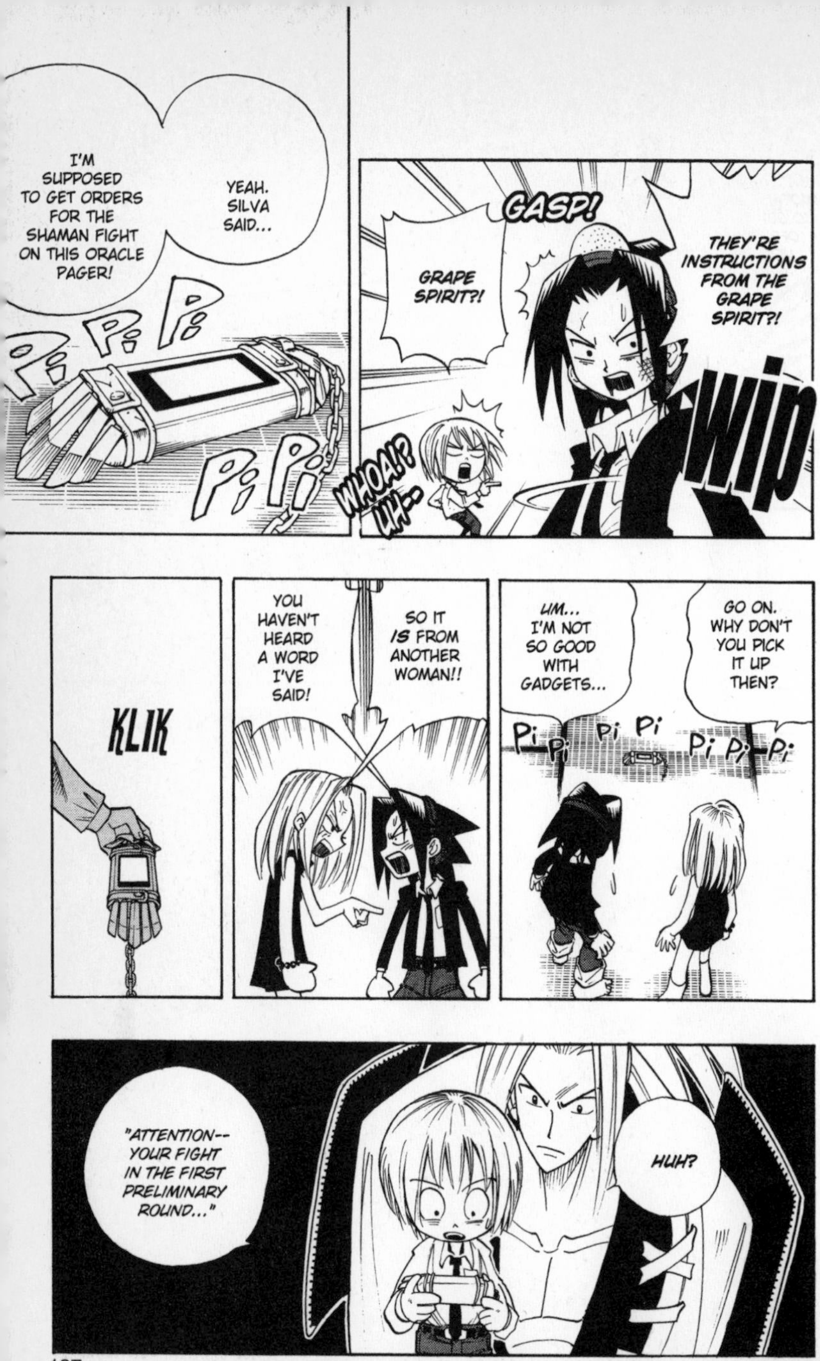
YEAH. SILVA SAID...
I'M SUPPOSED TO GET ORDERS FOR THE SHAMAN FIGHT ON THIS ORACLE PAGER!
Pi Pi Pi Pi Pi
GASP!
THEY'RE INSTRUCTIONS FROM THE GRAPE SPIRIT?!
GRAPE SPIRIT?!
WIP
WHOA!? UH-
GO ON. WHY DON'T YOU PICK IT UP THEN?
UM... I'M NOT SO GOOD WITH GADGETS...
Pi Pi Pi Pi Pi Pi Pi
SO IT *IS* FROM ANOTHER WOMAN!!
YOU HAVEN'T HEARD A WORD I'VE SAID!
KLIK
HUH?
"ATTENTION-- YOUR FIGHT IN THE FIRST PRELIMINARY ROUND..."

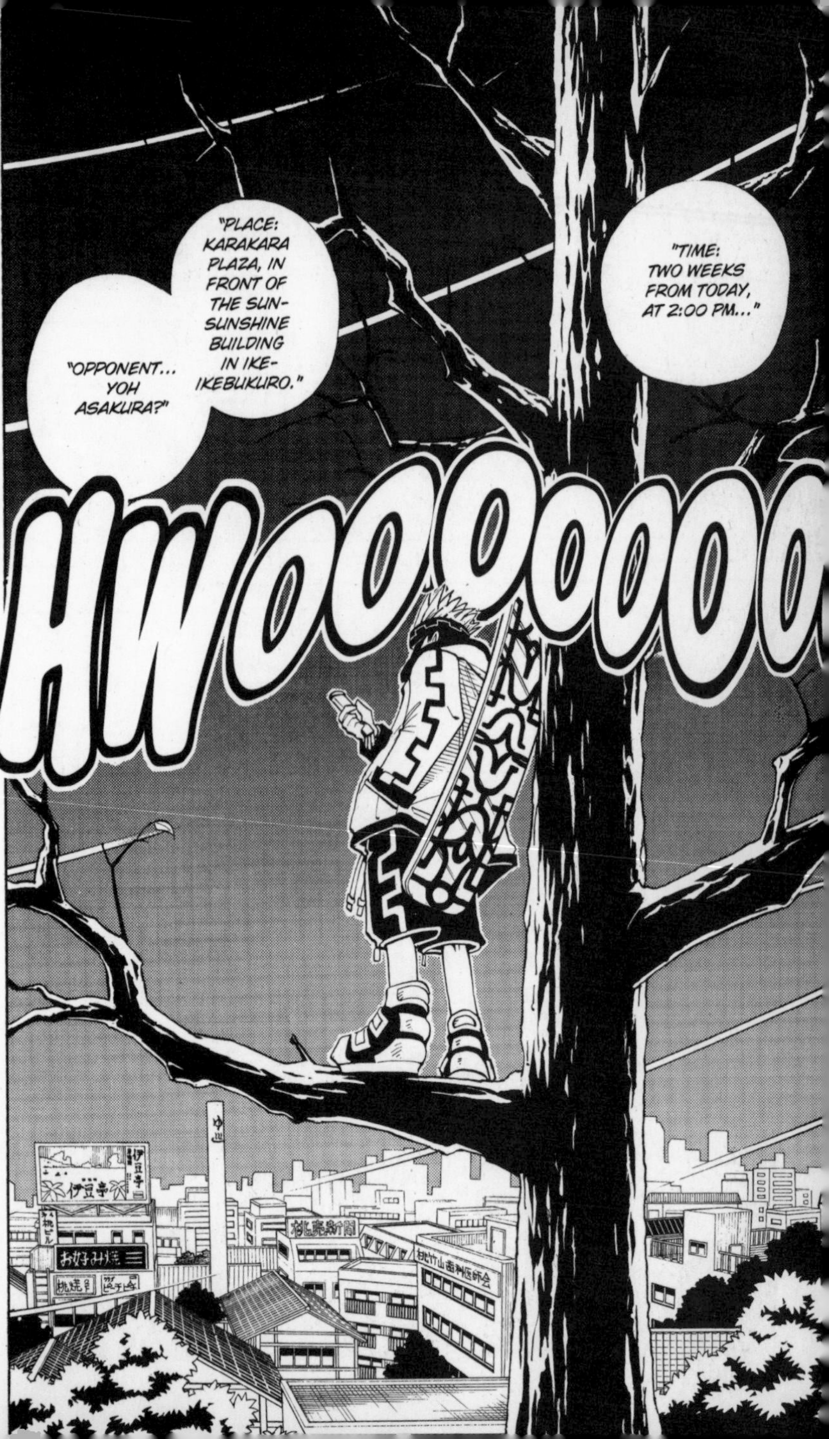
"TIME: TWO WEEKS FROM TODAY, AT 2:00 PM..."
"PLACE: KARAKARA PLAZA, IN FRONT OF THE SUN-SUNSHINE BUILDING IN IKE-IKEBUKURO."
"OPPONENT... YOH ASAKURA?"
HWOOOOOOO

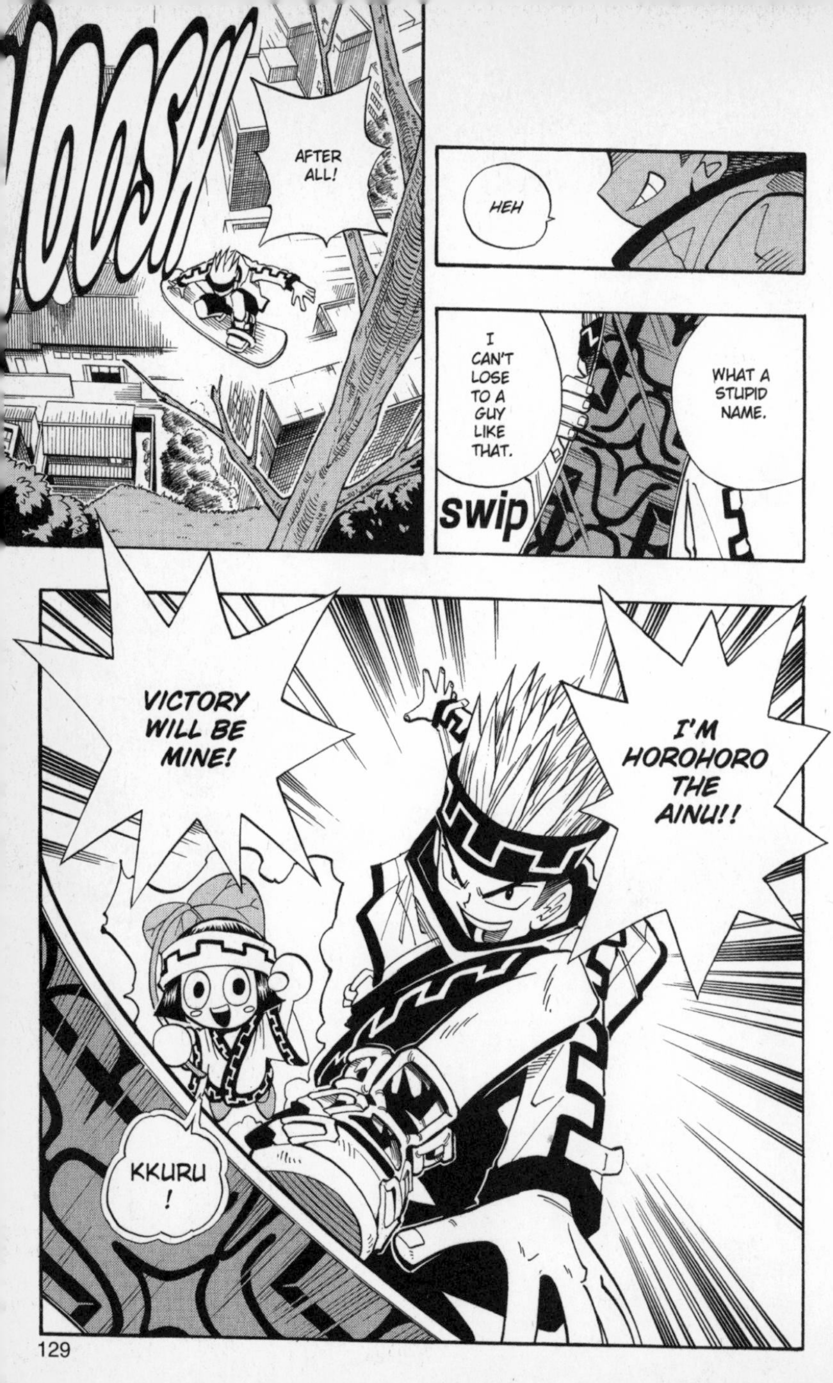
HEH
WHAT A STUPID NAME.
I CAN'T LOSE TO A GUY LIKE THAT.
swip
AFTER ALL!
I'M HOROHORO THE AINU!!
VICTORY WILL BE MINE!
KKURU!

SHAMAN
KING
4

ORACLE
PROJECTOR

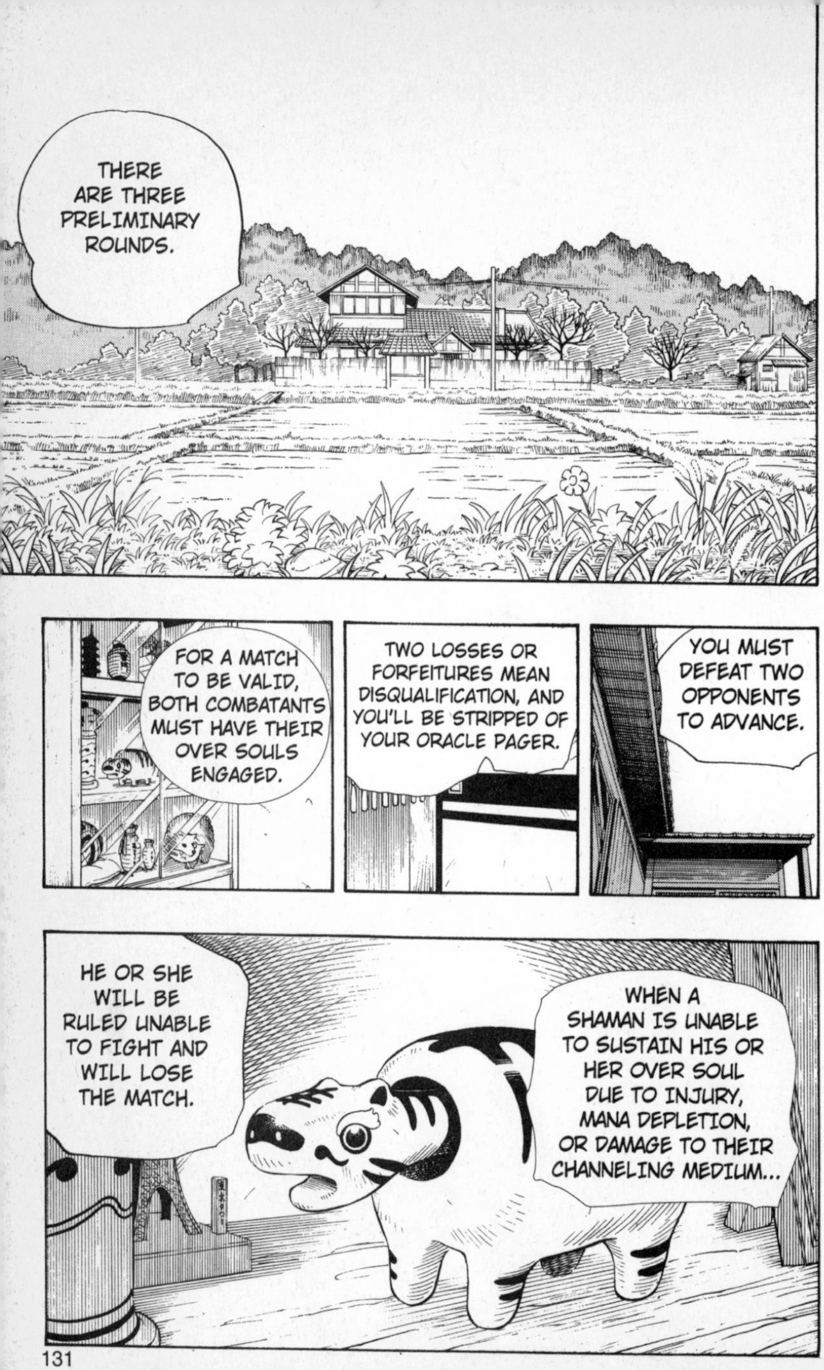
THERE ARE THREE PRELIMINARY ROUNDS.
YOU MUST DEFEAT TWO OPPONENTS TO ADVANCE.
TWO LOSSES OR FORFEITURES MEAN DISQUALIFICATION, AND YOU'LL BE STRIPPED OF YOUR ORACLE PAGER.
FOR A MATCH TO BE VALID, BOTH COMBATANTS MUST HAVE THEIR OVER SOULS ENGAGED.
WHEN A SHAMAN IS UNABLE TO SUSTAIN HIS OR HER OVER SOUL DUE TO INJURY, MANA DEPLETION, OR DAMAGE TO THEIR CHANNELING MEDIUM...
HE OR SHE WILL BE RULED UNABLE TO FIGHT AND WILL LOSE THE MATCH.

Reincarnation 33: Horohoro

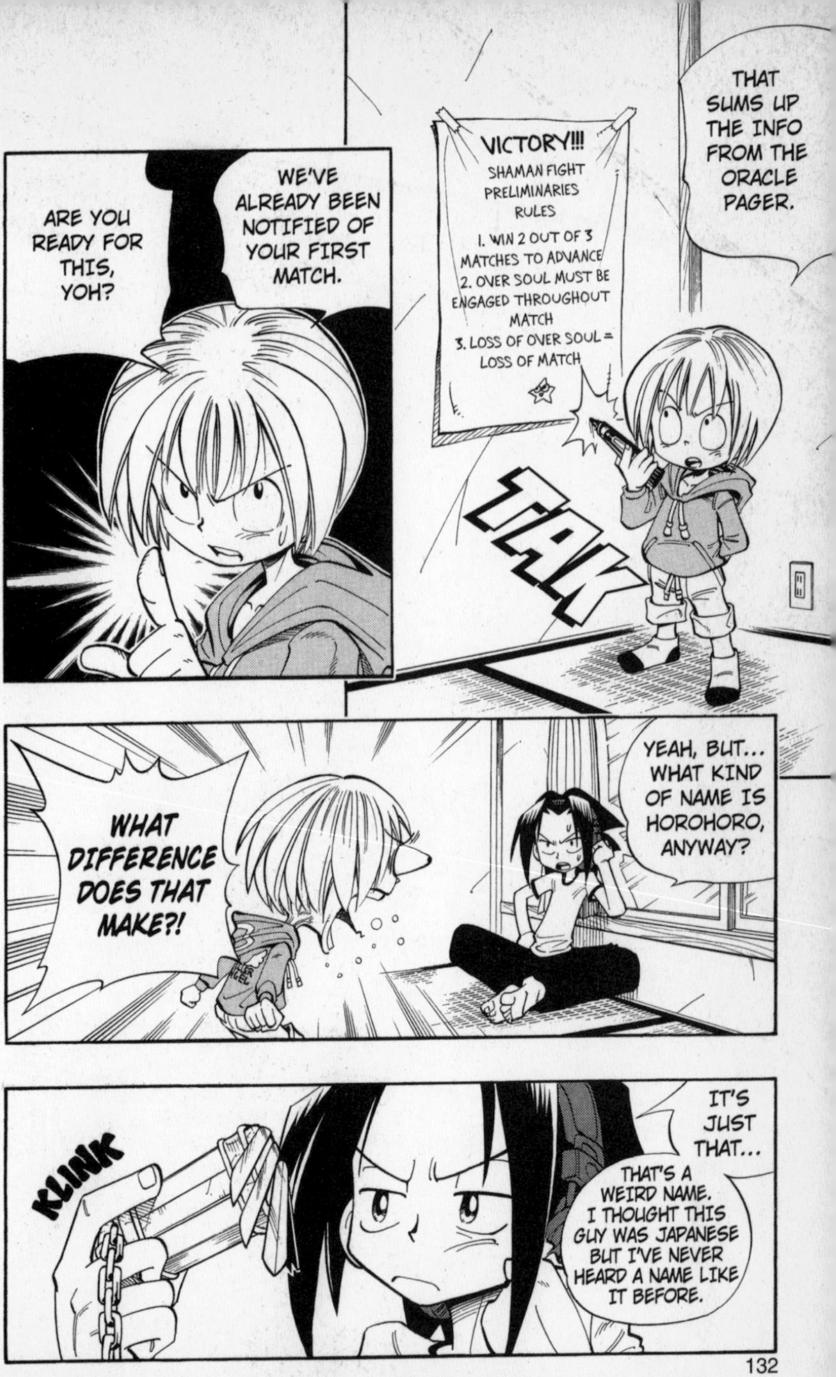
THAT SUMS UP THE INFO FROM THE ORACLE PAGER.
VICTORY!!!
SHAMAN FIGHT PRELIMINARIES RULES
1. WIN 2 OUT OF 3 MATCHES TO ADVANCE
2. OVER SOUL MUST BE ENGAGED THROUGHOUT MATCH
3. LOSS OF OVER SOUL = LOSS OF MATCH
TAK
WE'VE ALREADY BEEN NOTIFIED OF YOUR FIRST MATCH.
ARE YOU READY FOR THIS, YOH?
YEAH, BUT... WHAT KIND OF NAME IS HOROHORO, ANYWAY?
WHAT DIFFERENCE DOES THAT MAKE?!
IT'S JUST THAT...
THAT'S A WEIRD NAME. I THOUGHT THIS GUY WAS JAPANESE BUT I'VE NEVER HEARD A NAME LIKE IT BEFORE.
KLINK

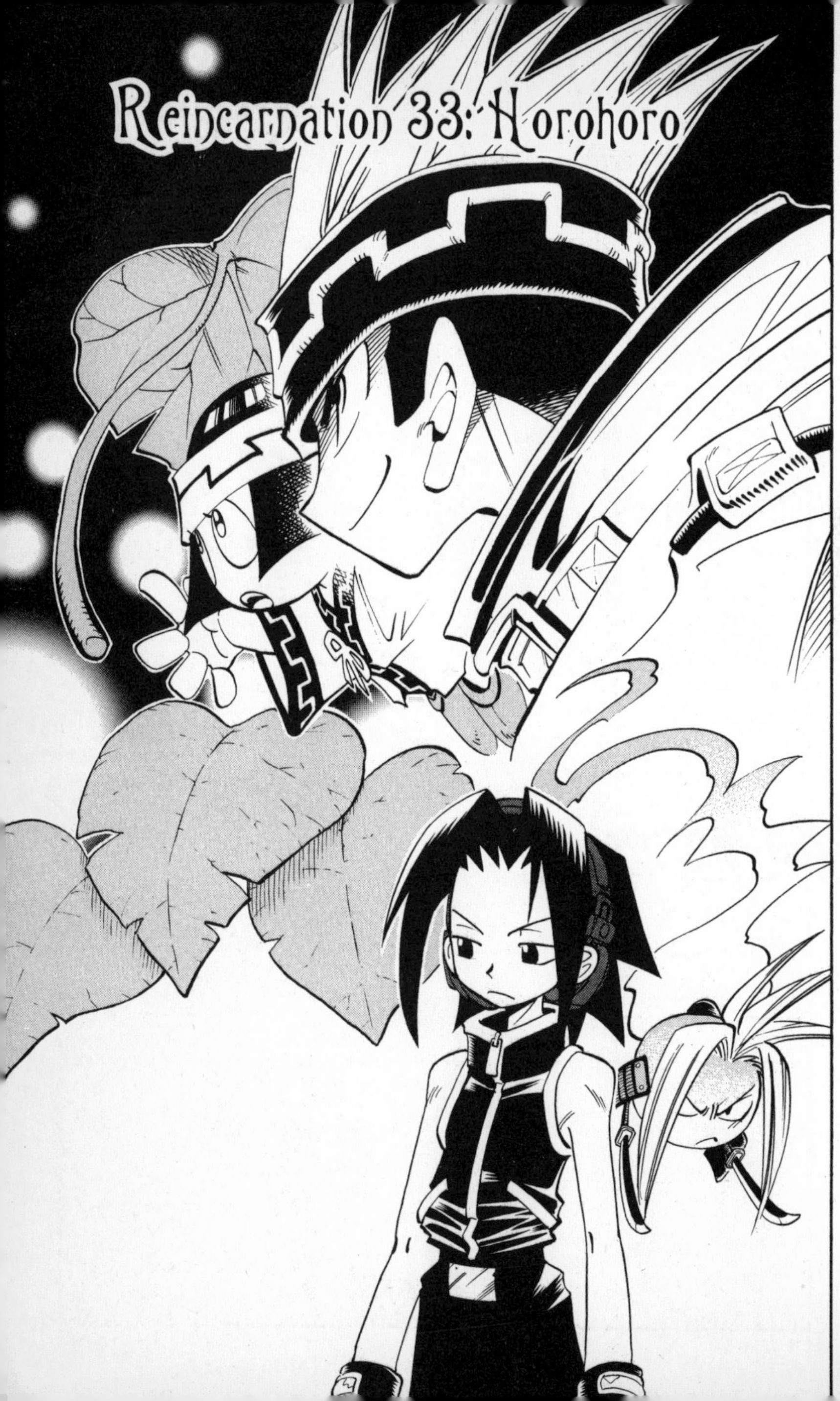
Reincarnation 33: Horohoro

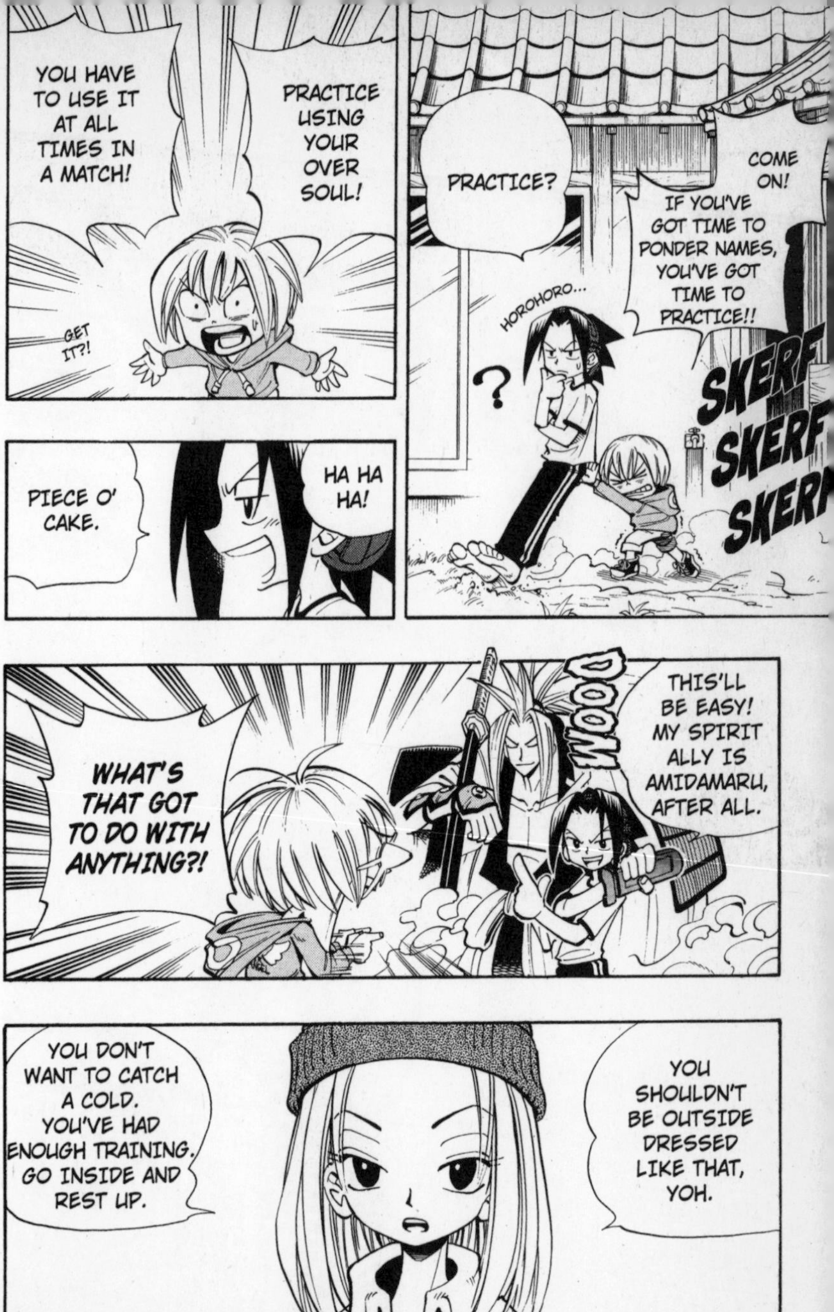
COME ON! IF YOU'VE GOT TIME TO PONDER NAMES, YOU'VE GOT TIME TO PRACTICE!!
PRACTICE?
HOROHORO...
SKERF
SKERF
SKER
PRACTICE USING YOUR OVER SOUL!
YOU HAVE TO USE IT AT ALL TIMES IN A MATCH!
GET IT?!
HA HA HA!
PIECE O' CAKE.
THIS'LL BE EASY! MY SPIRIT ALLY IS AMIDAMARU, AFTER ALL.
DOOOM
WHAT'S THAT GOT TO DO WITH ANYTHING?!
YOU SHOULDN'T BE OUTSIDE DRESSED LIKE THAT, YOH.
YOU DON'T WANT TO CATCH A COLD. YOU'VE HAD ENOUGH TRAINING. GO INSIDE AND REST UP.

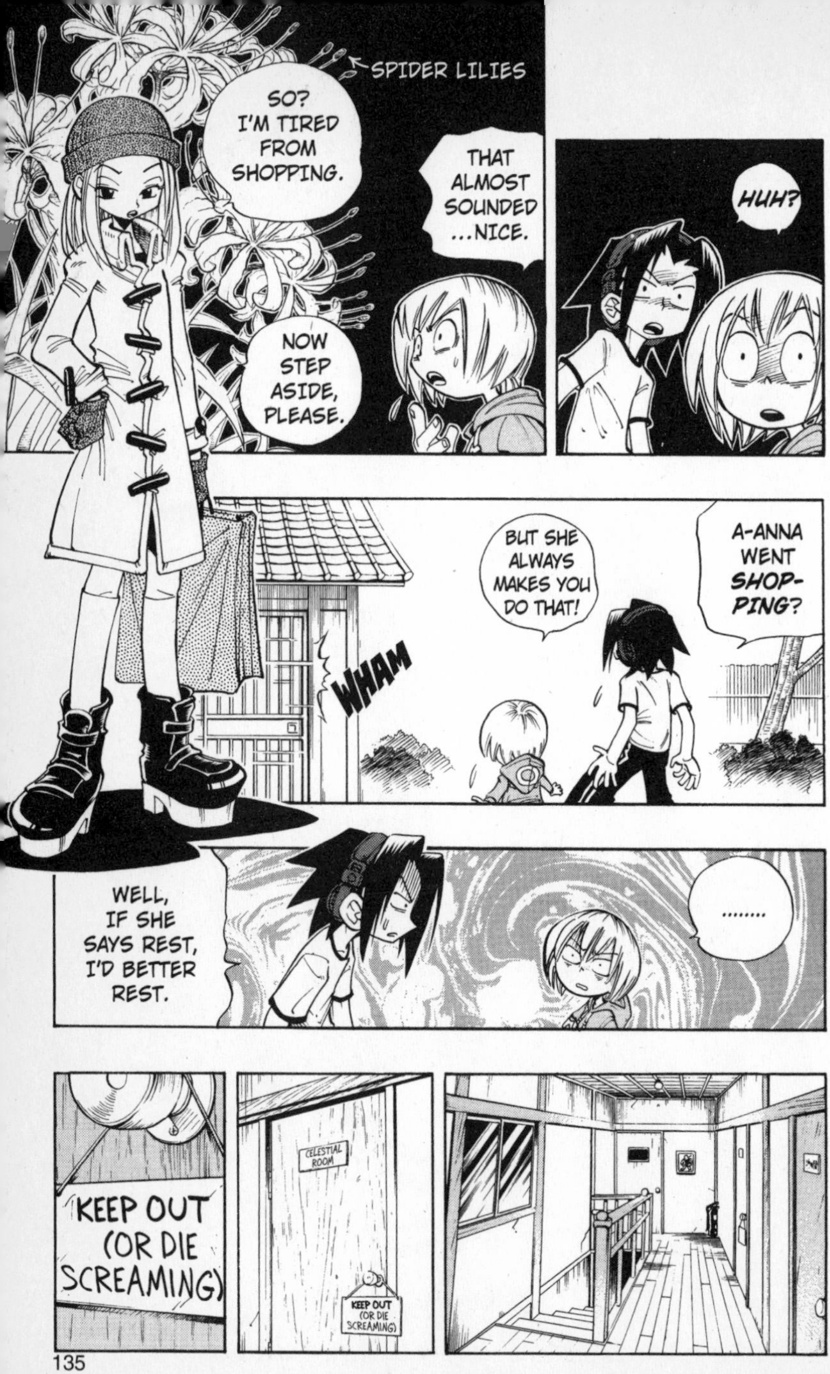
SPIDER LILIES
SO? I'M TIRED FROM SHOPPING.
THAT ALMOST SOUNDED ...NICE.
NOW STEP ASIDE, PLEASE.
HUH?
WHAM
A-ANNA WENT SHOPPING?
BUT SHE ALWAYS MAKES YOU DO THAT!
WELL, IF SHE SAYS REST, I'D BETTER REST.
....
KEEP OUT (OR DIE SCREAMING)
CELESTIAL ROOM
KEEP OUT (OR DIE SCREAMING)

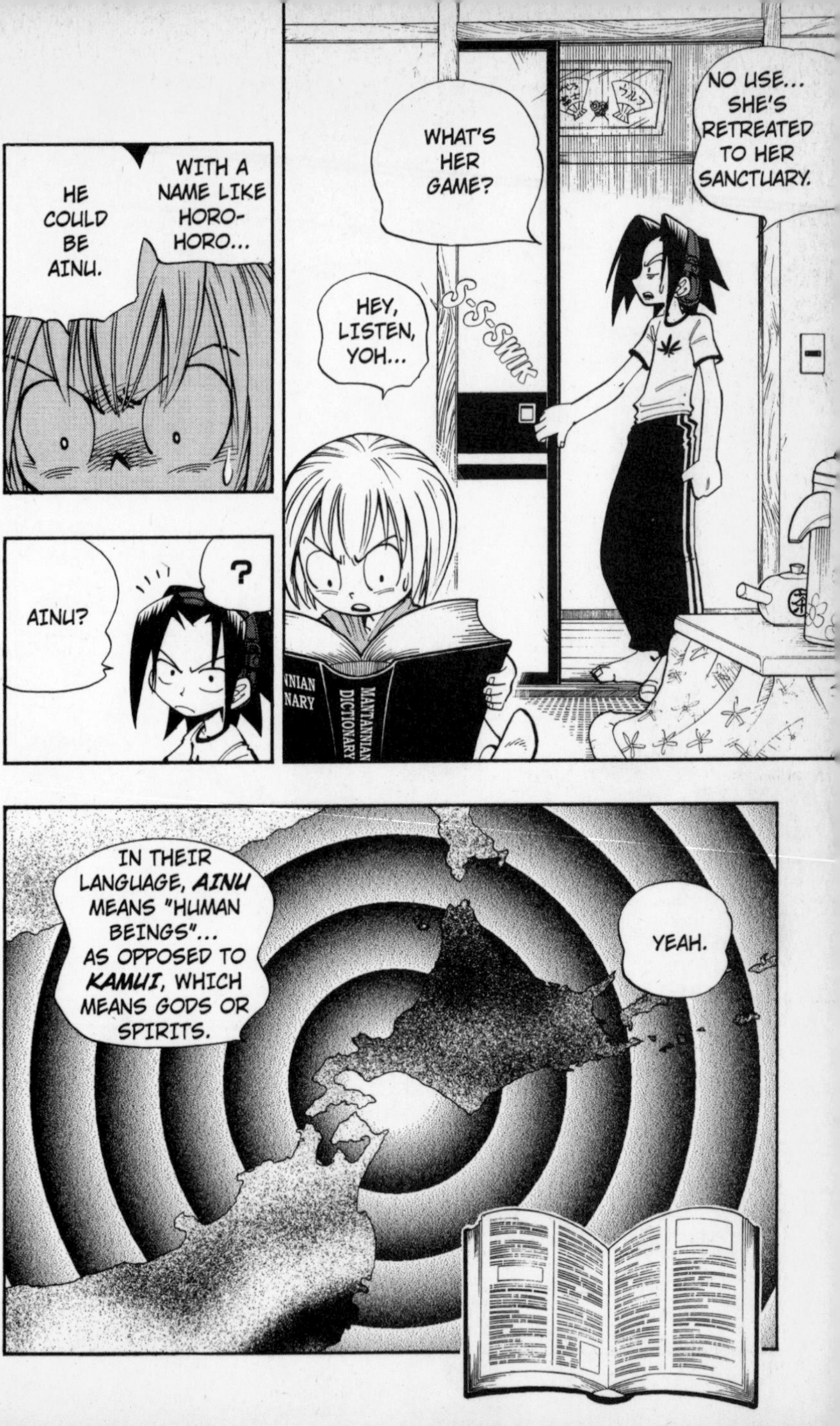
NO USE... SHE'S RETREATED TO HER SANCTUARY.
WHAT'S HER GAME?
S-S-SWIK
HEY, LISTEN, YOH...
MANTANNIAN DICTIONARY
WITH A NAME LIKE HORO-HORO...
HE COULD BE AINU.
?
AINU?
IN THEIR LANGUAGE, AINU MEANS "HUMAN BEINGS"... AS OPPOSED TO KAMUI, WHICH MEANS GODS OR SPIRITS.
YEAH.

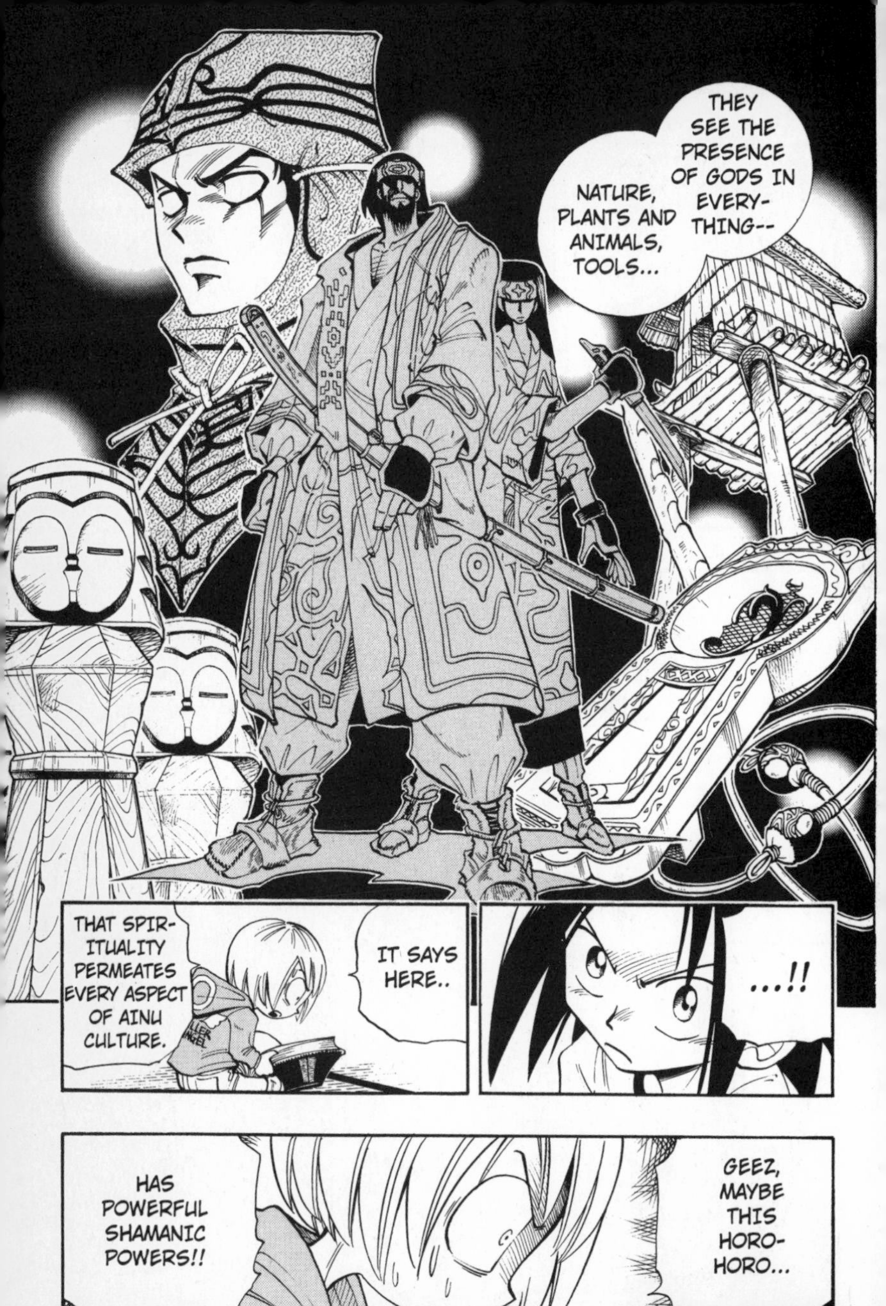
THEY SEE THE PRESENCE OF GODS IN EVERY-THING--
NATURE, PLANTS AND ANIMALS, TOOLS...
...!!
IT SAYS HERE..
THAT SPIR-ITUALITY PERMEATES EVERY ASPECT OF AINU CULTURE.
GEEZ, MAYBE THIS HORO-HORO...
HAS POWERFUL SHAMANIC POWERS!!

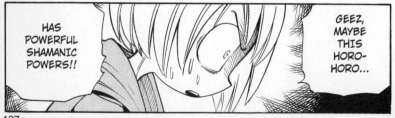

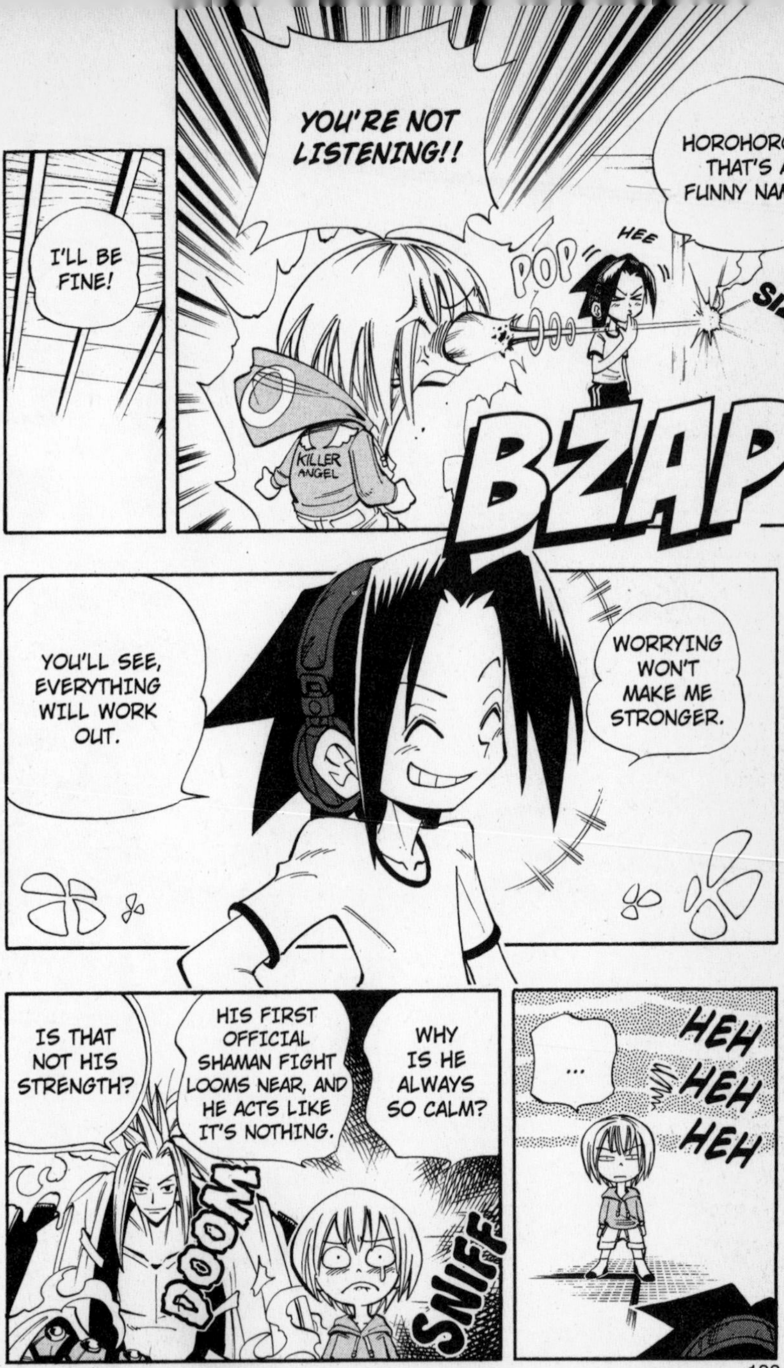
HOROHORO-- THAT'S A FUNNY NAME.
YOU'RE NOT LISTENING!!
HEE
POP
SIZZ
KILLER ANGEL
BZAP
I'LL BE FINE!
WORRYING WON'T MAKE ME STRONGER.
YOU'LL SEE, EVERYTHING WILL WORK OUT.
...
HEH HEH HEH
WHY IS HE ALWAYS SO CALM?
HIS FIRST OFFICIAL SHAMAN FIGHT LOOMS NEAR, AND HE ACTS LIKE IT'S NOTHING.
IS THAT NOT HIS STRENGTH?
DOOM
SNIFF

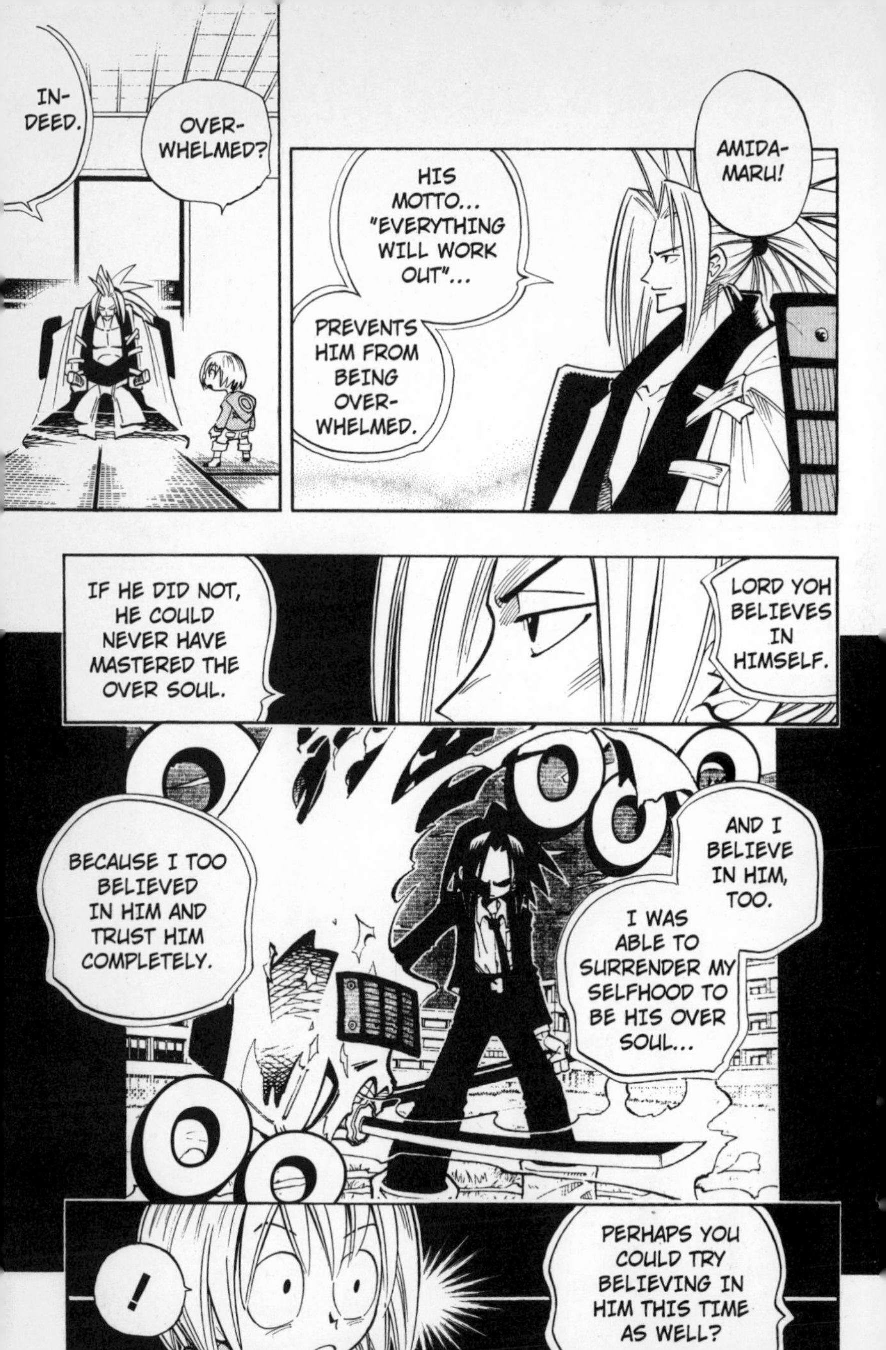
AMIDA-MARU!
HIS MOTTO... "EVERYTHING WILL WORK OUT"...
PREVENTS HIM FROM BEING OVER-WHELMED.
OVER-WHELMED?
IN-DEED.
LORD YOH BELIEVES IN HIMSELF.
IF HE DID NOT, HE COULD NEVER HAVE MASTERED THE OVER SOUL.
AND I BELIEVE IN HIM, TOO.
I WAS ABLE TO SURRENDER MY SELFHOOD TO BE HIS OVER SOUL...
BECAUSE I TOO BELIEVED IN HIM AND TRUST HIM COMPLETELY.
PERHAPS YOU COULD TRY BELIEVING IN HIM THIS TIME AS WELL?
!

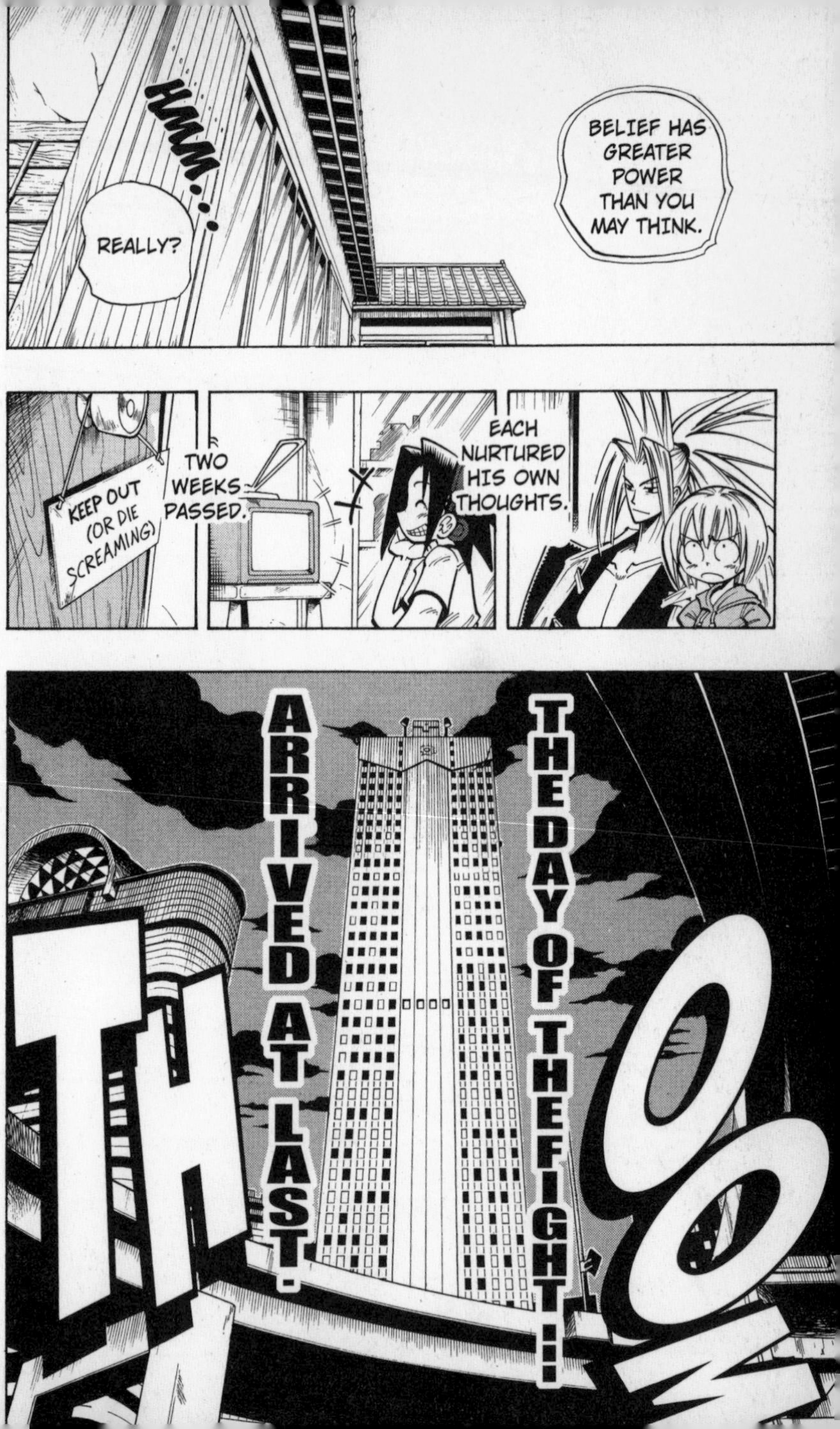

BELIEF HAS GREATER POWER THAN YOU MAY THINK.
HMMM...
REALLY?
EACH NURTURED HIS OWN THOUGHTS.
TWO WEEKS PASSED.
KEEP OUT (OR DIE SCREAMING)
THE DAY OF THE FIGHT...
ARRIVED AT LAST.
THOOM

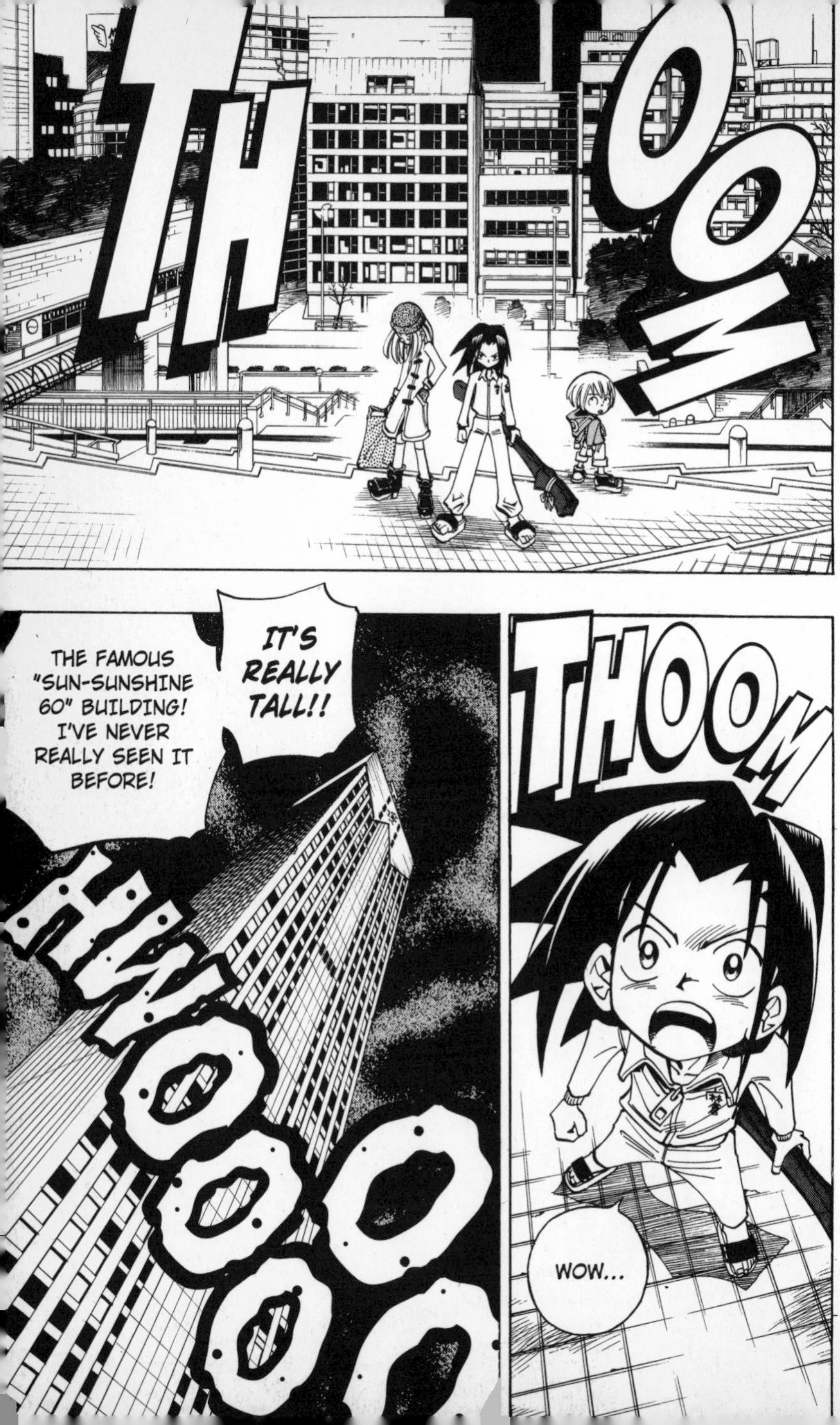
THOOM
THOOM
WOW...
IT'S REALLY TALL!!
THE FAMOUS "SUN-SUNSHINE 60" BUILDING! I'VE NEVER REALLY SEEN IT BEFORE!

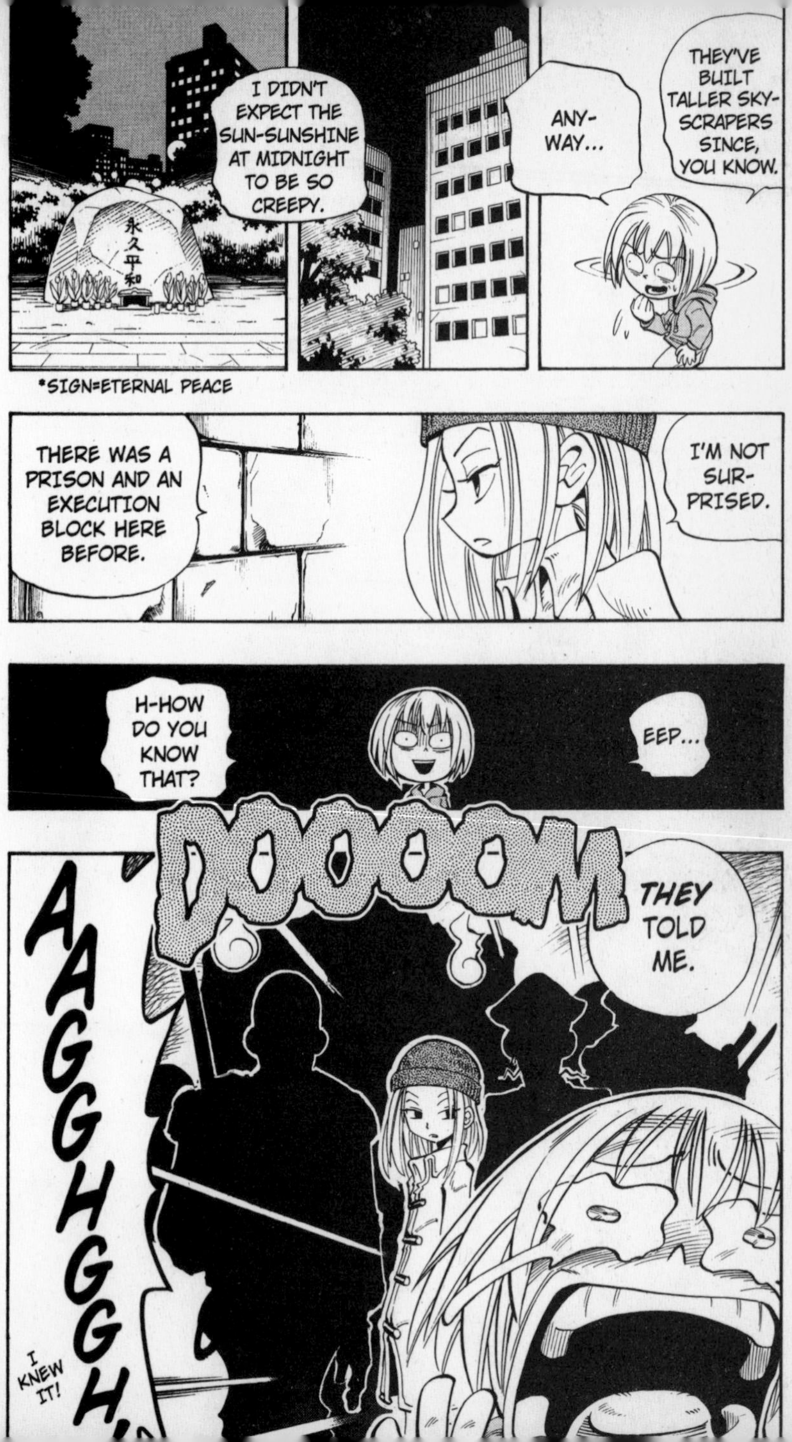
THEY'VE BUILT TALLER SKY-SCRAPERS SINCE, YOU KNOW.
ANY-WAY...
I DIDN'T EXPECT THE SUN-SUNSHINE AT MIDNIGHT TO BE SO CREEPY.
永久平和
*SIGN=ETERNAL PEACE
I'M NOT SUR-PRISED.
THERE WAS A PRISON AND AN EXECUTION BLOCK HERE BEFORE.
EEP...
H-HOW DO YOU KNOW THAT?
DOOOOM
THEY TOLD ME.
AAGGHGGGH!
I KNEW IT!

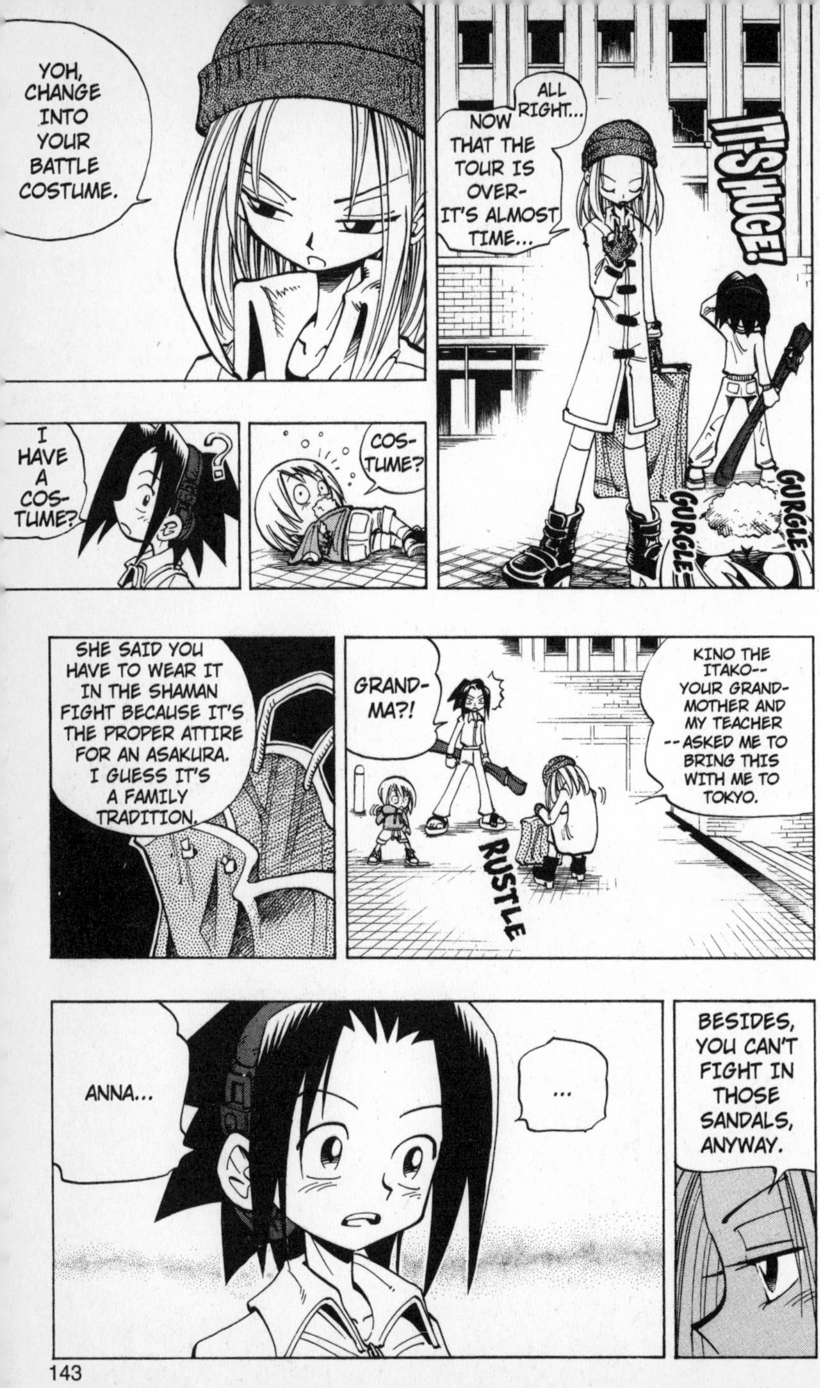
ALL RIGHT...
NOW THAT THE TOUR IS OVER- IT'S ALMOST TIME...
IT'S HUGE!
GURGLE
GURGLE
YOH, CHANGE INTO YOUR BATTLE COSTUME.
COS-TUME?
I HAVE A COS-TUME?
KINO THE ITAKO-- YOUR GRAND-MOTHER AND MY TEACHER --ASKED ME TO BRING THIS WITH ME TO TOKYO.
GRAND-MA?!
RUSTLE
SHE SAID YOU HAVE TO WEAR IT IN THE SHAMAN FIGHT BECAUSE IT'S THE PROPER ATTIRE FOR AN ASAKURA. I GUESS IT'S A FAMILY TRADITION.
BESIDES, YOU CAN'T FIGHT IN THOSE SANDALS, ANYWAY.
...
ANNA...

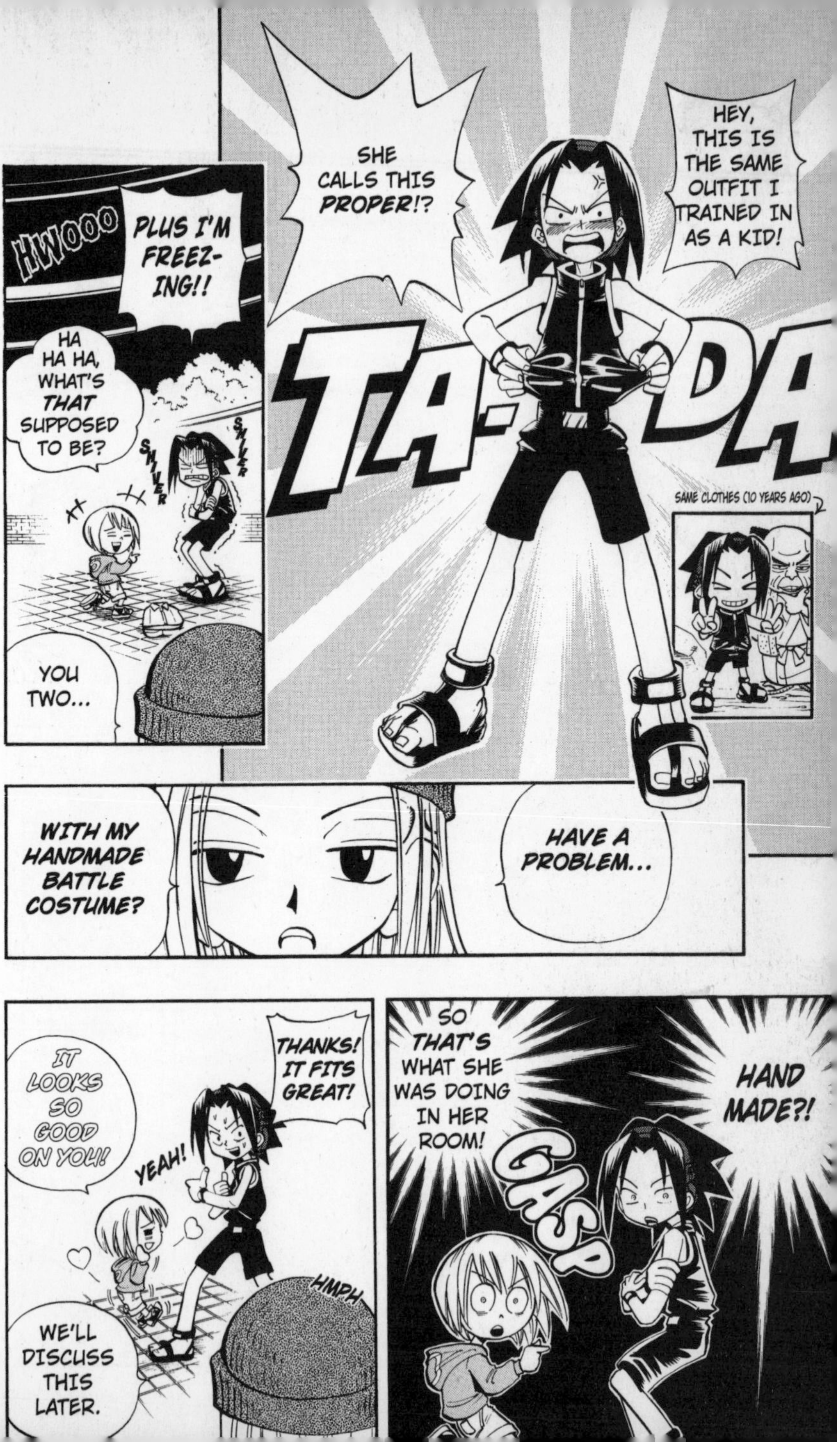
HEY, THIS IS THE SAME OUTFIT I TRAINED IN AS A KID!
SHE CALLS THIS PROPER!?
TA-DA
SAME CLOTHES (10 YEARS AGO)
HWOOO
PLUS I'M FREEZ-ING!!
HA HA HA, WHAT'S THAT SUPPOSED TO BE?
SHIVER
SHIVER
YOU TWO...
HAVE A PROBLEM...
WITH MY HANDMADE BATTLE COSTUME?
HAND MADE?!
SO THAT'S WHAT SHE WAS DOING IN HER ROOM!
GASP
THANKS! IT FITS GREAT!
IT LOOKS SO GOOD ON YOU!
YEAH!
HMPH
WE'LL DISCUSS THIS LATER.

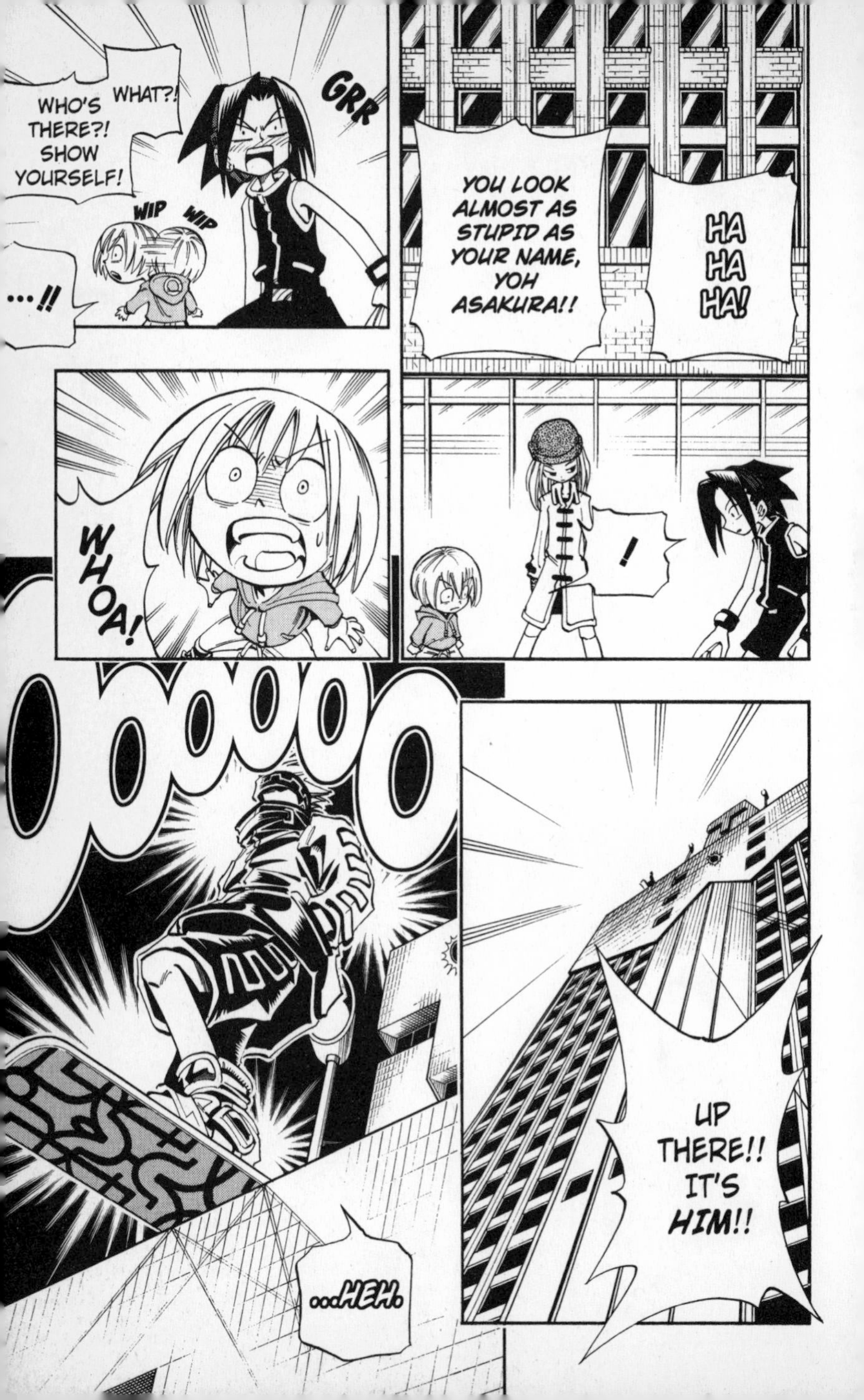

HA HA HA!
YOU LOOK ALMOST AS STUPID AS YOUR NAME, YOH ASAKURA!!
GRR
WHAT?!
WHO'S THERE?! SHOW YOURSELF!
WIP WIP
...!!
!
WHOA!
UP THERE!! IT'S HIM!!
...HEH...

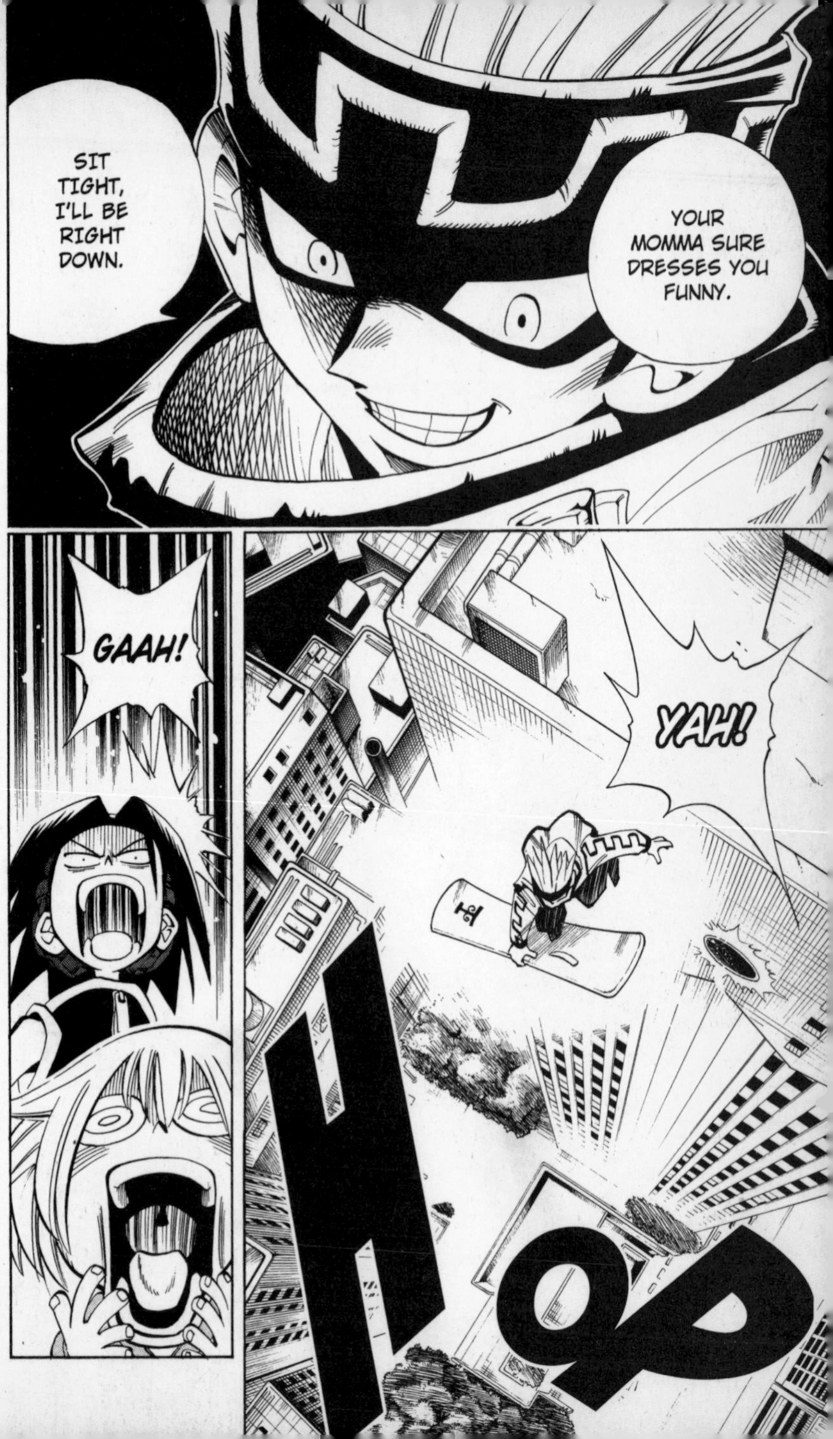
YOUR MOMMA SURE DRESSES YOU FUNNY.
SIT TIGHT, I'LL BE RIGHT DOWN.
YAH!
HOP
GAAH!

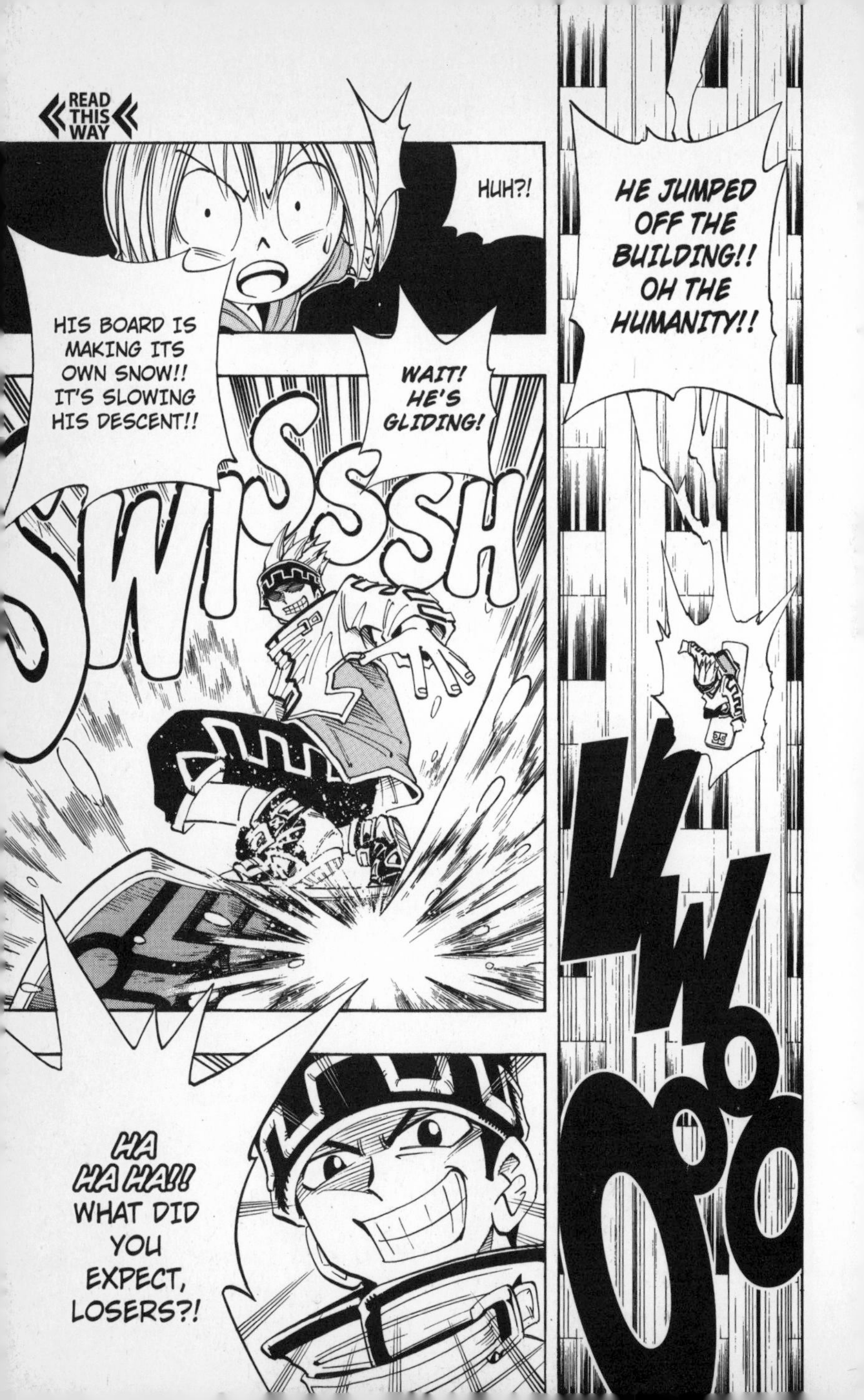
READ THIS WAY
HE JUMPED OFF THE BUILDING!! OH THE HUMANITY!!
HUH?!
WAIT! HE'S GLIDING!
HIS BOARD IS MAKING ITS OWN SNOW!! IT'S SLOWING HIS DESCENT!!
SWISSH
HA HA HA!! WHAT DID YOU EXPECT, LOSERS?!

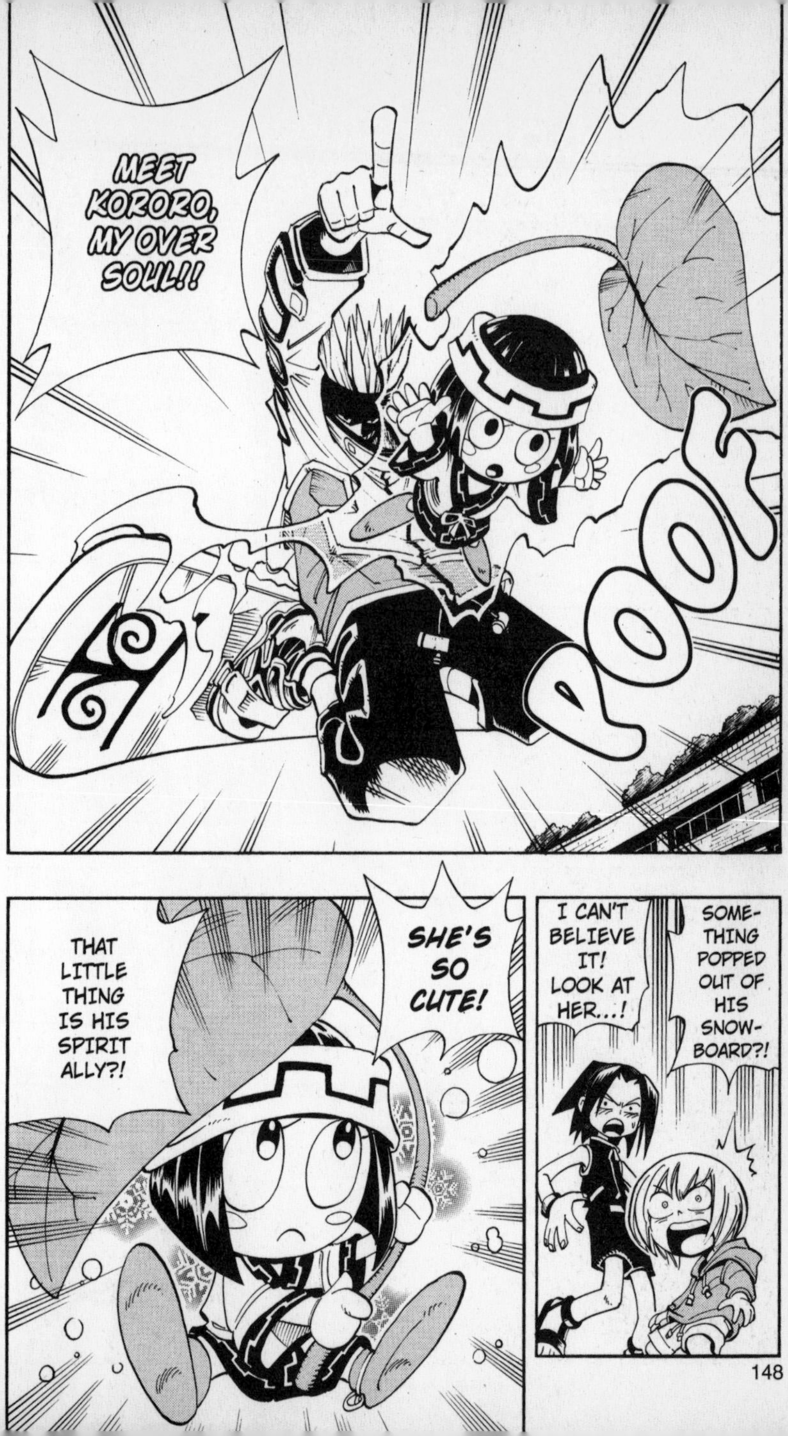
MEET KORORO, MY OVER SOUL!!
POOF
SOMETHING POPPED OUT OF HIS SNOWBOARD?!
I CAN'T BELIEVE IT! LOOK AT HER...!
SHE'S SO CUTE!
THAT LITTLE THING IS HIS SPIRIT ALLY?!

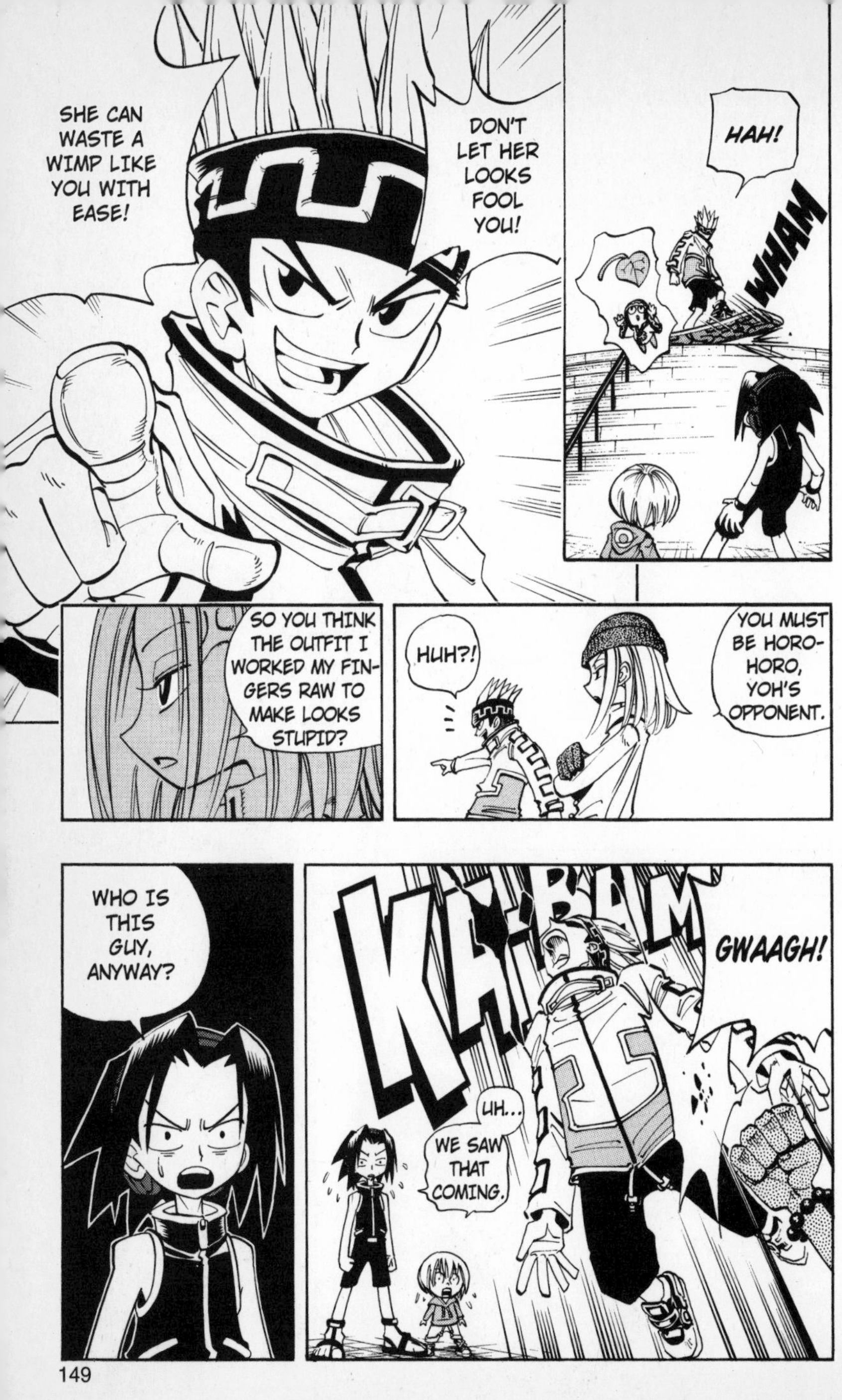
HAH!
WHAM
DON'T LET HER LOOKS FOOL YOU!
SHE CAN WASTE A WIMP LIKE YOU WITH EASE!
YOU MUST BE HORO-HORO, YOH'S OPPONENT.
HUH?!
SO YOU THINK THE OUTFIT I WORKED MY FINGERS RAW TO MAKE LOOKS STUPID?
KA-BAM
GWAAGH!
UH...
WE SAW THAT COMING.
WHO IS THIS GUY, ANYWAY?

SHAMAN KING CHARACTER FILE No.17

カリム

kalim

1999

(JULY)

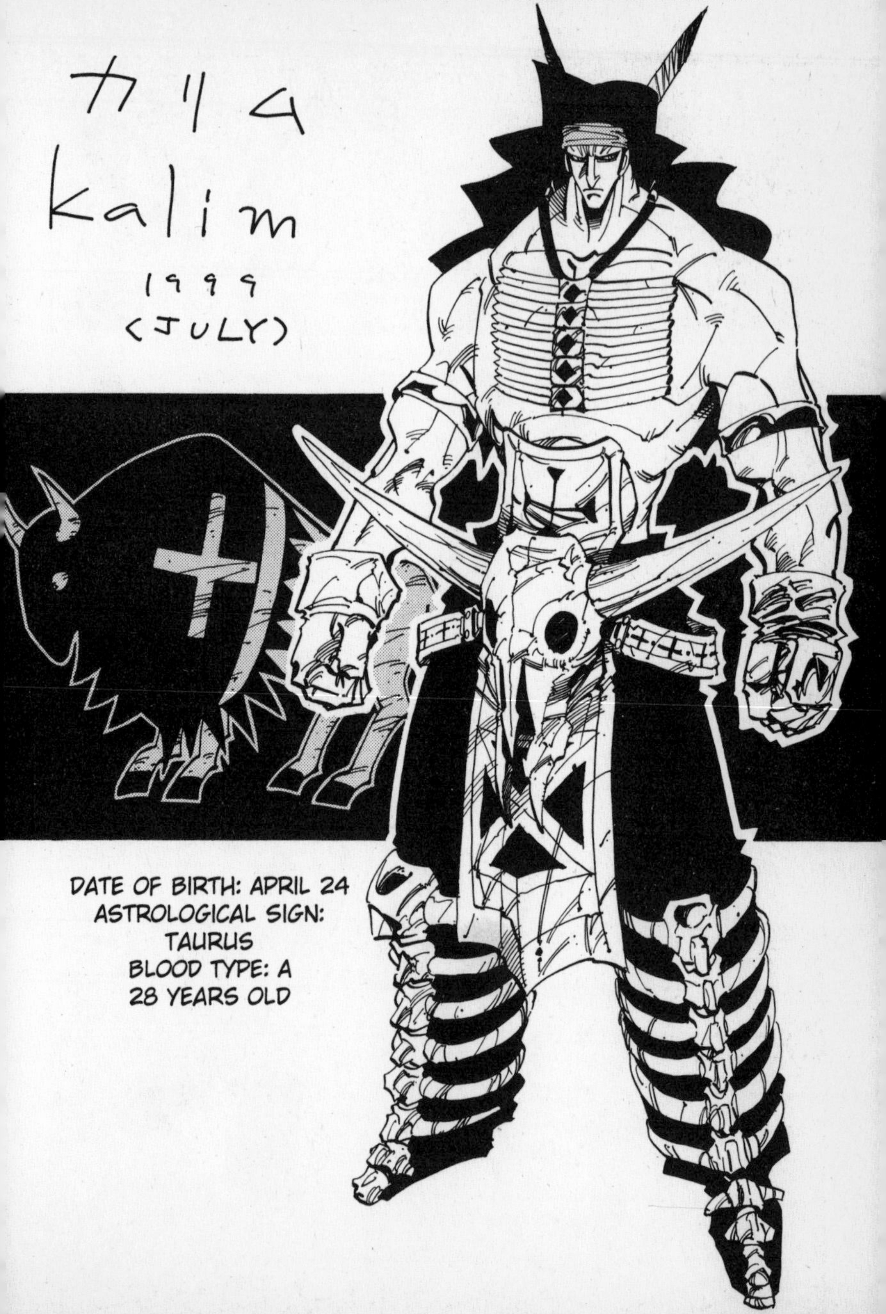

DATE OF BIRTH: APRIL 24

ASTROLOGICAL SIGN: TAURUS

BLOOD TYPE: A

28 YEARS OLD

Reincarnation 34: The Powers Of Kororo

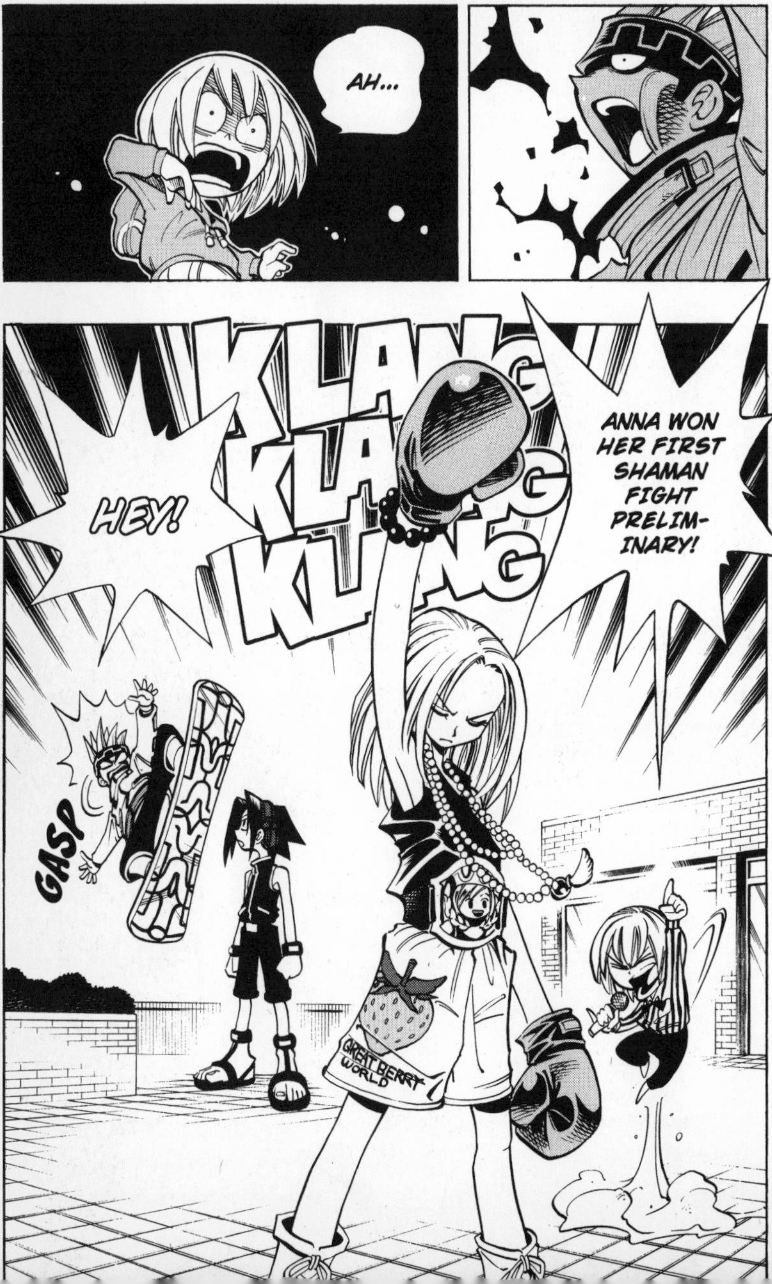
AH...
ANNA WON HER FIRST SHAMAN FIGHT PRELIM-INARY!
KLANG
KLANG
KLING
HEY!
GASP

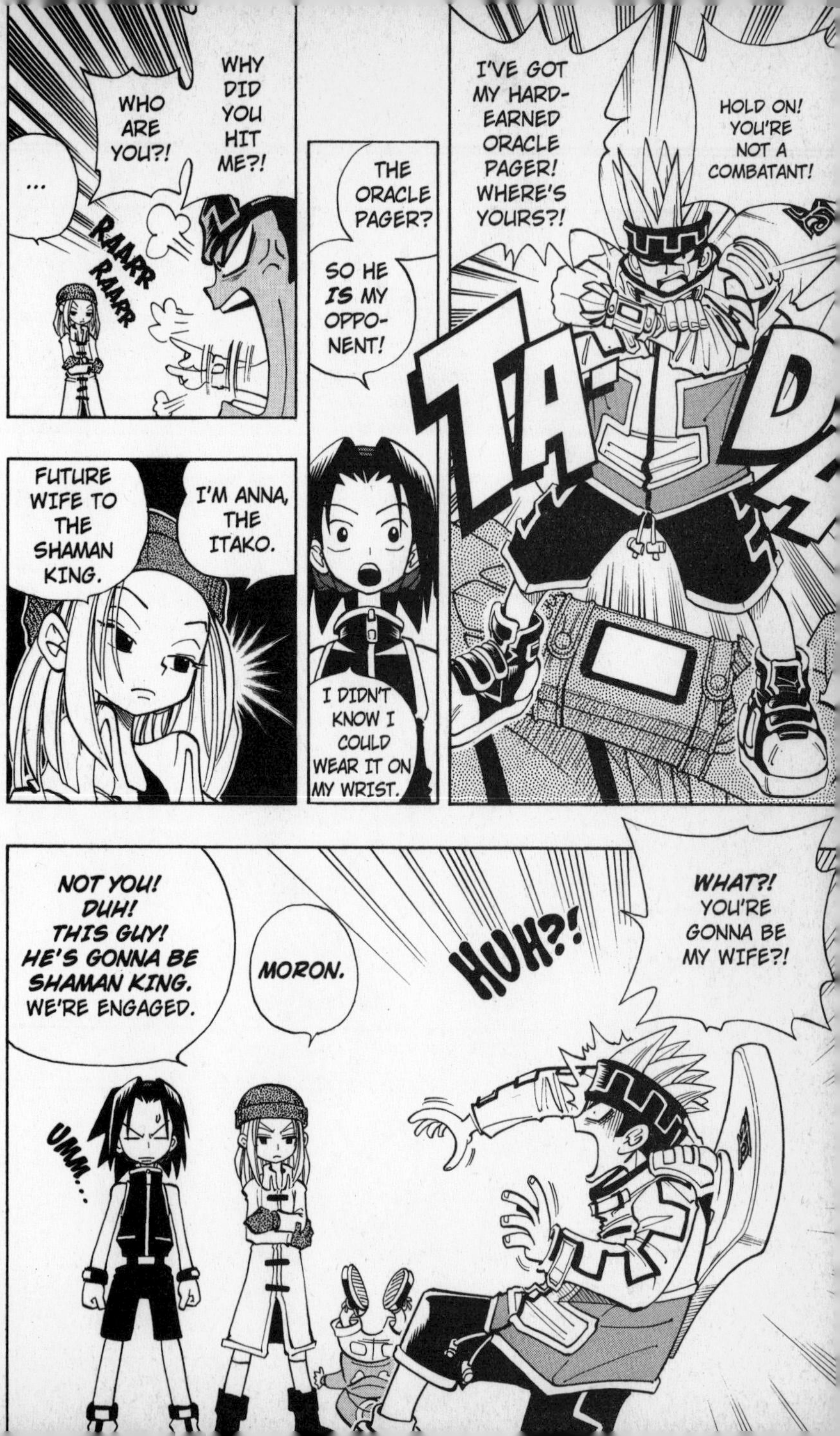
HOLD ON! YOU'RE NOT A COMBATANT!
I'VE GOT MY HARD-EARNED ORACLE PAGER! WHERE'S YOURS?!
TA-D
THE ORACLE PAGER?
SO HE *IS* MY OPPONENT!
I DIDN'T KNOW I COULD WEAR IT ON MY WRIST.
WHY DID YOU HIT ME?!
WHO ARE YOU?!
...
RAAARR RAAARR
I'M ANNA, THE ITAKO.
FUTURE WIFE TO THE SHAMAN KING.
WHAT?! YOU'RE GONNA BE MY WIFE?!
HUH?!
MORON.
NOT YOU! DUH! THIS GUY! HE'S GONNA BE SHAMAN KING. WE'RE ENGAGED.
UMM...

Reincarnation 34: The Powers of Kororo

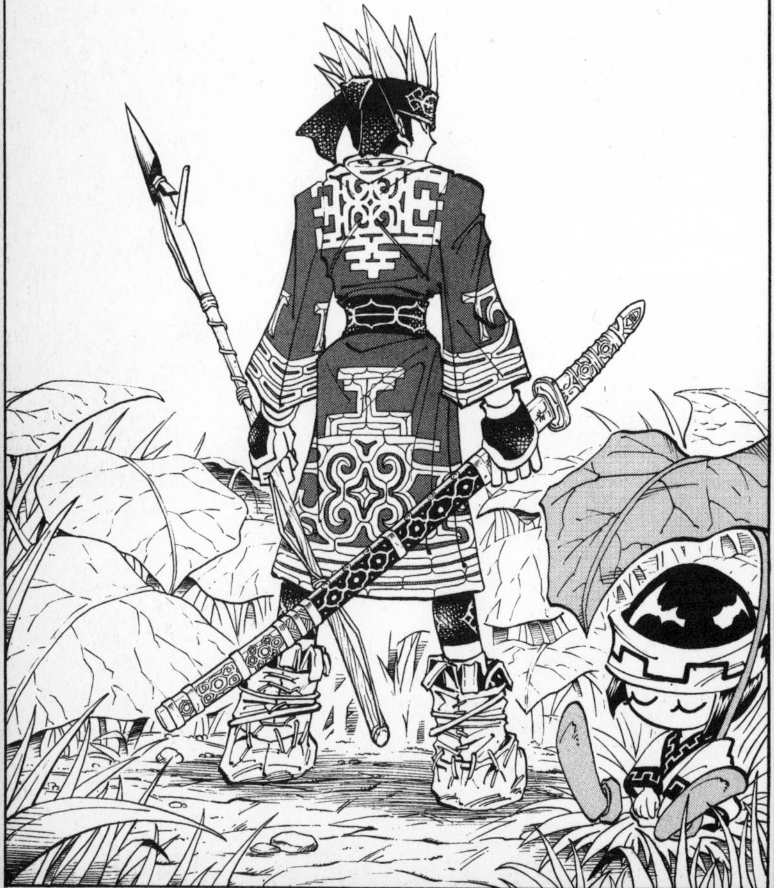

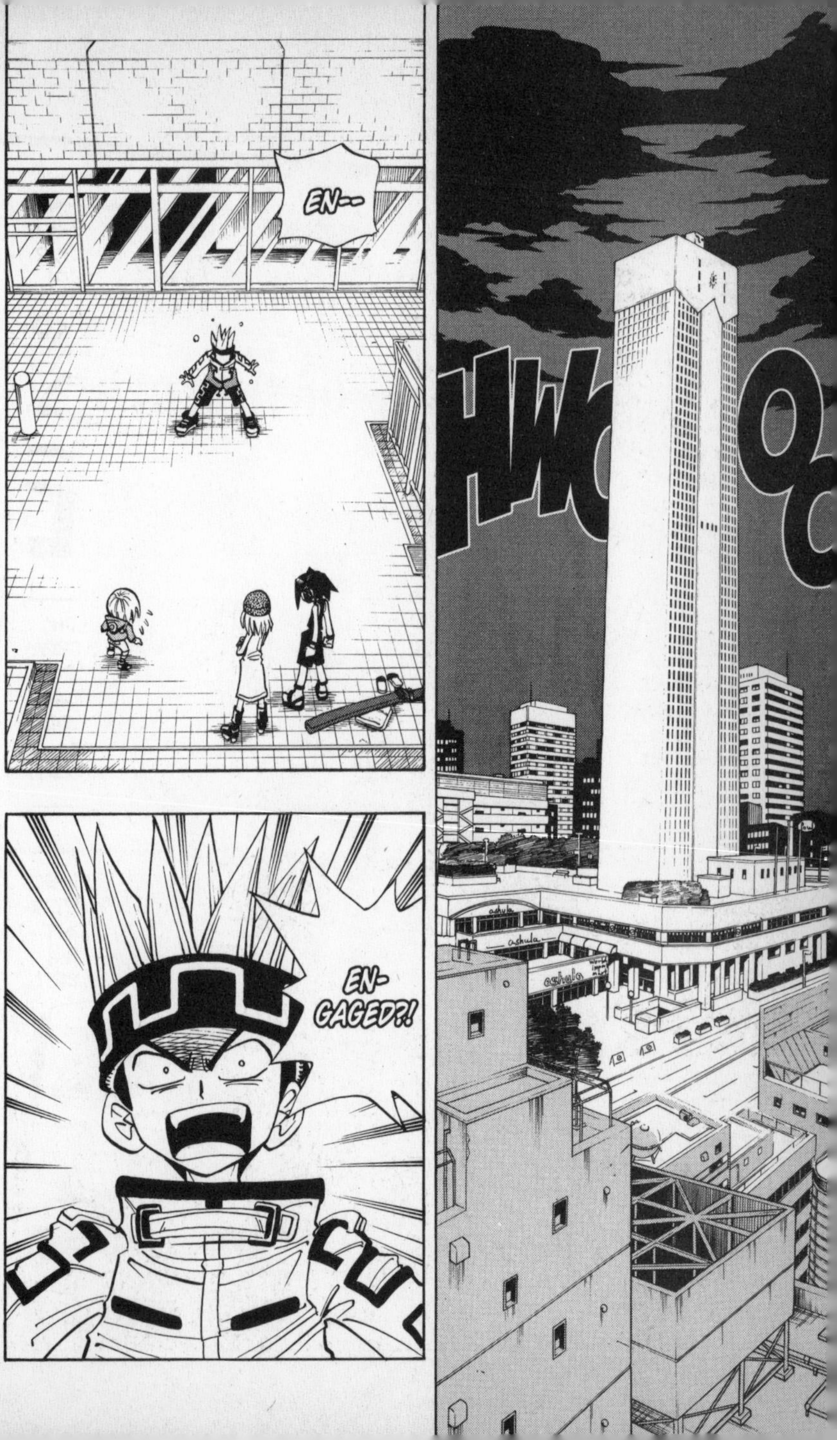
EN--
EN-GAGED?!

READ THIS WAY

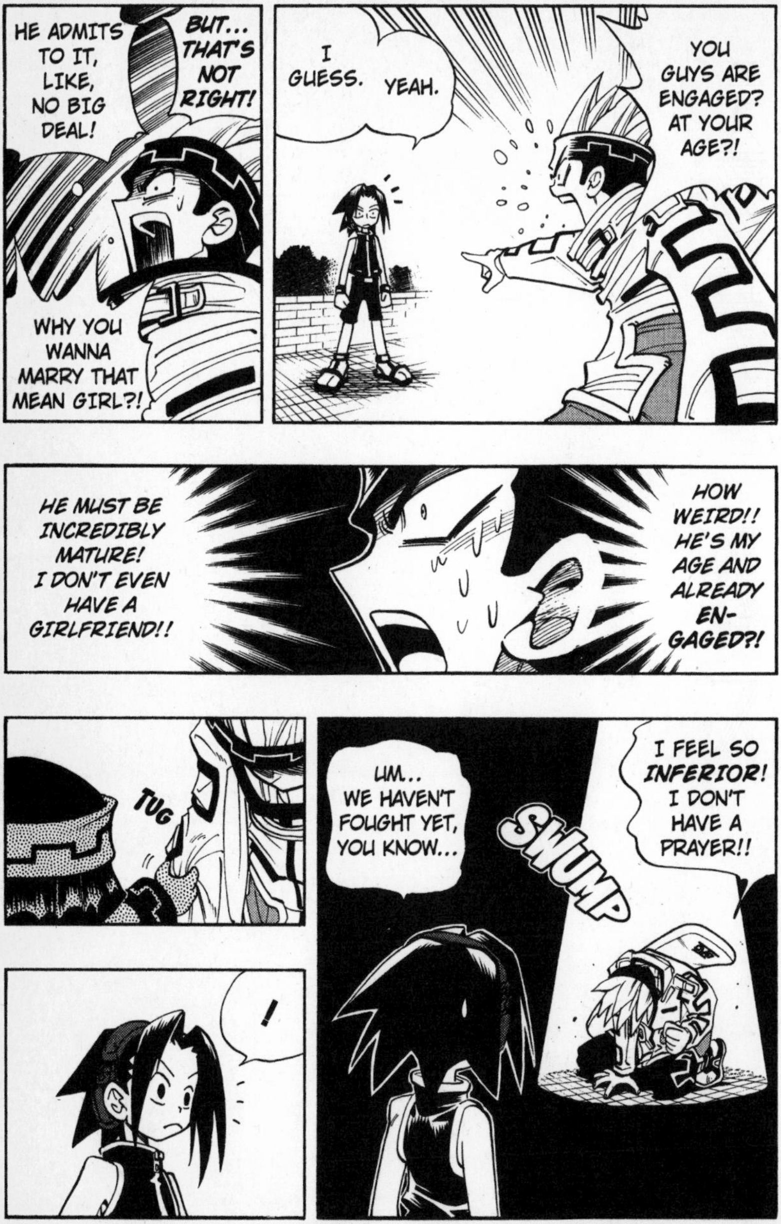
YOU GUYS ARE ENGAGED? AT YOUR AGE?!
I GUESS.
YEAH.
BUT... THAT'S NOT RIGHT!
HE ADMITS TO IT, LIKE, NO BIG DEAL!
WHY YOU WANNA MARRY THAT MEAN GIRL?!
HOW WEIRD!! HE'S MY AGE AND ALREADY EN-GAGED?!
HE MUST BE INCREDIBLY MATURE! I DON'T EVEN HAVE A GIRLFRIEND!!
I FEEL SO INFERIOR! I DON'T HAVE A PRAYER!!
SWUMP
UM... WE HAVEN'T FOUGHT YET, YOU KNOW...
TUG
!

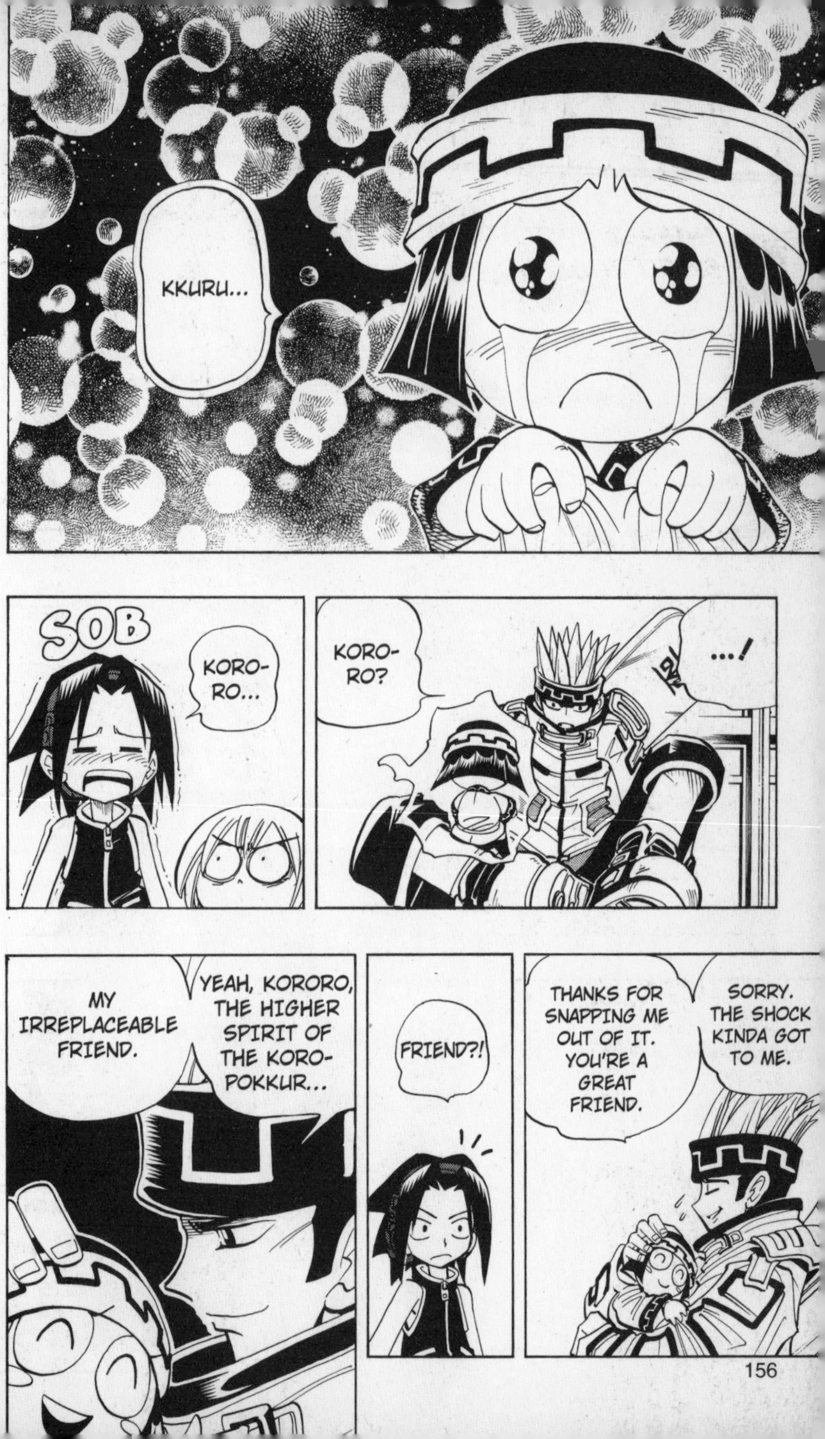
KKURU...
...!
KORO-RO?
SOB
KORO-RO...
SORRY. THE SHOCK KINDA GOT TO ME.
THANKS FOR SNAPPING ME OUT OF IT. YOU'RE A GREAT FRIEND.
FRIEND?!
YEAH, KORORO, THE HIGHER SPIRIT OF THE KORO-POKKUR...
MY IRREPLACEABLE FRIEND.

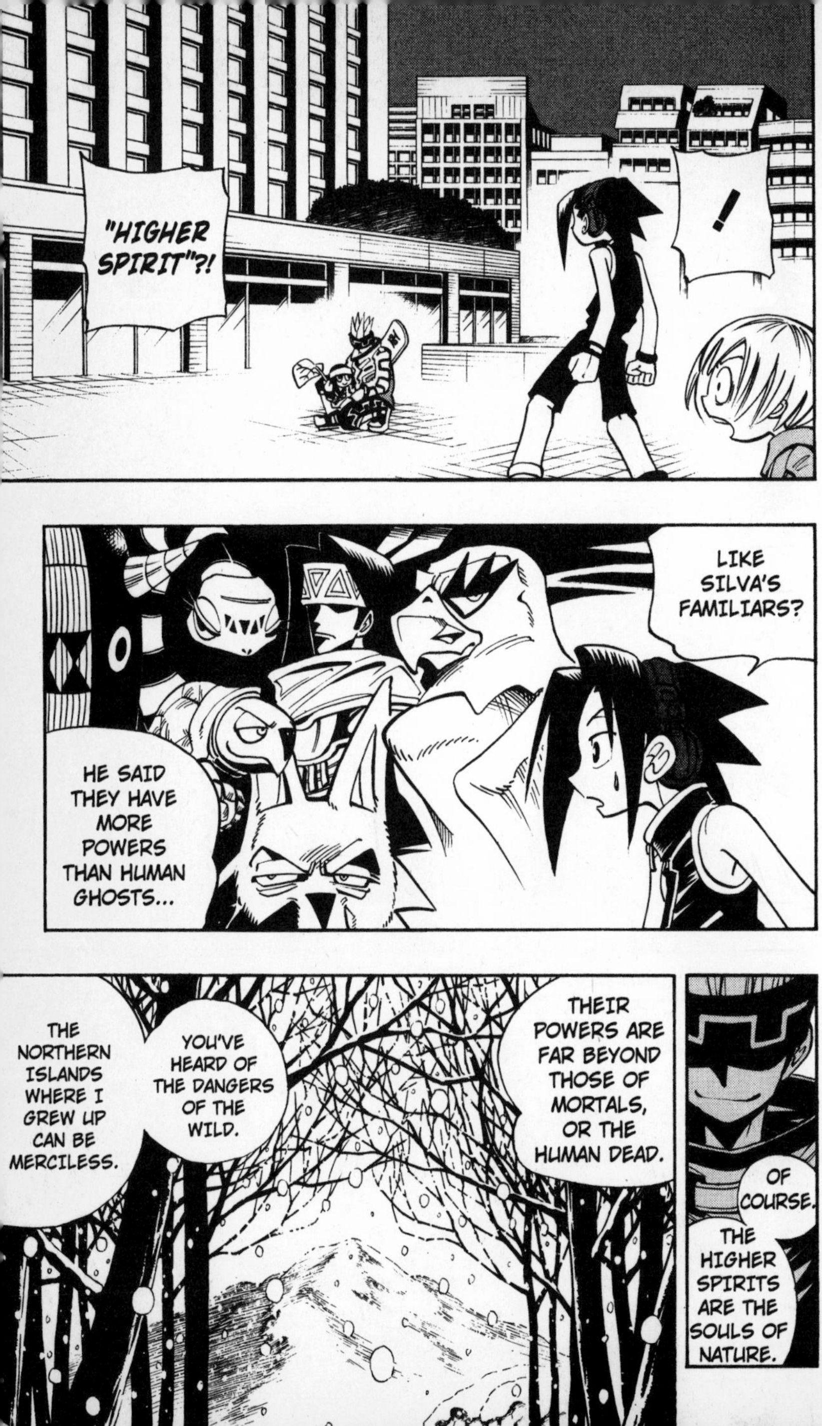
!
"HIGHER SPIRIT"?!
LIKE SILVA'S FAMILIARS?
HE SAID THEY HAVE MORE POWERS THAN HUMAN GHOSTS...
OF COURSE.
THE HIGHER SPIRITS ARE THE SOULS OF NATURE.
THEIR POWERS ARE FAR BEYOND THOSE OF MORTALS, OR THE HUMAN DEAD.
YOU'VE HEARD OF THE DANGERS OF THE WILD.
THE NORTHERN ISLANDS WHERE I GREW UP CAN BE MERCILESS.

READ THIS WAY

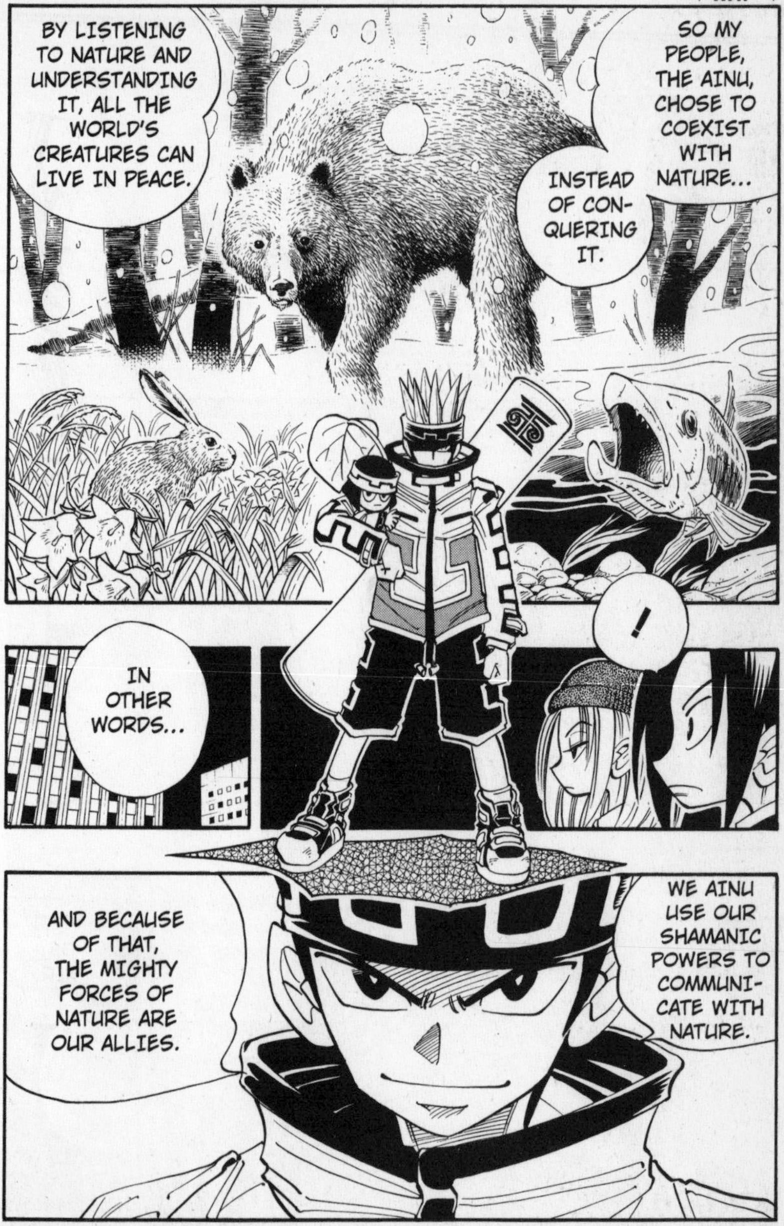

SO MY PEOPLE, THE AINU, CHOSE TO COEXIST WITH NATURE...
INSTEAD OF CON-QUERING IT.
BY LISTENING TO NATURE AND UNDERSTANDING IT, ALL THE WORLD'S CREATURES CAN LIVE IN PEACE.
!
IN OTHER WORDS...
WE AINU USE OUR SHAMANIC POWERS TO COMMUNI-CATE WITH NATURE.
AND BECAUSE OF THAT, THE MIGHTY FORCES OF NATURE ARE OUR ALLIES.

READ THIS WAY

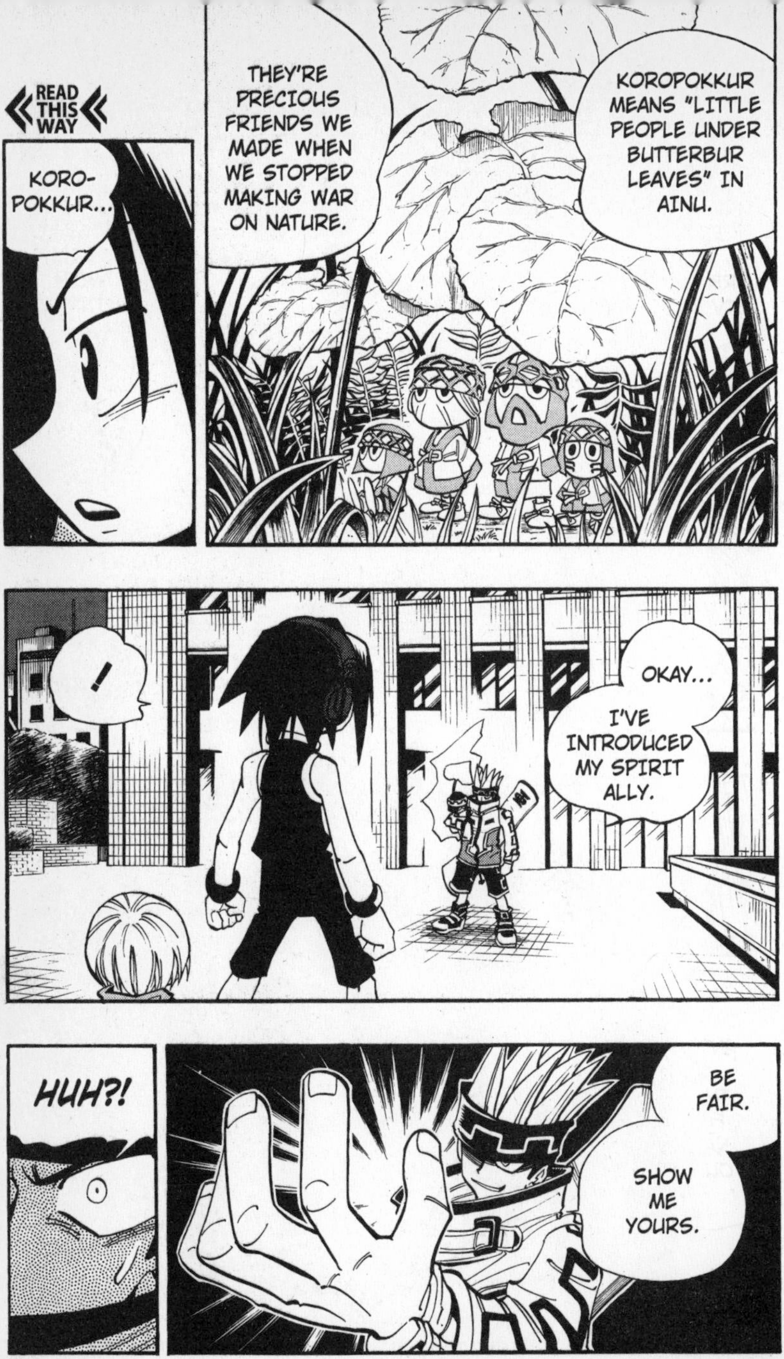

KOROPOKKUR MEANS "LITTLE PEOPLE UNDER BUTTERBUR LEAVES" IN AINU.
THEY'RE PRECIOUS FRIENDS WE MADE WHEN WE STOPPED MAKING WAR ON NATURE.
KORO-POKKUR...
OKAY...
I'VE INTRODUCED MY SPIRIT ALLY.
!
BE FAIR.
SHOW ME YOURS.
HUH?!

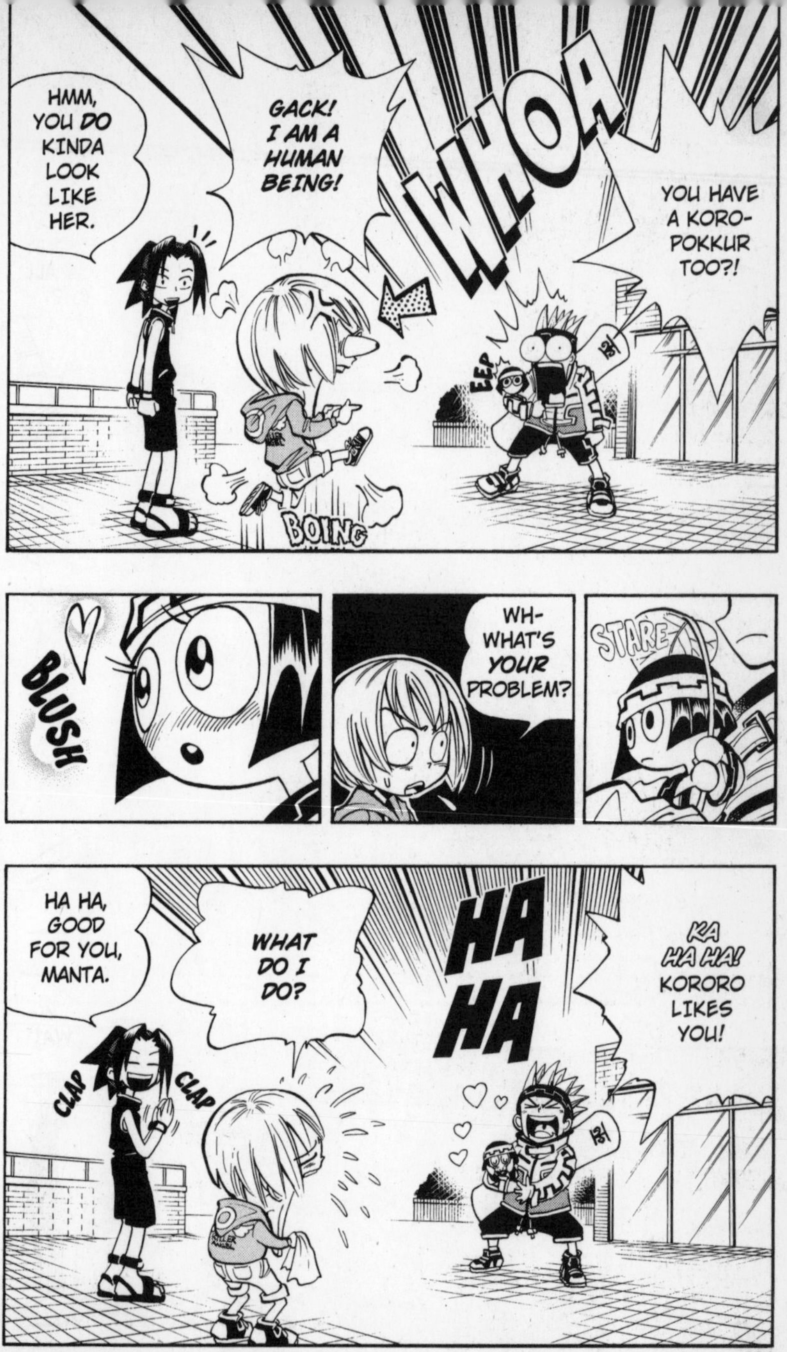
WHOA
YOU HAVE A KORO-POKKUR TOO?!
GACK! I AM A HUMAN BEING!
HMM, YOU DO KINDA LOOK LIKE HER.
EEP
BOING
STARE
WH-WHAT'S YOUR PROBLEM?
BLUSH
KA HA HA! KORORO LIKES YOU!
HA HA
WHAT DO I DO?
HA HA, GOOD FOR YOU, MANTA.
CLAP CLAP

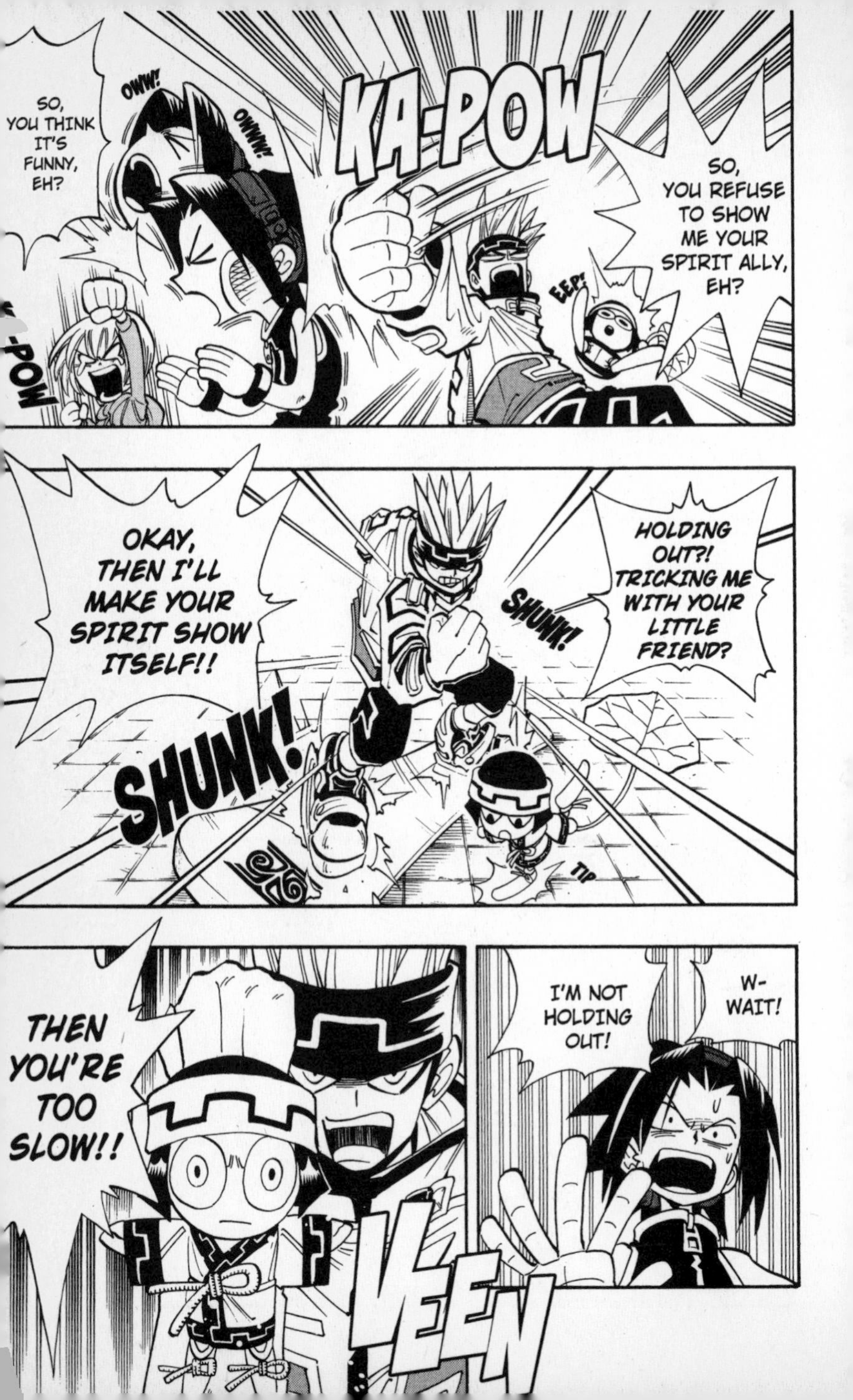
SO, YOU REFUSE TO SHOW ME YOUR SPIRIT ALLY, EH?
KA-POW
EEP!
OWWW!
OWW!
SO, YOU THINK IT'S FUNNY, EH?
-POW
HOLDING OUT?! TRICKING ME WITH YOUR LITTLE FRIEND?
SHUNK!
OKAY, THEN I'LL MAKE YOUR SPIRIT SHOW ITSELF!!
SHUNK!
TIP
W- WAIT!
I'M NOT HOLDING OUT!
THEN YOU'RE TOO SLOW!!
VEEN

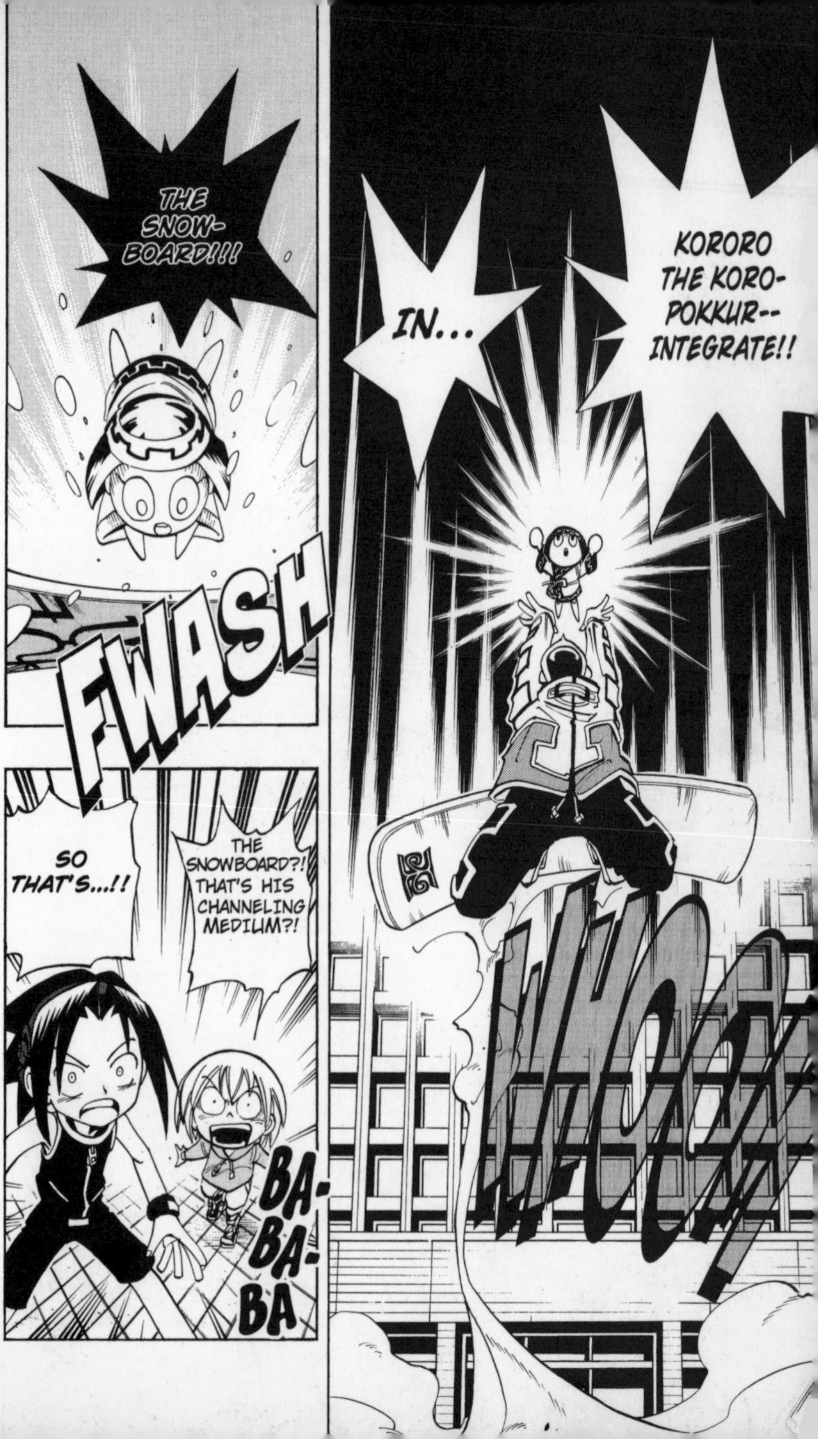
KORORO THE KORO-POKKUR-- INTEGRATE!!
IN...
THE SNOW-BOARD!!!
FWASH
THE SNOWBOARD?! THAT'S HIS CHANNELING MEDIUM?!
SO THAT'S...!!
BA-BA-BA-BA

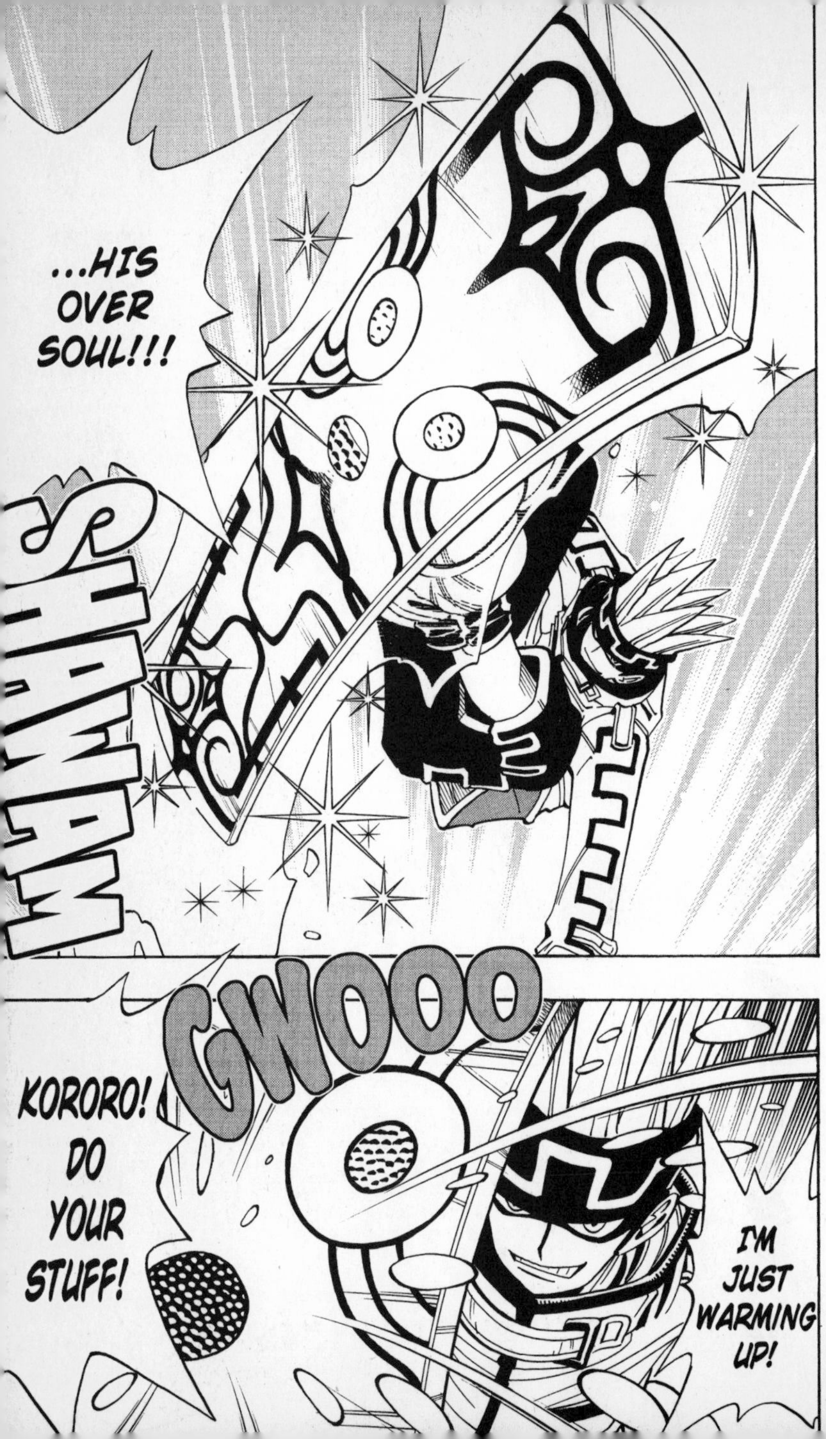
...HIS OVER SOUL!!!
SHWAM
GWOOO
I'M JUST WARMING UP!
KORORO! DO YOUR STUFF!

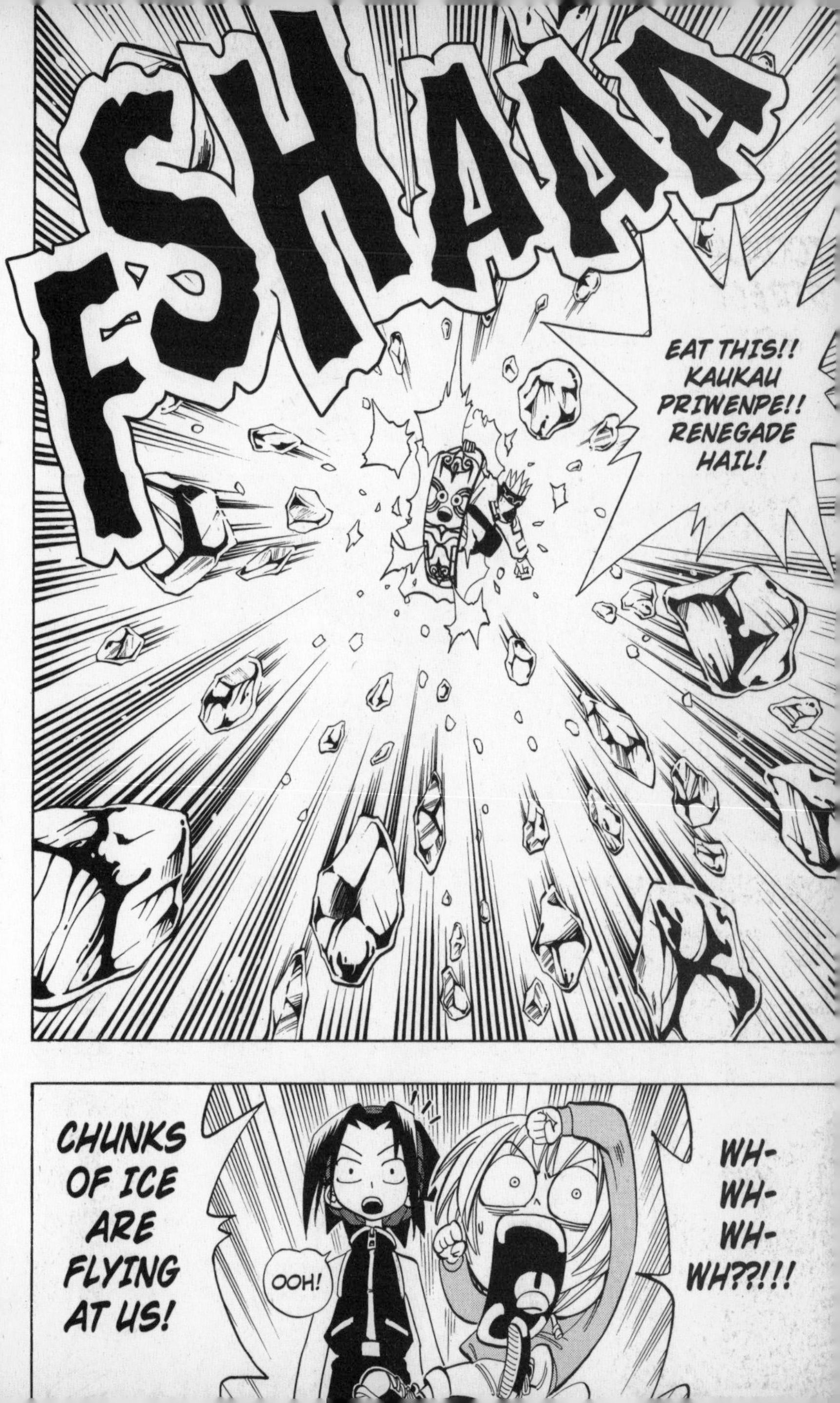
FSHAAA
EAT THIS!! KAUKAU PRIWENPE!! RENEGADE HAIL!
WH-WH-WH-WH??!!!
OOH!
CHUNKS OF ICE ARE FLYING AT US!

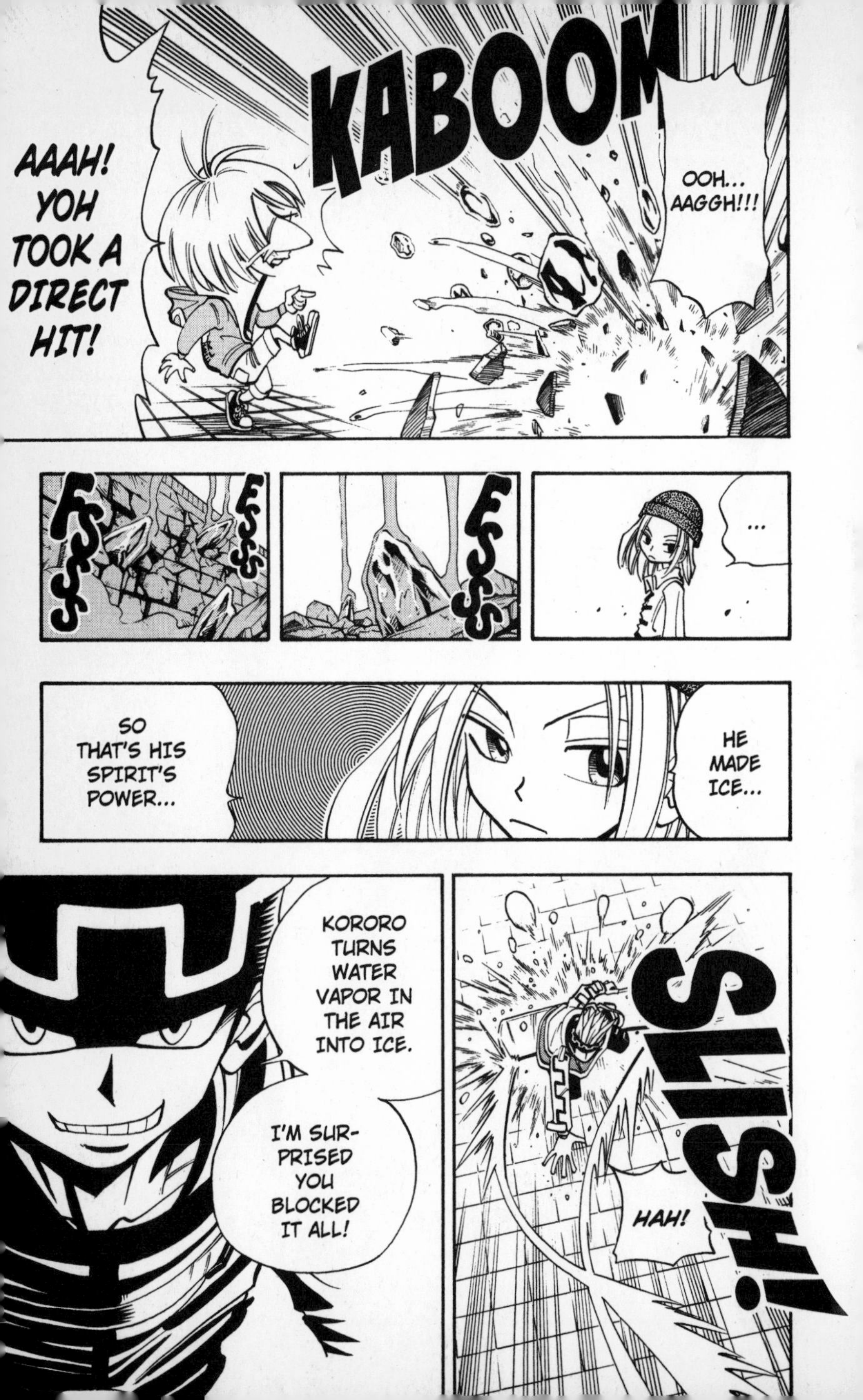
KABOOM
OOH... AAGGH!!!
AAAH! YOH TOOK A DIRECT HIT!
...
FSSS
FSSS
FSSS
HE MADE ICE...
SO THAT'S HIS SPIRIT'S POWER...
SHSH!!
HAH!
KORORO TURNS WATER VAPOR IN THE AIR INTO ICE.
I'M SUR-PRISED YOU BLOCKED IT ALL!

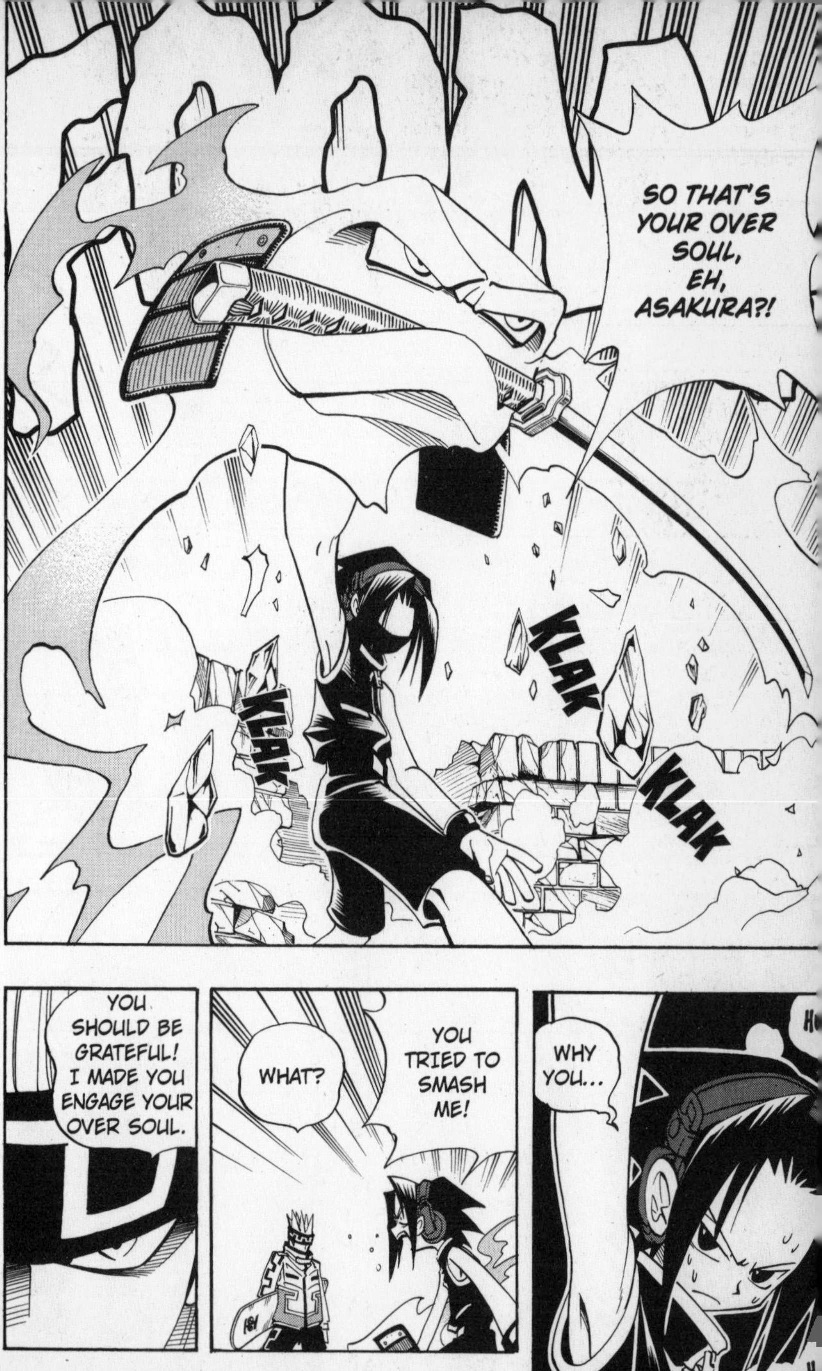
SO THAT'S YOUR OVER SOUL, EH, ASAKURA?!
KLAK
KLAK
KLAK
WHY YOU...
HUFF
YOU TRIED TO SMASH ME!
WHAT?
YOU SHOULD BE GRATEFUL! I MADE YOU ENGAGE YOUR OVER SOUL.

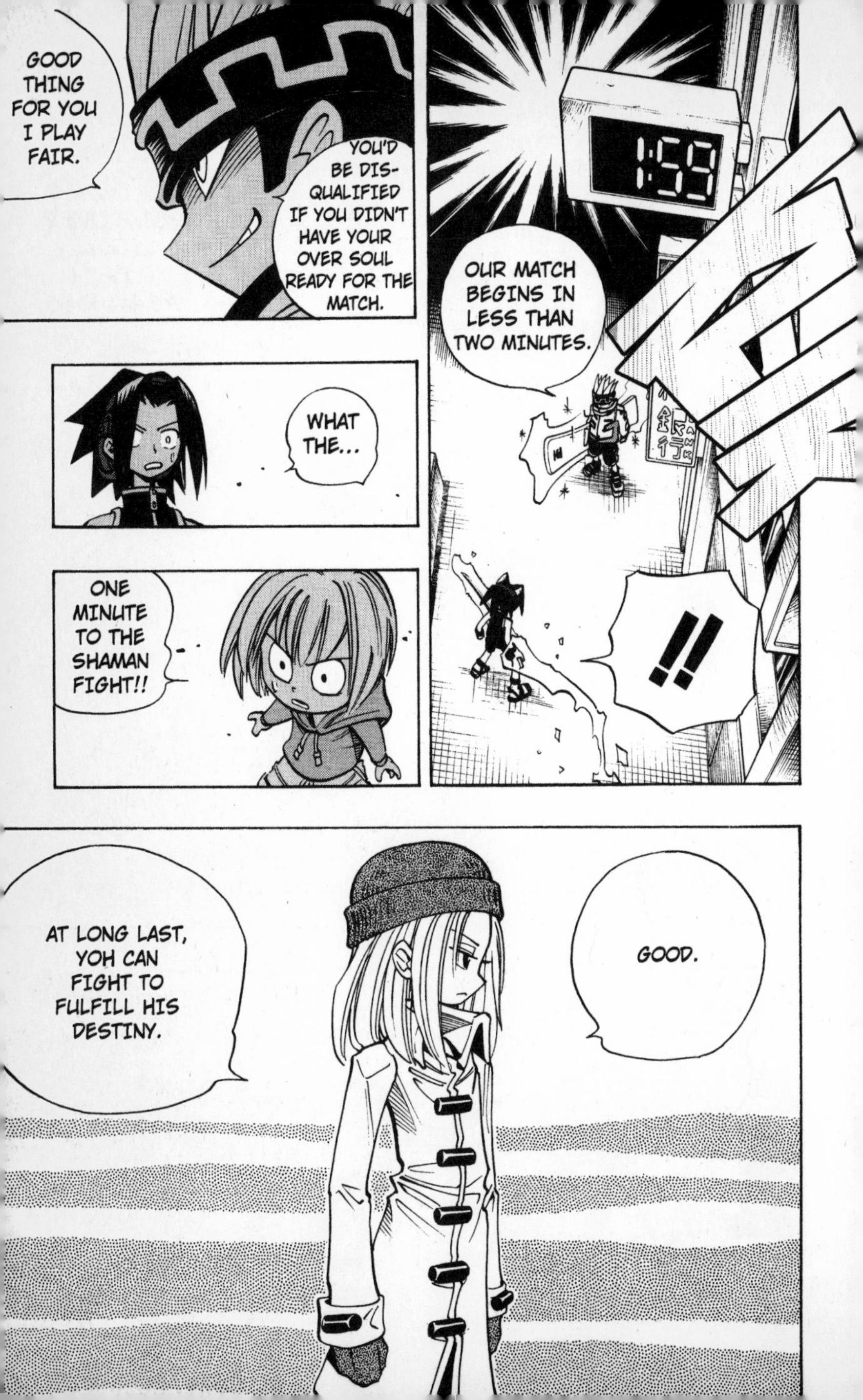
1:59
OUR MATCH BEGINS IN LESS THAN TWO MINUTES.
!!
YOU'D BE DIS-QUALIFIED IF YOU DIDN'T HAVE YOUR OVER SOUL READY FOR THE MATCH.
GOOD THING FOR YOU I PLAY FAIR.
WHAT THE...
ONE MINUTE TO THE SHAMAN FIGHT!!
GOOD.
AT LONG LAST, YOH CAN FIGHT TO FULFILL HIS DESTINY.

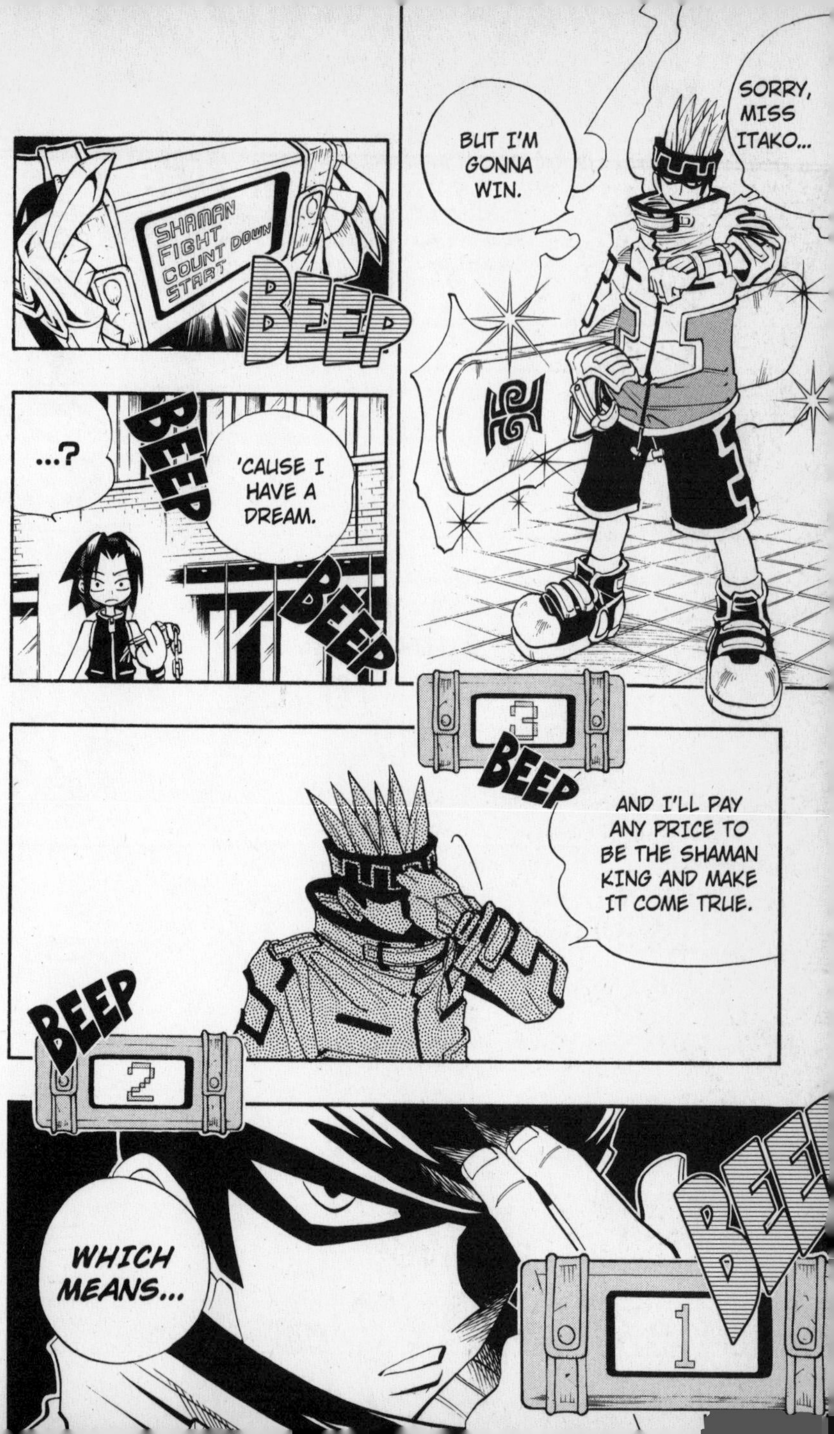
SORRY, MISS ITAKO...
BUT I'M GONNA WIN.
SHAMAN FIGHT COUNT DOWN START
BEEP
BEEP
BEEP
'CAUSE I HAVE A DREAM.
...?
3
BEEP
AND I'LL PAY ANY PRICE TO BE THE SHAMAN KING AND MAKE IT COME TRUE.
BEEP
2
BEE
1
WHICH MEANS...

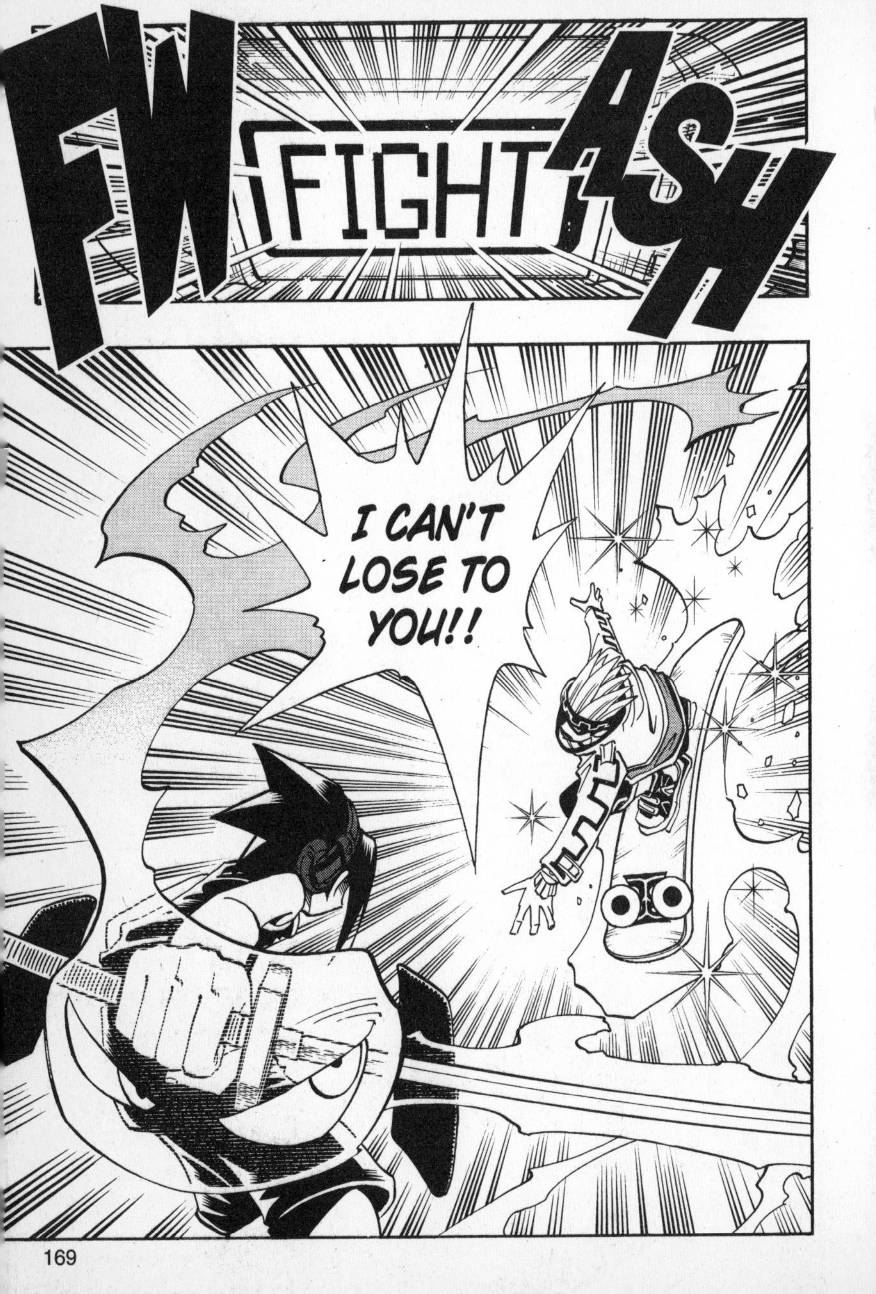
FWASH
FIGHT
I CAN'T LOSE TO YOU!!

SHAMAN KING CHARACTER FILE No.18

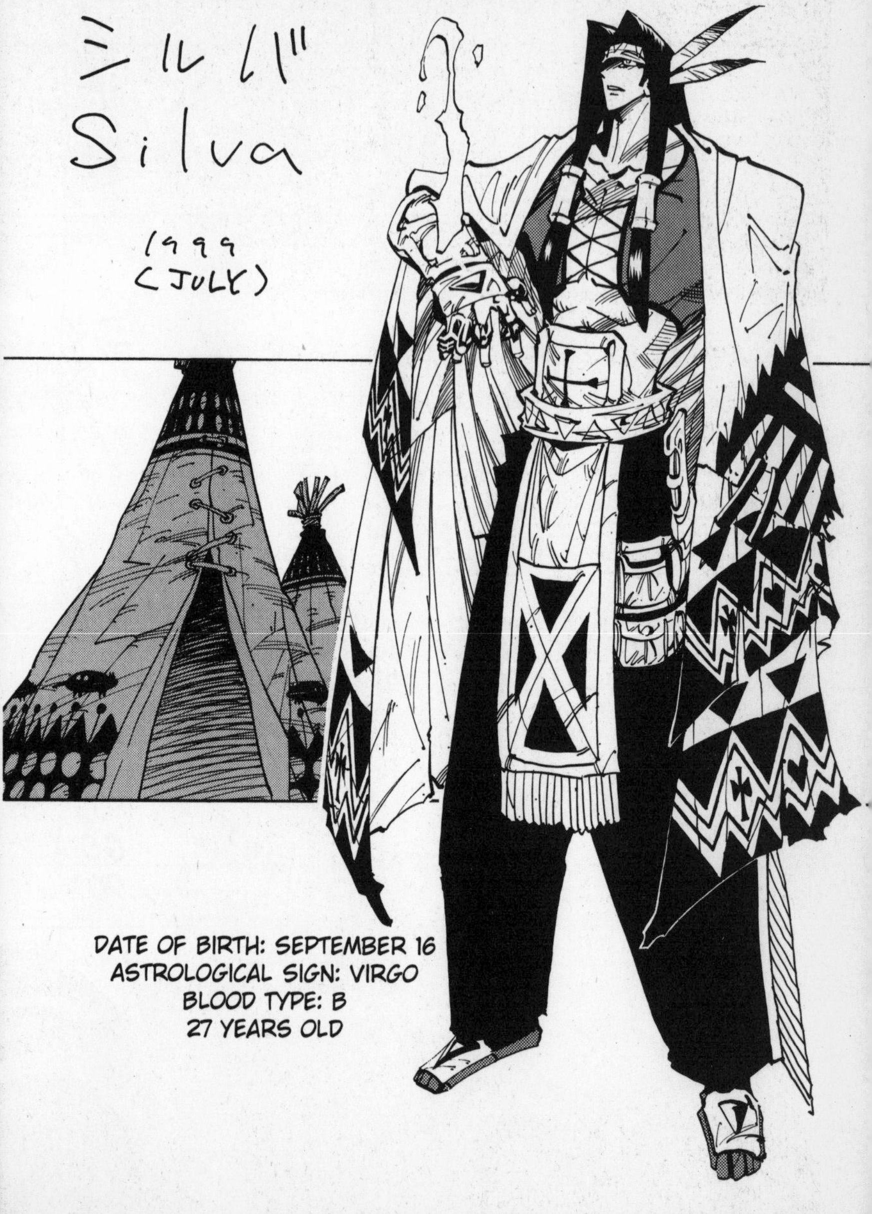
シルバ
Silva
1999
(JULY)

DATE OF BIRTH: SEPTEMBER 16
ASTROLOGICAL SIGN: VIRGO
BLOOD TYPE: B
27 YEARS OLD

READ THIS WAY

Reincarnation 35: Horohoro's Dream

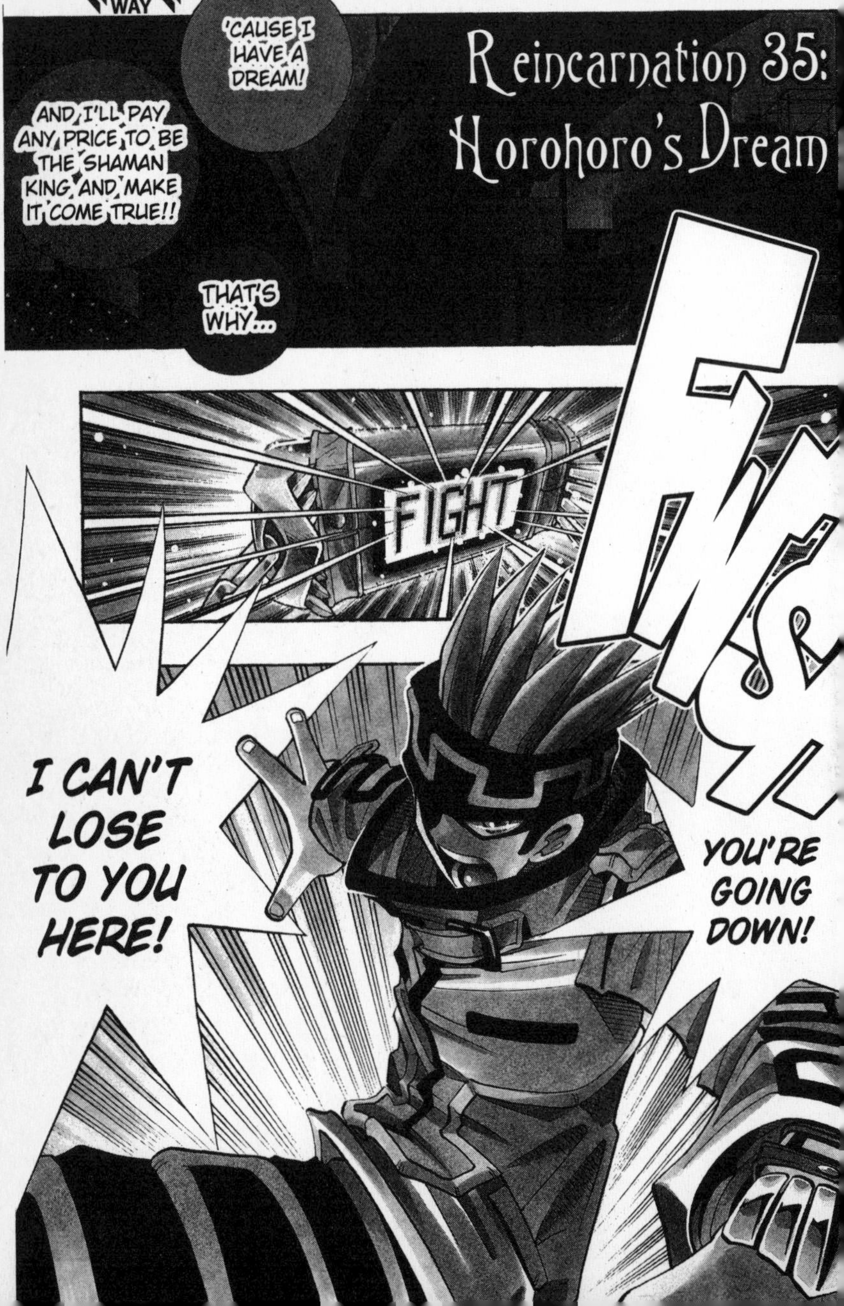

'CAUSE I HAVE A DREAM!
AND I'LL PAY ANY PRICE TO BE THE SHAMAN KING AND MAKE IT COME TRUE!!
THAT'S WHY...
FIGHT
YOU'RE GOING DOWN!
I CAN'T LOSE TO YOU HERE!

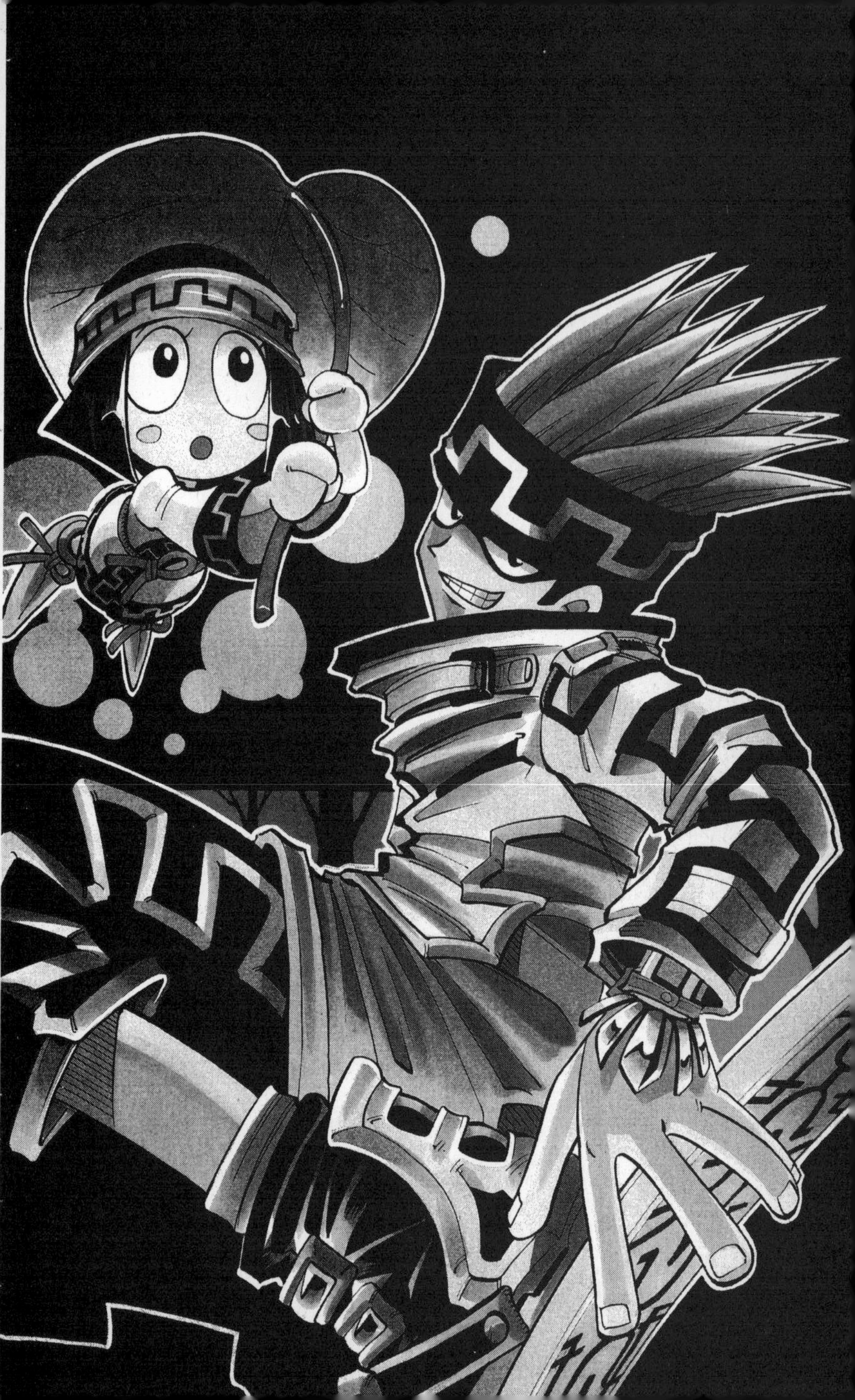

Reincarnation 35: Horohoro's Dream

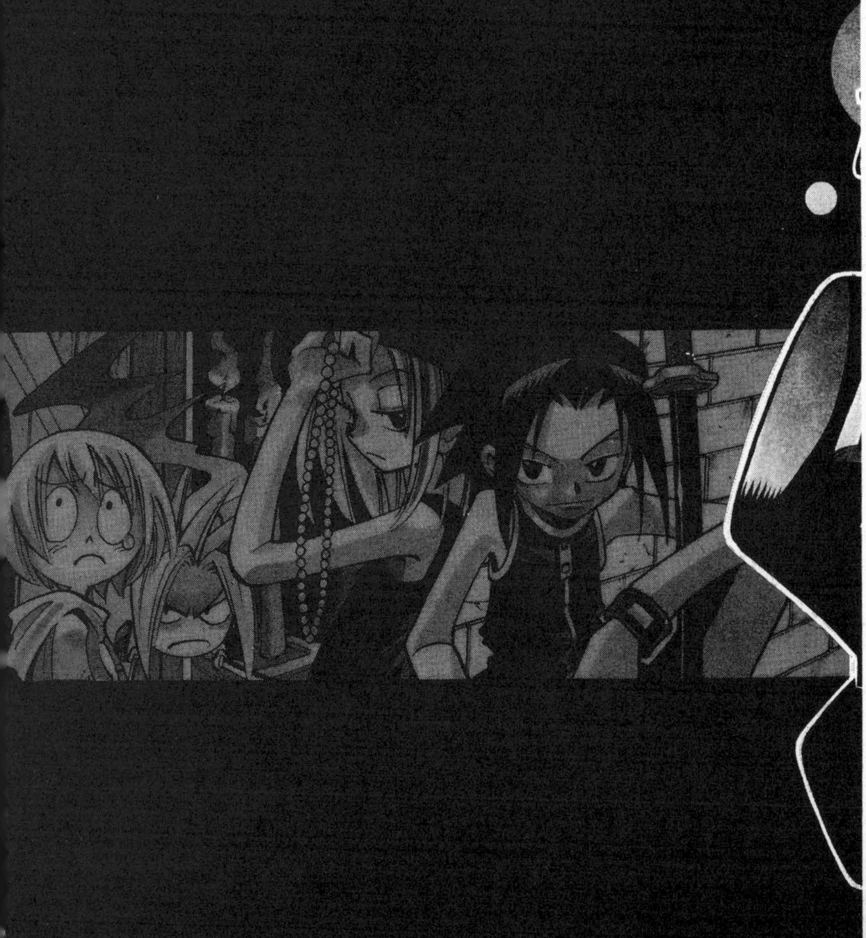

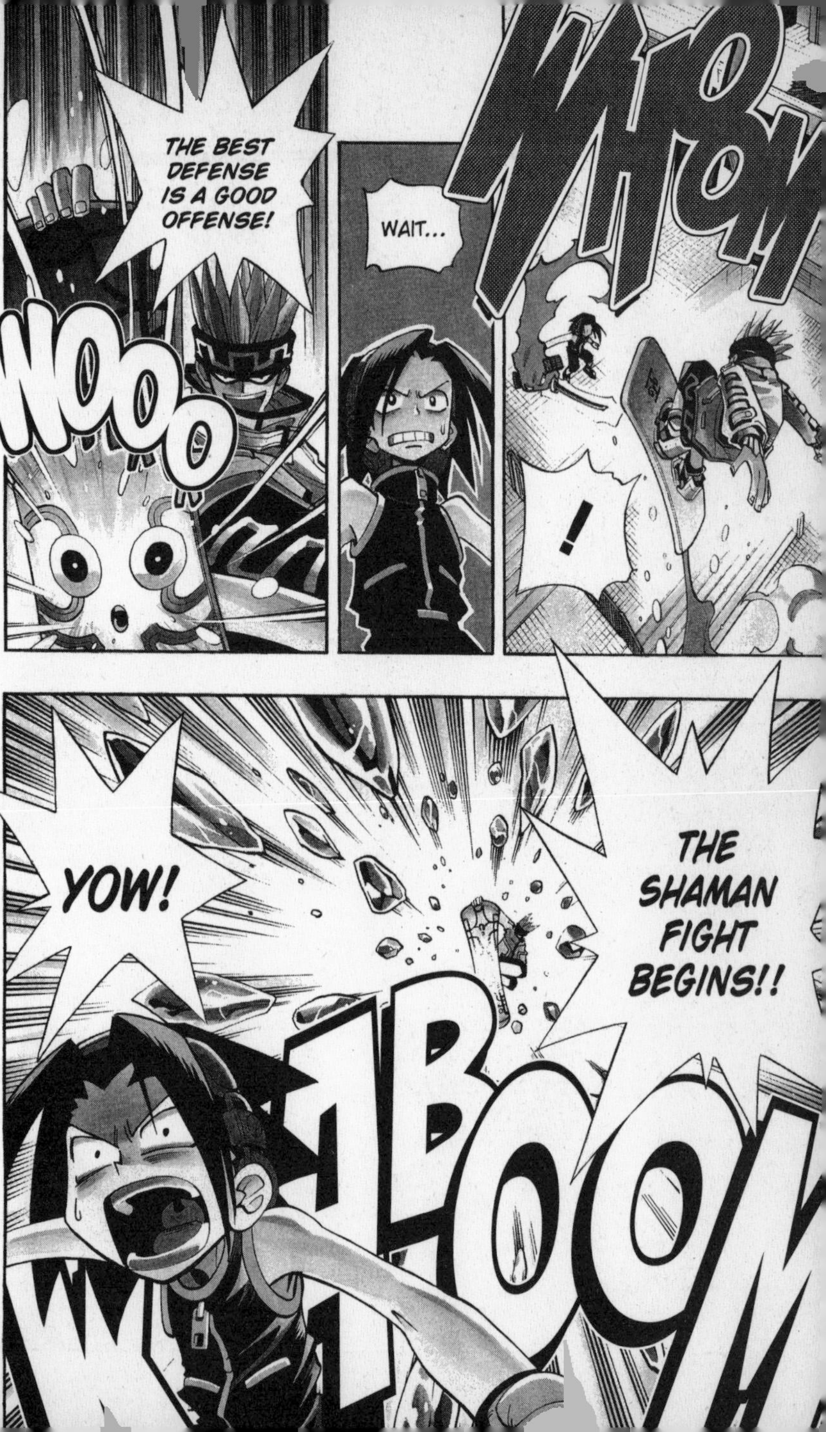
!
WAIT...
THE BEST DEFENSE IS A GOOD OFFENSE!
WOOO
THE SHAMAN FIGHT BEGINS!!
YOW!

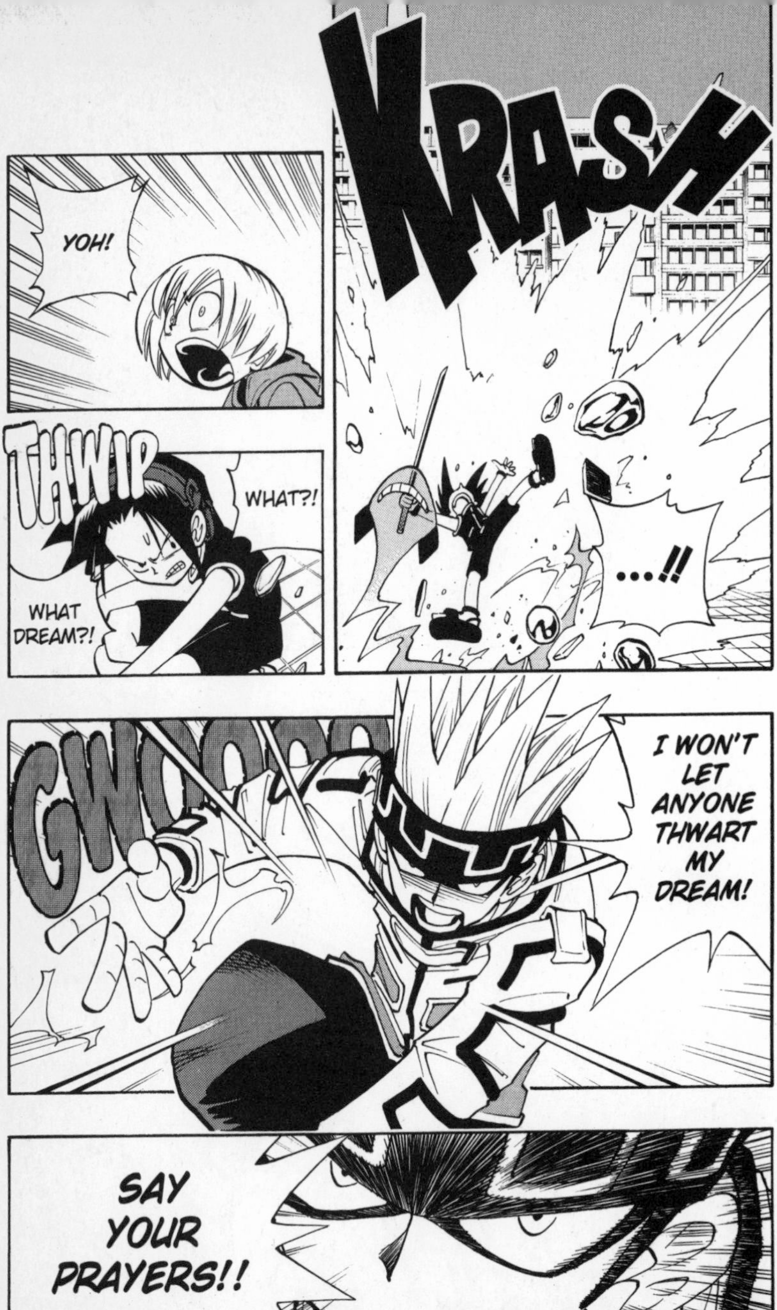
KRASH
...!!
YOH!
THWIP
WHAT?!
WHAT DREAM?!
GWOOOO
I WON'T LET ANYONE THWART MY DREAM!
SAY YOUR PRAYERS!!

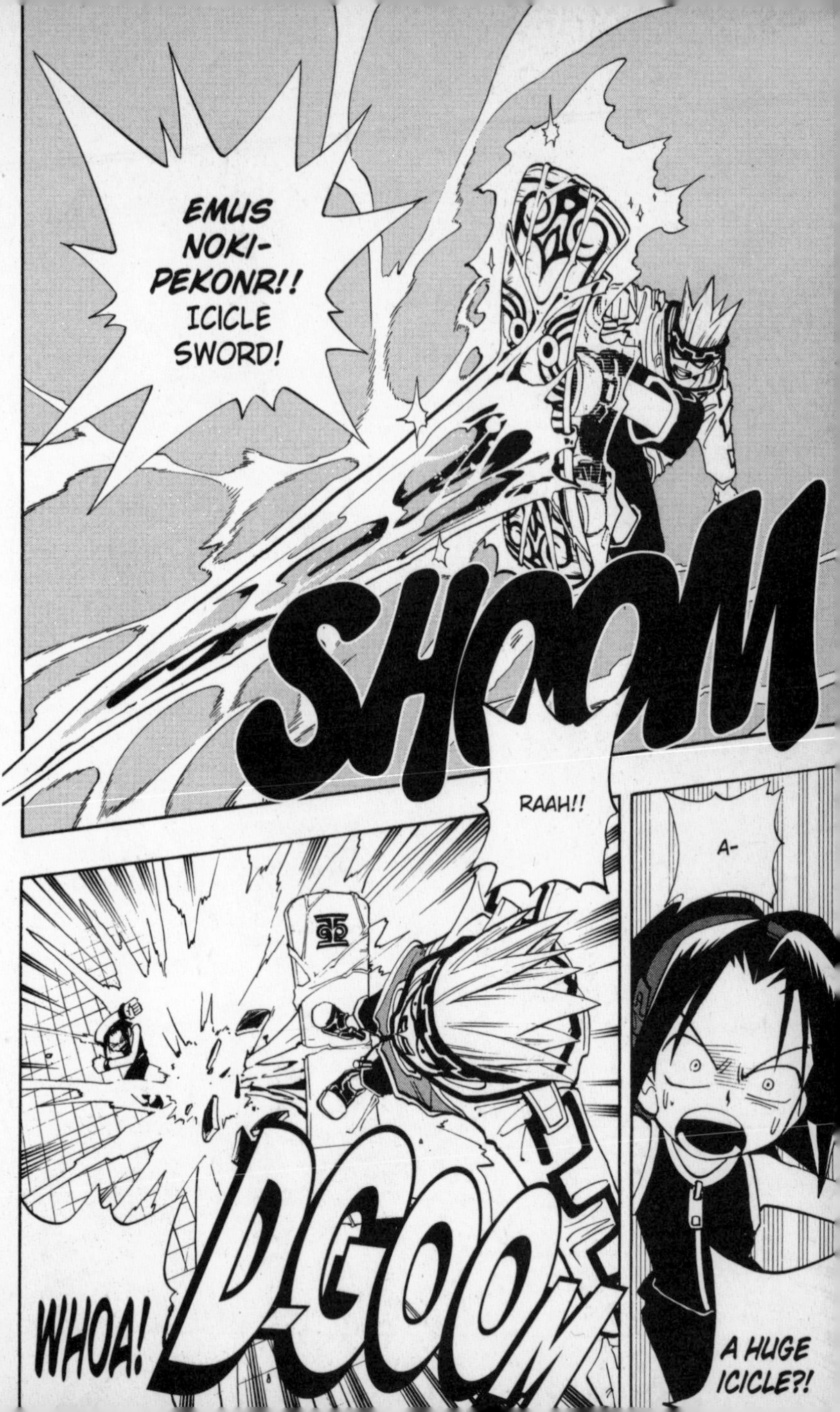
EMUS NOKI-PEKONR!! ICICLE SWORD!
SHOOM
A-
A HUGE ICICLE?!
RAAH!!
DGOOM
WHOA!

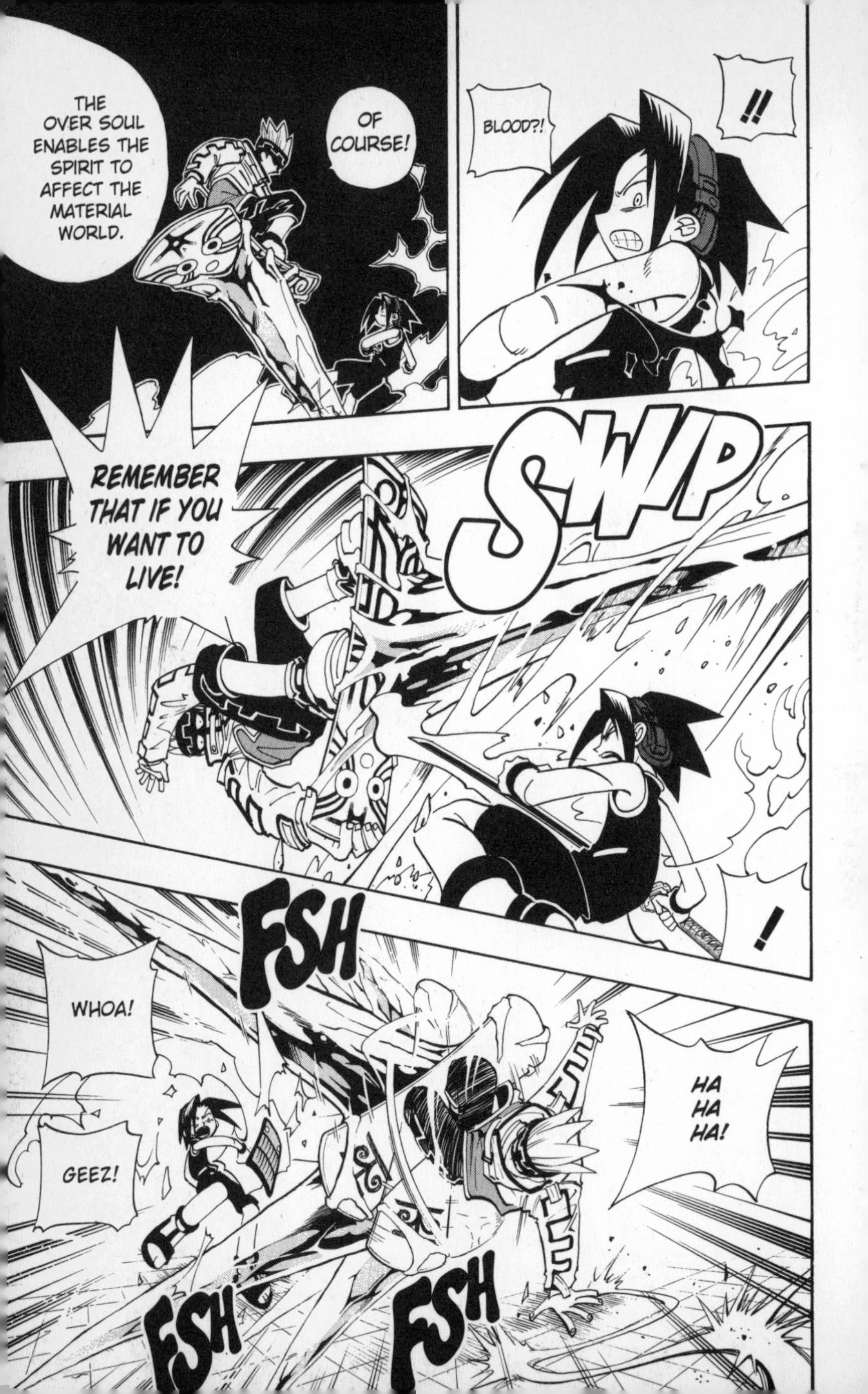
!!
BLOOD?!
OF COURSE!
THE OVER SOUL ENABLES THE SPIRIT TO AFFECT THE MATERIAL WORLD.
SWIP
REMEMBER THAT IF YOU WANT TO LIVE!
!
HA HA HA!
FSH
WHOA!
GEEZ!
FSH
FSH

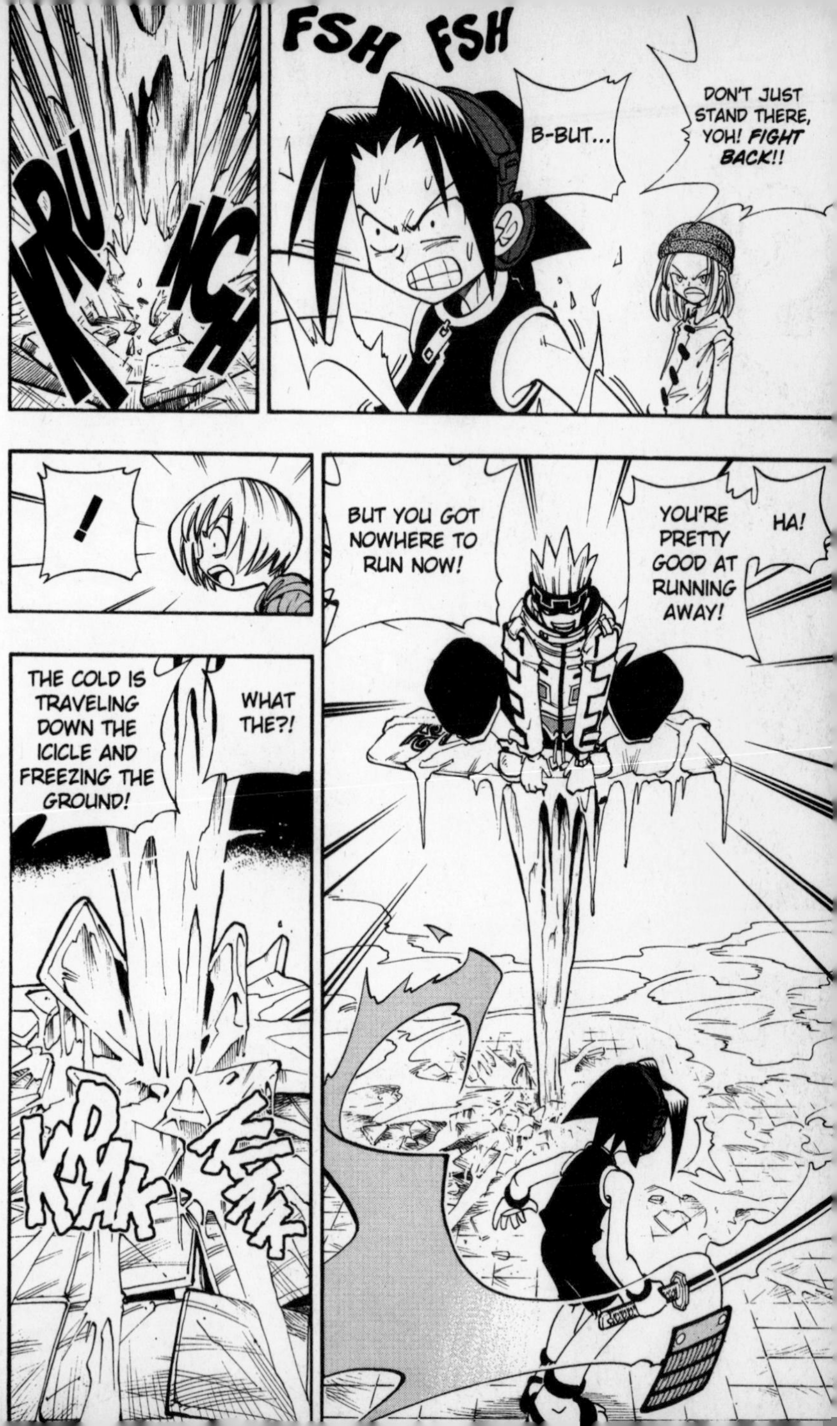
FSH FSH
DON'T JUST STAND THERE, YOH! FIGHT BACK!!
B-BUT...
KRUNCH
HA!
YOU'RE PRETTY GOOD AT RUNNING AWAY!
BUT YOU GOT NOWHERE TO RUN NOW!
!
WHAT THE?!
THE COLD IS TRAVELING DOWN THE ICICLE AND FREEZING THE GROUND!
KRAK

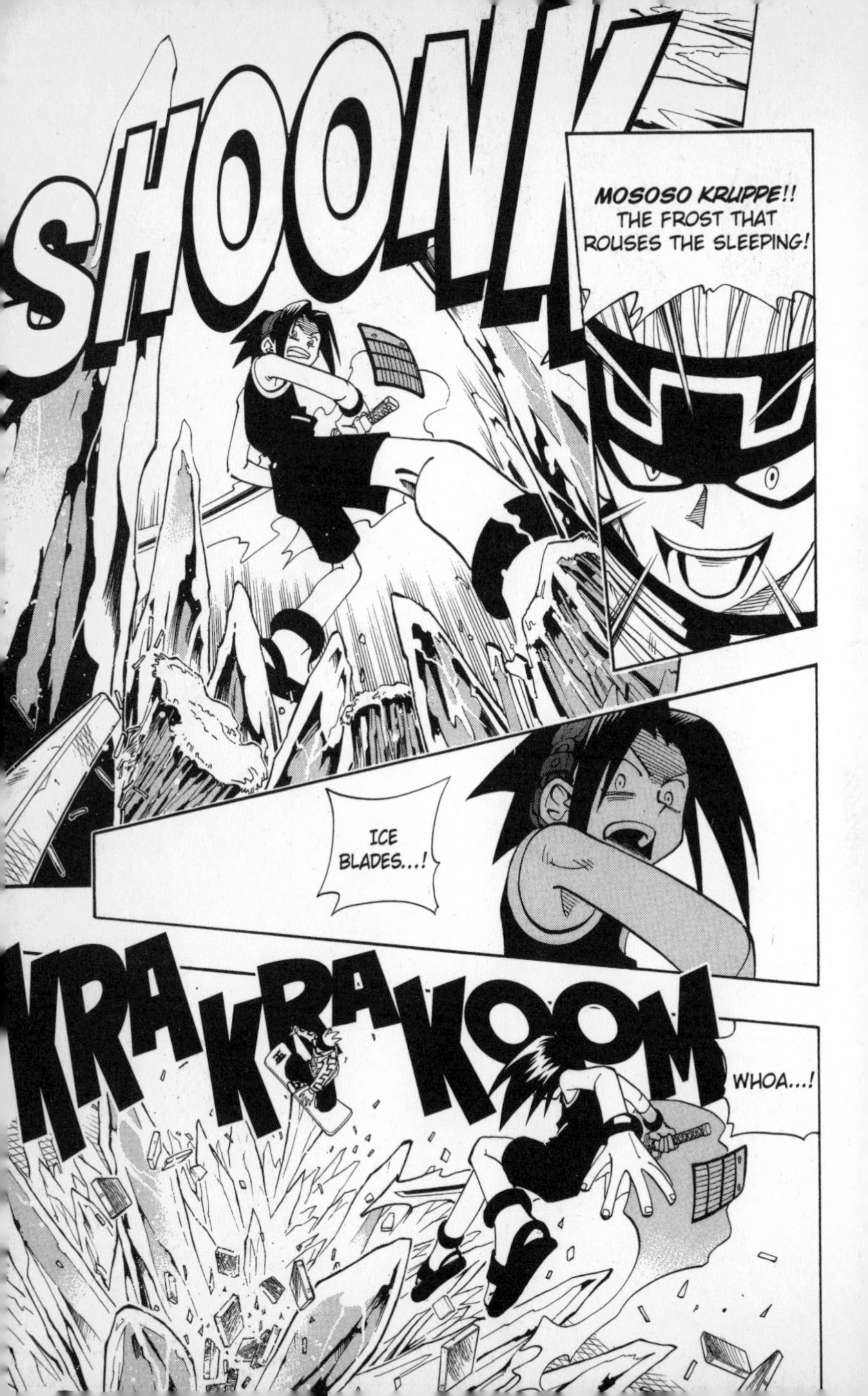
MOSOSO KRUPPE!! THE FROST THAT ROUSES THE SLEEPING!
SHOONK
ICE BLADES...!
WHOA...!
KRAKRAKOOM

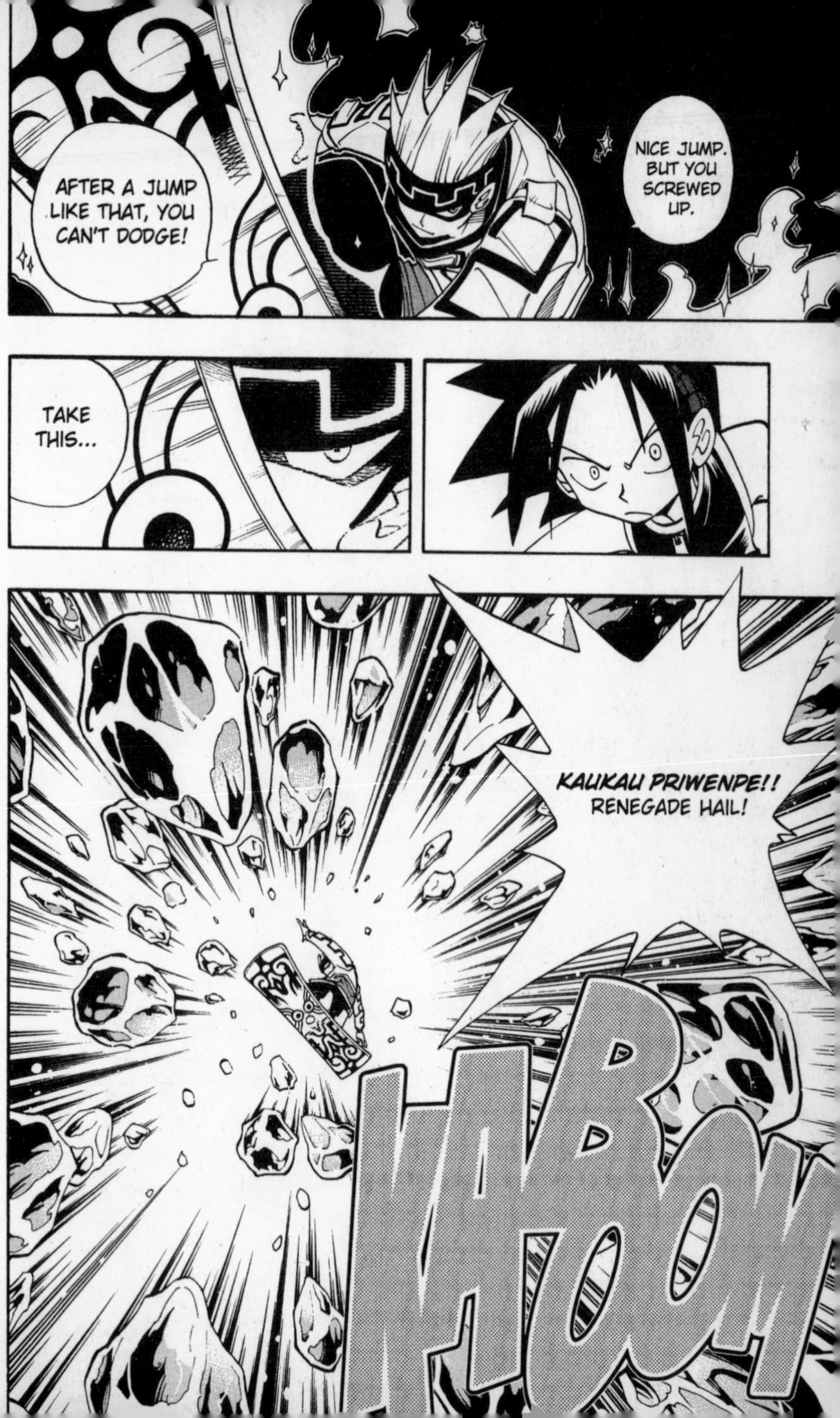
NICE JUMP. BUT YOU SCREWED UP.
AFTER A JUMP LIKE THAT, YOU CAN'T DODGE!
TAKE THIS...
KAUKAU PRIWENPE!! RENEGADE HAIL!
KABOOM

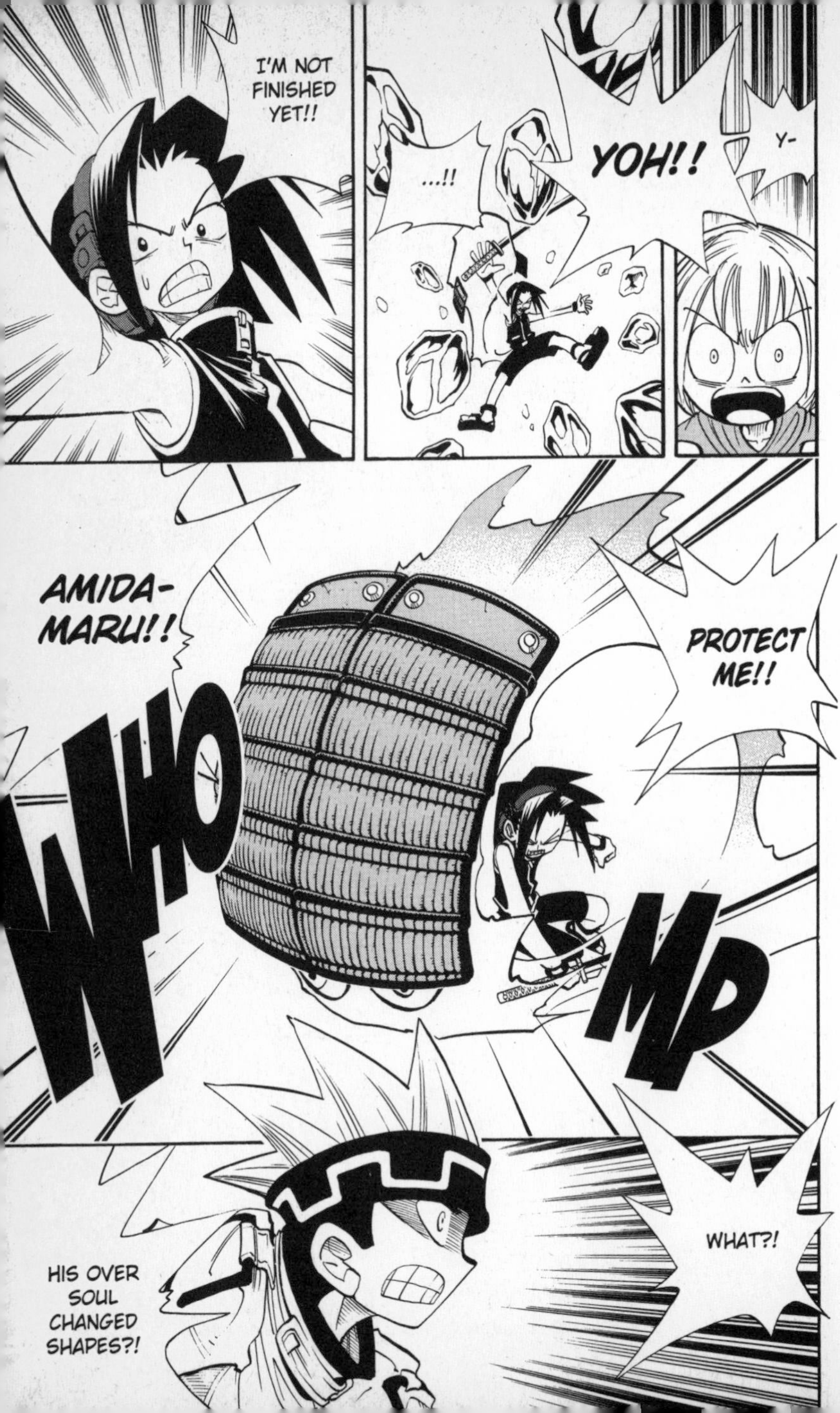
Y-
YOH!!
...!!
I'M NOT FINISHED YET!!
AMIDA-MARU!!
PROTECT ME!!
WHOMP
WHAT?!
HIS OVER SOUL CHANGED SHAPES?!

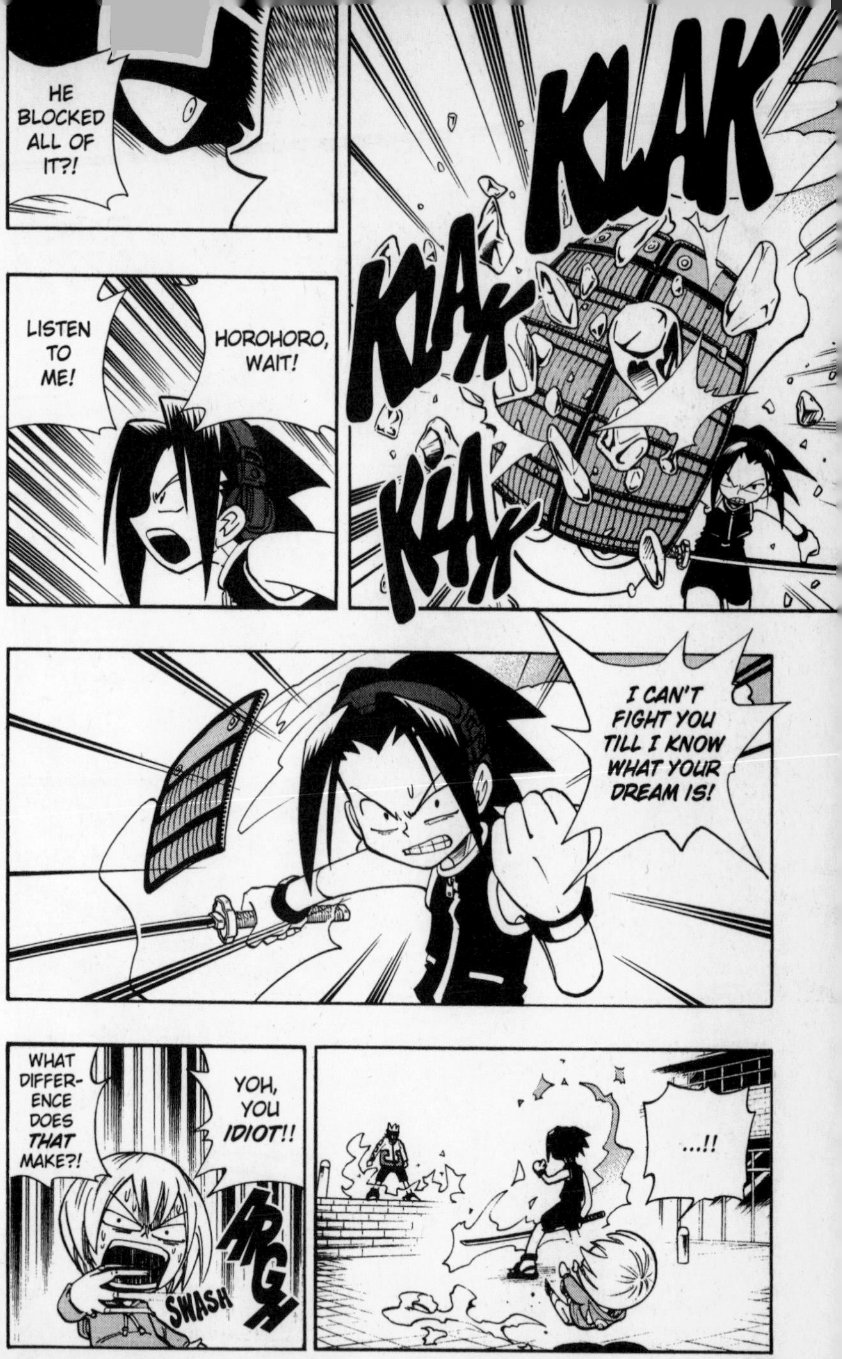
KLAK
KLAK
KLAK
HE BLOCKED ALL OF IT?!
HOROHORO, WAIT!
LISTEN TO ME!
I CAN'T FIGHT YOU TILL I KNOW WHAT YOUR DREAM IS!
...!!
YOH, YOU IDIOT!!
WHAT DIFFER-ENCE DOES THAT MAKE?!
ARGH
SWASH

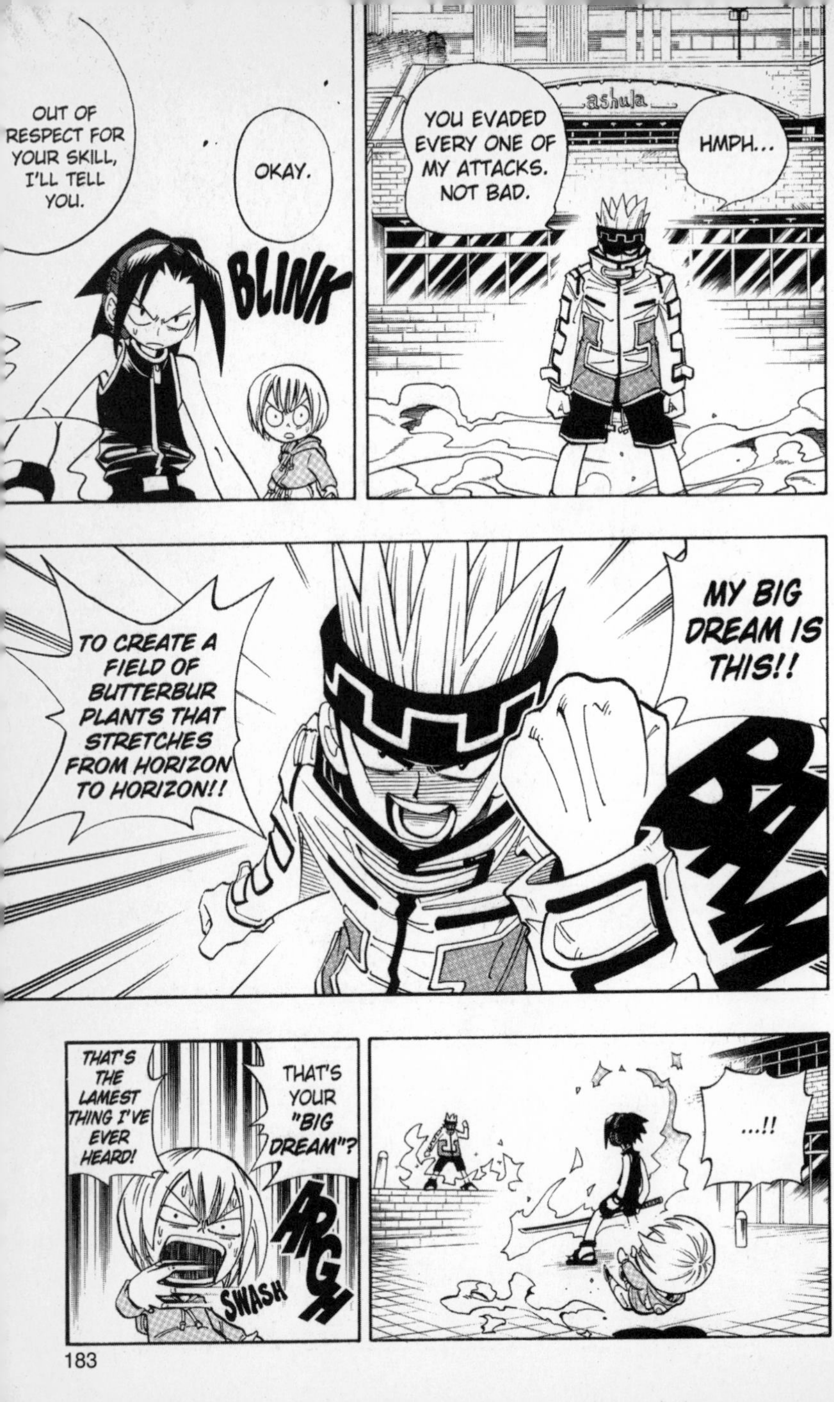
HMPH...
YOU EVADED EVERY ONE OF MY ATTACKS. NOT BAD.
OKAY.
OUT OF RESPECT FOR YOUR SKILL, I'LL TELL YOU.
BLINK
MY BIG DREAM IS THIS!!
TO CREATE A FIELD OF BUTTERBUR PLANTS THAT STRETCHES FROM HORIZON TO HORIZON!!
BAM
...!!
THAT'S YOUR "BIG DREAM"?
THAT'S THE LAMEST THING I'VE EVER HEARD!
ARGH
SWASH

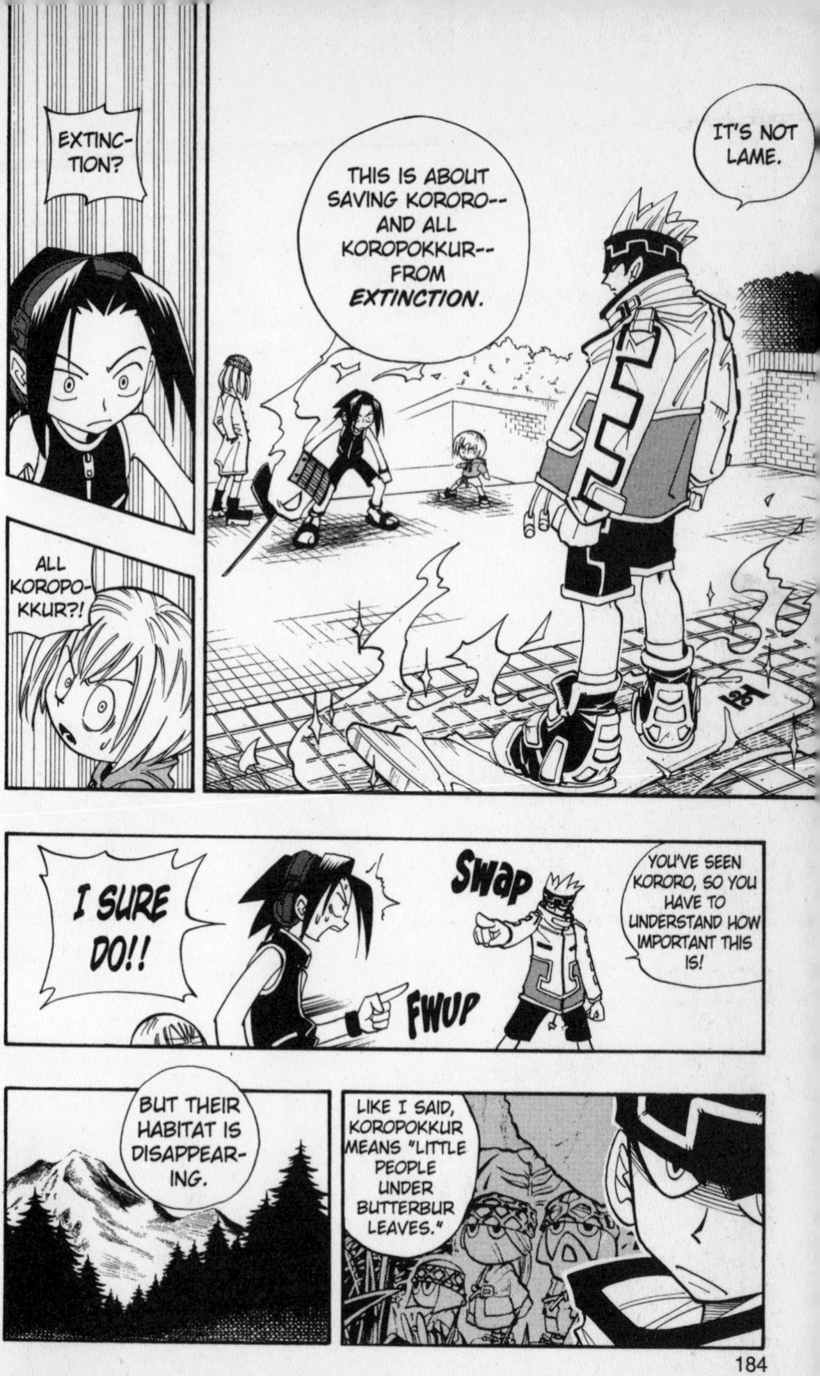
IT'S NOT LAME.
THIS IS ABOUT SAVING KORORO-- AND ALL KOROPOKKUR-- FROM *EXTINCTION*.
EXTINC-TION?
ALL KOROPO-KKUR?!
YOU'VE SEEN KORORO, SO YOU HAVE TO UNDERSTAND HOW IMPORTANT THIS IS!
SWAP
I SURE DO!!
FWUP
LIKE I SAID, KOROPOKKUR MEANS "LITTLE PEOPLE UNDER BUTTERBUR LEAVES."
BUT THEIR HABITAT IS DISAPPEAR-ING.

READ THIS WAY

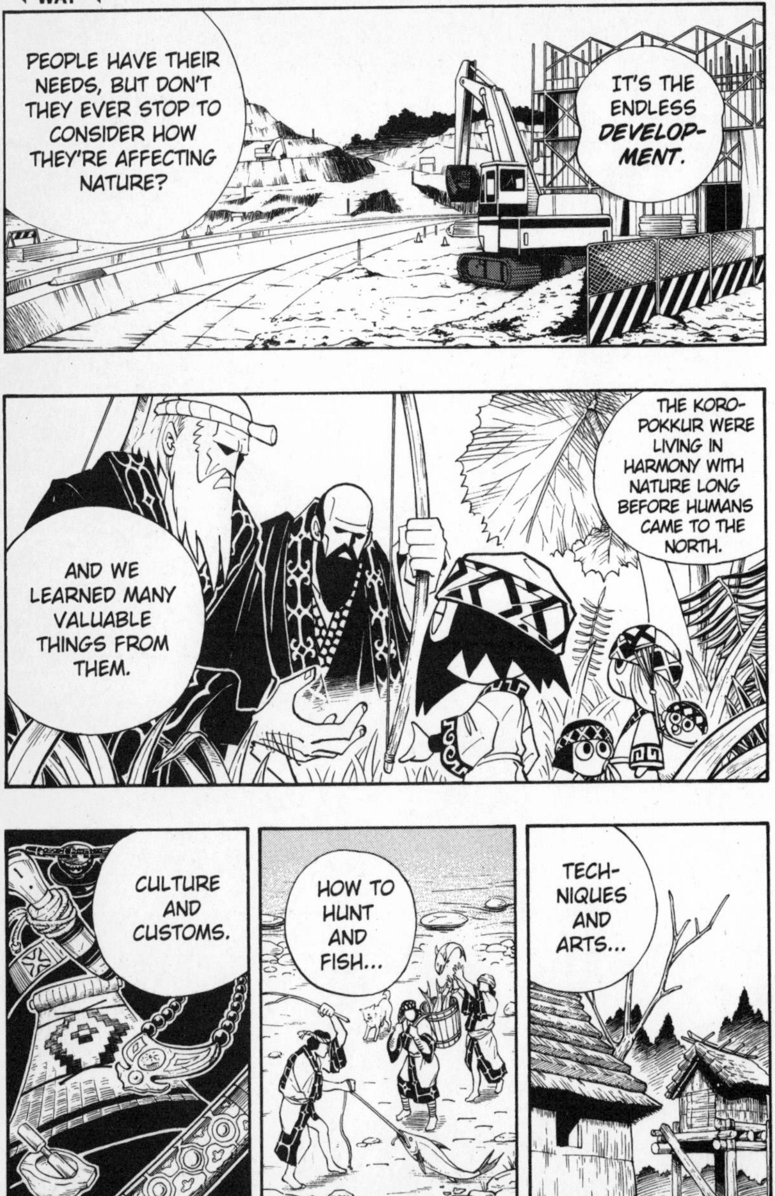

IT'S THE ENDLESS DEVELOP-MENT.
PEOPLE HAVE THEIR NEEDS, BUT DON'T THEY EVER STOP TO CONSIDER HOW THEY'RE AFFECTING NATURE?
THE KORO-POKKUR WERE LIVING IN HARMONY WITH NATURE LONG BEFORE HUMANS CAME TO THE NORTH.
AND WE LEARNED MANY VALUABLE THINGS FROM THEM.
TECH-NIQUES AND ARTS...
HOW TO HUNT AND FISH...
CULTURE AND CUSTOMS.

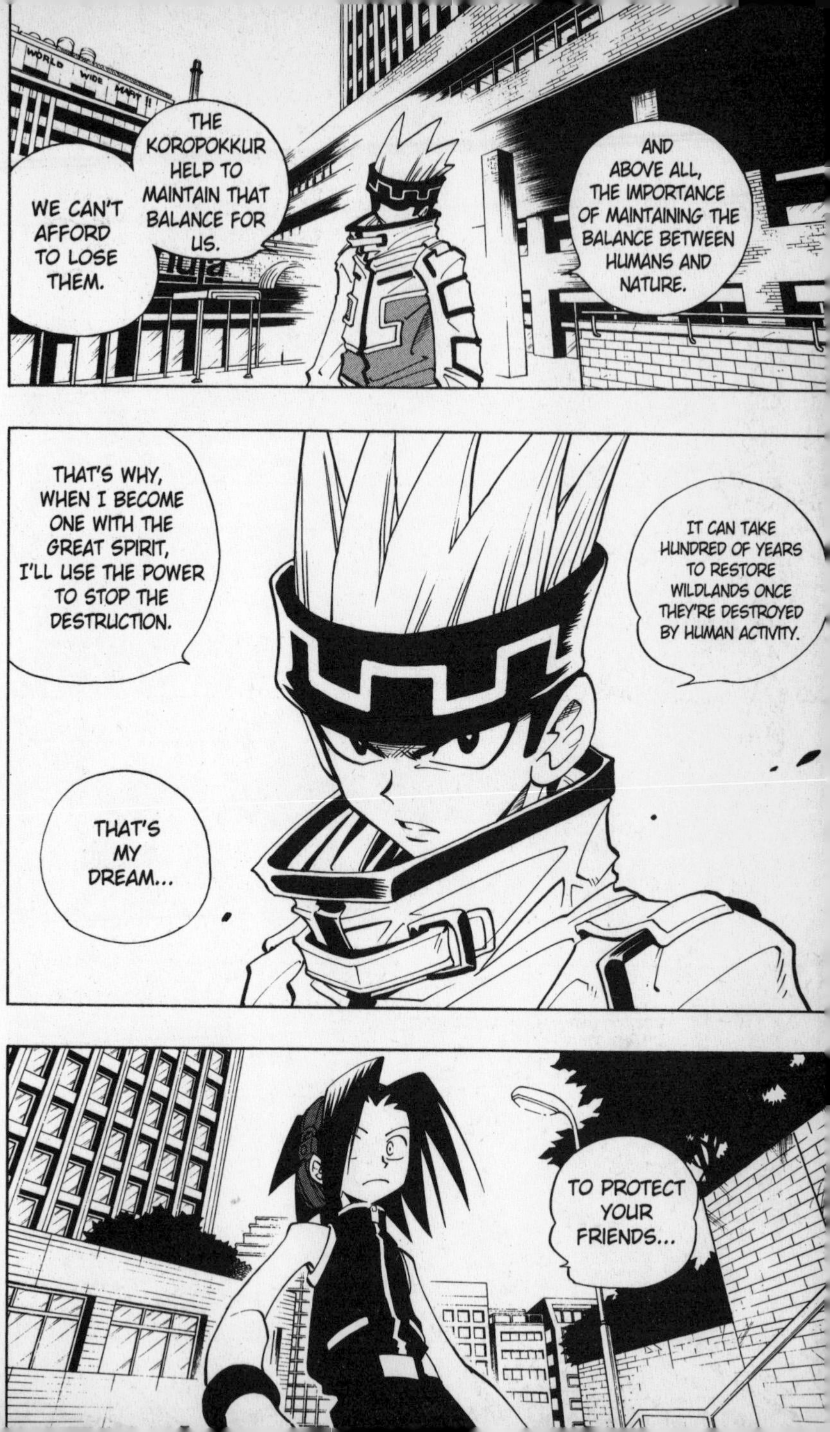
AND ABOVE ALL, THE IMPORTANCE OF MAINTAINING THE BALANCE BETWEEN HUMANS AND NATURE.
THE KOROPOKKUR HELP TO MAINTAIN THAT BALANCE FOR US.
WE CAN'T AFFORD TO LOSE THEM.
WORLD WIDE MART!!
IT CAN TAKE HUNDRED OF YEARS TO RESTORE WILDLANDS ONCE THEY'RE DESTROYED BY HUMAN ACTIVITY.
THAT'S WHY, WHEN I BECOME ONE WITH THE GREAT SPIRIT, I'LL USE THE POWER TO STOP THE DESTRUCTION.
THAT'S MY DREAM...
TO PROTECT YOUR FRIENDS...

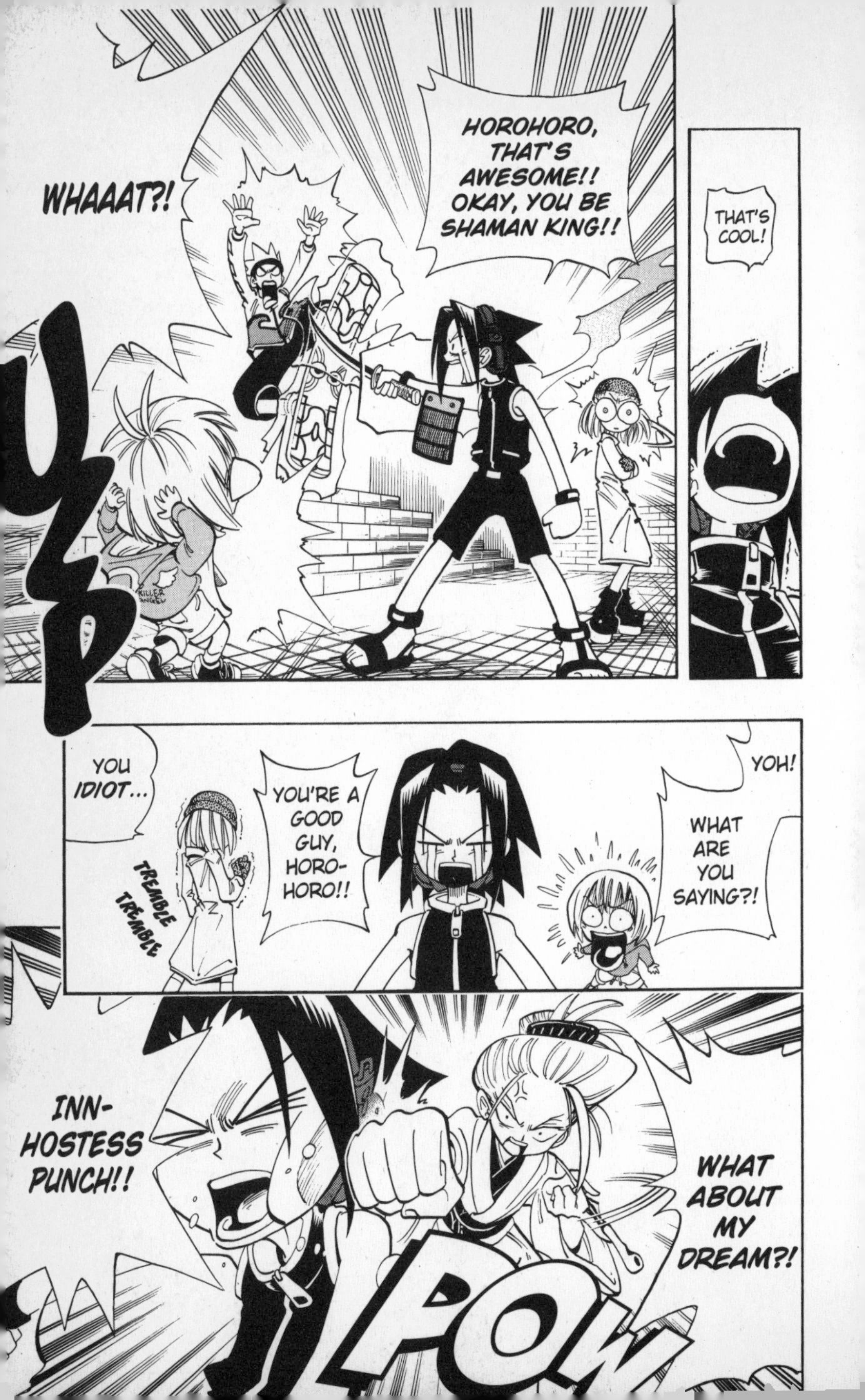
THAT'S COOL!
HOROHORO, THAT'S AWESOME!! OKAY, YOU BE SHAMAN KING!!
WHAAAT?!
YOH!
WHAT ARE YOU SAYING?!
YOU'RE A GOOD GUY, HORO-HORO!!
YOU IDIOT...
TREMBLE TREMBLE
WHAT ABOUT MY DREAM?!
INN-HOSTESS PUNCH!!
POW

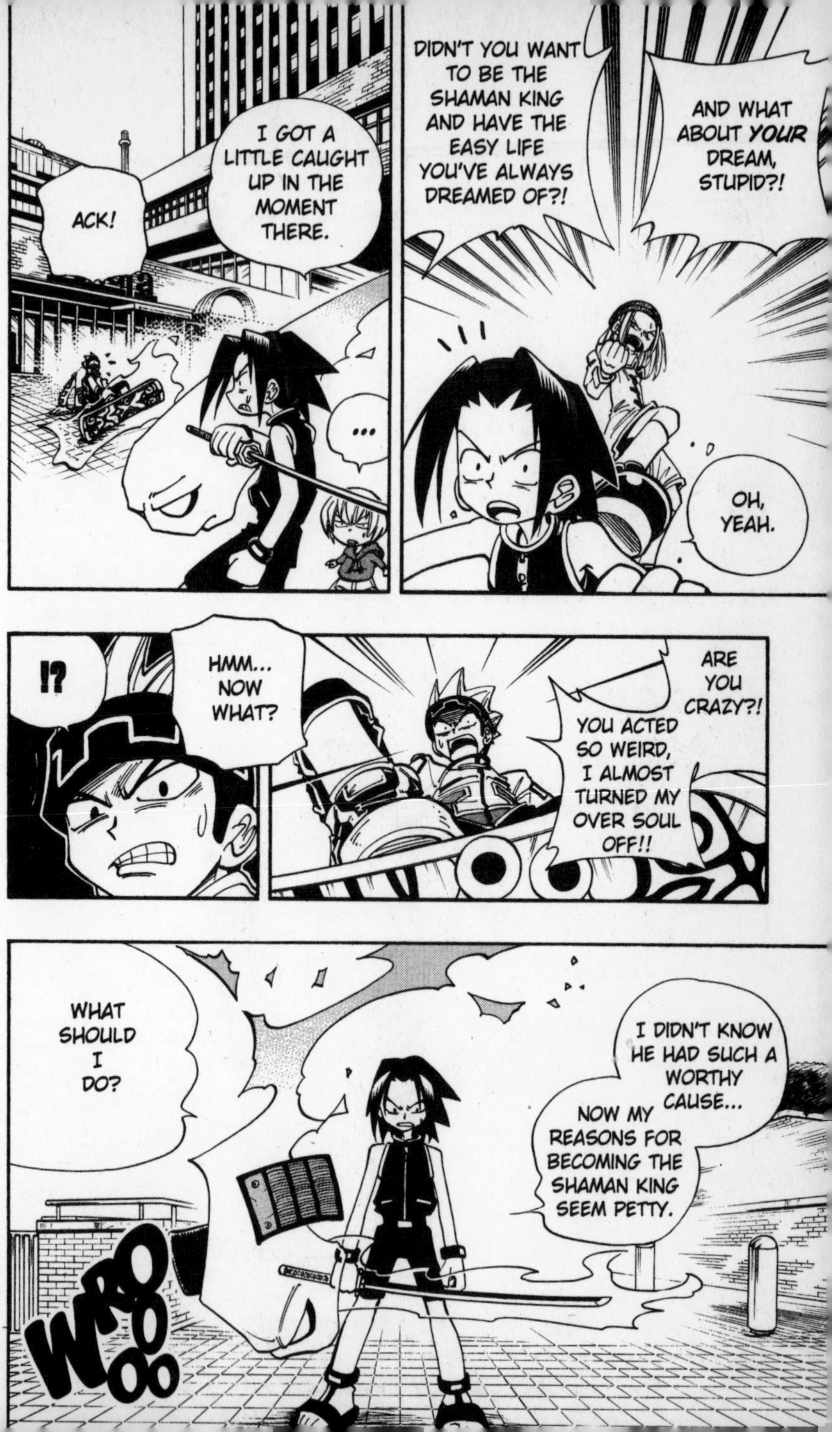
AND WHAT ABOUT ***YOUR*** DREAM, STUPID?!
DIDN'T YOU WANT TO BE THE SHAMAN KING AND HAVE THE EASY LIFE YOU'VE ALWAYS DREAMED OF?!
OH, YEAH.
I GOT A LITTLE CAUGHT UP IN THE MOMENT THERE.
ACK!
...
ARE YOU CRAZY?!
YOU ACTED SO WEIRD, I ALMOST TURNED MY OVER SOUL OFF!!
HMM... NOW WHAT?
!?
I DIDN'T KNOW HE HAD SUCH A WORTHY CAUSE...
NOW MY REASONS FOR BECOMING THE SHAMAN KING SEEM PETTY.
WHAT SHOULD I DO?
WROOOO

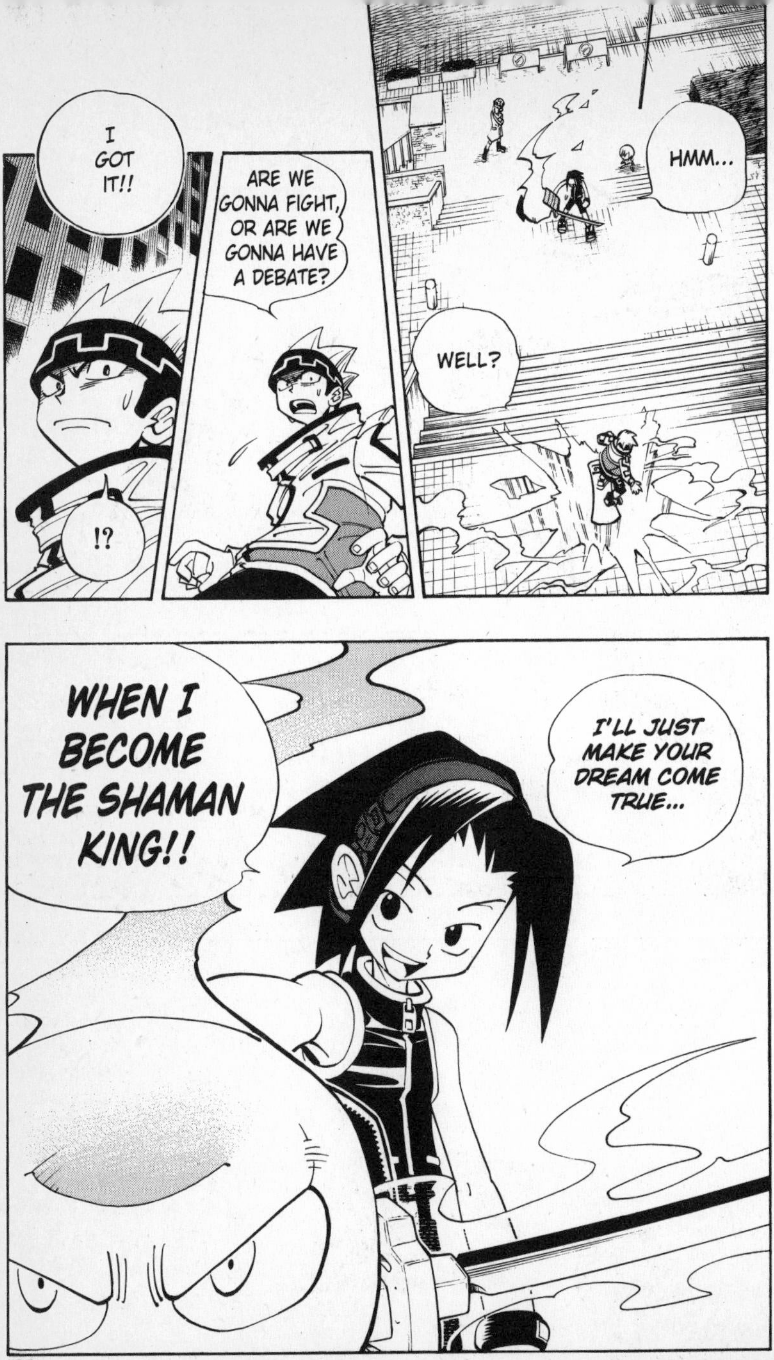
HMM...
WELL?
ARE WE GONNA FIGHT, OR ARE WE GONNA HAVE A DEBATE?
I GOT IT!!
!?
I'LL JUST MAKE YOUR DREAM COME TRUE...
WHEN I BECOME THE SHAMAN KING!!

TO BE CONTINUED IN *SHAMAN KING* VOL. 5!

SHAMAN KING CHARACTER FILE No.19

シルバーアームズ

SILVER ARMS

500 YEARS POSTMORTEM

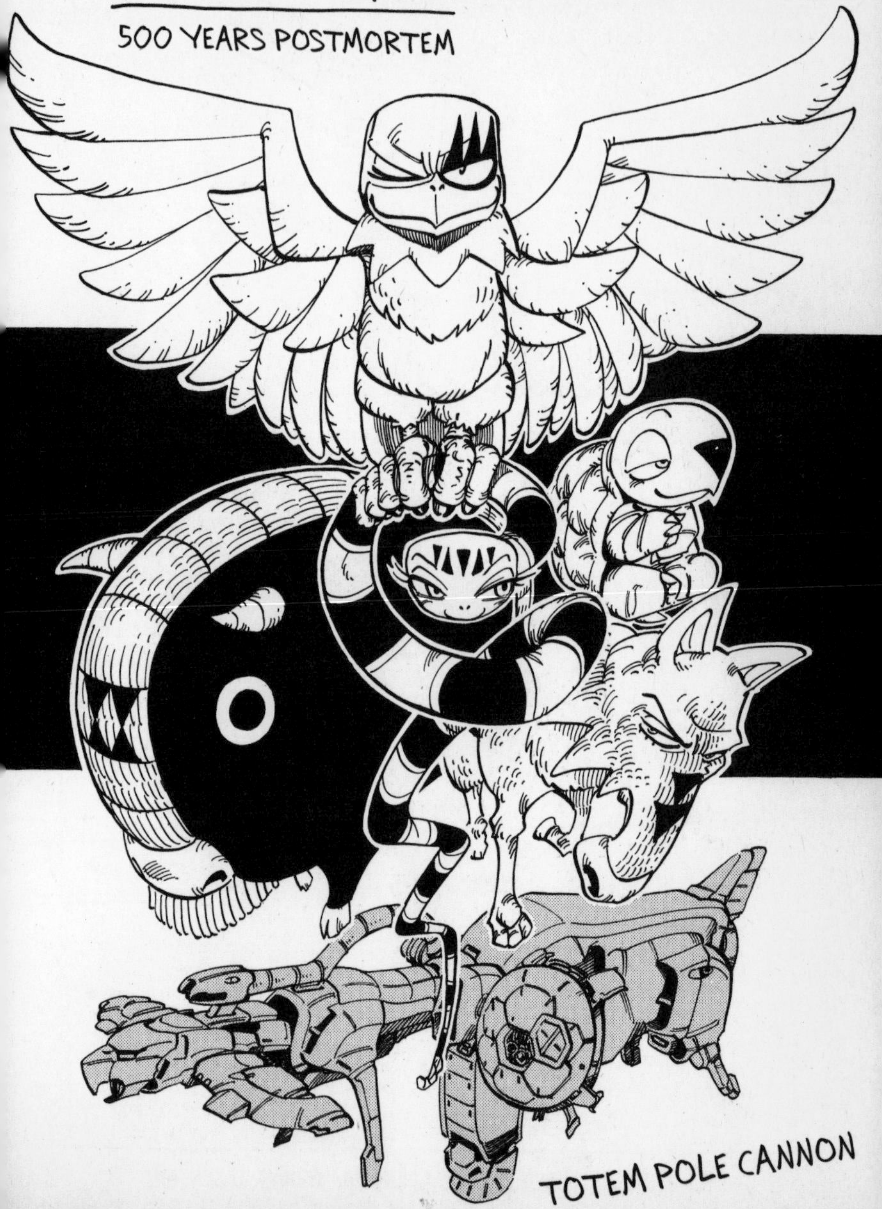

TOTEM POLE CANNON

SPECIAL BONUS

DIAGRAM OF THE TOTEM POLE CANNON

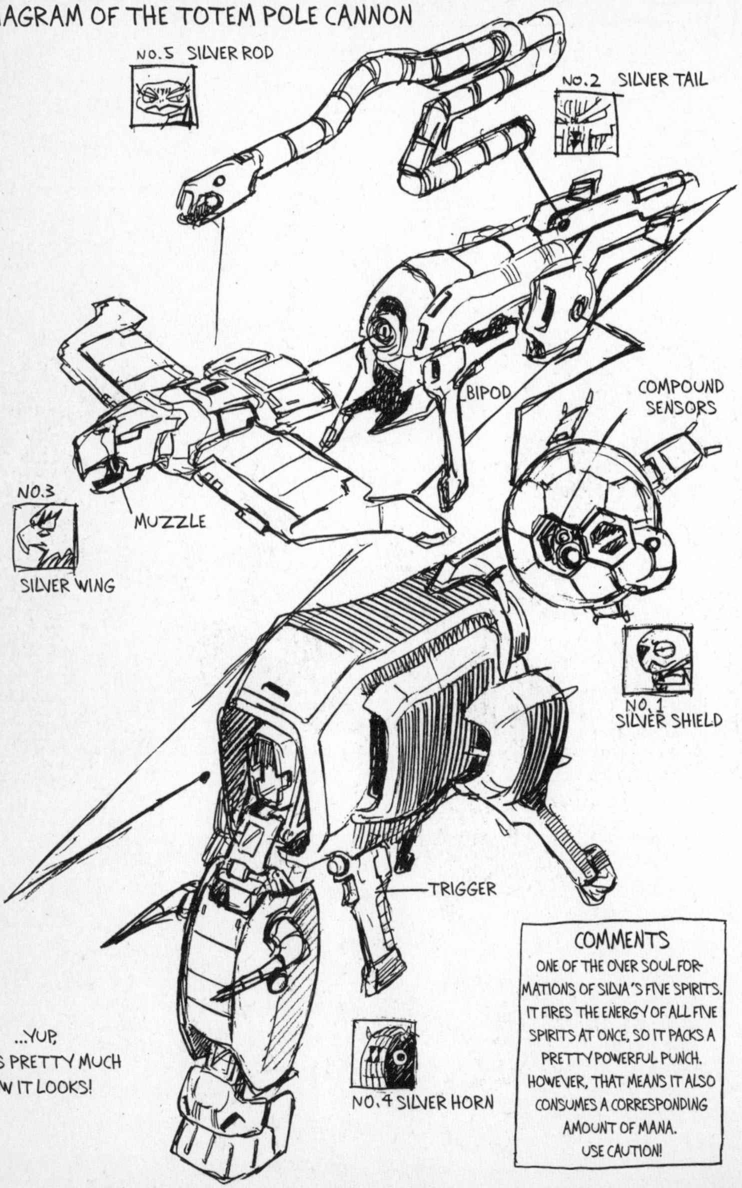
NO.5 SILVER ROD
NO.2 SILVER TAIL
BIPOD
COMPOUND SENSORS
NO.3
MUZZLE
SILVER WING
NO.1 SILVER SHIELD
TRIGGER
NO.4 SILVER HORN

...YUP, THIS IS PRETTY MUCH HOW IT LOOKS!

COMMENTS

ONE OF THE OVER SOUL FORMATIONS OF SILVA'S FIVE SPIRITS. IT FIRES THE ENERGY OF ALL FIVE SPIRITS AT ONCE, SO IT PACKS A PRETTY POWERFUL PUNCH. HOWEVER, THAT MEANS IT ALSO CONSUMES A CORRESPONDING AMOUNT OF MANA. USE CAUTION!

IN THE NEXT VOLUME...

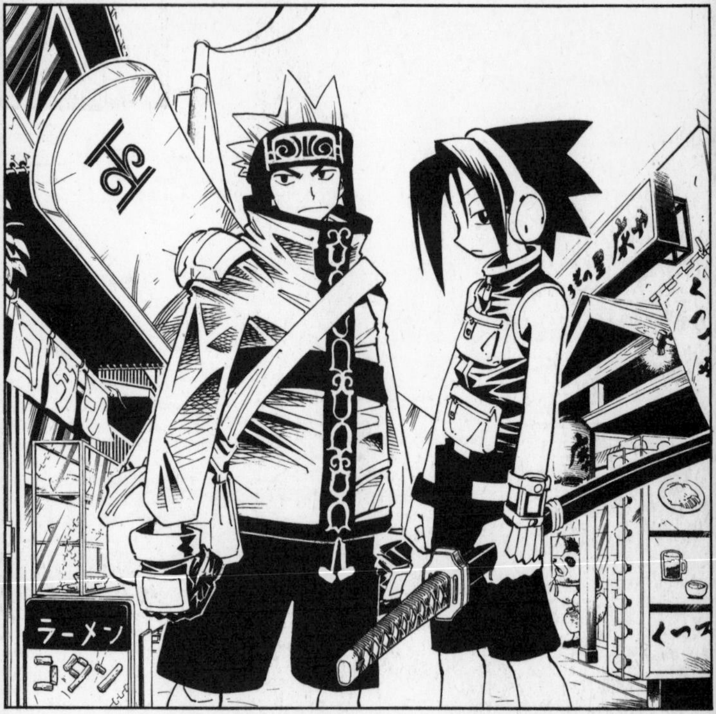
ラーメン
コタン

Snow and hail rain upon Tokyo as Yoh, the prodigal shaman of Japan, fights Horohoro, the ice-wielding shaman of the Ainu! The winner will have a shot at the Shaman King and get to write the history books... but lose two battles in a row and you'll be disqualified from the competition! But just losing might be the least of Yoh's problems as Horohoro unleashes an avalanche to send Yoh into his own personal Ice Age!

COMPLETE OUR SURVEY AND LET US KNOW WHAT YOU THINK!

☐ Please check here if you DO NOT wish to receive information or future offers from VIZ

Name: _____

Address: _____

City: _____ State: _____ Zip: _____

E-mail: _____

☐ Male ☐ Female Date of Birth (mm/dd/yyyy): ___ / ___ / ___ (Under 13? Parental consent required)

What race/ethnicity do you consider yourself? (please check one)

☐ Asian/Pacific Islander   ☐ Black/African American   ☐ Hispanic/Latino

☐ Native American/Alaskan Native ☐ White/Caucasian   ☐ Other: _____

What SHONEN JUMP Graphic Novel did you purchase? (indicate title purchased)

_____

What other SHONEN JUMP Graphic Novels, if any, do you own? (indicate title(s) owned)

_____

_____

Reason for purchase: (check all that apply)

☐ Special offer   ☐ Favorite title   ☐ Gift

☐ Recommendation   ☐ Read in SHONEN JUMP Magazine

☐ Other_____

Where did you make your purchase? (please check one)

☐ Comic store   ☐ Bookstore   ☐ Mass/Grocery Store

☐ Newsstand   ☐ Video/Video Game Store   ☐ Other: _____

☐ Online (site: _____)

Do you read SHONEN JUMP Magazine?

☐ Yes ☐ No **(if no, skip the next two questions)**

Do you subscribe?

☐ Yes ☐ No

If you do not subscribe, how often do you purchase SHONEN JUMP Magazine?

☐ 1-3 issues a year

☐ 4-6 issues a year

☐ more than 7 issues a year

What genre of manga would you like to read as a SHONEN JUMP Graphic Novel?
(please check two)

☐ Adventure ☐ Comic Strip ☐ Science Fiction ☐ Fighting

☐ Horror ☐ Romance ☐ Fantasy ☐ Sports

Which do you prefer? (please check one)

☐ Reading right-to-left

☐ Reading left-to-right

Which do you prefer? (please check one)

☐ Sound effects in English

☐ Sound effects in Japanese with English captions

☐ Sound effects in Japanese only with a glossary at the back

THANK YOU! Please send the completed form to:

VIZ Survey
42 Catharine St.
Poughkeepsie, NY 12601

All information provided will be used for internal purposes only. We promise not to sell or otherwise divulge your information.

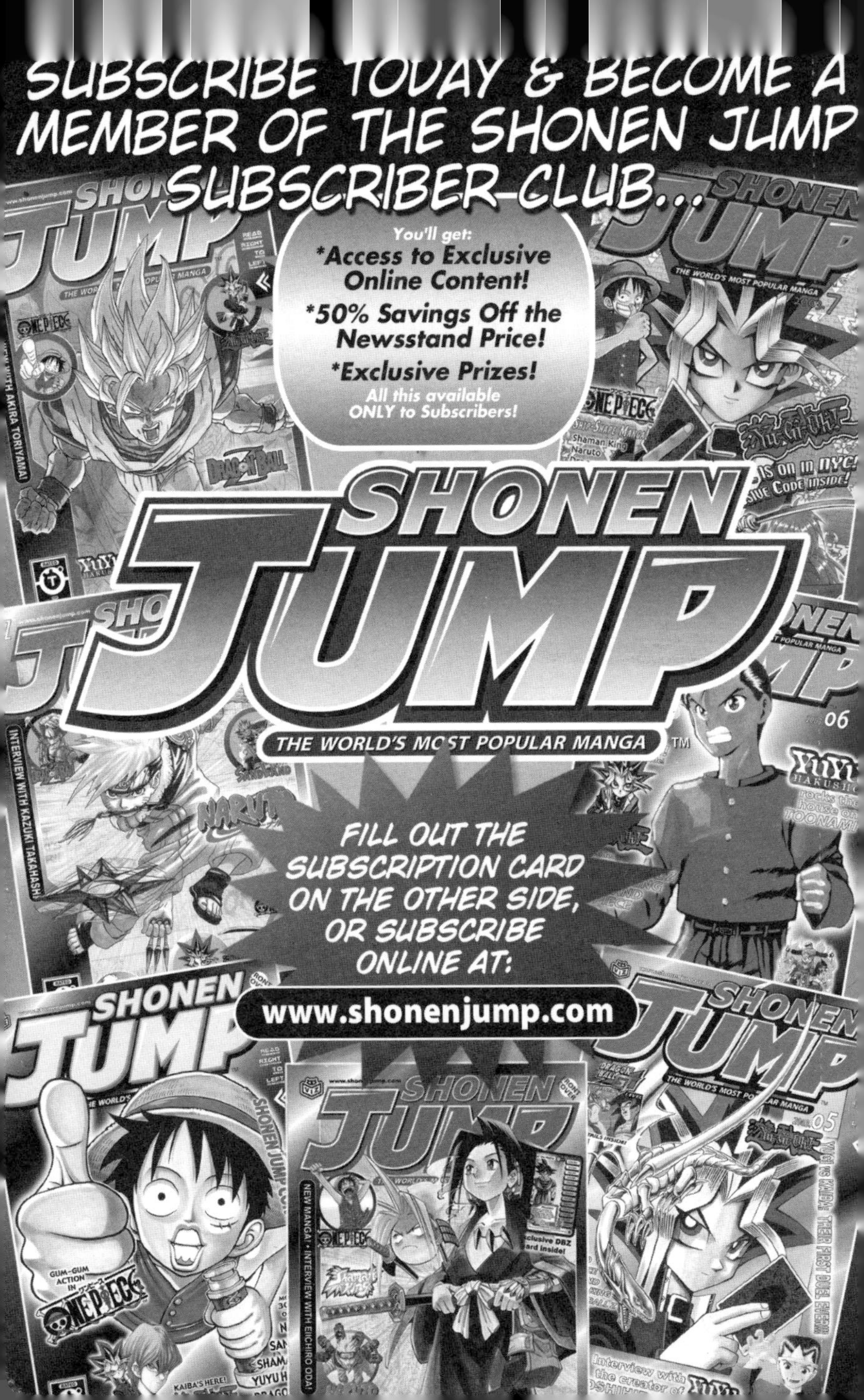
SUBSCRIBE TODAY & BECOME A MEMBER OF THE SHONEN JUMP SUBSCRIBER CLUB...
You'll get:
*Access to Exclusive Online Content!
*50% Savings Off the Newsstand Price!
*Exclusive Prizes!
All this available ONLY to Subscribers!
SHONEN JUMP
THE WORLD'S MOST POPULAR MANGA ™
FILL OUT THE SUBSCRIPTION CARD ON THE OTHER SIDE, OR SUBSCRIBE ONLINE AT:
www.shonenjump.com